# Do you want to

# Speak Spanish?

### A SIMPLE, PRACTICAL METHOD TO SPEAK SPANISH BY MEANS OF PHONETICAL PRONUNCIATION

### LATEST EDITION CORRECTED AND ENLARGED

Containing all the words required in daily life, as well as a comprehensive English-Spanish dictionary with imitated pronunciation.

## EDITORIAL RAMON SOPENA, S.A.

© EDITORIAL RAMON SOPENA, S.A.
C/ Córcega, 60 - 08029 BARCELONA
Tel.: 93 322 00 35
Fax. 93 322 37 03
e-mail: edsopena@infonegocio.com
Depósito Legal: B-22038-MMII
Impreso en EDIM, S.C.C.L.
Printed in Spain

ISBN 84-303-1175-0

# Index

# INDISPENSABLE INSTRUCTIONS
## TO BE STUDIED BEFORE USING
## THIS BOOK

In the imitated pronunciation:

u    is always like u in *cut, up*, etc., never as in *put, bull*.

        Ex. *under* (Sp. anda = come on).

r    at the end of a syllable is not pronounced, as in *far, better*.

        Ex. *arger* (Sp. haga = do, make).

rr   is always to be pronounced (as in Scotch), tomo*rr*ow.

        Ex. *Kyerreh* (Sp. quiere = want). In some cases the *r*. is overlined instead of being doubled. The sound is the same.

g    always hard, as in *get, give*.

        Ex. *gérrer* (Sp. guerra = war), *gissárr* (Sp. guisar = cook).

th   always hard, as in *think*. Never as in *this, the*.

        Ex. Looth (Sp. luz = light).

e    alone or followed by a vowel, as in *he, me*.

        Ex. *e* (Sp. y = and), cumbeo (Sp. cambio = change).

e    in all other cases is pronounced as in *let, send*.

        Ex. Pwéddeh (Sp. puede = can).

i    alone as in English. In all other cases, as in *it, middle*.

y    as in English.

oo  always short, as in foot, good. Never as in food, boon.

A full stop (.) in the middle of a word is to facilitate the pronunciation and to give each part its full value.

ACCENTS. The real tonic accent is always the last. When we have placed two or more in one word, the last must be the strongest.

The Spanish vowels have one invariable sound, though they may be slightly longer in some words than in others.

*a*   has the sound of *u* in *up, under*. Ex. anda (under), bata (butter).

       Imitated pronunciation: u.

*ar*  is pronounced as in Enghsh, but sounding the *r* as in Scotland.

| | |
|---|---|
| *arr* | has the U (as in *up*) cound, but with the *r* rolled. Comp. *caro* (caroh) and *carro* (curroh). |
| *i* | short *i* as in *it, pin*. Ex. visto (vîstoh), dinero (di-náiroh). |
| | long *e* as in *me, feed*. Ex. pino (peenoh), hilo (éeloh). |
| *e* | short *e* as in *fed, get*. Ex. me (meh), éste (ésteh). |
| *o* | short *o* as in *not, gone* (never as in *go, home*). Ex. no (noh). |
| | a little longer, like *or* in some words. Ex. coma (cormer). |
| u | short *oo*, as in *foot, look*. Ex. mucho (moochoh), punto (poontóh), longer, as in *spoon, food*. Ex. tuyo (tooyoh), luna (loonah). |
| *y* | as in English. Ex. yeso (yéssoh). |
| *ay* | English *i* or *y*. Ex. ái! (I). |
| *oi, oy* | as in English. Ex. doy (doy), boina (bóina). |
| *au* | English *ow* in *now*. Ex. aula (owler). |

*Consonants differing from the English*

| | |
|---|---|
| c | As in English before *a o u*. Ex. cubo (cooboh), caro (caroh). |
| | Hard *th*, as in *thank*, before e and i. Ex. cesto (thés-toh), cinco (thinkoh). |
| ch | As in English. Ex. chico (cheekoh), techo (téchoh). |
| d | Initial as in English; final very soft, sometimes like *th* in *the*. Ex. venid (vennéǝ the), sed (seth). |
| g | Before *a, o, u* as in English. Before *e, i,* like Scotch *ch* in *loch*. Ex. general (hhenerál). |
| h | Always mute. |
| j | Like *g* before *e* and *i,* or German *ch* in *ach!* Ex. jefe (hhéffeh). |
| ll | Like *lli* in *billiard, million*. Ex. Estrella (estrélya). |
| ñ | Like *ny* in *canyon*. Ex. Niña (ninya), Baño (bunnyo). |
| r | Stronger than in English, and always pronounced. Ex. caro (cároh), perro (pairroh). |
| s | Always sharp, as in *see, wants*. Ex. libros (léǝbross). |
| z | Like English th hard, as in *thank, which*. Ex. zoro (thorroh), paz (path or puth). |
| au | English oe as in now. Ex. palau (pallów). |

# At the travel agency

## En la agencia de viajes

**Good morning. 1** Buenos días. **2** *Bwénnoss déarss.*

**I want to leave for England, France, the United States on the... 1** Deseo salir para Inglaterra, Francia, los Estados Unidos... el día... **2** *Dessáyoh sulléarr púrrer inglutérrer, frúnthea, loss estárdoss... el déar...*

**I want to go by plane. 1** Me interesa ir en avión. **2** *Meh interrésser éar en uvvión.*

**I would like to leave next week. 1** Me gustaría salir la semana próxima. **2** *Meh göösterréar sulléarr lah semúnner próximer.*

**Could you make me a plan of the journey and give me an estimate? 1** ¿Podría hacerme un itinerario del viaje y presupuesto? **2** *Padréar utháirmeh oon ittínnerrrário del vee.úhheh e presoopwéstoh?*

**A contract journey. 1** Un viaje a «forfait». **2** *Oon vee.úhheh ah forfeh.*

**Is it to be a return trip? 1** ¿Ha de ser ida y vuelta? **2** *Ar deh sair ēēder e vwélter?*

**No, one way, as I may be going from there to another country. 1** Sólo ida, pues es posible que desde allí me dirija a otro país. **2** *Sāwloh ēēder, pwess ess posēēbleh keh meh dirrēēher ah āwtroh pice.*

**Do you want hotels included? 1** ¿Ha de ser con hoteles incluidos? **2** *Ah deh seir con awtéless incloo.ēēdos?*

*En la agencia de viajes*

**All inclusive with second class hotels. 1** Todo completo y en hoteles de segunda categoría. **2** *Tawdo compléttoh e en awtélles deh segöönder cúttegorréar.*

**How many days do you want to spend on the journey? 1** ¿Cuántos días desea destinar a ese viaje? **2** *Kwúntoss déarss dessáyer destinárr ah ésseh vee.úhheh?*

**Is your passport in order? 1** ¿Tiene el pasaporte en regla? **2** *Tyénneh el pússerpórrteh en régler?*

**I only require the visas of the... consulates. 1** Sólo me faltan los visados de los consulados de... **2** *Sälo meh fúllteh loss visscárdoss deh loss cónsoolárdoss deh...*

**What does that all come to? 1** ¿Cuánto cuesta todo? **2** *Kwúntoh kwestes tawdoh?*

**If I cannot go, will you return me the fares? 1** De no poder salir, ¿me devolverán el importe del billete? **2** *Dek non poddáair sulléëerr, meh devvólvairrëëan el imporrteh del billyétteh?*

**Yes, but you must give us twentyfour hours notice. I shall deduct 10% (1). 1** Sí, pero ha de avisarnos con veinticuatro horas de antelación. Se le deducirá el 10 por ciento (2). **2** *See, péhroh deh uvvissárnoss, con vénteh kwúttroh órass deh úntilutheón. Seh leh deddoothëërrár el dé.eth por thyéntoh.*

**I want a first class two berth cabin. 1** Deseo un camarote de primera para... con dos literas. **2** *Dessáyoh oon cummerrótte deh primáirrer púrrer... Con doss lëëeteruss.*

**I'm sorry, there's only one first left, with one berth, and a second with four. 1** Lo siento, sólo quedan de primera con una litera y de segunda con cuatro. **2** *Loh syéntoh, säwloh kéhdun deh primairroh con ööner lëëterer e deh segöönder con kwúttroh.*

**Yes sir. There's also a swimming pool, gymnasium, orchestra and bar. 1** Sí, señor, y también

---

*En la agencia de viajes*

piscina, gimnasio, orquesta y bar. **2** *See, senyórr, e tumbyéen pisthéener, hymnárseó, orrkéster e barr.*

**How much does it cost? 1** ¿Cuánto vale? **2** *Kwúntoh várleh?*

**All right, I'll come for my ticket tomorrow. 1** Perfectamente, mañana pasaré a recoger el pasaje. **2** *Pairféctaménteh, múnnyúnner pusserréh ah recohháirr el pussúhheh.*

**Please send the tickets to the hotel. The porter will pay for them** (1). **1** Haga el favor de enviarme el pasaje al hotel, allí lo abonará el conserje (2). **2** *Árger el fuvvórr deh énviarrmeh el pussúhheh awtél, úlyéé loh ubbónnerráy ul consáirrheh.*

**I want to take a pleasure trip to... 1** Quisiera hacer un viaje de recreo por... **2** *Keesáirer utháir oon ve.úhheh deh reccreóh porr...*

**What towns do you advise me to visit? 1** ¿Qué ciudades me aconseja que visite? **2** *Kéh theoodárdess meh úkkonséhher keh visséeteh?*

**This is the best moment to go to... 1** Estamos en la mejor época para ir a... **2** *Estármoss en lah mehhór éppocker púrrer ear ah...*

**Could you arrange me a combined, journey for...? 1** ¿Podría combinarme un viaje para...? **2** *Podréar combinárrmeh oon veúhheh púrrer...?*

**Yes sir. I'll arrange you a route that you'll like. 1** Sí, señor, le haré un itinerario que le agradará. **2** *See, senyyórr. Len urráy oon ittínnerrárrio keh leh uggrúdderrár.*

**I would like to visit the... region. 1** Quisiera visitar la región... **2** *Kissáirer víssitárr lah réh-heón...*

**We have fortnightly trips to... with visits to monuments, picturesque spots, etc. 1** Tenemos viajes quincenales para..., con visita a monumentos, museos, lugares pintorescos, etc. **2** *Tennémoss ve.úhhess kínthennárless púrrer... con vissééeter oh mónuméntoss, moosáyoss, loogárress pintorréscoss, etcétera.*

---

(1) See heading **The sea voyage,** for more information.
(2) Más información en el epígrafe **Viaje en barco.**

*Viaje en automóvil*

**Book me two seats for... ...'s car. 1** Resérveme dos plazas para el autocar del día... **2** *Ressáirvameh doss plúthuss púrrer el ōwtocárr del déar...*

**Have you any leaflets? 1** ¿Me podría facilitar folletos turísticos? **2** *Meh podréar futhillitárr follléttoss toorísticoss?*

**How much do I owe you? 1** ¿Cuánto le debo? **2** *Kwúntoh leh débboh?*

# Journey by car

## Viaje en automóvil

---

**The car**                          **El automóvil**

---

**The bumpers, 1** El parachoques. **2** *El púrra.tchóckess.*

**The radiator. 1** El radiador. **2** *El rúddier.dórr.*

**The wheel. 1** La rueda. **2** *Lah roo.édda.*

**The spare wheel. 1** La rueda de recambio. **2** *Lah roo.édda deh reh.cúmbeoh.*

**The tyre, the cover. 1** El neumático o la cubierta. **2** *El nayo.mútticoh or lah coobayáirter.*

**The inner tube. 1** La cámara. **2** *Lah cúmmerer.*

**The lamps. 1** Los faros. **2** *Loss faross.*

**The registration number. 1** La matrícula. **2** *Lah muttríckoolah.*

**The door. 1** La portezuela. **2** *La pórrteh.thooéller.*

**The boot. 1** El departamento para equipajes. **2** *El departamyéntoh púrra ékkipúkhes.*

**The tank. 1** El tanque de gasolina. **2** *El túnkeh deh gazzoleener.*

**The steering wheel. 1** El volante. **2** *El vollúnteh.*

**The horn. 1** La bocina. **2** *La bothēēner.*

**The petrol gauge. 1** El indicador de gasolina. **2** *El indicadórr deh gazzoleener.*

*Viaje en automóvil*

**The oil gauge. 1** El indicador de aceite. **2** *El indicadórr deh atháiteh.*

**The temperature gauge. 1** El indicador de temperatura. **2** *El indicadórr de temperatõõrer.*

**The contact. 1** El contacto. **2** *El contúctoh.*

**The lamp switch. 1** El interruptor de los faros. **2** *El interrooptór deh loss fáross.*

**The accelerator. 1** El acelerador. **2** *El uthélleradórr.*

**The gear change stick. 1** La palanca del cambio de marchas. **2** *Lah pullúnker del cumbeoh deh mártchass.*

**The hand brake. 1** La palanca del freno. **2** *Lah pullúnca del frénnoh.*

**The accelerator pedal. 1** El pedal del acelerador. **2** *El paydáhl dehl uthélleradórr.*

**The clutch. 1** El embrague. **2** *El embrárgeh.*

**The ventilator. 1** El ventilador. **2** *El véntiladórr.*

**The air filter. 1** El filtro de aire. **2** *El filtroh deh íreh.*

**The battery or the accumulator. 1** La batería o el acumulador. **2** *La butteréar oh el acoõõmooladórr.*

**The differential. 1** El diferencial. **2** *El differentheál.*

**The chassis. 1** El bastidor. **2** *El bustidórr.*

**The motor. 1** El motor. **2** *El mottórr.*

**The spark plugs. 1** Las bujías. **2** *Luss bookhéas.*

**The condensor. 1** El condensador. **2** *El condensadórr.*

**The valves. 1** Las válvulas. **2** *Luss vúlvoolers.*

**The carburettor. 1** El carburador. **2** *El cárrbooradórr.*

**The bearings. 1** Los cojinetes. **2** *Loss cokhinétterr.*

**The crankshaft. 1** El cárter. **2** *El cárrterr.*

**The oil pump. 1** La bomba de aceite. **2** *Lah bómba deh atháyteh.*

**The torque rod. 1** La biela. **2** *Lah be.élla.*

**The piston. 1** El pistón. **2** *El pistón.*

**The dynamo. 1** La dínamo. **2** *Lah dēēnamoh.*

**The coil. 1** La bobina. **2** *Lah bobbēēner.*

**The driving axle. 1** El eje de transmisión. **2** *El ékheh deh trunsmissión.*

**The cam shaft. 1** El árbol de leva. **2** *El árrbul deh läiver.*

*Viaje en automóvil*

**The wheel plates. 1** Los platos de las ruedas. **2** *Loss plártoss deh luss roo.éduss.*

**The radio, the aerial. 1** La radio, la antena. **2** *Lah rárdioh, la unténner.*


## At the border
## En la frontera

**Here we are at the border. 1** Ya estamos en la frontera. **2** *Yah esstármos en lah frontáirer.*

**We have to pass the customs. 1** Hemos de pasar por la aduana. **2** *Emmos deh pussárr porr lah úddoo.wúnner.*

**Passports please. 1** Los pasaportes, por favor. **2** *Loss pússer.pórrtess porr fúvvórr.*

**Here you are. 1** Tenga usted. **2** *Ténger oostéh.*

**Entry visa, exit visa, permit to stay. 1** El visado de entrada, de salida, de estancia para dos meses, de tránsito. **2** *El vissárdoh deh entrárda, deh sulleeder, der esstunthea, púrra doss messess, deh transitoh.*

**Please show me your car papers. 1** Hagan el favor de enseñarme la documentación del automóvil. **2** *Uckee lah tyéénneh Áymoss del buskhárr del cotcheh?*

**Here they are. 1** Aquí la tiene usted. **2** *Uckéé lah tyénneh oostéh.*

**Have we to get out of the car? 1** ¿Hemos de bajar del coche? **2** *Aymos deh buhkárrdel cotcheh?*

**That's all right. 1** Está en regla. **2** *Esstráh en régla.*

**Your international driving licence. 1** El permiso internacional de conducción. **2** *El permissoh internúthionúl deh condóôctheeón.*

**The triptych. 1** El tríptico. **2** *El trípticoh.*

**The temporary export licence. 1** El cuaderno de exportación temporal. **2** *El kwuddáirnoh deh exportatheeón temporúll.*

**The temporary import permit. 1** La tarjeta de admisión provisional. **2** *Lah tarkhétter deh údmissión provissionúll.*

*Viaje en automóvil*

**Where is the exchange office?** (1) **1** ¿Dónde está la oficina de cambio de moneda? (2). **2** *Dóndeh esstár la offithēēner de cúmbeoh deh monehder?*

**Will you please change me... into Spanish money.** **1** Haga el favor de cambiarme... en moneda del país. **2** *Árger el fuvvór deh cumbiárrmeh... en munéhder del pahēēss.*

**What rate have you given me? 1** ¿Qué cambio ha cotizado? **2** *Keh cumbeoh ah cóttithárdoh?*

**Thank you. 1** Muchas gracias. **2** *Mōōtchus grártheuss.*

**Where can I buy a road map? 1** ¿Dónde puedo comprar un mapa de carreteras? **2** *Dóndeh pwédoh comprárr oona múpper deh cúrretáirruss?*

**At a book shop at the end of this street. 1** En una librería que hay al final de esta calle. **2** *En oona lēēbrarēēa keh i ull finúll deh ésster cúllyeh.*

## On the road
## En el trayecto

**Could you please tell me which is the road to... 1** ¿Haría el favor de indicarme la carretera general de...? **2** *A réar el fuvvorr deh indicármeh lah curretáirer khenerúll deh...?*

**Is there a petrol pump near here? 1** ¿Hay cerca de aquí un surtidor de gasolina? **2** *I tháirrker deh uckēē oon sōōtidórr deh gússolēēner?*

**Follow the road and you will come to a service station. 1** Siguiendo la carretera encontrará una esta-

---

*Viaje en automóvil*

ción de servicio. **2** *Sigyéndoh lah curretáirra encontraráh oon estáh.theón deh sairr.veethio.*

**I want to fill up. The tank is nearly empty. 1** Deseo repostar. El depósito del coche está casi vacío. **2** *Dessáyoh reppostár.El deppósitoh del cótcheh esstah cusee vatheeoh.*

**How much shall I put? 1** ¿Qué cantidad desea le ponga? **2** *Keh cunti.dárd dessáyer leh póngoh?*

**Put in 40 litres of petrol and. 1** Ponga 40 litros de gasolin. **2** *Pónger kwurrénter leetross deh gússolee ener.*

**Do you want the car greasing? 1** ¿Desea engrasar el coche? **2** *Dessáyer engrussárr el cótcheh?*

**It's not necessary. 1** No es necesario. **2** *Nóh ess nethessarrioh.*

**Please see if the tyres are hard enough. 1** Haga el favor de revisar la presión de aire de los neumáticos. **2** *Árger el fuvvór deh revvisárr lah presseeón deh ireh deh loss náyoo.mútticos.*

**Put some water in the radiator. 1** Ponga agua en el radiador. **2** *Pónger úggwer en el rúddier.dórr.*

**Tell the mechanic to come. 1** Diga al mecánico que venga. **2** *Deeger úll mecúnnicoh keh vénger.*

**What is it, sir? 1** ¿Qué desea? **2** *Keh dessáir?*

**Will you please look at the ignition? 1** ¿Quiere revisar el encendido? **2** *Kee.áiry revvisárr el énthen.deedoh?*

**Do you notice any defect? 1** ¿Qué deficiencia observa? **2** *Keh déffy.thee.énthia obsáirrver?*

**The off (right) headlight does'nt light. 1** Que no se enciende el faro derecho. **2** *Keh nóh seh énthee.-éndeh el fárroh derétchoh.*

**That's all right now. 1** Ya está arreglado. **2** *Yáh estáh arreglárdoh.*

**Mechanic, please look over the carburettor, the lighting, the engine, the suspension and the brakes. 1** Mecánico, haga el favor de revisar la carburación, el encendido, el motor, la suspensión, los frenos. **2** *Mecúnnicoh, árger el fuvvór deh révisárr lah cárrboorrúthee.ón, el enthendeedoh, el mottórr, lah soospénsee.ón, loss frénnoss.*

**How much will that be? 1** ¿Cuánto es? **2** *Kwúntoh és?*

*Viaje en automóvil*

**I want a sparking plug and a new tyre. 1** Deseo una bujía, un neumático nuevo. **2** *Dessáyoh ōōna boohéer, oon náyoo.mútticoh nooévvoh.*

**Test the battery. 1** Compruebe la batería. **2** *Cómproo.ébbeh las butterr̄ēēr.*

**See to the brakes and the steering gear. 1** Arrégleme los frenos, la dirección. **2** *Urréglumméh loss frénnoss, lah diréck.theón.*

**The car won't start. 1** El coche no arranca. **2** *El cótcheh noh urrúncker.*

**The starter doesn't work properly. 1** El arranque no funciona bien. **2** *El urrúnckeh noh foon.theóner bee.én.*

**The carburettor needs seeing to. 1** El carburador precisa un reglaje. **2** *El cárrbooradór preth̄ēēser oon regláh.heh.*

**The radiator leaks. 1** El radiador pierde. **2** *El rárdee.uddór peeáirdeh.*

**The motor has seized. 1** El motor está agarrotado. **2** *El mottórr estáh uggúrrer.tárdoh.*

**The clutch does not work. 1** El embrague no funciona. **2** *El embrárgay nóh foon.theórner.*

**The fuses are burnt. 1** Se han quemado los fusibles. **2** *Sayún kehmárdoh loss foos̄ēēbless.*

**It needs new lamps. 1** Necesita lámparas nuevas. **2** *Netthess̄ēēter lúmperrus nwáivus.*

**How long will the repairs take? 1** ¿Cuánto tiempo durará la reparación? **2** *Kwúntok tee.émpoh d̄ōōrerráh lah réppurrútheoón.*

**How many kilometers is it to... 1** ¿Cuántos kilómetros hay hasta...? **2** *Kwúntoss killómmetross i usster...?*

**Is there a motorway? 1** ¿Hay autopista? **2** *I owtoh.pister?*

**Is the road good or is it very rough? 1** ¿Es buena la carretera o está muy accidentada? **2** *Es mwénner la cúrretáirer oh esstáh m̄ōōy úkthedentárder?*

**Are there many bends? 1** ¿Hay muchas curvas? **2** *I m̄ōōtchuss corrvus?*

**No. It's fairly level as far as. 1** No. Hasta... es bastante recta. **2** *Nóh. Ussterr... es busstúnteh récter.*

**After kilometer... the Port rise begins, with many**

*Viaje en automóvil*

**dangerous bends. 1** A partir del kilómetro... empieza la subida del Puerto... con muchas curvas peligrosas. **2** *Upparteer del killómmetroh... empyéther lah soobééder del pwáirrtoh... con móótchuss óórrvus pelligrósseras.*

**Is the summit of the Port very high? 1** ¿Está a mucha altura la cima del Puerto...? **2** *Esstár ar móótcher ulltóórer la théémer del pwáirrtoh?*

**1.400 meters above sea level. 1** A 1.400 metros sobre el nivel del mar. **2** *Ar méél kwúttron thee.éntos métros sobbreh el nivvéll del marr.*

**It the road tarred? 1** ¿La carretera está alquitranada? **2** *Lah cúrretáirer estár úllkittrunnárder.*

**Is it narrow? 1** ¿Es estrecha? **2** *Es esstrétcher?*

**Dangerous? 1** ¿Peligrosa? **2** *Pelligrórser?*

**Snowed over? 1** ¿Nevada? **2** *Nevvárder?*

**Frozen? 1** ¿Helada? **2** *Ellárder?*

**What is this district called? 1** ¿Cómo se llama esta comarca? **2** *Cómmor sel lyármer éssster cumárker?*

**Is it flat, mountainous? 1** ¿Es llana, montañosa? **2** *Es lyárner, móntunn yáwser?*

**How far is the station, the hotel, the Post Office, the telephone, the river, the bridge, the garage, the Police Station? 1** ¿A qué distancia está la estación, el hotel, la estafeta de Correos, el teléfono, el río, el puente, el garaje, la Comisaría de Policía? **2** *Ah kéh distúnthear estár lah estúh.theón, estúh.theón, ellor.tél, lah estuffetter deh corráyoss, el telléffonnóh, el réo, el pwénteh, el gurrúheh, las commissarear deh polli.théar?*

**Thanks for your information. 1** Muchas gracias por su información. **2** *Moochus grártheus porr soo informártheón.*

**Can you tell me whether there is a motel near here? 1** ¿Puede decirme si hay un parador cerca? **2** *Pwéddeh dethéarmeh see i onn púrrer.dórr tháirker?*

**At four kilometers beyond the next village. 1** A cuatro kms. pasado el primer pueblo que viene. **2** *Ah kwúttro killómetros pussardoh el primáir pwébloh keh ve,eny.*

*Viaje en automóvil*

**Waiter, we want lunch (1). 1** Camarero, deseamos almorzar (2). **2** *Cummerráiror, dessayármos úllmorrtharr.*

**Make us two bags for supper. 1** Prepárenos dos bolsas de comida para la cena. **2** *Preppárrennos dos bolsers deh commēēder púrrer lah thénner.*

**Is there a repair garage in this village? 1** ¿Hay en este pueblo algún taller de reparación de coches? **2** *I en éste pwéblor ullgoon tullyáir deh reppurruthéo deh cótches?*

**Yes, on the first crossing on the right. 1** Sí, en la primera travesía a la derecha. **2** *See, en lah primmáirrer travvessēēr úllah derrétcher.*

**The car has broken down... miles from here. 1** Mi coche está con avería a... kms. de aquí. **2** *Me cótcheh estár con uvverēēr ah..., killómmettros deh ukkee.*

**Mechanic, will you please look at my engine? 1** Mecánico, míreme el motor. **2** *Mekkúnnich, meerer el mottórr.*

**What is the matter? 1** ¿Qué le pasa? **2** *Kéh leh pússer?*

**There's a funny noise. Listen! 1** Que se oye un ruido extraño. Observe. **2** *Keh sélleh ōāīyeh oon roōēēdor extrúnnyor. Obsáirrveh.*

**Of course. The fourth rod is melted. 1** Efectivamente. Tiene la cuarta biela fundida. **2** *Effecteever.menteh. Tee.enneh lah kwarrter bee.éllar foondēēder.*

**What a nuisance. Get it mended as soon as possible. 1** Qué contrariedad. Haga el arreglo lo antes que pueda. **2** *Keh contrárreadud. Árger el úrrégloh loh úntess keh pwedder.*

**It will take a day to finish. 1** Tardaré un día en dejar terminada la reparación. **2** *Tarrderreh oon dēēar en dehár tairminárdoh lah réppurrútheon.*

**Well, it can't be helped. I will come back tomorrow.**

---

(1)   See heading **At the restaurant.**
(2)   Consultar el epígrafe **En el restaurante.**

*Viaje en automóvil*

**1** Si no hay otro remedio qué le vamos a hacer. Volveré mañana. **2** *See noh i órtrroh remáidio keh leh vármos ar uthéirr? Volverréh munnyúnner.*

**Is it all right now? 1** ¿Qué, ha quedado bien? **2** *Kee? ar keddárdoh b%%.en?*

**Yes, sir. I have cleaned the cylinder head, too. It was full of carbon dust. 1** Sí, señor. De paso he limpiado la culata que estaba llena de carbonilla. **2** *See sennyórr. Deh pussoh eh limpe.ardoh lah coolárter keh estárber ylénner deh carrbonn%%lyah.*

**I shall have to speed up, to see whether I can catch up some of the time lost. 1** Tendré que aumentar la velocidad, para ver si recupero algo este retraso. **2** *Tendreh keh ówmentárr lah velóssidud, púrrer váir see reco%%pairoh úlgod ésteh retrússoh.*

**Which is the straightest road to get to the coast? 1** ¿Cuál es la carretera más recta para alcanzar la costa? **2** *Kwúll ess lah cúrrettáirer muss réctoh púrrer úllcunthárr lah coster?*

**Which is the nicest beach round here? 1** ¿Qué playa es la más bonita en esta parte? **2** *Keh plýer ess lah múss bonn%%ter en ésster párrteh?*

**How long does it take to go to...? 1** ¿Cuánto tiempo se necesita para ir a...? **2** *Kwúntoh tee.émpoh seh nethesseeter púrrer earr ah...?*

**Which is the best road for... 1** ¿Cuál es la mejor carretera para ir a...? **2** *Kwúll ess lah mehórr curretáirer púrrer ear ah...?*

**Is there any monument, historical church or anything else worth visiting in this village? 1** ¿Hay en este pueblo algún monumento, templo histórico u otra cosa típica dignos de visitarlos? **2** *I en ésteh pwébloh úllg%%n monooméntoh, témploh isstóricoh oo áwtrrer córser típica dignoss deh vissitarrloss?*

**No, but in the next place there is a very famous museum of antiquities. 1** No, pero en la próxima localidad... hay un museo antiguo muy célebre. **2** *Noh, páiroh en lah prxima 'loccúllidud... i oon moosáyoh untigwoh m%%ee théllebreh.*

**Are we near the balneary? 1** ¿Estamos cerca

*Viaje en automóvil*

del balneario...? **2** *Estarmus tháirrca del búniá-rrio...?*

**This is a very pretty village. 1** Este pueblo es muy bonito. **2** *Éssteh pwébloh es mṏoee bonëëtoh.*

**It's an important tourist centre. 1** Es una importante estación turística. **2** *Ess oon imporrtúnteh estuthón toorística.*

**Large numbers of visitors come here in the summer. 1** En la época de calor afluyen a él una numerosísima colonia de veraneantes. **2** *En lah éppoker deh cullórr ufflooen en el noomairrosíssimer colónnia deh vérrenee.úntess.*

**Where do you advise me to stay overnight? 1** ¿Qué localidad me recomienda para pernoctar? **2** *Kéh loccullidúd meh reckommyénder púrrer páirrnoctarr?*

**Can you tell me how to get to the high road to... 1** ¿Podría indicarme qué dirección debo tomar para salir a la carretera general de...? **2** *Poddrréar indicarrmch ken dirréctheón débboh tommárr púrrer sullëërr úller currettáirer hennerrúll deh...*

**Is there much traffic on this road? 1** ¿Hay mucha circulación por esta carretera? **2** *I mootcher théercooltheón porr éster curretáirrer?*

**Yes, a lot of lorries, buses and cars go by every day. 1** Sí, diariamente pasan muchos camiones, autocares y automóviles. **2** *See, de.írerménteh pussen mõõtchoss cúmmeóness, ówtocárress ee ówtommóvvilless.*

**Are we far from... ? 1** ¿Falta mucho para llegar a...? **2** *Fullter mõõtchoh púrrer lyegárr ah...?*

**Excuse me. I want some water for the radiator.Can you tell me where there is a tap near here? 1** Oiga. Necesito agua para el radiador. ¿Podría decirme dónde hay una fuente cerca? **2** *Óyger, nethissëëtoh úggwer púrrer el rúddierdórr. Poddréar dethermeh dóndeh i ṏõner fwénteh tháirrker?*

*Viaje en automóvil*

### In case of an accident
### En caso de accidente

**Where is the nearest Police Station?** 1 ¿Dónde está la comisaría de Policía más próxima? 2 *Dóndeh estár lah commissarréar deh pollithéar muss próxima?*

**Please call a doctor.** 1 Haga el favor de llamar a un médico. 2 *Árger.el fuvvórr deh lymmárr ah oon méddico.*

**There has been an accident... miles from here, and some people are seriously injured.** 1 Se ha producido un accidente a... kilómetros de aquí y hay heridos graves. 2 *Seh ar prodootheedoh oon ackthidénteh ah ... killómetross deh uckēē ee i erē̄edoss grárvess.*

**There are some slightly injured.** 1 Hay heridos leves. 2 *I erē̄edoss lévvess.*

**There is some material damage.** 1 Hay daños materiales. 2 *I dúnnyoss muttairy.úlless.*

**Where is the nearest hospital?** 1 ¿Dónde está el hospital más próximo? 2 *Dóndeh esstár el ospittúll muss próximoh?*

**Please telephone for an ambulance.** 1 Sírvase telefonear a una ambulancia. 2 *Sē̄errver seh telephónniárr ah oona úmbullúnthear.*

**Are you injured?** 1 ¿Está Vd. herido? 2 *Estar oostéh errē̄edoh?*

**My Insurance Company is... Here is the policy.** 1 Mi Compañía de Seguros es... Aquí está la póliza. 2 *Me compunyéar deh segō̄oross es... Ukkē̄ē estár lah pollither.*

**Did you witness the accident?** 1 ¿Ha sido Vd. testigo del accidente? 2 *Ar sē̄edoh oostéh testē̄ēgoh del úkthidénteh?*

**Do you mind giving evidence?** 1 ¿No tiene inconveniente en hacer de testigo? 2 *Noh tē̄ē.eny inconvenee.énty en utháir deh testē̄ēgoh?*

**Will you give me your name and address?** 1 ¿Pue-

*Viaje en avión*

de decirme su nombre y señas de donde vive?
**2** *Pwéddeh dethēērr meh soo nómbreh i sénnyuss deh dóndeh vēēveh?*

**Can you tow my car in? It has broken down... miles from here. 1** ¿Puede Vd. remolcar mi coche? Está con avería a... kilómetros de aquí. **2** *Pwédeh oostéh remmolcarr me cotcheh? Estár con uvverréar ah... killómmetros deh uckee.*

---

| **Journey by air** | **Viaje en avión** |
|---|---|

---

**At the air line office**
**En la oficina de la compañía de aviación**

---

**Is there any space in the first plane tomorrow for... ? 1** ¿Hay plazas para el primer avión de mañana con destino a...? **2** *I plúthers púrrer el primair uvvión deh munyúnner con destēēnoh ah?*

**Yes, sir. How many seats do you want? 1** Sí, señor; ¿cuántas quiere? **2** *See, senyórr. Kwuntuss kyáireh?*

**Give me one for M... 1** Déme una a nombre de... **2** *Démmeh ōōner ah nómbreh deh...*

**How much is it? 1** ¿Cuánto es? **2** *Kwúntoh ess?*

**At what time does the plane leave for... ? 1** ¿A qué hora sale el avión para...? **2** *Ah keh āwrer sárleh el uvviún púrrer...?*

**At half past two exactly. 1** A las dos y media en punto. **2** *Ulluss dóssy méddier en pōōntoh.*

**When must we be at the airport? 1** ¿Con cuánta antelación se ha de estar en el aeropuerto? **2** *Con kwúntah úntellútheón sayár deh estár en el íro.-pwáirtoh?*

**Half an hour before-hand. 1** Es suficiente con media hora. **2** *Es soofithiénteh con méddier órrah.*

**Is the airport very far from the town? 1** ¿Está muy apartado el aeropuerto de la ciudad? **2** *Estár mooy úpparr.tárdoh el iro.pwáirtoh de lah théoodúd?*

**Not very. 35 minutes by car from the Company's office. 1** No mucho. Hay unos 35 minutos en coche desde las oficinas de la compañía. **2** *Noh mŏŏtchon. I ōōnoss trénter e thínkoh minootoss en cótcheh desseh luss óffiithēēnuss deh lah cómpunnēēr.*

**Passengers must be at the terminal at the time stated on the ticket. 1** Conforme se indica en las instrucciones del billete, a... han de estar los pasajeros en la estación terminal. **2** *Cónfórmeh seh indēēker en luss instrōōcktheeóness del bilyétth, ah... un deh estárr loss pússuh.háiross en lah estútheon táirrminnúll.*

**That is, an hour before the plane leaves. 1** ¿O sea, una hora antes de la salida del avión? **2** *Or sáyer, ōōner āwrer úntess de lah sullēēder del uvvión?*

**That's right. 1** Eso es. **2** *Essoh ess.*

**Porter, will you attend to my luggage? 1** Mozo, ¿quiere despachar mi·equipaje? **2** *Mórtoh, cáirreh desputchárr me ecki.púhheh?*

**At once, sir, Have you got your ticket? 1** En seguida. ¿Tiene el billete? **2** *En seggēēder. Tyénéh el bilyétteh?*

**Yes. Here it is. 1** Sí, tome usted. **2** *See, tórmer oostéh.*

**You had better have a label on your bags with your name on it. 1** Es conveniente que las maletas lleven una etiqueta con su nombre. **2** *Es convenivénth keh luss mullétuss lyévvun oona étty kétter con soo nómbreh.*

**If you are crossing the ocean, I would advise you to put the things you need most in a hand bag. 1** Haciendo un viaje transoceánico le aconsejo lleve en la valija de mano lo que pueda serle más necesario. **2** *Uthyéndoh oon vee.iúhheh trúnsotheánnicoh leh uccanséccoh lyéveh en la vullēēher deh márnoh law keh pwédder sáirleh muss néthessárrioh.*

**Why? 1** ¿Por qué? **2** *Pórrkéh?*

**Because the baggage hold is not accessible to passengers during the flight. 1** Porque las bodegas, que es donde van los equipajes, no son accesibles al pasaje durante el vuelo. **2** *Pórrkeh luss*

*Viaje en avión*

boddégguss, keh ess dondeh vun loss ekkipuhhess, noh son úck.thesseebl=ess doorúnteh el vwélloh.

**Thanks for your advice.** 1 Gracias por sus consejos. 2 Grútheus porr soos conséhhoss.

**You will have to pay... for excess luggage.** 1 Deberá abonar..., por exceso de equipaje. 2 Debberrár úbbohnárr... por extheéssoh deh ékkipúhheh.

**How much free luggage is allowed?** 1 ¿Qué peso admiten libre de pago? 2 Keh péssoh udmēēten lēēbreh deh párgoh.

**Fifteen kilos per person.** 1 Hasta quince kilos por persona. 2 Ússter kíntheh kēēloss porr páirsāwner.

**Up to twenty kilos.** 1 Hasta veinte kilos. 2 Ússer vénteh kēēloss.

**What hand luggage is allowed?** 1 ¿Qué equipaje está permitido llevar a mano? 2 Keh ékki.p; hheh estár paimittēēdoh lyevvárr ah múnnoh?

**At the airport**
**En el aeropuerto**

**The plane for...?** 1 ¿El avión para...? 2 El uv-vión porr...?

**Don't worry. The loud speaker will warn you.** 1 No se preocupe, el altavoz ya le avisará. 2 Noh seh pre.ocōōpeh, el ultervóth yar leh uvvēēsarráh.

**I will wait in the bar.** 1 Esperaré entretanto en el bar. 2 Espérreréh entreh.túntoh en el barr.

**You have to pass the Customs, too** (1). 1 Además ha de pasar por la aduana (2). 2 Uddemúss ar deh pussár porr lah úddoo.únner.

**At what time will we get to...?** 1 ¿A qué hora llegaremos a...? 2 Ah keh āwrer lyeggurráimuss ah...?

---

(1) See heading **At the frontier.**
(2) Consultar el epígrafe **En la frontera.**

*Viaje en avión*

**Do we fly direct? 1** ¿Hacemos el vuelo directo?
**2** *Utháimoss el vwélloh diŕréctoh?*

**No. We make a stop at... 1** No, hacemos escala en...
**2** *Noh, uthaymoss esscúller en...*

**Hurry up! The loud speaker is calling us. 1** Dése
prisa, que nos llaman por el altavoz. **2** *Désseh
prēēser, keh noss yármun por el áltervóth.*

**I am quite excited. 1** Estoy un poco emocionado.
**2** *Estóy oon pórcor emmóthionárdoh.*

**Have you never flown? 1** ¿No ha hecho ningún viaje
en avión? **2** *Noh ar étchoh ningōōn vee.húhheh en
uvvión?*

**It's my fifth or sixth flight, but I always feel excited
when we take off. 1** Es mi quinto o sexto vuelo,
pero siempre me impresiona cuando subo. **2** *Es mi
kíntoh oh séxtoh vooéloh, páiroh syémpreh meh
imprésseóner kwúndoh sōōboh.*

**Are we to go up in that three engined plane?
1** ¿Hemos de subir en aquel trimotor? **2** *Aymoss
deh soobéar en ukkél treemottór?*

**No, I think the officer is taking us to that other
bi-plane. 1** No, parece que el empleado se dirige
a ese otro bimotor. **2** *Noh, purrétheh keh el ém-
play.árdoh seh dirēēheh ah ésseh āwthoh bee.-
mottór.*

### On the plane

### En el avión

**The motors are starting up. 1** Ya se ponen en marcha los motores. **2** *Yah seh pónnen en márrtcher
loss mottóress.*

**We are leaving punctually to the minute (exactly
on time). 1** Salimos a la hora fijada. **2** *Sullēēmoss
ullah āwrer fihárder.*

**Don't forget to fasten your lifebelt that is on your
seat. 1** No olvide abrocharse el cinturón de seguridad que está en su butaca. **2** *Noh olvēēedeh
úbbrotchárrseh el thíntoorón deh segōōridúd keh
estár en soo bootúcker.*

*Viaje en avión*

**That's true. I must remember to do that. 1** Es verdad, debo tener en cuenta esta medida de precaución. **2** *Es vaird.r débboh tennáir en kwénter éster meděeder deh precǎwtheón.*

**May smoke? 1** ¿No podemos fumar? **2** *Noh podémmos foomárr?*

**Not now. Only when we are in full flight. 1** Ahora no. Cuando estemos en pleno vuelo. **2** *Uh.órer noh. Kwundoh estáimuss en pláinoh vooéloh.*

**We can hear the noise of the motors very loudly in this plane. 1** Se oye mucho el ruido de los motores en este avión. **2** *Seh óyeh mǒotchoh el rooěedoh de los mottórres en ésteh uvvión.*

**The heat makes me worse. 1** Me molesta más el calor que hace. **2** *Meh molléster múss el cullórr keh útheh.*

**You can regulate the air by the air intake beside your seat. 1** Puede regular la aireación por la toma de aire, situada junto a su butaca. **2** *Pwéddeh regoolárr lah íreh.;theón porr lah tómmer deh íreh sittooárder hǒontoh ar soo bootúcker.*

**Are we still far? 1** ¿Falta mucho para llegar? **2** *Fúllter mǒotchon púrrer lyegárr?*

**No, we have fifteen minutes to go. 1** No, tan sólo unos quince minutos. **2** *Noh, tun sawlaw oonos kíntheh minootoss.*

**I'm feeling a bit sick. 1** Estoy algo mareado. **2** *Estóy úlgoh múrreh.árdoh.*

**Ask the stewardess to look after you. 1** Solicite asistencia de la azafata. **2** *Sollithěěteh ússisténthea dellah úther.fárta.*

**The plane is going down. We are arriving. 1** El avión está descendiendo. Ya llegamos. **2** *El uvvión estáh déssthendee.éndoh. Yah lyégármoss.*

**I advise you to move your jaw, as if you were chewing, so as to avoid trouble withyour ear drum, and to button your life belt. 1** Le recomiendo que haga movimientos de masticación para evitar molestias en su tímpano, y que se abroche el cinturón de seguridad. **2** *Leh reecommiéndoh keh árger movvimyéntoss deh músticútheón púrrer evvitárr molléstius en soo tímpunnoh,*

*Viaje en avión*

*e keh seh ubbrótcheh el thíntoorón* ⃰ *deh seggō̄ oridúd.*

**We have already landed. 1** Ya hemos tomado tierra.
**2** *Yah áymos tommádoh tyérrer.*

## The airport
## El aeropuerto

**Terminal. 1** Estación terminal. **2** *Esstuthión tairminúll.*
**Bus. 1** Autocar. **2** *Outohcarr.*
**Airport. 1** Estación aérea. **2** *Estutheón ah.áiria.*
**The pilot. 1** El piloto. **2** *El pillllóttoh.*
**The mechanic. 1** El mecánico. **2** *El meckúnnicoh.*
**The radio operator. 1** El radiotelegrafista. **2** *El rárdioh.télligruffíster.*
**The bi-plane. 1** El bimotor. **2** *El bee.mottórr.*
**The three engine plane. 1** El trimotor. **2** *El tree.mottór.*
**The four engine plane. 1** El cuatrimotor. **2** *El kwúttre.mottórr.*
**The small plane. 1** La avioneta. **2** *Lah úvvionétter.*
**The helicopter. 1** El helicóptero. **2** *El élicópterroh.*
**The runway. 1** Las pistas de aterrizaje. **2** *Luss písters deh utterri.thúhheh.*
**The airport. 1** El aeropuerto. **2** *El ah.áiroh.pwáirrtoh.*
**The motors. 1** Los motores. **2** *Loss mottórress.*
**The jet plane. 1** El avión de propulsión chorro. **2** *El uvveón deh propoolseón.*
**The seats. 1** Las butacas. **2** *Luss bootúcuss.*
**The berths. 1** Las literas. **2** *Luss lēēteruss.*
**The windows. 1** Las ventanillas. **2** *Luss ventuuíllvus.*
**The propellers. 1** Las hélices. **2** *Luss élly.thess.*
**The wings. 1** Las alas. **2** *Luss arluss.*
**The vertical rudder. 1** El timón de dirección. **2** *El timmón deh directheón.*
**The horizontal rudder 1** El timón de profundidad. **2** *El timmón de proffoondidud.*
**The fuselage, the body 1** El fuselaje. **2** *El foosillúhheh.*

*Viaje en barco*

**The undercarriage. 1** El tren de aterrizaje. **2** *El tren deh uttérrithúhheh.*

**The cockpit (pilot cabin). 1** La cabina del piloto, la carlinga. **2** *Lah cubbēēner del pillóttoh, lah carrlínger.*

**The hangar. 1** El hangar. **2** *El ungárr.*

**The stewardess. 1** La azafata. **2** *Lah úttherfárter.*

**The safety belt. 1** El cinturón de seguridad. **2** *El thintoorrón deh seggōōridúd.*

---

| The sea voyage | Viaje en barco |
|---|---|

---

**At the shipping company's office**

**En la oficina de la compañía de navegación del consignatario**

**I want a passage to... On what days does the boat sail? 1** Deseo un pasaje para... ¿Qué días sale barco? **2** *Dessáyoh oon pussúhheh púrrer... Keh dēēuss sárleh barrcoh?*

**Every Thursday. 1** Los jueves de cada semana. **2** *Loss hwévves deh cárther semmúnner.*

**There is a regular service. 1** Hay servicio regular. **2** *I sairvēēthioh reggoolárr.*

**Splendid. Please book me for next week. Can you tell me the name of the ship? 1** Magnífico. Déme una plaza para el de la próxima semana. ¿Puede decirme el nombre del buque? **2** *Mugnífficoh. Démmeh ōōner plúther púrrer el deh lah próximersemm únner. Pwédeh dethēērmeh el nómbreh del bōōkeh?*

**The... sails next week. 1** La semana que viene saldrá el... **2** *Lah semúnner keh vyenneh suldrár el...*

**An economy ticket. 1** Pasaje clase turística. **2** *Pussúhheh clússeh toorística.*

**What cabin do you want? 1** ¿Qué camarote desea usted? **2** *Keh kummerrótteh dessáfer oostéh.*

*Viaje en barco*

**What classes are available? 1** ¿Qué clases tiene disponibles? **2** *Keh clússess tyéneh disponĕĕbless?*

**There are first, second, third and luxury class cabins available. 1** Hay camarotes de primera, segunda, tercera y de lujo. **2** *I cúmmerróttess deh prímmáirer, segŏŏnder, tairtháire e del lŏŏhoh.*

**Give me a first class with one berth, but not a hot one. 1** Déme uno de primera, con una litera, pero que no sea caluroso. **2** *Demme ŏŏnoh deh primmáirer, conŏŏner lĕĕterer, páiroh keh noh sáyer cullerãwsoh.*

**This one here on the cabin plan is just what you want. 1** Éste que le señalo en el plano de distribución de cabinas reúne esa condición. **2** *Ésteh keh leh senyúlloh en el plárnoh deh dístribŏŏtheón deh cubbĕĕnuss reh.díŏŏneh ésser conthión.*

**Whereabouts is it? 1** ¿Dónde está situado? **2** *Dóndeh estar sitooárdoh?*

**The middle of the ship, on the port side. 1** En el centro del barco y a babor. **2** *En el théntroh del barrcoh y ar búbbórr.*

**How much is it? 1** ¿Cuánto vale? **2** *Cw;ntoh várleh?*

**All right, book it for me, please. 1** Bien, resérvemelo. **2** *Byen, resáirrvemmelloh.*

**Can you give me a few labels for my luggage? 1** ¿Puede, usted, darme algunas etiquetas para el equipaje? **2** *Pw;ddeh oostéh dármeh ulgóónuss éttikéttus purrer el ékkipúhheh?*

**How many pieces have you? 1** ¿Cuántos bultos lleva? **2** *Kwúntoss bŏŏltoss lyévver?*

**Here you are. These are for the luggage you want to keep with you in the cabin, and these are for the luggage to go into the hold. 1** Tome usted. Éstas son para los bultos que quiera tener en el camarote, y éstas otras para los de bodega. **2** *Tómmeh osstéh. Ésson púrrer loss bŏŏltoss keh kyáirer tennáirr en el cúmmerróteh, e ésstuss awtros púrrer loss deh boddégger.*

**At what time does the ship sail? 1** ¿A qué hora sale el buque? **2** *Ah keh wãrer sárleh el bŏŏkeh?*

**At seven, eight, half past nine, a quarter to ele-**

*Viaje en barco*

**ven, in the morning. 1** A las siete, ocho, nueve y media, once menos cuarto, de la mañana. **2** *Ah luss sḗḗ.etty. ótchoh, noo.évveh e méddier, óntheh ménnos kwarrtoh e kwuttroh de lah munyúnnah.*

**At a quarter past two, at three twenty-two, a quarter past four in the morning. 1** A las dos y quince, las tres y veintidós. las cuatro y cuarto de la tarde. **2** *Ah luss doss e kíntheh luss tres e ventidóss, luss kwúttroh e kwárrtoh de lah tárrdeh.*

**At midday, at midnight. 1** A mediodía. A media noche. **2** *Ah méddioh déar. Ah méddioh nótcheh.*

**How long is the crossing? 1** ¿Cuánto tiempo dura la travesía? **2** *Kwúntoh tyémpoh dōōrra lah trúvvairséer?*

**On what day and at what time does the ship get to...? 1** ¿Qué día llega el barco a..., y a qué hora? **2** *Keh déear lyégger el barrkoh ah..., e ah keh āwrer?*

**How often does it stop? 1** ¿Cuántas escalas hace? **2** *Kwúntuss escúllus útheh?*

**Five times. It stops at the following places. 1** Cinco. Toca en los siguientes puertos... **2** *Thinkoh. Tóccer en loss siggyéntess pwáirtoss...*

**From which quay does it leave? 1** ¿De qué muelle sale? **2** *Deh keh mwélyeh sárleh?*

**From the International Marine Station. 1** De la estación marítima internacional. **2** *Deh lah esstútheón murríttimmer internútheonúll.*

**Do we have to be at the port much beforehand? 1** ¿Se ha de estar en el puerto con mucha antelación? **2** *Seh ar deh estár en el pwáirtoh con mōōtcher úntilúthión?*

**Two hours before sailing. 1** Dos horas antes de la salida. **2** *Doss āwrers úntess deh lah sullḗḗder.*

**How much do I owe you? 1** ¿Cuánto le debo? **2** *Kwútoh leh débboh?*

**Here you are, and thanks for your information. 1** Tome usted, y muchas gracias por su información. **2** *Tómmeh oostéh e mōōtchus grútheus porr soo informutheón.*

## At the port
## En el puerto

**Here we are at the quay. 1** Ya estamos en el muelle.
   **2** *Yah estármoss en el mwéllyeh.*
**Where's the boat? 1** ¿Dónde está el barco? **2** *Dóndeh estár el barrcoh?*
**Its this one. 1** Es ése de ahí. **2** *Ess éssy deh ahéē.*
**It's a magnificent transatlantic. 1** Es un transatlántico magnífico. **2** *Ess onn trúnsutlúnticoh.*
**And up to date. It was launched last year. 1** Y moderno. Fue botado el pasado año. **2** *E modáirnoh. Fweh bottárdoh el únyoh pussárdoh.*
**They are still loading. 1** Todavía están haciendo las operaciones de carga. **2** *Tóddervéar estún uthyéndoh luss óppairútheónes deh carrger.*
**There are two hours before they raise the anchor. 1** Es que faltan casi dos horas para levar anclas. **2** *Ess keh fúltun cússy dóssāwrers púrrer lyevvárr úncluss.*
**Porter, here are my bags. These are for the hold and these are for cabin No. 35. 1** Mozo, tenga mis maletas. Éstas han de ir a la bodega, y éstas otras colóquelas en el camarote 35. **2** *Mǎwthaw, ténger mees mulléttus. Ésstuss hun deh ear ah lah boddégger, e éstuss āwtruss colóckehlúss en el cummerrotteh trénty-thinkoh.*
**There's a lot of traffic in the port. 1** Este puerto tiene mucho movimiento. **2** *Este pwárirtoh tyénneh mǒǒtchoh móvvimyéntoh.*
**There are no warships. 1** No hay ningún buque de guerra. **2** *Noh i ningǒǒn bǒǒkeh de gérrer.*
**Because they all left for manoeuvres yesterday.
   1** Porque ayer salió toda la flota de maniobras.
   **2** *Pórrkeh ayáir sullióh tāwder la flótter deh múnniāwbruss.*
**But there are several cargo boats and tankers.
   1** En cambio hay varios barcos de carga y petroleros. **2** *En cúmbioh i varrioss bárrcoss deh carrger e pétrolláiross.*
**They are finishing the loading. 1** ¿Están terminando la carga? **2** *Estún táirminúndoh lah cárrger?*

*Viaje en barco*

**Yes, passengers may go aboard. 1** Sí, los pasajeros ya pueden subir a bordo. **2** *See, loss pússerháiross yah pwédden soobéér ah bórrdoh.*

**Porter, come aboard with me. 1** Mozo, acompáñeme al barco. **2** *Mawthaw, uccompúnyerméh ul bárrcoh.*

**Take care, sir. Hold the railing firmly. 1** Tenga cuidado, señor. Cójase bien a la barandilla de la pasarela. **2** *Ténger kweedárdoh, senyórr. Cóhherseh byén ah lah búnderríllyer deh lah pussaréller.*

## On board
## En el barco

**On what side is my cabin? 1** ¿Por qué lado está mi camarote? **2** *Porr keh lárdoh, estár me kúmmerrótteh?*

**It's forward. Go along that corridor and you'll come to it. 1** Está hacia proa. Siga aquel pasillo y lo encontrará. **2** *Estár úthier piáwer. Seeger ukkéll pússéélyoh e loh encóntrarrár.*

**Is that a good place? 1** ¿Es buen sitio? **2** *Ess bwén séétioh?*

**One of the best. Those below deck are hotter. 1** Es uno de los mejores. Los que están bajo cubierta son más calurosos. **2** *Ess óónoh dehloss mehhórress. Loss keh estún búhhoh coobyáirth son múss cúlooróssoss.*

**This deck is very roomy. 1** Esta cubierta es muy espaciosa. **2** *Estah coobyártoh es móöy esputhiáwser.*

**What a lovely room! 1** Este salón es precioso. **2** *Ésteh sullón es prétháwsoh.*

**You will like the smoking room better. 1** Le gustará más el salón de fumar. **2** *Leh goostaréar múss el sullón deh foomárr.*

**Where is the dining room, the bar, the library, the sick bay, the hair dresser's, the gymnasium, the tea room, the swimming pool, etc.? 1** ¿Dónde está el comedor, el bar, la biblioteca, la enferme-

*Viaje en barco*

ría, la peluquería, el gimnasio, el salón de té, la piscina, etc.? **2** *Dóndeh estáh el cómmidórr; el barr, lah bibliotékker, lah enfairmerréar, lah péllookerréar, el himnússio, el sullon deh lah, pistheener, etc.?*

**My cabin is rather large. 1** Mi camarote es bastante grande. **2** *Me cúmmerrótte es bustúnteh grúndeh.*

**Mine is smaller, but comfortable. 1** El mío es más pequeño, pero confortable. **2** *El méoh es múss pekkényoh, péhroh confort!rbleh.*

**The berths are cosy. 1** Las literas son cómodas. **2** *Luss lĕĕterus son cómmodus.*

**Steward, get me a deck chair, please. 1** Oiga, mozo, proporcióneme una silla de cubierta. **2** *Óyger, mãwthaw, propórtheónermeh ŏŏner síllyer deh coobyáirter.*

**How much is that? 1** ¿Cuánto es? **2** *Kwúntoh ess?*

**Steward, I want my dinner on deck, in my cabin. 1** Camarero, sírvame la comida en cubierta, en el camarote. **2** *Cummerráiroh, sĕĕrvermeh lah commĕĕder en coobyáirter, en el cúmmerrãwteh.*

**Steward, I am on a diet and want a special meal. Who attends to that? 1** Camarero, estoy a régimen y deseo una comida especial. ¿Quién se cuida de esto? **2** *Cummeráiroh, estóy ah réhimen a dessáyoh ooner commĕĕder espéthiúl. Kee.én seh kwĕĕder deh éstoh?*

**The second steward. I will tell him. 1** El segundo mayordomo. Ahora le avisaré. **2** *El segŏŏndoh mýorrdãwmoh. Uh.óra leh uvvíssarréh.*

**Are you feeling sick? 1** ¿Está usted mareado? **2** *Estah oostéh múrriardoh?*

**I'm never seasick. 1** Nunca me mareo. **2** *Nŏŏnker meh murráyoh.*

**Does she rock a lot? 1** ¿Se mueve mucho este barco? **2** *Seh, mooáyveh mŏŏtchoh ésteh bárrcoh?*

**No, only a little in heavy sea. 1** No, un poco sólo cuando hay mar gruesa. **2** *Noh, oon pãwcoh sãwloh kwúndoh i marr gruéssoh.*

**The sea is a little choppy. 1** El mar está picado. **2** *El marr estáh pickárdoh.*

**She is pitching somewhat, and yet there are no**

*Viaje en barco*

**waves. 1** El barco cabecea algo, y, sin embargo, no hay olas. **2** *El bárrcoh cubbetháyer úlgoh, y, sin embárrgoh, noh i āwlerss.*

**There is a ground swell. 1** Es que hay mar de fondo. **2** *Ess keh i marr deh fóndoh.*

**This rocking is almost unbearable. 1** Este movimiento de balanceo es casi insoportable. **2** *Ésteh móvimyéntoh deh búllonthávoh ess cssy insupporrtárbleh.*

**I'm feeling dizzy. I'm beginning to be sick. 1** Siento náuseas. Empiezo a marearme. **2** *Syéntoh nāwsayerss. Empyéthoh ah murreármeh.*

**I have a headache. 1** Siento dolor de cabeza. **2** *Syéntoh dollorr deh cubbéther.*

**Its the beginning of seasickness. 1** Eso es principio de mareo. **2** *Éssoh ess el printhíppioh deh murráyoh.*

**Now the sea looks like a pool of oil. 1** Ahora el mar parece una balsa de aceite. **2** *Ah.órer el marr purrétheh ooner búllser deh utháyteh.*

**Have you any binoculars? 1** ¿Tiene usted unos prismáticos? **2** *Tyénneh oostéh ōōnoss prismútticóss?*

**I can see a ship on the horizon. It looks like a cargo boat. 1** En el horizonte se divisa un barco. Parece de carga. **2** *En el orrithónteh ser divēēser oon bárrcoh. Purrétheh de cárrger.*

**I would like to be on land. 1** Tengo ya ganas de pisar tierra. **2** *Téngoh yah gúnners deh pissarr tyérrer.*

**At dawn tomorrow we shall reach... 1** Mañana, al alba, llegaremos a... **2** *Munnyúnner, al úllber, lyégarráymoss ah...*

**Come over to starboard. 1** Venga usted a estribor. **2** *Vénger osstéh ah éstribórr.*

**What's happening? 1** ¿Qué ocurre? **2** *Keh ucōōrreh?*

**What a magnificent sunset! 1** Hay una puesta de sol magnífica. **2** *I ooner pwéster deh sol mugníffiker.*

**Oh! its wonderful. I have never seen anything like it. 1** ¡Oh!, es admirable. No recuerdo haber visto cosa semejante. **2** *Oh! ess údmirárbleh. Noh rekwairdoh ubbáirr vistoh cāwser semmihúnteh.*

**What speed is she doing? 1** ¿A qué velocidad nave-

*Viaje en barco*

ga este barco? **2** *Ah kéh velóthidúd nuváiger ésteh bárrcoh?*

**Twenty miles an hour. 1** A veinte millas por hora. **2** *Ah vénteh míllyuss porr óra.*

**Is that a lot? 1** ¿Es mucho? **2** *Ess mōōhchoh?*

**It's about 37 kilometres an hour, but other times she does a better day's run. 1** Representan unos 37 kilómetros por hora. Pero otras veces hace mejor singladura. **2** *Represéntun oonoss tréntithinkoh killómmetross porr óra. Péhroh āwtruss véthess útheh myórr sin gladōōrah.*

**Does she burn coal? 1** ¿Va con carbón? **2** *Vah con carrbón?*

**Nowadays ships burn gas-oil or petroleum. 1** Hoy día los barcos van con gasoil y petróleo. **2** *Oy dear loss bárrcos vun con gússoil e petrólleo.*

**The compass. 1** La brújula. **2** *Lah brōōhoolah.*

**The rudder. 1** El timón. **2** *El teemón.*

**The propellor, the funnel, the smoke the breeze. 1** El ventilador, la chimenea, el humo, la brisa. **2** *El véntilladórr, la chimmenáyer, el ōōmoh, lah brēēsser.*

**Where's the swimming pool? 1** ¿Dónde está la piscina? **2** *Dóndeh estáh lah pisthēēner?*

**Which, the open air or the covered one? 1** ¿Cuál, la cubierta o la descubierta? **2** *Kwull, lah coobyáirter oh lah désscoobyárter?*

**At what time shall we arrive? 1** ¿A qué hora llegaremos? **2** *Ah keh óra lyéggarráymos?*

**I must see a doctor. Where is he? 1** Tengo necesidad de ver al médico. ¿Dónde está? **2** *Téngoh nethéssidud deh váir ull médicoh. Dóndeh estár?*

**In the sick bay. 1** En la enfermería. **2** *En lah enfáirrmerréar.*

**The pilot has taken over. 1** El práctico se ha hecho cargo del barco. **2** *El prúcticoh seh ar étchoh carrgoh del bárrcoh.*

**We are coming into the harbour. 1** Estamos entrando ya en el puerto. **2** *Estármos estrúndoh en el pwáirtoh.*

**The tugs have also taken over. 1** Los remolcadores también han entrado en acción. **2** *Loss remólcadérress túmby.én un entrárdoh en úctheōn.*

*Viaje en barco*

## The port
## El puerto

---

**The quay.** 1 El muelle. 2 *El mwéllyeh.*
**The marine station.** 1 La estación marítima. 2 *Lah estutheón murrítimmer.*
**The cranes.** 1 Las grúas. 2 *Luss groo.uss.*
**The sheds.** 1 Los tinglados. 2 *Loss tinglárdoss.*
**The boat, ship.** 1 El barco, el buque, el paquebote. 2 *El bárrcoh, el bŏ̄okeh, el púkkborth.*
**The transatlantic.** 1 El transatlántico. 2 *El trúnsutlúnticoh.*
**The motor ship.** 1 La motonave. 2 *Lah móttonárveh.*
**The ferry boat.** 1 El barco transbordador. 2 *El bárrcoh trunssbórderdórr.*
**The cargo boat.** 1 El barco de carga. 2 *El bárrcoh deh cárrger.*
**The fishing boat.** 1 El barco pesquero. 2 *El bárrcoh pesscáiroh.*
**The warships:** 1 Los barcos de guerra: 2 *Loss bárrcoss deh gherrer:*
**The battle ship.** 1 El acorazado. 2 *El uccórrerthárdoh.*
**The cruiser.** 1 El crucero. 2 *El crootháiroh.*
**The destroyer.** 1 El destructor. 2 *El destrooctórr.*
**The torpedo boat.** 1 El torpedero. 2 *El torrpedáiroh.*
**The mine layer.** 1 El minador. 2 *El meenadórr.*
**The submarine.** 1 El submarino. 2 *El soobmaiēēnoh.*
**The supply ship.** 1 El buque nodriza. 2 *El bookeh nodrēēther.*
**The aeroplane carrier.** 1 El portaaviones. 2 *El pórrter.uvvióness.*
**The coast guard ship.** 1 El guardacostas. 2 *El gwarrder.cóstuss.*
**The training ship.** 1 El barco-escuela. 2 *El bárrcoh escwéller.*
**The speed lanch.** 1 La lancha rápida. 2 *Lah lúncher rúppidder.*
**The tanker.** 1 El petrolero. 2 *El petrolláiroh.*
**The canoe.** 1 La canoa. 2 *Lah cunnóa.*
**The sailing ship.** 1 El velero. 2 *El velláirroh.*
**The tug boat.** 1 El remolcador. 2 *El remolcadórr.*

*Viaje en barco*

**The yacht.** 1 El yate. 2 *El yútteh.*
**The lighter.** 1 La chalana. 2 *Lah tchullúnner.*
**The dock.** 1 La dársena. 2 *Lah dárrsenner.*
**The sea plane.** 1 El hidroavión. 2 *El íddroh.uvvõn.*
**The anchor.** 1 El áncora. 2 *El úncorah.*
**The chain.** 1 La cadena. 2 *La cuddáiner.*
**The deck.** 1 La cubierta. 2 *Lah coobyáirter.*
**The bridge.** 1 El puente de mando. 2 *El pwénteh deh múndo.*
**The cabin.** 1 El camarote. 2 *El cúmmmerrótteh.*
**The hold.** 1 La bodega. 2 *Lah boddáiger.*
**The bow.** 1 La proa. 2 *Lah prãwer.*
**The stern.** 1 La popa. 2 *Lah pópper.*
**Port side.** 1 Babor. 2 *Bubborr.*
**Starboard.** 1 Estribor. 2 *Esstreeborr.*
**The hatchway.** 1 La escotilla. 2 *Lah escottílyer.*
**The rudder.** 1 El timón. 2 *El timmón.*
**The propellor.** 1 La hélice. 2 *La éllitheh.*
**The keel.** 1 La quilla. 2 *Lah killyer.*
**The boilers.** 1 Las calderas. 2 *Luss culldáiruss.*
**The funnels.** 1 La chimenea. 2 *Lah chemmináir.*
**The siren.** 1 La sirena. 2 *Lah sirrénner.*
**The foremast.** 1 El trinquete. 2 *El trinkétteh.*
**The mizzen mast.** 1 La mesana. 2 *La messúnner.*
**The mast.** 1 El mástil. 2 *El músteill.*
**The aerials for the radio.** 1 Los cables de la radio. 2 *Loss cárbless de lah rárdioh.*
**The lifeboat,** 1 El bote salvavidas. 2 *El bórteh súlvervẽēduss.*
**The life ring.** 1 El salvavidas. 2 *El salvervẽēduss.*
**The life saving jacket** 1 El chaleco salvavidas. 2 *El tchulléckoh súlvervẽēduss.*
**The captain.** 1 El capitán. 2 *El cuppitún.*
**The first officer.** 1 El primer oficial. 2 *El primmáir offitheúl.*
**The purser.** 1 El sobrecargo. 2 *El sóbreh.cérgoh.*
**The chief steward.** 1 El primer mayordomo (jefe de la despensa). 2 *El primáir myorrdãwmoh (héffeh dellah dispénser).*
**The head waiter (second steward).** 1 El segundo mayordomo (jefe del comedor). 2 *El segoondoh my.or.dãwmoh (héffeh del commidórr).*

Viaje en tren

**The pilot. 1** El piloto. **2** *El pillóttoh.*
**The engineer. 1** El maquinista. **2** *El múkkinnister.*
**The seaman (sailor). 1** El marinero. **2** *El murrináiroh.*
**The waiter. 1** El camarero. **2** *El cummerráiroh.*
**The waitress. 1** La camarera. **2** *Lah cummerráirah.*

---

| **The train journey** | **Viaje en tren** |
| --- | --- |

---

### At the station
### En la estación

**The station. 1** La estación. **2** *Lah estútheón.*
**The platform. 1** El andén. **2** *El undén.*
**The tracks. 1** Las vías. **2** *Luss véarss.*
**The rails. 1** Los raíles. **2** *Loss ríless.*
**The shelter. 1** La marquesina. **2** *Lah marrkesséēner.*
**The train. 1** El tren. **2** *El tren.*
**The engine. 1** La locomotora. **2** *Lah lāwcawmottórrah.*
**The van. 1** El furgón. **2** *El foorrgón.*
**The coaches, carriages. 1** Los vagones. **2** *Los vuggónness.*
**The electric rail. 1** El autovía. **2** *El ōūtaw.vēēr.*
**The windows. 1** Las ventanillas. **2** *Luss véntunníllyuss.*
**The engine driver. 1** El maquinista. **2** *El múkkiníster.*
**The stoker. 1** El fogonero. **2** *El fóggonnáiroh.*
**The station master. 1** El jefe de estación. **2** *El héffeh deh estútheón.*
**The inspector. 1** El revisor. **2** *El revvisórr.*
**The emplovee. 1** El empleado. **2** *El empleárdoh.*
**The pointsman. 1** El guardagujas. **2** *El gwárrder.uggōōhuss.*
**The guard. 1** El factor. **2** *El fuctór.*
**The porter. 1** El mozo. **2** *El mãwthaw.*

*Viaje en tren*

**The timetable. 1** El cuadro de horarios. **2** *El kwódroh deh orrárrioss.*
**The passenger. 1** El viajero. **2** *El vēēaháiroh.*
**The truck. 1** El baúl. **2** *El bah.ōōl.*
**The suit case. 1** La maleta. **2** *Lah mullétter.*
**The luggage. 1** El equipaje. **2** *El ékkipúhheh.*
**The electric wire. 1** El cable eléctrico. **2** *El cárbleh eléctricoh.*
**The smoke. 1** El humo. **2** *El ōōmoh.*
**Porter, have my luggage registered to... 1** Mozo, facture mi equipaje para... **2** *Mawthaw, fuctōōreh me ékkipúhheh púrrer...*
**You must get your ticket first, sir. 1** Primero debe sacar el billete, señor. **2** *Primmáiroh débbeh succár el bylyétteh, senyórr.*
**Give me the ticket. 1** Déme usted el billete. **2** *Démmeh oostéh el billyéte.*
**At which window do I get a ticket to...? 1** ¿En qué ventanilla despachan los billetes para...? **2** *En kéh véntuuníllyer despútchun billéttess púrrer...?*
**Where is the window? 1** ¿Dónde está la ventanilla? **2** *Dóndeh estár lah véntunníllyer?*
**Are you selling tickets to... 1** ¿Despachan aquí billetes para...? **2** *Despútchun ukkēē billyéttes púrrer...?*
**Three firsts please. 1** Déme tres primeras. **2** *Démmeh tress primáirass.*
**How much is it? 1** ¿Cuánto es? **2** *Kwúntoh ess?*
**How much is a ticket to...? 1** ¿Cuánto vale un billete para...? **2** *Kwúntoh várleh oon billyétte púrrer...?*
**First, second, third, couchette, sleeping car, pullman. 1** En primera, en segunda, en tercera, en coche cama, en coche pullman. **2** *En primmáirer, en seggōōnder, en tairrtháirer, en cótcheh cúmmer, en cotcheh pōōlmun?*
**A half ticket. 1** Un billete medio. **2** *Onn billyétteh méddioh.*
**Combined ticket. 1** Billete combinado. **2** *Billyéteh combinárdoh.*
**Family ticket. 1** Billete familiar. **2** *Billyétteh fummílliárr.*
**Do I have to change? 1** ¿Hay transbordo en el trayecto? **2** *I trunssbórdoh en el raryéctoh?*

*Viaje en tren*

**No, you don't have to change. 1** No, señor, no tiene usted que cambiar de tren. **2** *Noh, senyórr. Noh tyénneh oostéh keh cúmbyár deh tren.*

**Yes, sir. At the border. 1** Sí, señor; en la frontera. **2** *See, senyórr, en lah frontáirer.*

**Changing trains is always very annoying. 1** Los cambios de tren son siempre muy molestos. **2** *Loss cúmbioss, deh tren son mōōy mollésstoss.*

**Lets go to the waiting room. 1** Vamos a la sala de espera. **2** *Vármoss úller súller deh esspáirer.*

**When does the train leave? 1** ¿A qué hora sale el tren? **2** *Ah keh óra sárleh el tren?*

**At twenty past three; at half past three; at quarter to four. 1** A las tres veinte; a las tres y media, a las cuatro menos cuarto. **2** *Ah luss tres vénteh; ah luss tres e méddier; úllus kwúttroh ménnoss kwárrtoh.*

**We have time for a drink. 1** Tengo tiempo de tomar algo en el bar. **2** *Tengoh tyémpoh deh tommárr úlgoh en el barr.*

**Which platform does it go from? 1** ¿De qué vía sale? **2** *Deh keh veer sárleh?*

**Platform No. 1, line 5. 1** Del andén número 1, vía 5. **2** *Del undén nōōmairoh ōōnoh, veer thínkoh.*

**Where is the book stall? I want to buy a timetable. 1** ¿Dónde está el quiosco de periódicos? Deseo comprar una guía de ferrocarriles. **2** *Dóndeh estár el keeóscoh deh perrióddiccoss? Dessáyoh comprárr ooner géar férroh.curr̄ēēless.*

**I'll wait here for you. 1** Yo le espero aquí. **2** *Yoh leh espáiroh ukk̄ēē.*

**In the meantime you can register your luggage. 1** Mientras tanto, puede usted facturar el equipaje. **2** *Myéntruss túntoh, pwéddeh oostéh fuctoorrárr el ékkipúhheh.*

**All right. See me to the comparment. 1** Bueno, acompáñeme al coche. **2** *Bwénnoh, uccompúnyermeh ull cótcheh.*

**Please put the bags in. 1** Haga el favor de subir las maletas. **2** *Árger el fuvvór deh soob̄ēēr luss mulléltus.*

**They are already in the compartment. 1** Ya están

*Viaje en tren*

colocadas en su departamento. **2** *Yah estún collocárduss en soo depártaméntoh.*

**Give me the luggage ticket. 1** Déme el talón del equipaje. **2** *Démmeh el tullón del ékkipúhheh.*

**This way. Seat 6 is yours. 1** Pase usted aquí; ocupa el asiento número 6. **2** *Pússeh oostéh ukk̄ēē; ocōō-per el usyéntoh n̄ōōmairoh sáiss.*

**Thanks. Here you are. 1** Tenga usted, y gracias. **2** *Ténger oostéh, e grútheus.*

**Good luck, sir. 1** Que tenga buen viaje. **2** *Keh ténger bwén vee.úhheh.*

## In the train

## En el tren

**First class. 1** Primera clase. **2** *Primáirer clússeh.*

**Second class. 1** Segunda clase. **2** *Seḡōōnder clússeh.*

**The compartment. 1** El departamento. **2** *El depártaméntoh.*

**This coach is very comfortable. 1** Este coche es muy cómodo. **2** *Ésteh cótcheh ess m̄ōōy cómmodoh.*

**There are also reserved seats. 1** También los hay reservados. **2** *Túmbee.én loss i resserrvárdoss.*

**Are we going very fast? 1** Llevamos mucha velocidad. **2** *Lyevvármoss m̄ōōcher vellóssidúd.*

**Sixty, seventy, eighty ninety, a hundred kilometers an hour. 1** Sesenta, setenta, ochenta, noventa, cien kilómetros por hora. **2** *Sessénter, setténter, otchénter, novénter, thee.én killómmetross por óra.*

**This window doesn't open, doesn't close. 1** Esta ventanilla no se puede abrir, no se puede cerrar. **2** *Ésstah véntun̄ēēlyer noh seh pwéddeh úbrrēērr, noh seh pwéddeh therrárr.*

**I am going to look a the timetable. 1** Voy a consultar la guía. **2** *Voy ah cónsooltárr lah géar.*

**Is there no restaurant no saloon car? 1** ¿No hay

coche restaurante, coche salón? **2** *Noh i cótcheh résstorrúnteh, cótche sullón?*

**There are, but only on the expresses. 1** Sólo lo lleva el expreso. **2** *Sāwlaw loh lyéver el expréssoh.*

**Yes, there's a restaurant car. 1** Sí, hay coche restaurante. **2** *See, i cótcheh réstorrúnth.*

**At what time is the first, second sitting? 1** ¿A qué hora sirven la primera, la segunda serie? **2** *Ah keh óra sēērvun lah preemáirrer, lah segōōnder sáirrier?*

**We shall go through a long tunnel. 1** Pronto pasaremos un largo túnel. **2** *Próntoh pusserráimus oon lárrgoh toonél.*

**You can't smoke here. 1** Aquí no se puede fumar. **2** *Ukee noh seh pwedde foomárr.*

**What a pretty country! 1** ¡Qué paisaje más bonito! **2** *Khe pie.súhheh múss bonnēētih.*

**Look at that house at the top of the mountain! 1** Fíjese en aquella casa que está en lo alto de la montaña. **2** *Fēēherseh en uckéllyer cússer keh estár en lo últoh déllah montúnyer.*

**Do you mind the window open? 1** ¿Le molesta que esté abierta la ventanilla? **2** *Leh mollésster keh estéh ubyáirter lah vénttunnílyer?*

**A lot of wind and dust comes in. 1** Entra mucho aire y mucho polvo. **2** *Entrrer mōōcher íry e mōōtchoh pólvoh.*

**Are you very tired? 1** ¿Tiene usted sueño? **2** *Tyénneh oostéh swénnyoh?*

**Yes, I want to sleep. 1** Sí, deseo dormir. **2** *See, dessáyoh dorrmeerr.*

**The bed's already made. 1** Ya está hecha la cama. **2** *Yah estár étcher lah cúmmer.*

**Excuse me, this seat is taken. 1** Perdone, este asiento está reservado. **2** *Pairdónneh, ésteh ussyéntoh estár resserrrvártoh...*

**If you wish, we can put out the light. 1** Si usted quiere podemos apagar la luz. **2** *See oostéh kyáireh poddémmoss uppergárr lah looth.*

**Yes, if you like. 1** Sí, si usted quiere. **2** *See, see oostéh kyáireh.*

**Good night! 1** ¡Buenas noches! **2** *Bwennuss notchess.*

*Viaje en tren*

**These suitcases are mine. 1** Estas maletas son mías. **2** *Ésstuss mulléttus son méuss.*

**Can I put my bags here? 1** ¿Puedo poner aquí mis maletas? **2** *Pwéddoh ponnáir ukkēē mees mulléttus?*

**This man is the inspector. 1** Este empleado es el revisor. **2** *Ésteh emplaiárdoh ess el revvissórr.*

**What a long journey! 1** ¡Qué viaje más largo! **2** *Keh veeúhheh múss larrgoh!*

**How many stations are there to...? 1** ¿Cuántas estaciones faltan para llegar a...? **2** *Kwúntuss estútheóness fúlltun púrrer lyeggarr ah...?*

**Four more. We shall be there in an hour. 1** Faltan cuatro. Llegaremos dentro de una hora. **2** *Fúlltun kwútthoh. Lyeggarráimuss dentroh deh ooner óra.*

**These are the suburbs of... 1** He aquí los alrededores de... **2** *Eh ukkēē loss ulréddedórress deh...*

**Ten minutes stop. 1** Diez minutos de parada. **2** *Dee.eth minōōtoss deh purrárder.*

**I'n going to the canteen (bar). 1** Voy a la cantina. **2** *Voy úllah cuntēēner.*

**What station is this? 1** ¿Qué estación es ésta? **2** *Kéh esttheón ess éster?*

**All aboard, please. 1** ¡Señores viajeros, al tren! **2** *Senyórres vēē.uhháirress, ull tren!*

**I want to get in. 1** Deseo subir. **2** *Dessáyoh soobēērr.*

**I want to get out. 1** Deseo bajar. **2** *Dessáyoh buhhárr.*

**I want to go to the toilet. 1** Deseo ir al retrete. **2** *Dessáyoh éarr ull rettrétteh.*

**I want to go to the lavatory. 1** Deseo lavarme. **2** *Dessáyoh luvvárrmeh.*

**I should like to get there soon. 1** Quisiera llegar pronto. **2** *Keesáirer lyeggárr próntoh.*

**We are getting there, thank Heavens. 1** Felizmente ya llegamos. **2** *Felleethménteh yah lyegármos.*

**We are there. 1** Ya hemos llegado. **2** *Yah áymoss lyegárdoh.*

**May I get out? 1** ¿Me permite bajar? **2** *Meh pairmēēteh buhhárr?*

**Good luck, gentlemen. 1** Buen viaje, señores. **2** *Bwén vee.úhheh, senyórr.*

*Viaje en tren*

## Changing trains
## Cambio de tren

---

**We have to change at the next station. 1** En la próxima estación debemos cambiar de tren. **2** *En lah próximah estútheón debbémoss cumbeárr deh tren.*

**We need'nt hurry. 1** No nos precipitemos. **2** *Noh nos prethíppitáimos.*

**Porter, which is the train for...? 1** ¡Mozo! Indíqueme el tren que va a... **2** *Máwthaw! Indéekermeh el tren keh vah ah...*

**You have fifteen minutes to wait. 1** Hay que esperar quince minutos. **2** *I keh ésperrárr kíntheh minõõtoss.*

**What a nuisance! 1** ¡Qué fastidio! **2** *Kéh fusstíddioh!*

**Is this our train? 1** ¿Debemos pasar a ese tren? **2** *Débbémos pussárr ah ésseh tren?*

**No, sir. It's one that will come come in on this line. 1** No, señor; a uno que vendrá por esta línea. **2** *Noh, senyórr; ah õõnoh keh vendrár porr éstah línnear.*

**Here comes the train. 1** Ya llega el tren. **2** *Yah lyegger el etren.*

**What a muddle! 1** ¡Qué confusión! **2** *Keh confõõsión!*

**Can we get in now? 1** ¿Podemos subir ya? **2** *Podémmos soobéer yahh?*

**Does this traing go directly to? 1** ¿Va este tren directo a...? **2** *Vah ésteh tren dirréctoh ah...?*

**Yes, sir. It's a direct train. 1** Sí, señor; es tren directo. **2** *See, senyórr, ess tren dirréctoh.*

**Do you like travelling by train? 1** ¿Le gusta a usted viajar en tren? **2** *Leh gõõster ah oostéh vea.hárr en tren?*

**Yes, but I don't like to spend the night. 1** Sí, pero pernoctar en él no tanto. **2** *See, péhroh pairnoctárr en él noh túntoh.*

**Direct train. 1** Tren directo. **2** *Tren diréctoh.*

**Express train. 1** Tren expreso. **2** *Tren expréssoh.*

**Fast train. 1** Tren rápido. **2** *Tren rúppidoh.*

**Mixed train. 1** Tren mixto. **2** *Tren míxtoh.*

**Mall train. 1** Tren correo. **2** *Tren corráyoh.*

*La llegada*

# The arrival
# La llegada

---

**By car**                                   **En automóvil**

---

**Constable, where is the. Hotel, please? 1** Guardia,
tenga la bondad de decirnos dónde está el Hotel...
**2** *Gwárrdear, ténger lah bondard deh dethéarrmeh
dónde estár el otél...*

**Could you tell me a first, second, third class hotel,
a boarding house (pension)? (1) 1** ¿Podría indicarme un hotel de primera categoría, de segunda,
de tercera, una pensión? (2). **2** *Poddréar indi-
carrméh oon otél deh primmáirer cuttégorréar, deh
segoonder, deh tairrtháirer, oona penseón?*

**I should like two rooms with a bath. 1** Quisiera dos
habitaciones con baño. **2** *Kissáirrer doss ubbitut-
hióness con búnnyoh.*

**Porter, is there a garage near here? 1** Conserje,
¿hay cerca un garaje? **2** *Consáirheh, i tháirrcker
oon gurrúhheh?*

**Do they take in cars? 1** ¿Admiten automóviles?
**2** *Udmeetun owtohmóvvilles?*

**The garage is full, but we can recommend you ano-
ther, that is... 1** Está el garaje completo, pero le re-
comendamos otro que está... **2** *Estár el gurrúhheh
compléttoh, páiroh leh reccumendármoss awtroh keh
estár...*

**What do they charge a day? 1** ¿Cuánto hacen pagar
por día? **2** *Kwúntoh úthen paggárr porr déar?*

**All right. Do I have to complete any form? 1**
Conforme. ¿Se ha de llenar alguna hoja-registro de

---

(1)    See heading **At the hotel.**
(2)    Consultar el epígrafe **En el hotel.**

*La llegada*

entrada? **2** *Confarrmeh. Seh ar deh lyennár ulgō oner ohher deh entrarder?*

**Yes, sir. Please give me the details. 1** Sí, señor. Haga el favor de darme los datos. **2** *See, senyórr. Úgger el fuvvórr deh dárrme loss dártoss.*

**My name and surname are... 1** Mi nombre y apellido son... **2** *Me nómbreh i sényuss son...*

**Registration number... 1** Matrícula... **2** *Muttríckooler...*

**Make... 1** Marca... **2** *Marrker...*

**I am staying at... 1** Me hospedo en... **2** *Meh ospéddoh en...*

**Grease the transmission, and speed change gear, the water feed and the dynamo. 1** Hagan engrase de la transmisión y caja de cambios, de la bomba de agua, de la dínamo, etc. **2** *Árgan engrússeh den lah trunsmisseón e cúhher deh cúmbeoss, deh lah bómber deh úggwer, deh lah dēēnermoh, etc.*

**Look over the brakes. 1** Revisen los frenos. **2** *Revēēsen loss frénnoss.*

**Please fill the petrol, oil tank. 1** Sírvase llenar el depósito de gasolina, de aceite. **2** *Sēērvusseh lyennárr el deppóssitoh deh gússollēēner, deh utháyteh.*

**Give me ten, fifteen, twenty, thirty litres of petrol. 1** Ponga diez, quince, veinte, treinta litros de gasolina. **2** *Pónger dee.eth, kíntheh, vénty, trénter lēētross deh gússolleener.*

**Fill the radiator. 1** Ponga agua en el radiador. **2** *Ponger úggwer en el rúddy.úddór.*

**Test the tyres. 1** Compruebe los neumáticos. **2** *Comproo.ébbeh loss náyoo.mútticoss.*

**The window cleaner does not work. 1** El limpiaparabrisas no funciona. **2** *El limpyer púrrer.brēēsus noh foontheóner.*

**Wash the car. 1** Laven el coche. **2** *Lúvvun el cótcheh.*

**I want to hire a car with, without a driver. 1** Deseo alquilar un automóvil con chófer, sin chófer. **2** *Dessayoh ulkillár oon óutommóvvil conn choffeur, sin choffeur.*

## By plane                                    En avión

**It's been a splendid trip. What do we have to do now? 1** El viaje ha sido excelente. ¿Qué trámites debemos cumplir? **2** *El vyúckeh ah sǟědoh éxthellenth. Kéh trúmmitess debéhmos koomplǟěrr?*

**We have to pass the Customs (1). We shall be warned by loud speaker. 1** Hemos de pasar por la aduana (2). Los altavoces ya nos avisarán. **2** *Áymos deh pussárr porr lah úddooúnner. Loss últrvóthess yah nos uvvissarrún.*

**In the meantime we can wait in the waiting room or at the bar. 1** Entre tanto puede esperar en la sala de espera, o en el bar. **2** *Entreh tuntoh pwéddeh ésperárr en las súllah deh espáirrer, oh en el barr.*

**Excuse me, where is the lavatory? 1** Oiga, señor, ¿dónde está el lavabo? **2** *Óyger, senyórr, dóndeh estár el luvvárboh?*

**Is the town very far? 1** ¿Está muy lejos la ciudad? **2** *Estár mooy léhhos lah theudúd?*

**About twenty minutes by the bus. 1** A unos treinta minutos en autocar. **2** *Ar ȫǒnoss trénter minnȫǒtos en ȫǔtocárr.*

**Can we get into the bus already? 1** ¿Podemos subir ya al autocar? **2** *Poddáymos soobǟěrr yah úl ȫǔtocárr?*

**No, not until the lugagge and the mail have been unloaded and put into the bus. 1** No, señor. Cuando hayan descargado los equipajes y el correo del avión y los hayan colocado en él. **2** *Noh, senyórr. Kwúndoh áhyun déscarrgárrdoh loss ékkipúhhes ee el corráyo del uvvión y los íyun collocárdoh en el.*

**Where do I get my luggage. 1** ¿Dónde he de retirar el equipaje? **2** *Dóndeh ay de rettirarr el ekkipúhheh?*

**At the airport office or at the town office, when the bus gets there. 1** Puede hacerlo en las oficinas del aeropuerto, o en la estación terminal cuando lle-

---

(1)   See heading **At the frontier.**
(2)   Consultar el epígrafe **En la frontera.**

*La llegada*

guemos con el autocar. **2** *Pwéddeh utháirloh en luss óffithẽẽnuss del íropwáirtoh, oh en la estúthíon táirminúll kwúndoh lyeggemos con el õũtocárr.*

**I had rather get it when we arrive in town. 1** Prefiero retirarlo en la ciudad, a la llegada. **2** *Preffyáirroh rettirárrloh en lah théudúd, ullah lyeggárder.*

**Passeengers for... please get into car No. 12, at the exit. 1** ¡Pasajeros de... para...! Hagan el favor de subir en el autocar número 12, situado en la salida. **2** *Pusserháiross deh... púrrer...! árgun el fuvvórr deh soobẽẽr en el õũtocárr nõõmeroh dótheh sittooárdoh en lahsullẽẽder.*

**Lets go. They are calling us by the loud speaker. Don't forget your suitcase. 1** Vamos, que nos llaman por el altavoz. No olvide su maletín. **2** *Vármoss, keh noss lyúm mun porr el últervóth. Noh ollveedeh soo mulleteen.*

**Where is the town station, in the centre or in a suburb? 1** ¿Dónde está la estación terminal, en el centro de la ciudad o en un barrio extremo? **2** *Dóndeh estár lah estútheón táirminúll, en el théntroh de lah thẽẽ.oodúd oh en oon búrrioh extráimoh?*

**They are generally in the centre, but this one is just outside. 1** Generalmente suelen estar en el centro, pero ésta se halla a la entrada. **2** *Hwnerallménteh swéllen estar en el théntroh, pairoh ésstar se úllyer ah la entrárder.*

**Can we get out now? 1** ¿Podemos bajar ya? **2** *Poddáimos buhhárr yah?*

**Yes, sir. We are there. 1** Sí, señor. Ya hemos llegado. **2** *See, senyórr. Yah hémmos lyeggárdoh.*

**Porter, here's my ticket. Get my luggage. 1** Mozo, tenga mi billete y retíreme el equipaje. **2** *Mawthaw, téngur me bilyétteh e retéererméh el ekkipúhheh.*

**I'll bring it at once. 1** En seguida se lo traigo. **2** *En seggheeder seh loh trýgoh.*

**Shall I put it in a taxi? 1** ¿Quiere que se lo coloque en un taxi? **2** *Kyáireh keh ser loh collóckeh e oon túxxy.*

**No, thank you. I'll take it myself. 1** No es necesario. Me lo llevaré yo. **2** *Noh es nethessário. Meh loh lyévvarréh yoh.*

**All right. Get one and put it in. 1** Bueno, búsque-me uno y póngalo dentro. **2** *Bwénno, bōōskehmeh ‾ ōōnoh e póngaloh déntroh.*

**Here's the taxi. Your things are inside. 1** Ahí tiene el taxi. Sus maletas están ya en su sitio. **2** *Ah.é tyénne el túxxy. Soos mulléttuss estún yah en soo seétioh.*

**Thanks. Here you are. 1** Gracias. Tome usted. **2** *Grú-theuss. Tómmeh oostéh.*

**Driver, take me to... Hotel. 1** Chófer. Lléveme al Hotel... **2** *Chofeur. Lyévermeh ull ottél...*

---

# By ship                                    En barco

**Will it be long before we go ashore, Captain? 1** ¿Tardaremos mucho en poder desembarcar, ofi-cial? **2** *Tardarráymos mōōtchoh en podáirr déssem-barrcárr, offíthial?*

**First we have to pass the medical and immigration officers, and then the Customs (1). 1** Antes hemos de pasar por los trámites de sanidad y de inmigración, y a continuación por la aduana (2). **2** *Úntess áymoss deh pussarr loss trmmitess deh súnnidúd edeh ínmiggrúthión e ah cóntinoo.útheón porr lah údderwúnner.*

**Porter, get my luggage from the cabin and from the hold. There are five pieces. Here is my ticket. 1** Mozo, retíreme el equipaje del camaro-te y de la bodega. Tengo cinco bultos. Aquí tiene mi pasaje. **2** *Māwthaw, retēērermeh el ékkipúh-heh del cúmmerrótteh e deh lah boddégger. Téngoh thínkoh bōōltoss. Ukkēē tyénneh me pussúhheh.*

**Here's all your luggage, sir. 1** Señor, aquí está todo su equipaje. **2** *Senyórr, ukkēē estár tāwdoh soo ékkipúhheh.*

**Can I take the luggage somewhere for you? 1** ¿Quiere

---

(1) See heading **At the frontier.**
(2) Consultar el epígrafe **En la frontera.**

*La llegada*

que le lleve el equipaje a algún sitio? **2** *Kyáireh keh leh lyévveh ekkipuhheh ah ulgoon seetioh?*

**Yes, to the Hotel... 1** Sí, al Hotel... **2** *See, ull awtél.*

**No, I'll see to it myself. Here you are. 1** No, ya me cuidaré yo de él. Tenga usted, y gracias. **2** *Noh, yah meh kwēēdurréh yóh deh el. Téngah oostéh, e grútheass.*

---

## By train                                    En tren

**Have we far to go yet? 1** ¿Falta mucho para llegar? **2** *Fúllter mōōtchoh púrrer lyegárr?*

**We are just arriving. 1** Estamos llegando ya. **2** *Estármos lyegúndoh yah.*

**Here we are. 1** Ya estamos. **2** *Yah estármos.*

**I'm going to get out. 1** Voy a bajar. **2** *Voy ah buhhárr.*

**Porter! Porter! 1** ¡Mozo! ¡Mozo! **2** *Māwthaw, māw-thaw!*

**Take my bags to a taxi. 1** Tome usted mis maletas, y búsqueme un taxi. **2** *Tómmeh oostéh mees múllétters e bōōskemmeh oon túcksy.*

**Take this suitcase, this rug, this small bag, etc. There are six pieces in all. 1** Tome usted estas maletas, esta manta, este maletín, etc. Entre todo hay seis bultos. **2** *Tómmeh oostéh meess mulléttus, éstah múnter, ésteh mulletēēn, etc. Éntreh tāwdoh i sáyss bōōltoss.*

**Do you want a taxi? 1** ¿Quiere usted un taxi? **2** *Kyáirreh oostéh oon túcksy?*

**Yes, find me one. 1** Sí, búsqueme uno. **2** *See, bōōskehméh ōōnoh.*

**Put the luggage in the taxi. 1** Coloque usted los bultos en el taxi. **2** *Collóckeh oostéh loss bōōltos en el túcksy.*

**There are six altogether. 1** Son seis en total. **2** *Son sáyss en totúll.*

**Wait, porter. Take this ticket and get the registered trunk. I'll wait for you in the taxi. 1** Espere, mozo; tome este talón, y sáqueme el baúl que viene facturado. Le espero dentro del auto. **2** *Esspérreh, māwthaw; tómmeh ésteh tullón e súckehmeh el*

*La llegada*

*bah.ōōl keh tyénneh fucvtoorárdoh. Loh esspáiroh déntroh del ówtoh.*

**How time flies!** 1 ¡Cómo pasa el tiempo! 2 *Cómmoh písser el tyémpoh!*

**Ah, here's the porter with my trunk..** 1 ¡Ah! ya está ahí el mozo y mi baúl. 2 *Ah! Yah estár uh.ēē el māwthaw e me bah.ōōl.*

**Put the trunk by the driver and the bags inside.** 1 Coloque el baúl al lado del chófer y las maletas en el interior. 2 *Collóckeh el bah.ōōl al lárdoh del choffeur e las mulléttus en el intáiriórr.*

**Here you are, porter.** 1 Tenga usted, mozo. 2 *Téngah oostéh, māwthaw.*

**Driver, to... Hotel.** 1 Chófer, al Hotel... 2 *Choffēū, al awtél...*

**Quickly, please, driver.** 1 Vaya de prisa. 2 *Váryer deh prēēser.*

**Drive slowly.** 1 Vaya despacio. 2 *Váryer despútheo.*

**Driver, have we much farther to go?** 1 Chófer, ¿falta mucho para llegar? 2 *Choffeur, fúllter mōōtchoh púrrer lyégarr?*

**No, we are just arriving.** 1 No, señor: llegaremos en seguida. 2 *Noh, senyórr. Lyéggaráymoss enseggeeder.*

**What's the name of this street?** 1 ¿Cómo se llama esta calle? 2 *Cómmoh seh lyármer éster cúllyeh?*

**And this one?** 1 ¿Y esta otra? 2 *E éster āwtrer?*

**And that building in the distance?** 1 ¿Y aquél edificio que se ve al fondo? 2 *E uckél eddifēētheo keh seh veh ull fóndoh?*

**There are a lot of cars here.** 1 Aquí hay muchos automóviles. 2 *Ukkēē i mōōtchoss ōwtommóvvi:ess.*

**The streets are full of poeple going to and fro.** 1 Las calles están llenas de gentes que van y vienen. 2 *Luss cúllyess estún lyénnuss deh héntess keh vun e vyénnun.*

**When shall we get there?** 1 ¿Cuándo llegaremos? 2 *Kwúndoh lyéggurráymoss?*

**We are there.** 1 Ya estamos. 2 *Yah esstármoss.*

**Driver, open the door, please.** 1 Chófer, abra la puerta. 2 *Choffeur, úbbrrer lah pwáirter.*

*La aduana   En la frontera*

**How much do I owe you? 1** ¿Cuánto le debo? **2** *Kwúntoh leh débboh?*

**The meter shows... 1** El taxímetro marca... **2** *El tucksímmetroh márrcer...*

**Here you are, and your tip. 1** Tenga el importe del trayecto, y la propina. **2** *Ténger el impórrteh del trayéctoh, e lah propëéner.*

# Customs
## At the border

## La aduana
## En la frontera

**The Customs. 1** La aduana. **2** *Lah adoo.únner.*

**The Customs officer. 1** El vista de aduana. **2** *El víster deh adoo.únner.*

**The porter. 1** El mozo. **2** *El mórthor.*

**The luggage. 1** El equipaje. **2** *El ekkipúkhy.*

**The trunk. 1** El baúl. **2** *El bah.ool.*

**The suit case. 1** La maleta. **2** *Lah mullétter.*

**The portmanteau. 1** El portamantas. **2** *El pórrter.múntuss.*

**The camera. 1** El aparato fotográfico. **2** *El upperrártoh forto.grúfficoh.*

**The bag. 1** El bolso. **2** *El bólsoh.*

**The portfolio. 1** La cartera. **2** *La carr.tãirer.*

**The walking stick. 1** El bastón. **2** *El bustón.*

**The umbrella. 1** El paraguas. **2** *El pah.rúg.wus.*

**The traveller. 1** El viajero. **2** *El veer.háirroh.*

**The inspection. 1** La revisión. **2** *Lah revisseón.*

**The passport. 1** El pasaporte. **2** *El pússa.porteh.*

**Your papers. 1** La documentación. **2** *La dóckoo.mentúthee.ón.*

**Where is the Customs office? 1** ¿Dónde está la oficina de aduana? **2** *Dóndeh estár la offitheena del ádoo.únner.*

**Please call me a Customs officer. 1** Llame, por

*La aduana    En la frontera*

favor, a un empleado de la aduana. **2** *Ll.yármer paw fuvvor ah oon emplayárdoh deh la ádoo.únner.*

**Passport please. 1** ¿Su pasaporte, por favor? **2** *Soo pússapórrteh, porr fuvvórr.*

**Here it is. 1** Tenga usted. **2** *Ténga oostéh.*

**Who is with you? 1** ¿Quién le acompaña? **2** *Kee.én lah acum.púnya.*

**My wife and daughter. 1** Mi mujer y mi hija. **2** *Me moohāĩrr e me ēēhher.*

**What is the purpose of your journey? 1** ¿Cuál es el objeto de su viaje? **2** *Kwúl es el obhétto deh soo vee.úhheh.*

**Holidays, touring, extension of studies, family affairs. 1** Vacaciones, turismo, ampliación de estudios, asuntos familiares. **2** *Vucca.theónis, tourísmoh, úmpli.uthión deh estōōdios, assōontos fumilli.áress.*

**Where were you born? 1** ¿Dónde ha nacido usted? **2** *Dondy ar nuthēeedoh oostéh?*

**Date of birth. 1** Fecha de nacimiento. **2** *Fétcher deh núthy.myéntoh.*

**I expect to stay... days in this country. 1** Pienso estar ... días en este país. **2** *Pyénsoh estár... deersen ésteh pi.ées.*

**All right. 1** Está todo conforme. **2** *Estár tóhdoh confórrmeh.*

**Entry permit (visa). 1** Visado de entrada. **2** *Visárdoh deh entrarda.*

**Permit to stay. 1** Visado de estancia. **2** *Visárdoh deh estunthia.*

**Transit visa. 1** Visado de tránsito. **2** *Visárdoh deh trúnsitoh.*

**Will the luggage be examined now? 1** ¿Revisarán en seguida el equipaje? **2** *Rehvisserán el ekki.púkhy.*

**Yes, sir. 1** Sí, señor. **2** *Sēē senyórr.*

**How many pieces have you? 1** ¿Cuántos bultos lleva usted? **2** *Kwúntoss bōōltoss lyéhver osstéh.*

**Four. 1** Llevo cuatro. **2** *Lléhvoh kwútroh.*

**Have you anything to declare? 1** ¿Tiene usted algo que declarar? **2** *Tyeneh oostéh úlgoh keh déklarárr.*

**No. 1** No, señor. **2** *Noh, senyórr.*

*La aduana    En la frontera*

**Please look. 1** Examine. **2** *Exummēēneh.*

**I have no tobacco, spirits. 1** No llevo tabaco, licores.
**2** *Noh lyévoh tabúckoh, lickóres.*

**I have two packets of cigarettes. 1** Tengo dos
paquetes de cigarrillos. **2** *Téngoh dos puckéttes
deh siggerríllyos.*

**Have you any money? 1** ¿Lleva moneda...? **2** *Lyever
monéhda.*

**Yes, I have six thousand... 1** Sí, llevo seis mil...
**2** *See, lyévoh sáis mil.*

**How much is allowed? 1** ¿Cuánto está permitido?
**2** *Kwúntoh estar pairmittēēdoh?*

**Up to two thousand per person. 1** Hasta dos mil...
por persona. **2** *Úster dos mil porr pairsãwna.*

**Will these formalities last long? 1** ¿Duran mucho
tiempo estos trámites? **2** *Dooran mõõchoh tyémpoh
éstos tráhmittes?*

**No, they will soon be over. 1** No, se terminan muy
pronto. **2** *No, tairmēēna mooy próntoh.*

**Porter, take the keys. 1** Mozo, tome usted las llaves.
**2** *Mãwthoh, tórmeh oostéh lars lyárves.*

**Come with me. 1** Acompáñeme usted. **2** *Uccúm.-
páhnyahmeh oostéh.*

**In this trunk I have personal clothing, linen, one
suit and two pairs of shoes. 1** En este baúl hay
prendas de mi uso personal, ropa blanca, un traje,
y dos pares de zapatos. **2** *En ésteh bah.õõl i prén-
ders deh me õõsoh pairsonárl, rãwper blúnca, oon
trárkne e dos páhres deh thupártos.*

**Please open this suitcase. 1** Haga el favor de abrir
esta maleta. **2** *Árger el fuvvórr deh ubbreer éster
mullétter.*

**Must I open this small bag? 1** ¿Debo abrir el
maletín? **2** *Débboh ubbreer el mulleteen?*

**Do you want me to open the trunk? 1** ¿Quiere usted
que abra el baúl? **2** *Kyairy oostéh keh ubbry el baool?*

**With pleasure. 1** Con mucho gusto. **2** *Con moochoh
goostoh.*

**Here you are. 1** Vea usted. **2** *Vair oostéh.*

**Is there anything dutiable. 1** ¿Hay algo que pague
derechos? **2** *I úlgoh keh párgeh derrétchos?*

**No, sir. All these things are duty free. 1** No, señor;

todos son artículos libres de derechos. **2** *Noh , senyar. Tawdos arrtícoolos lēēbres deh derréchos.*

**May I shut the bag? 1** ¿Puedo cerrar la maleta? **2** *Pwédoh therrarr lah mullétter?*

**Yes, that's all. 1** Sí, hemos terminado. **2** *See, éhmos tairminahdoh.*

**How much duty have I to pay? 1** ¿Cuánto he de pagar de derechos? **2** *Kwúntoh áydeh puggár?*

**Porter, take the keys and lock my baggage. 1** Mozo, tome la llave y cierre mi equipaje. **2** *Mawthoh, tommeh lah lyarveh e thérreh me écky.púkheh.*

**Is this the passport officer, please? 1** Por favor, ¿ese señor es el vista? **2** *Porr fuvvor, essy senyrr ess el visēēterr?*

**No, he is the Customs Collector. 1** No, es el administrador. **2** *Noh, es el udmínistradórr.*

**See me to the train. 1** Acompáñeme al tren. **2** *Ukkum.púnyameh ul trén.*

**What class, sir? 1** ¿Qué clase tiene usted? **2** *Keh clússeh tyénéh osstéh?*

**First, second, third class. 1** Primera, segunda, tercera clase. **2** *Primāīrer, segōōnder, tairthāīr clússeh.*

**Where to? 1** ¿Dónde va? **2** *Dóndeh váh?*

**To... 1** Voy a... **2** *Voy ah...*

**Then I will find you a direct coach. 1** Entonces le buscaré un coche directo. **2** *Entónthess leh booscurréh oon cótcheh diréctoh.*

**Here is your seat and here are your bags. 1** He aquí su sitio. Ahí están sus maletas. **2** *Eh ukkēē soo sēētioh. Ukkee esstún sooss mullétters.*

**There are two, three, four, five pieces. 1** Son dos, tres, cuatro, cinco bultos. **2** *Son dós, trés, kwúttroh, thínkoh búlltoss (booltoss).*

**Right. 1** Está bien. **2** *Esstár bee.en (byen).*

**Here you are, porter. 1** Tome usted, mozo. **2** *Tómmeh oostéh, mawthoh.*

**Thank you, sir. 1** Muchas gracias, señor. **2** *Mōōchus grárthius, senyór.*

# At the hotel
# At the boarding house

# En el hotel
# En la pensión

| At the hotel | En el hotel |
|---|---|

**The hall. 1** El vestíbulo. **2** *El vestíbbooloh.*
**The porter. 1** El portero. **2** *El porrtáirroh.*
**The clerk. 1** El conserje. **2** *El consáir.heh.*
**The buttons. 1** El botones. **2** *El bottóness.*
**The management. 1** La dirección. **2** *Lah diréctheón.*
**The reception office. 1** La oficina de recepción. **2** *Lah óffithéēner deh rethéptheón.*
**The cash desk. 1** La caja. **2** *Lah cúhher.*
**The interpreter. 1** El intérprete. **2** *El intlirrpretteh.*
**The waiter. 1** El camarero. **2** *El cumáirroh.*
**The waitress. 1** La camarera. **2** *Lah cúmmerráirer.*
**The lift. 1** El ascensor. **2** *El ústhensórr.*
**The stair case. 1** La escalera. **2** *Lah ésculláirer.*
**The american bar. 1** El bar americano. **2** *El barr ummericúnnoh.*
**The dining room. 1** El comedor. **2** *El cómmidórr.*
**The smoking room. 1** El fumador. **2** *El foomerdórr.*
**The library. 1** La biblioteca. **2** *Lah bíbliotécker.*
**The first floor. 1** El primer piso. **2** *El primáirr pēēsoh.*
**The rooms. 1** Las habitaciones. **2** *Luss úbbitúthioness.*
**The inner and outer rooms. 1** Las habitaciones interiores y exteriores. **2** *Luss úbbitathióness intáirioress e extáiriórress.*
**The corridor. 1** El pasillo. **2** *El pússilloh.*
**The bath room. 1** El cuarto de baño. **2** *El kwárrtoh deh búnyoh.*
**The lavatory. 1** El lavabo. **2** *El luvvánhboh.*

**The electric bell. 1** El timbre eléctrico. **2** *El tímbreh eléctricon.*

**The management? 1** ¿La administración? **2** *Lah údministrútheón?*

**I booked a room for M... 1** Tengo reservada una habitación a nombre de... **2** *Téngo réssairvárdoh oon úbbitútheón ah nómbreh deh...*

**I'm sorry I couldn't get here sooner. 1** Siento no haber podido llegar antes. **2** *Syéntoh noh ubbáir podoéedoh lyeggárr úntess.*

**I want a single bedded room. 1** Deseo una habitación con una cama. **2** *Desséo comer úbbitútheón con ooner cúmmmer.*

**I want a single bedded room and a bath room. 1** Deseo una habitación con una cama y cuarto de baño. **2** *Desséoh ooner ubbitútheón con ooner cúmmer e kwúrrtoh deh búnyoh.*

**Two communicating rooms. 1** Dos habitaciones con comunicación interior. **2** *Doss úbbitútheónes con commöonicútheón intáirriórr.*

**A double bedded room. 1** Una habitación con dos camas o cama de matrimonio. **2** *Ooner; bitútheón con doss cúmmers oh cúmmers oh cúmmer deh múttrimónio.*

**I want the room with or without board. 1** ¿Desea la habitación sola o con pensión? **2** *Dessáir lah úbbitutheón sǎwlah oh con penseón?*

**How much is the room? And the board? 1** ¿Cuánto importa la habitación? ¿Y la pensión? **2** *Kwuhtoh impórrter lah úbbitútheón? E lah penseón?*

**Everything included? 1** ¿Todo incluido? **2** *Tǎwdoh ínclooo.éēdoh?*

**No, there's the 10% for service. 1** No, falta el diez por ciento del servicio. **2** *Noh, fúlter el dǒē.eth porr thyéntoh del sáirvēētheo.*

**This way, please sir. 1** Pase por aquí, señor. **2** *Pússy porr uckéē, senyórr.*

**Step into the lift. 1** Haga el favor de entrar en el ascensor. **2** *Úgger el fuvvórr deh entrárr en el usthensórr.*

**Do you like this room? 1** ¿Le gusta esta habitación? **2** *Leh gǒoster éster úbbitútheón?*

**It's all right. It's light. I'll take it. 1** Está bien. Es clara. Me quedo con ella. **2** *Estár bién. Es cléroh. Meh kéddoh con élyer.*

**Will you please fill in the registration form in the office. 1** Deberá llenar la hoja de registro de viajeros, en la conserjería. **2** *Débberrár lyennárr lah óhher de rehisstroh deh véaháiross, en el consáirherréar.*

**Will you fill in the form, porter? 1** ¿Quiere llenar la hoja, conserje? **2** *Káireh lyennárr lah óhher consáirheh?*

**Name and surname, please. 1** ¿Su nombre y apellido, por favor? **2** *Soo nómbre e úppelyēēdoh, porr fuvvórr.*

**Age. 1** ¿Edad? **2** *Eddud?*

**Thirty. 1** Treinta años. **2** *Trénter únyoss.*

**Married, single, widower. 1** Casado. Soltero. Viudo. **2** *Cussardoh. Soltáiroh. Vyúdoh.*

**Your profession? 1** ¿Su profesión? **2** *Soo profession?*

**Manufacturer. 1** Industrial. **2** *Indōōtriál.*

**Reason for journey? 1** ¿Motivo del viaje? **2** *Motte.-vóh delvyúhhy?*

**Pleasure. 1** Recreo. **2** *Reccráyoh.*

**Coming from? 1** ¿Procedencia? **2** *Préthedénthea?*

**Thank you. Where is your luggage? The boy will take it to your room. 1** Muchas gracias. ¿Dónde tiene el equipaje? El botones se lo llevará a su habitación. **2** *Mootchuss grútheuss. Dóndeh tyénneh el ékkiphhe? El bottóness loh lyévvararr ah soo úbbitatheón.*

**Can you tell me where the... consulate is? 1** ¿Podría indicarme dónde está el consulado de...? **2** *Pordéar indiccármeh dóndeh estár el consoolárdoh de...*

**Have my luggage sent up. 1** Haga subirme el equipaje. **2** *Úgger soobéarme el ékkipúhheh.*

**Where is the bath? 1** ¿Dónde está el baño? **2** *Dóndeh estár el búnnyoh?*

**In the corridor. The last door on the right. 1** En el pasillo. La última puerta a la derecha. **2** *En el pussílyoh. Lah ōōltimmer peváirter uller derrétcher.*

**Is the office open yet? I want to leave some money there. 1** ¿Está ahora abierta la caja del hotel? Deseo entregar cierta cantidad. **2** *Estar ah.óra ubyáirter lah cúhher del awtel? Dessáyoh éntreggárr tháirter kuntidúd.*

**Will you keep this money for me, please? Here is my card. Room No... 1** ¿Quiere guardarme usted ese dinero? Ahí tiene mi tarjeta. El número de habitación es el... **2** *Kyaireh gwarrdármme oostéh ésseh dinairo? Uh.ée tyénne me tarrhétter. El noomairoh deh úbbitthón es el...*

**Here is the receipt. 1** Tenga el recibo. **2** *Tenger el retheeboh.*

**Thank you. 1** Muchas gracias. **2** *Móotchus grútheus.*

**Can you tell me where there is a garage near the hotel? 1** ¿Puede decirme dónde hay un garaje cerca del hotel? **2** *Pwéddeh dethéerme dóndeh i con gurrúhheh tháirker del awtél?*

---

## At the boarding house      En la pensión

**The hall. 1** El recibidor. **2** *El rethíbbidórr.*
**The room. 1** La habitación. **2** *Yah úbbitúthón.*
**The bath. 1** El baño. **2** *El búnnyoh.*
**The bedroom. 1** El dormitorio. **2** *El dórrmitório.*
**The dining room. 1** El comedor. **2** *El cómmidórr.*
**The table. 1** La mesa. **2** *La messer.*
**The chairs. 1** Las sillas. **2** *Lus síllyus.*
**The carpet. 1** La alfombra. **2** *Lah afolómbrer.*
**The lamp. 1** La lámpara. **2** *Lah lúmperrer.*
**The clock. 1** El reloj de pared. **2** *El réllóh deh purréth.*
**The pictures. 1** Los cuadros. **2** *Loss kwúdross.*
**The radio. 1** La radio. **2** *Lah rárdio.*
**The radiator. 1** El radiador de la calefacción. **2** *El rúddierdór deh lah cúllefúctheón.*
**The sideboard. 1** El aparador. **2** *El uppúrrerdórr.*
**The sitting room. 1** La sala de estar. **2** *La súller deh esstár.*
**The piano. 1** El piano. **2** *El pyúnnoh.*
**The sofa. 1** El sofá. **2** *El sofár.*

**The armchairs. 1** Los sillones. **2** *Loss sillyóness.*
**The bookcase. 1** La biblioteca. **2** *Lah bibliotécker.*
**The books. 1** Los libros. **2** *Loss lẽẽbross.*
**Have you any rooms free? 1** ¿Tienen habitaciones libres? **2** *Tyénnen úbbittutheóness lẽẽbress.*
**I should like one for a fortnight. 1** Desearía una para dos semanas. **2** *Déssairréarrooner púrrer dos semmunnerss.*
**We have one available on the second floor. 1** Nos queda disponible una en el segundo piso. **2** *Noss kéddah disponnebleh ooner en el segõõnder pẽẽsoh.*
**Is there a lift? 1** ¿Hay ascensor? **2** *I ústhensórr?*
**How much is full board? 1** ¿Cuánto cuesta la pensión completa? **2** *Kwúnter kwéster lan pensión complétter?*
**Please have my suitcase brought up to the room. 1** Sírvase hacerme subir la maleta a la habitación. **2** *Seervvusseh úthairme soobeer lah mullétter ah lah úbbitútheón.*
**I should like to have a shower. 1** Desearía tomar una ducha. **2** *Déssairéar tomárr ooner dõõtcher.*
**At what time is breakfast? 1** ¿A qué hora se desayuna? **2** *A ken óra seh desahyõõner?*
**There is no fixed time. Whenever you like. 1** No hay hora fija. A la que usted desee. **2** *Noh i óra fẽẽher. Ulláh keh oostéh dessayer.*
**And lunch? 1** ¿La hora del almuerzo? **2** *Lah óra del ulmwáirthoh.*
**At two. 1** A las dos. **2** *A luss doss.*
**And the supper? 1** ¿Y la de la cena? **2** *E lah deh lah thénner?*
**At half past nine. 1** A las nueve y media. **2** *A luss nwévveh a méddier.*
**I don't want full board, only the room. 1** No me interesa la pensión completa, sino únicamente la habitación. **2** *Noh meh interrésser lah pénsión complétter, seenoh õõnicaménte lah úbbitútheón.*
**Where is the telephone? 1** ¿Dónde tienen el teléfono? **2** *Dõndeh, tyénnen el telléffonnóh?*
**May I phone? 1** ¿Puedo telefonear? **2** *Pwéddoh telleffónneárr?*

**Do you like the room, sir? 1** ¿Le gusta la habitación, señor? **2** *Leh gööster lah úbbitatheón, senyor?*

**Yes, I think it's very comfortable. 1** Sí, la encuentro muy confortable. **2** *See, lah enkwéntroh mooy cónfortúbbleh.*

**I find the bed rather hard. 1** La cama la encuentro algo dura. **2** *Lah cúmmer la encuéntroh úlgoh d͞óórah.*

---

## Going to bed                                    Al acostarse

**The bedroom. 1** El dormitorio. **2** *El dormittórrio.*

**The bed. 1** La cama. **2** *Lah cúmmer.*

**The double bed. 1** La cama de matrimonio. **2** *Lah cúmmer deh múttrimónio.*

**The pillow. 1** La almohada. **2** *Lah úllmohúdder.*

**The large pillow. 1** El almohadón. **2** *El úllmohuddón.*

**The spring matress. 1** El somier. **2** *El sómmieh.*

**The sheets. 1** Las sábanas. **2** *Lus súbbbunnuss.*

**The blanket. 1** La manta. **2** *Lah múnter.*

**The coverlet. 1** La colcha. **2** *Lah cóltcher.*

**The elderdown quilt. 1** El edredón. **2** *El édruddón.*

**The carpet, the mat. 1** La alfombra, alfombrilla. **2** *Lah úlfómbrer, úllfombríllyer.*

**The night table. 1** La mesita de noche. **2** *Lah messéeter deh nótcheh.*

**The armchairs. 1** Los sillones. **2** *Loss sillyóness.*

**The cupboard. 1** El armario. **2** *El armarrio.*

**The armchairs. 1** Las butacas. **2** *Luss bootuccuss.*

**The dressing table. 1** El tocador. **2** *El tóccerdórr.*

**The alarm clock. 1** El despertador. **2** *El despáirtudorr.*

**Please wake me at six, half past seven... 1** ¿Hará el favor de despertarme a las seis, a las siete y media...? **2** *Úrrer el fuvvórr deh déspairtárrmeh ah luss sée.etty e méddier.*

**Have a bath ready for me. 1** Téngame preparado el baño. **2** *Téngermeh preparráhdoh el búnnyoh.*

**How do you like the water, very hot? 1** ¿Cómo desea el agua, muy caliente? **2** *Cómmoh dessáyer el úgwer, mooy cullyenteh?*

**No, warm. 1** No, templada. **2** *Noh, templárdoh.*

**Cold water. 1** Agua fría. **2** *Ugwer freer.*

**Can you clean my shoes? 1** ¿Podrán limpiarme los zapatos? **2** *Podrún limpiárrme loss thuppártoss.*

**Yes, sir. Leave them in the corridor in front of your door. 1** Sí, señor. Déjelos en el pasillo en su misma puerta. **2** *See, senyórr. Déheh loss en el pussíllyoh en soo mísmer pwértah.*

**Please leave them at the foot of the bed. 1** Haga el favor de dejarlos a los pies de la cama. **2** *Árger el fuvvórr deh dehhárloss ah loss pé.es deh lah cúmmer.*

**Is this the call bell? 1** ¿Este es el timbre para llamar? **2** *Éste ess el tímbreh púrrer lyamárr?*

**Yes, sir. 1** Sí, señor. **2** *See, senyórr.*

**I am cold. Put another blanket on the bed. 1** Siento frío. Póngame otra manta en la cama. **2** *Syéntoh frēēoh. Pongermeh āwtrer múnter en lah kúmmer.*

**I'm tired. I shall sleep well. 1** Estoy cansado. Dormiré bien. **2** *Estóy cunsárdoh. Dorrmirréh byen.*

**What do you generally have for breakfast, sir? 1** ¿Qué acostumbra a tomar el señor para desayunar? **2** *Keh uccóstōōmbrer ah tommárr el senyórr púrrer déssa-yoonárr?*

**Coffee. 1** Café. **2** *Cufféh.*

**Chocolate. 1** Chocolate. **2** *Chócolárteh.*

**Ham and eggs, marmalade, coffee and milk. 1** Huevos con jamón, mermelada y café con leche. **2** *Wévoss con humón, máirmalárder e cufféh con létcheh.*

**Coffee and milk, a roll and butter. 1** Café con leche, un panecillo y mantequilla. **2** *Cufféh con letcheh, oon púnnithíllyoh e múntikíllyer.*

**Will you close the balcony, the window, please? 1** Cierre el balcón, la ventana, por favor. **2** *Thiérreh el bulcón, lah ventúnner, por fuvvórr.*

**There is a lot of noise. One can't sleep. 1** Hacen mucho ruido, no se puede dormir. **2** *Úthen mōōtchoh roo,ēēdoh, noh seh pwéddeh dormeerr.*

## Getting up                                      Al levantarse

**Good morning, sir. Have you slept well? 1** Buenos días, señor, ¿ha descansado bien? **2** *Bwénnoss déuss, senyór. Ah déscunsardoh bé,en.*

**Very well. 1** Muy bien. **2** *Móöy bé,en.*

**What's the time? 1** ¿Qué hora es? **2** *Keh óra ess?*

**Eight o'clock. 1** Las ocho. **2** *Luss ótchoh.*

**I had an unbroken sleep. 1** He dormido toda la noche en un sueño. **2** *Eh dorrmëëdoh tãwder lah nótcheh en oon swénnqyoh.*

**Do you want your breakfast? 1** ¿Quiere usted el desayuno? **2** *Kyérreh oostéh el déssayöönoh?*

**Yes, bring it at once. 1** Sí, tráigamelo en seguida. **2** *See, trygermehlóh en seggëëder.*

**No, I shall come down later. 1** No, ya bajaré luego. **2** *Noh, yah búhherráy lwéggoh.*

**You're up very early. 1** Ha madrugado usted mucho. **2** *Ah múdroogárdoh oostéh möötchoh.*

**Yes. It's my habit. I don't like to lose the morning. 1** Sí, es mi costumbre. Quiero aprovechar la mañana. **2** *See, es me costöömbreh. Kyáirroh pprovet-chárr lah munnyúnner.*

**Do you know the town? 1** ¿Conoce usted la ciudad? **2** *Connátheh oostéh lah théodúd?*

**It's the first time I've been here. 1** Es la primera vez que vengo. **2** *Es lah primmáirer veth keh véngoh.*

**I want a guide who speaks... 1** Desearía un guía que hable... **2** *Déssairréar oon géar keh úbbleh...*

**You can arrange that in the office. 1** Puede usted encargarlo en la administración. **2** *Pwéddeh oostéh encarrgárrloh en lah udministrútheón.*

**Is there a hairdresser in the hotel? 1** ¿Hay peluquero en el hotel? **2** *I péllookáiroh en el awtél?*

**At what time is dinner? 1** ¿A qué hora se come? **2** *A keh óra se cáwmeh?*

**At what time is supper? 1** ¿A qué hora se cena? **2** *Ah keh óra se thénner?*

**Ask if there are any letters for me. 1** Pregunte si hay cartas para mí. **2** *Pregoonteh see i cárrtuss pórrer me.*

**If anybody asks for me, tell them I shall be back**

**inmediately. 1** Si pregunta alguien por mí digá usted que volveré en seguida. **2** *See pregŏŏnter úlgee.en porr me, dĕĕger oostéh beh vólverreh en seggeeder.*

---

## The bath                  El baño

---

**The bath. 1** La bañera. **2** *Lah bunnyáirer.*
**The taps. 1** Los grifos. **2** *Loss griffos.*
**The shower bath. 1** La ducha. **2** *Lah dŏŏtcher.*
**The lavatory. 1** El water o lavabo. **2** *El vútterr oh luvvárboh.*
**The mirror. 1** El espejo. **2** *El espéhhoh.*
**The towels. 1** Las toallas. **2** *Luss to.úllyuss.*
**The towel rack. 1** El toallero. **2** *El twulláiroh.*
**The soap. 1** El jabón. **2** *El hubbón.*
**The soap box. 1** La jabonera. **2** *Lah jubbonnáirer.*
**The sponge. 1** La esponja. **2** *Lah espónher.*
**The tooth brush. 1** El cepillo para los dientes. **2** *El théppíllyoh púrrer loss dyéntess.*
**The tooth paste. 1** La pasta dentífrica. **2** *Lah puster dentíffrickeker.*
**The comb. 1** El peine. **2** *El páyneh.*
**The hair brush. 1** El cepillo para el cabello. **2** *El theppíllyoh púrrer el cubbéllyoh.*
**The bidet. 1** El bidé. **2** *El bíddeh.*
**The friction glove. 1** El guante para fricción. **2** *El gwúnteh púrrer fríctheón.*
**Bath salts. 1** Sales para baño. **2** *Sárless púrrer búnnyoh.*
**Massage brush. 1** Cepillo para masaje. **2** *Theppíllyoh púrrer mussúhheh.*
**Talcum powder. 1** Polvos de talco. **2** *Pólvoss deh túlcoh.*
**Can I have a bath? 1** ¿Puedo bañarme? **2** *Pwédde hbunyárrmeh?*
**Yes, sir, The bath is ready. 1** Sí, señor; el baño está preparado. **2** *See, senyorr. El búnnyoh estar prepurrárdoh.*
**Is the bath being got ready? 1** ¿Está preparado el baño? **2** *Estár preparrádoh el búnnyoh?*

**As soon as you like.** 1 Cuando usted guste. 2 *Kwúndo oostéh bŏŏsteh.*

**Get the towels and soap ready for me.** 1 Prepáreme usted jabón y toallas. 2 *Prepárrermeh hubbón e twúllvuss.*

**You'll find everything in the bathroom.** 1 Todo lo encontrará usted en el cuarto. 2 *Tawdoh loh encóntrarrár oostéh en el kwártoh.*

**Do you want the bath warm?** 1 El baño lo tomo con agua templada. 2 *El búnnyoh lo tómmoh con úggwer templárdah.*

**If you want a shower bath...** 1 Si usted quiere una ducha... 2 *See kyérreh oostéh ooner dŏŏtcher fréer?*

**No. In the morning I prefer a bath.** 1 No, por la mañana prefiero un baño. 2 *Noh, porr lah munnúnner prefyáiroh oon búnnyoh.*

**If you like you can have a luke warm bath.** 1 Puede usted tomar, si gusta, un baño tibio. 2 *Pwéddeh oostéh tommarr, see gooster, oon búnnyoh tibbioh.*

**I had rather. Cold water doesn't suit me.** 1 Lo prefiero. No me prueba el agua fría. 2 *Loh prefyáiroh. No meh prwébber el uggwer fréer.*

**After the bath I shall shave.** 1 A la salida del baño me afeitaré. 2 *Úller sullĕĕder del búnnyoh meh uffaiteréh.*

**This towel is small.** 1 Esta toalla es pequeña. 2 *Éster twúllyer es peckényoh.*

---

## Breakfast                                    El desayuno

**Waiter, coffee and milk, sugar, plum, strawberry, apricot, peach jam.** 1 Camarero, café con leche, azúcar, mermelada de ciruelas, de fresas, de albaricoque, de melocotón. 2 *Cummerráiroh, cúffeh con létcheh, úthhher, mairmalárder den thirru.éllus, deh fréssuss, deh úlberry, cóckeh, deh méllacottón.*

**Bring me a roll.** 1 Tráigame un panecillo. 2 *Trýgermeh oon punnithíllyoh.*

**This milk is cold.** 1 Esta leche está fría. 2 *Éster létcheh estar fréoh.*

**Give me some fresh water. 1** Déme agua fresca.
**2** *Démmer úgwer frésker.*
**I want some toast. 1** Quiero pan tostado. **2** *Kyáirrah pun tostárdoh.*
**I want chocolate with milk. 1** Quiero chocolate y leche. **2** *Kyáirroh chocolárteh e lécheh.*
**Give me some rusks. 1** Déme bizcochos. **2** *Démmeh biicótchoss.*
**Bring me an omelette. 1** Tráigame una tortilla. **2** *Trýgermeh ooner torrtíllyer.*
**Fried eggs, ham and eggs. 1** Huevos fritos, huevos con jamón. **2** *Wévvoss frēētoss, wévvoss con hummón.*
**Toast. Honey. 1** Tostadas. Miel. **2** *Tosstarduss. Myél.*
**One cup of coffee, please. 1** Un café. **2** *Oon cufféh.*
**Butter. 1** Mantequilla. **2** *Múntikillyer.*
**Bring me some toothpicks. 1** Tráigame mondadientes. **2** *Trygermeh mónder.dyéntess.*
**A packet of cigarettes. 1** Un paquete de cigarrillos. **2** *Oon puckétteh deh thíggarríllyoss.*
**Give me a match, please. 1** Déme un fósforo. **2** *Démmeh oon fósforróh.*
**How much do I owe you? 1** ¿Cuánto debo? **2** *Kwúntob débboh?*

---

## The meals                    Las comidas

---

**At what time is dinner? 1** ¿A qué hora sirven la comida? **2** *Ah keh óra sēērvun luss cumééderss?*
**At what time is supper? 1** ¿A qué hora sirven la cena? **2** *Ah keh óm seervun lah thénner?*
**Can one go to the dining room? 1** ¿Se puede pasar al comedor? **2** *Seh pwéddeh pussárr al comméhdórr?*
**Waiter, where can I sit? 1** Camarero, ¿dónde me siento? **2** *Cummerráiroh, dóndeh meh syéntoh?*
**Are you alone? 1** ¿Va usted solo? **2** *Var oostéh sawloh?*
**How many are you? 1** ¿Cuántos son ustedes? **2** *Kwúntos son oostéddess?*

**You will be alright here. 1** Aquí estará usted bien.
**2** *Ukke éstarrár oostéh byén.*

**You can sit at this table. 1** En esta mesa pueden sentarse. **2** *En éster mésser pwédden sen-
tárrseh.*

**May I serve you? 1** ¿Quiere usted que le sirvan?
**2** *Kyérreh oostéh keh leh sēērven?*

**No, a little later. 1** No; un poco más tarde. **2** *Noh.
Oon pāwcoh múss tárdeh.*

**Yes, at once. I'm in a hurry. 1** Sí, en seguida, tengo
prisa. **2** *See, en seggeeder. Téngoh prēēser.*

**Give me the menu. 1** Déme el menú. **2** *Lémmeh el
maynóo.*

**Give us some hors d'oeuvres first, then a good
soup, fish, vegetables, chicken or veal cutlet,
beefsteak; etc., pudding, coffee and liqueurs
(1). 1** Sírvanos primero entremeses. Luego una
buena sopa, pescado, legumbres, pollo o chuletas
de ternera, bistec, etc., y postres, café y licores (2).
**2** *Seervanoss primmairoh éntreh.méssess. Lwéggoh ooner bwenner sāwper, pescárdoh, póllyoh oh
chooléttuss deh táirnairer, bissteck, etc., e pos-
tress, cuffé e lickórress.*

---

## Services                              Servicios

### The washing
### Lavado de la ropa

---

**Waiter, don't forget to have my clothes washed.
1** Camarero, no olvide de hacer lavar mi ropa.
**2** *Cummeráirer, noh olvēēdeh deh uttháir luvvárr me
rāwper.*

**It is at the foot of the bed. 1** Está a los pies de la
cama. **2** *Estár ah loss lé.ess de lah cummer.*

---

(1)  Fusher information under the heading **At the restaurant**.
(2)  Más información en el epígrafe **En el restaurante**.

**Here is the list. 1** Aquí tiene usted la lista. **2** *Ukkee tyénneh oostéh lah lísta.*

**There are two shirts. 1** Hay dos camisas. **2** *I doss cummēēsuss.*

**Four pairs of socks. 1** Cuatro pares de calcetines. **2** *Kwúttroh páress deh cúlthtēēness.*

**Two pants. 1** Dos calzoncillos. **2** *Doss cúlthetēēness.*

**Eight handkerchiefs. 1** Ocho pañuelos. **2** *Ochoh púnyoo.élloss.*

**Two vests. 1** Dos camisetas. **2** *Doss cummisséttus.*

**Two pyjamas. 1** Dos pijamas. **2** *Doss pihúmmus.*

**When do you want this back? 1** ¿Cuándo quiere esta ropa? **2** *Kwúndoh kyérreh éster rawper?*

**In one, two, three, four days. 1** Dentro de uno, dos, tres, cuatro días. **2** *Déntroh deh doss, tress, kwúttroh déars.*

**As soon as possible. 1** Lo antes posible. **2** *Loh úntess possēēbleh.*

**I will try to manage it. 1** Procuraré complacerle. **2** *Procōōrrarrréh cómpluthéirleh.*

## To write a letter

### Para escribir una carta

---

**To write a letter 1** Para escribir una carta **2** *Púrrer escribeerr ooner cárrter*

**Waiter, bring me some paper and an envelope. 1** Camarero, tráigame papel y sobre. **2** *Cummeráirroh trýgermeh puppél e sóbreh.*

**I don't need a pen. 1** No necesito pluma. **2** *Noh nethessēētoh plōōmer.*

**What day is it today? 1** ¿Qué día es hoy? **2** *Keh déar ess hoy?*

**What is the date? 1** ¿A cuántos estamos? **2** *Ah kwúntoss estármoss?*

**Where can I post these letters? 1** Dígame dónde puedo echar estas cartas. **2** *Dēēgermeh dóndeh pwéddoh etchárr éstuss cártuss?*

**Where is the nearest post box? 1** ¿Dónde está el buzón más próximo para echar estas cartas?

**2** *Dóndeh estár el boothón múss próximoh púrrer etchárr éstuss cárrtuss?*

**Please post this letter. 1** Écheme esta carta al correo. **2** *Etchérmeh éstuss cárrtuss ul corráyoh.*

**Don't forget to put the stamps on. 1** No olvide de poner los sellos de franqueo. **2** *Noh olvéēdeh deh ponnáir loss sélyoss deh frunkáyoh.*

**Telephone**

**Teléfonos**

---

**Exchange. 1** Cambio. **2** *Kahmbyoh.*

**Supplementary No... 1** Supletorio núm... **2** *Sooplettórrioh nōōmerroh...*

**The receiver. 1** El aparato. **2** *El úppérrártoh.*

**The ear phone. 1** El auricular. **2** *El awriccoolárr.*

**n.°, one, two, three, four, five, six, seven, eight, nine, o, Mr... 1** Número uno, dos, tres, cuatro, cinco, seis, siete, ocho, nueve, cero, señor... **2** *nōōmerro oonoh, doss, tress, kwúttroh, thinkoh, sáyis, sée.etteh, ótchoh, nwévveh, tháiroh, senyórr...*

**I want a long distance call to number... at... 1** Deseo una conferencia con el número... de... **2** *Dessáyoh onner conferrénthier con el nōōmeroh... deh...*

**Will it be long? 1** ¿Tardará mucho? **2** *Tárdarráh mōōtchoh?*

**Where is the phone booth? 1** ¿Dónde está la cabina de teléfonos? **2** *Dóndeh estár lah kahbéenah deh telléffonnóss?*

**May I use this telephone? 1** ¿Puedo usar este teléfono? **2** *Pwéddoh oosárr éste telléffonóh?*

**Hello, hello. 1** ¡Oiga! Oiga! **2** *Oyger! Oyger!*

**Yes? 1** ¡Dígame! **2** *Dēēgermeh!*

*En el restaurante*

# At the restaurant

# En el restaurante

---

**The table** **La mesa**

**The table cloth. 1** El mantel. **2** *El muntéll.*
**The serviette. 1** La servilleta. **2** *Lah sairvilyétter.*
**The plate. 1** El plato. **2** *El plúttoh.*
**The glass. 1** El vaso. **2** *El vússoh.*
**The wine glass. 1** La copa. **2** *Lah cópper.*
**The liqueur glass. 1** La copita. **2** *Lah coppḗēter.*
**The spoon. 1** La cuchara. **2** *Lah cootchúrrer.*
**The desert spoon. 1** La cucharilla. **2** *Lah cootcherríl-yer.*
**The fork. 1** El tenedor. **2** *El ténnedórr.*
**The knife. 1** El cuchillo. **2** *El cootchílyoh.*
**The wine. 1** El vino. **2** *El vēēnoh.*
**Champagne. 1** El champán. **2** *El shumpúnyer.*
**Water. 1** El agua. **2** *El úgwer.*
**Mineral water. 1** El agua mineral. **2** *El úgwer minerúll.*
**Oil. 1** El aceite. **2** *El utháiteh.*
**Vinegar. 1** El vinagre. **2** *El vinúggreh.*
**Beer. 1** La cerveza. **2** *Lah trairvéther.*
**Milk. 1** La leche. **2** *Lah létcheh.*
**Bread. 1** El pan. **2** *El pun.*
**Mustard. 1** La mostaza. **2** *Lah mostúther.*
**The salt pot. 1** El salero. **2** *El sulláirroh.*
**Pepper. 1** La pimienta. **2** *Lah pimmyénter.*
**The chair. 1** La silla. **2** *Lah síllyer.*
**Cold, hot, warm. 1** Frío, caliente, tibio. **2** *Fréo, cul-yénteh, tíbbea.*
**Toothpicks. 1** Los mondadientes. **2** *Loss món-derdyéntess.*
**The menu, the card. 1** El menú. **2** *El mennōō.*

*En el restaurante*

---

## The dinner                                                    La comida

**Waiter, we should like a table near the window.**
1 Camarero, desearíamos una mesa junto a la ventana. 2 *Cummerráirroh, déssairéarmoss ooner mésser hõõntoh úller ventúnner.*

**Where can we sit?** 1 ¿Dónde podemos sentarnos?
2 *Dóndeh poddémmoss sentárrnoss?*

**How many are you?** 1 ¿Cuántos son ustedes?
2 *Kwúntoss son oostéddess?*

**Can't we have that table?** 1 ¿No podemos ocupar aquella mesa? 2 *Noh poddémmos occoopárr uckéllyan mésser?*

**I'm sorry. It's reserved.** 1 Lo siento. Está reservada.
2 *Loh syéntoh. Estár ressairrvárdah.*

**Waiter, give me the dinner, please.** 1 Camarero, sírvame el cubierto. 2 *Cummerráirroh, sẽẽrrvummeh el coobyáirrtoh.*

**Waiter, give me the menu, please.** 1 Camarero, déme la carta. 2 *Cummerráirroh, démmeh lah cárrter.*

**Bring us some hors d'oeuvres.** 1 Tráiganos entremeses variados. 2 *Trygernoss éntremessess vurreárdoss.*

**Ham, sausage, butter, tuna, olives.** 1 Jamón, salchichón, mantequilla, atún, aceitunas... 2 *Hummón, sulsitchon, muntikíllyer, uttõõn, uthehtõõnuss.*

**Do you want our special salad?** 1 ¿Desean los señores ensaladilla, especialidad de la casa? 2 *Dessányun loss senyórress ensúlluddíllyer, espéthiúllidúd, deh lah cússer?*

**Then some normandy sole.** 1 A continuación sírvanos lenguado a la normanda. 2 *Ah contínooútheón sẽẽrvunnoss lengwárdoh ah lah norrmúnder.*

**Right, sir.** 1 Perfectamente, señor. 2 *Pairfécterménteh, senyórr.*

**We will make you a paella that you will like.** 1 Les prepararemos una paella que les gustará. 2 *Less prepúrrarráymoss ooner py.élyer keh less foosterráh.*

**What else would you like?** 1 ¿Qué más desean los señores? 2 *Keh muss dessáyun loss senyórress?*

*En el restaurante*

**Veal cutlets and fried potatoes. 1** Unas chuletas de ternera con patatas fritas. **2** *Oonuss chooléttus deh tairnáirrer con puttártess frẽẽtuss.*

**For me, chicken and salad. 1** A mí pollo asado con unas hojitas de lechuga. **2** *Ah me pólyoh ussárdoh con õõuuss onhẽẽtuss deh letchõõger.*

**An for me, some roman hake with a little lemon. 1** Y a mí, merluza a la romana con un poquito de limón. **2** *E ah me, mairrlõõther ah lah rommúnner con oon pockẽẽtoh deh limmón.*

**Waiter, bring me another plate, a fork and a glass. 1** Camarero, tráigame otro plato, un tenedor, un vaso. **2** *Cummerráirroh, trygermeh óttroh plúttoh, oon tennedórr. oon vússoh.*

**What would you like to drink? 1** ¿Qué desean beber los señores? **2** *Keh dessáyun bebbáirr loss senyórress?*

**Champagne. 1** Champán. **2** *Shumpúnyer.*

**White wine, red wine. 1** Vino blanco, vino tinto. **2** *Vẽẽnoh blúncoh, vẽẽnoh tíntoh.*

**Have you any favourite brand? 1** ¿Tienen preferencia por una marca determinada? **2** *Tyénnen preferrénthea porr ooner márrker dettáirminnárder?*

**No, so long as it's good. Don't forget to bring a bottle of mineral water, too. 1** No, que sea bueno. No olvide de traer también una botella de agua mineral. **2** *Noh, keh sáyer bwénnoh. Noh olvẽẽdeh deh try.áirr tumbyén ooner bottéllyer deh úgwer minnerrúll.*

**Do you want anything else? 1** ¿Desean algo más los señores? **2** *Dessáyun úlgoh múss loss senyórress?*

**No, bring the pudding. 1** No, sírvanos los postres. **2** *Noh, sẽẽrvunnos loss póstress.*

**Bring me some Roquefort and strawberries. 1** Tráigame queso Rocafort y fresas. **2** *Trýgermeh késsoh rocfórt o fréssuss.*

**For me, some pears and ice cream. 1** A mí, peras y un helado. **2** *Ah me, péhruss e oon ellárdoh.*

**The same for me. 1** A mí lo mismo. **2** *Ah me loh míssmoh.*

**I prefer pudding. 1** Yo prefiero dulces. **2** *Yoh prefyáirroh dõõlthess.*

*En el restaurante*

**Serve coffee afterwards. 1** Después sírvanos café.
**2** *Despwéss sëërrvunnoss cufféh.*
**Do you want liqueurs? 1** ¿Quieren licores? **2** *Kyáir-run lickórress?*
**Yes, some digestive, a good brand. 1** Sí, algún es-tomacal de buena marca. **2** *See, ulgöön estómmuc-cúll deh bwénner márrker.*
**Waiter, the bill, please. 1** Camarero, traiga la cuenta.
**2** *Cummerráirroh trýger lah kwénter.*

---

**List of dishes**                   **Lista de platos**

**Hors d'oeuvres**
**Entremeses**

---

**Olives. 1** Aceitunas. **2** *Uthettoónerss.*
**Anchovies. 1** Anchoas. **2** *Untchóuss.*
**Pork sausage. 1** Chorizo. **2** *Tchorrëëthoh.*
**Ham. 1** Jamón. **2** *Hummón.*
**Butter. 1** Mantequilla. **2** *Muntekílyer.*
**Mortadella (sausage). 1** Mortadela. **2** *Mórrtuddéller.*
**Oysters. 1** Ostras. **2** *Óstruss.*
**Sausage. 1** Salchichón. **2** *Sulsitchón.*
**Sardines. 1** Sardinas. **2** *Sarrdëënerss.*

**Soups**
**Sopas**

---

**Rice. 1** Arroz. **2** *Urróth.*
**Broth, consomé. 1** Caldo, consomé. **2** *Cúldoh, con-somméh.*
**Noodles. 1** Fideos. **2** *Fiddáyoss.*
**Macaroni. 1** Macarrones. **2** *Muckerrónness.*
**Bread. 1** Pan. **2** *Pun.*

*En el restaurante*

**Vegetables and greens**
**Legumbres y verduras**

---

**Onions. 1** Cebollas. **2** *Thebóllyuss.*
**Cabbage. 1** Coles. **2** *Cólless.*
**Cauliflower. 1** Colifor. **2** *Colliflórr.*
**Asparagus. 1** Espárragos. **2** *Espúrrergoss.*
**Spinach. 1** Espinacas. **2** *Espinnúckuss.*
**Chick peas. 1** Garbanzos. **2** *Garrbúnthoss.*
**Broad beans. 1** Habas. **2** *Úbbuss.*
**Beans dried, fresh. 1** Judías secas, tiernas. **2** *Hoo-déass séckuss, tyáirnuss.*
**Lettuce. 1** Lechuga. **2** *Letchō̄ger.*
**Lentils. 1** Lentejas. **2** *Lentéhhuss.*
**Potatoes. 1** Patatas. **2** *Puttúttuss.*
**Mushrooms. 1** Setas. **2** *Séttuss.*

**Paste**
**Pastas**

---

**Canalones. 1** Canalones. **2** *Cúnnalónness.*
**Noodles. 1** Fideos. **2** *Fiddáyoss.*
**Macaroni. 1** Macarrones. **2** *Muckerrónness.*
**Ravioli. 1** Raviolis. **2** *Ruvviólless.*

**Eggs**
**Huevos**

---

**Hard. 1** Duros. **2** *Dōōross.*
**Fried. 1** Fritos. **2** *Frēētoss.*
**Boiled. 1** Pasados por agua. **2** *Pussárdoss porr úgwer.*
**Omelette. 1** Tortilla. **2** *Torrtíllyer.*

*En el restaurante*

## Game and Poultry
## Aves y caza

---

**Partridge. 1** Perdiz. **2** *Pairdeéth.*
**Quail. 1** Codorniz. **2** *Coddorrnééth.*
**Rabbit. 1** Conejo. **2** *Connéhhoh.*
**Hare. 1** Liebre. **2** *Lyébbreh.*
**Duck. 1** Pato. **2** *Púttoh.*
**Turkey. 1** Pavo. **2** *Púvvoh.*
**Pigeon. 1** Pichón. **2** *Pitchón.*
**Chicken. 1** Pollo. **2** *Pólyoh.*

## Fish and shell fish
## Pescados y marisco

---

**Muscles. 1** Almejas. **2** *Ulméhhuss.*
**Eels. 1** Anguilas. **2** *Ungéélerss.*
**Tuna. 1** Atún. **2** *Uttóōn.*
**Cod. 1** Bacalao. **2** *Buckerlów.*
**Gilthead. 1** Bonito. **2** *Bonnéétoh.*
**Squids. 1** Calamares. **2** *Cullermárress.*
**Lobster. 1** Langosta. **2** *Lungóster.*
**Prawns. 1** Langostinos. **2** *Lungostéénoss.*
**Mussels. 1** Mejillones. **2** *Mehhillyónness.*
**Hake. 1** Merluza. **2** *Mairrlóóther.*
**Barnicles. 1** Percebes. **2** *Pairrsébbess.*
**Small fry. 1** Pescadilla. **2** *Pescuddílyer.*
**Squids. 1** Pulpos. **2** *Póōlposs.*
**Salmon. 1** Salmón. **2** *Sulmón.*
**Red mullet. 1** Salmonete. **2** *Sulmonnétteh.*
**Trout. 1** Truchas. **2** *Trútchuss.*

*En el restaurante*

## Meat
## Carnes

---

**Beef. 1** Buey. **2** *Bweh.*
**Pork. 1** Cerdo. **2** *Tháirdoh.*
**Mutton. 1** Cordero. **2** *Corrdáirroh.*
**Veal. 1** Ternera. **2** *Tairrnáirrer.*
**Cow. 1** Vaca. **2** *Vúcker.*
**Pork chops. 1** Costillas de cerdo. **2** *Costíllyerss deh tháirrdoh.*
**Fillet of veal. 1** Filetes de ternera. **2** *Filléttess deh tairrnáirrah.*
**Veal pie. 1** Empanada de ternera. **2** *Empunnárder de tairrnáirrah.*
**Lamb cutlet. 1** Chuleta de cordero. **2** *Tchoolétter deh corrdáirroh.*
**Fillet of beet, beaf steak. 1** Filete de buey, bistec. **2** *Fillétteh deh bweh, bistéc.*
**Lamb's foot. 1** Pierna de carnero. **2** *Pyáirrner deh carrnáirroh.*
**Loin of pork. 1** Lomo de cerdo. **2** *Lómmoh deh tháirrdoh.*
**Loin of veal. 1** Lomo de ternera. **2** *Lómmoh deh tairrnáirrer.*
**Roast. 1** Asado. **2** *Ussárdoh.*
**Tripe. 1** Callos. **2** *Cúllyoss.*
**Sweetbread. 1** Lechón. **2** *Letchón.*
**Tongue. 1** Lengua. **2** *Léngwer.*
**Kidneys. 1** Riñones. **2** *Rinyónness.*
**Brain. 1** Sesos. **2** *Séssoss.*

## Roast dishes
## Asados

---

**Roast beef and mashed potatoes. 1** Asado de vaca con puré de patatas. **2** *Ussárdoh deh vúcker con poorréh deh puttúttuss.*

*En el restaurante*

**Beef steak and salad. 1** Bistec con ensalada. **2** *Bistéc con ensullárder.*
**Chicken. 1** Pollo. **2** *Póllyoh.*


## Cheeses
## Quesos

---

**Camembert. 1** Camembert. **2** *Cúmmumbáir.*
**Gruyère. 1** Gruyére. **2** *Grooyáirr.*
**Dutch cheese. 1** Holanda. **2** *Ollúnder.*
**Roquefort. 1** Roquefort. **2** *Rosckfórr.*
**Swiss cheese. 1** Suizo. **2** *Swēéthon.*


## Dessert
## Postres

---

**Sweets, pudding. 1** Dulces. **2** *Dōōlthess.*
**Custard. 1** Flan. **2** *Flun.*
**Fruit** (1). **1** Fruta (2). **2** *Frōōter.*
**Ice creams. 1** Helados. **2** *Ellárdoss.*
**Coffee. 1** El café. **2** *El cufféh.*
**Tea. 1** El té. **2** *El teh.*
**Sugar. 1** El azúcar. **2** *El uthúcker.*
**Liqueur. 1** El licor. **2** *El lickórr.*


**Matches. 1** Las cerillas. **2** *Luss therríllyuss.*
**The cigar. 1** El cigarro. **2** *El thiggúrroh.*
**The cigarettes. 1** Los cigarrillos. **2** *Loss th:gurríllyoss.*
**The ash tray. 1** El cenicero. **2** *El thénnitháirroh.*

---

(1)  See the heading **At the fruit shop.**
(2)  Véase el epígrafe **En la frutería.**

*En el restaurante*

---

## The tea                                    El té

---

**Waiter, give me a tea please. 1** Camarero, sírvame
un té. **2** *Cummarráirroh, sĕĕrvummeh oon teh.*
**Plain tea? 1** ¿Té sólo? **2** *Teh sólloh?*
**With milk. 1** Con leche. **2** *Con létcheh.*
**Will you have some bread and butter? 1** ¿Quiere
usted pan y mantequilla? **2** *Kyérreh oostéh pun e
muntekíllyer?*
**No, I had rather have some dry cakes. 1** No, prefiero algunas pastas secas. **2** *Noh, prefyáirroh ulgŏŏ-
nera pústers séccus.*
**Give me some fresh water. 1** Déme agua fresca.
**2** *Démmeh úgwer frésker.*
**Give me a little more sugar. 1** Sírvame un poco más
de azúcar. **2** *Sĕĕrryvummeh oon ccoh múss deh
uthŏŏker.*
**I like my tea strong and very hot. 1** El té me gusta
fuerte y muy caliente. **2** *El teh meh gŏŏster fwáirteh
e mooy cullyénteh.*
**Toast. 1** Pan tostado. **2** *Pun tostárdoh.*
**Honey, jam. 1** Miel, mermelada. **2** *Myél, máirrmullár-
der.*
**Hot water. 1** Agua caliente. **2** *Úgwer cullyénteh.*
**Weak, strong tea. 1** Té flojo, fuerte. **2** *Teh flóhhoh,
fwáirrteh.*
**I want the complete tea. 1** Deseo un té completo. **2**
*Dessáyoh oon the compléttoh.*
**How much is that? 1** ¿Cuánto vale? **2** *Kwántoh
vúlleh?*

# In town
## En la ciudad

**The City** 1 La ciudad 2 *Lah théudáh*
**The street.** 1 La calle. 2 *Lah cúllyeh.*
**The Promenade.** 1 El paseo. 2 *El pussáyoh.*
**The Avenue.** 1 La avenida. 2 *Lah úvveneeder.*
**The Passage.** 1 El pasaje. 2 *El pussúhheh.*
**The Square.** 1 La plaza. 2 *Lah plúther.*
**The Lane.** 1 El callejón. 2 *El cúllyehhón.*
**The gardens.** 1 Los jardines. 2 *Loss hardeeness.*
**The source.** 1 La fuente. 2 *Lah fwénteh.*
**The fountain.** 1 El surtidor. 2 *El sootidórr.*
**The road.** 1 La calzada. 2 *La culthárder.*
**The pavement.** 1 La acera. 2 *El utháiroh.*
**The lights.** 1 El semáforo. 2 *El semmúfforoh.*
**The traffic policemen.** 1 El guardia urbano, el guardia de tráfico. 2 *El gwardia oorbúnnoh, el gwárdia deh trúfficoh.*
**The trees.** 1 Los árboles. 2 *Loss árrbolless.*
**The bus.** 1 El autobús. 2 *El ōwtobooss.*
**The tram.** 1 El tranvía. 2 *El trunvéar.*
**The trolley bus.** 1 El trolebús. 2 *El trólleybooss.*
**The overhead wires.** 1 El cable eléctrico. 2 *El cárbleh eléctrico.*
**The tube (underground).** 1 El metro. 2 *El méttroh.*
**The car.** 1 El automóvil, el auto. 2 *El owtomóvvil, el awtoh.*
**The taxi.** 1 El taxi. 2 *El túxi.*
**The car.** 1 El coche. 2 *El cétcheh.*
**The road car.** 1 El autocar. 2 *El owtocárr.*
**The lorry.** 1 El camión. 2 *El cumión.*
**The small lorry.** 1 La camioneta. 2 *Lah cummionnétter.*
**The motor cycle.** 1 La motocicleta. 2 *Lah mawtorthickkletter.*

*En la ciudad*

**The tricycle. 1** El triciclo. **2** *El treethíckloh.*
**The bicycle. 1** La bicicleta. **2** *Lah beethiclétter.*
**The pedestrians. 1** Los peatones. **2** *Loss páyertónness.*
**The building. 1** El edificio. **2** *El éddifééthio.*
**The house. 1** La casa. **2** *Lah cússer.*
**The tower. 1** La torre. **2** *Lah tórreh.*
**The door. 1** La puerta. **2** *Lah pwáirter.*
**The balconies. 1** Los balcones. **2** *Loss bulcónness.*
**The windows. 1** Las ventanas. **2** *Luss ventúnnuss.*
**The verandas. 1** El porche. **2** *El porchay.*
**The roof. 1** El tejado. **2** *El tehhárdoh.*
**The lightning conductor. 1** El pararrayos. **2** *El púrrerryóss.*
**The district. 1** Un barrio. **2** *Oon barrio.*
**The Town Hall. 1** El Ayuntamiento. **2** *El ahyööntermyéntoh.*
**The County Council. 1** La Diputación. **2** *Lah díppootúthión.*
**The Consulate. 1** El consulado. **2** *El consoolárdoh.*
**The University. 1** La universidad. **2** *Lah oonivársidúd.*
**The Library. 1** La biblioteca. **2** *Lah bíbliotecker.*
**The Museum. 1** El museo. **2** *El moosáyoh.*
**The Post and Telegraph Office. 1** Correos y Telégrafos. **2** *Corráyoss e telléggruffóss.*
**The Telephone company. 1** Compañía de teléfonos. **2** *Kompahnyée: ah dech telléffoss.*
**The tourist office. 1** La oficina de turismo. **2** *Lah offitheener deh toorrismoh.*
**The hospital. 1** El hospital. **2** *El ospitúll.*
**The Cathedral. 1** La catedral. **2** *La cúttidrúll.*
**The church. 1** La iglesia. **2** *Lah iggléssia.*
**The bank. 1** El banco. **2** *El búnckoh.*
**The restaurant. 1** El restaurante. **2** *El restorúnteh.*
**The chemist's. 1** La farmacia. **2** *Lah farmúthea.*
**The public house. 1** El bar. **2** *El barr.*
**The hotel. 1** El hotel. **2** *El awtél.*
**The prison. 1** La cárcel. **2** *Lah carrthel.*
**The police station. 1** La comisaría de policía. **2** *Lah cómmissarréar deh pollithéa.*
**The boarding house. 1** La pensión. **2** *Lah pensión.*
**The shop. 1** La tienda. **2** *Lah tyénder.*
**The stores. 1** Los grandes almacenes. **2** *Loss grúndess úllmuthénness.*

*En la ciudad*

**The cinema. 1** El cine. **2** *El thínneh.*
**The theatre. 1** El teatro. **2** *El tayártroh.*
**The circus. 1** El circo. **2** *El thēērrcoh.*
**The entertainments hall. 1** La sala de fiestas. **2** *Lah súller deh fyestuss.*
**The night club. 1** El club nocturno. **2** *El cloob noctōōrrnoh.*
**The stadium, the sports ground. 1** El estadio, el campo de deportes. **2** *El estárdio, el cúmpoh deh depórrtess.*
**The fair. 1** Las atracciones. **2** *Luss uttrúcthéones.*
**The station. 1** La estación. **2** *Lah estúthión.*
**The bull ring. 1** La plaza de toros. **2** *Lah plúther deh tāwross.*
**The port. 1** El puerto. **2** *El pwáirtoh.*
**The shipping company. 1** La compañía de navegación. **2** *Lah companyía deh núvviguthión.*
**The air line. 1** La compañía de aviación. **2** *Lah companyía deh ve.úhhes.*
**The travel agency. 1** La agencia de viajes. **2** *Lah uhhénthea de vyúhhes.*
**The newspaper stand. 1** El quiosco de periódicos. **2** *El keeéscoh deh pēērióddicoss.*
**The tobacconist's. 1** El estanco. **2** *El estúnckoh.*
**The hairdresser. 1** La peluquería. **2** *Lah péllookerrea.*
**The market. 1** El mercado. **2** *El maircárdoh.*

**Asking the way**
**Para pedir una dirección**

**Excuse me. Is... street far from here? 1** Usted perdone. ¿Está muy lejos la calle de...? **2** *Ostéh pairdonneh. Estár mooy léhhoss lah cúllyeh deh...?*

**No, sir. The third on the left. 1** No, señor; la tercera calle, a la izquierda. **2** *No, senyórr. Lah tairtháirer cúllyeh ah lahithkyáirder.*

**Round that corner. 1** Al doblar aquella esquina. **2** *Ull dobblárr ukkéllyer esskẽener.*

**Many thanks. 1** Muchas gracias. **2** *Mõõcthuss grútheuss.*

**Is it near the... Hotel? 1** ¿Está cerca el Hotel de...? **2** *Estár tháirker el awtél deh...?*

**Quite far. Quite near. Take the first, second, third street on the right. 1** Está lejos. Está cerca. Tome usted la primera, la segunda, la tercera calle a la derecha. **2** *Estár léhhoss. Estár tháirker. Tómme oostéh las primáirer, lah seggõõnder, lah tairtháirer cúllyeh ah lah derrétcher.*

**Go straight on along this street. 1** Siga usted esta misma calle. **2** *Sẽẽger oostéh éstah mísmer cúllyeh.*

**Constable, can you tell me where the... consulate is? 1** Guardia, ¿puede decirme dónde está el consulado...? **2** *Gwárrdia. Pwéddeh dethéarrmeh dóndeh estár el cónsoolárdoh?*

**In.. Avenue. 1** En la avenida de... **2** *En lah úvvenẽẽder deh...*

**How can I get there? 1** ¿Qué combinación puedo hacer para ir? **2** *Keh cómbinúthion pwéddoh utháir púrrer ah...?*

**Take... tram, the bus, the subway. 1** Tome el tranvía..., el autobús, el metro. **2** *Tómmeh el trunvéar..., el owtobõõss, el méttroh.*

**Where is St... Church, Square... Avenue, The Town Hall, the Hotel, the bull ring... Museum, the Tourist Office? 1** ¿Dónde está la iglesia de..., la plaza de... la avenida de..., el Ayuntamiento, la comisaría de policía, el Hotel..., la plaza de toros, el museo de..., la oficina de turismo...? **2** *Dóndeh estár lah igglessia deh..., lah plúther deh..., lah úvvenẽẽder deh..., el ahyõõntamyéntoh, lah commissaréar deh póllithéar, el awtél..., lah plúther deh tówrross, el moosáyoh deh..., lah óffithẽẽner deh toorrísmo?*

**What tram, bus, subway must I take to get to...? 1** ¿Qué tranvía, autobús, metro, he de coger para ir a...? **2** *Keh trunveer, owtobooss, méttroh eh deh cohháir púrrer éar ah...?*

*En la ciudad*

**How can I get to the theatre? 1** ¿Cómo podré ir al teatro...? **2** *Cómoh podréh éarr ul tayúttroh...?*

**Is it far? 1** ¿Está lejos? **2** *Estár léhhoss?*

**About how far is it? 1** ¿Qué distancia aproximada hay? **2** *Keh distúnthear uppróximárder i?*

**Where is the tram, the bus stop? 1** ¿Dónde está la parada del tranvía, del autobús...? **2** *Dóndeh estár lah purrárder del trunvéar, del owtobōōs?*

## The appointment

### La cita

**Hello, friend! 1** ¡Hola, amigo! **2** *Óhlah! ummēēgoh.*

**Ah, it's you, old man. 1** ¡Ah! ¿Es usted, amigo? **2** *Ah! Ess oostéh, ummēēgoh?*

**How do you like this town? 1** ¿Cómo le prueba esta ciudad? **2** *Cómmoh leh prwébber éstah thé.oodúd?*

**Very well. 1** Muy bien. **2** *Mooy be.én.*

**How long have you been here? 1** ¿Desde cuándo está usted aquí? **2** *Désdeh kwúndoh estár oostéh ukkēē?*

**Three days. 1** Desde hace tres días. **2** *Désdeh úttheh tres déars.*

**I didn't know. 1** No lo sabía. **2** *Noh loh subbéar.*

**You have given me a very pleasant surprise. 1** Me ha dado una sorpresa muy agradable. **2** *Meh ah dárdoh ooner sorprésser mooy úggruddárbleh.*

**How long will you be here? 1** ¿Cuánto tiempo se quedará usted en...? **2** *Kwúntoh tyémpoh seh kédderrár oostéh en...?*

**I don't know exactly yet. 1** No lo sé aún exactamente. **2** *Noh loh seh ahōōn exúctaménteh.*

**I expect to be here at least a week. 1** Pienso permanecer por lo menos una semana. **2** *Pyénsoh páirmmunnehtháir porr loh ménnos ooner semúnner.*

**Will you have supper with me today? 1** ¿Cenará usted conmigo hoy? **2** *Thennerrár oostéh con mēēgoh oy?*

*En la ciudad*

**With great pleasure. 1** Con mucho gusto. **2** *Con mŏŏtchoh gŏŏstoh.*

**I'm sorry, but it's quite impossible today. 1** Lo siento mucho, pero hoy me es imposible. **2** *Loh syéntoh mŏŏtchot, péhroh oy me ess impossĕĕbleh.*

**When can I have the pleasure of having supper with you? 1** ¿Cuándo podré tener el gusto de cenar con usted? **2** *Kwúndoh poddréh tennáirr el gŏŏtoh deh thennárr con oostéh? ah luss étchoh e máddea.*

**Tomorrow. 1** Mañana. **2** *Munnyúnner.*

**Where and at what time may I expect you? 1** ¿Dónde y a qué hora quiere que le espere? **2** *Dóndeh e ah keh óra kyáireh keh leh espáireh?*

**At... restaurant at half past eight. 1** En el restaurante... a las ocho y media. **2** *En el réstorrúnteh... ah luss ótchoh e méddea.*

**Good, without fail. 1** Bien, no faltaré. **2** *Byén, noh fullterréh.*

**Until tomorrow. 1** Hasta mañana. **2** *Ússter munnyúnne.*

**Until tomorrow, my friend. 1** Hasta mañana, amigo mío. **2** *Ú.sster munnyúnner ummĕĕgoh méoh.*

## Greetings
## El saludo

---

**Good morning, sir. 1** Buenos días, señor. **2** *Byénnoss déarss, senyórr.*

**Did you have a good night? 1** ¿Qué tal ha pasado la noche? **2** *Keh tull ar pussárdoh lah nótcheh?*

**Very good. And you? 1** Muy bien, ¿y usted? **2** *Mooy be.én e oostéh?*

**Splendid. 1** Perfectamente. **2** *Pairféctamenteh.*

**Is your family well? 1** ¿Sigue bien su familia? **2** *Sĕĕgeh be.én soo fummílyer?*

**They are all in the best of health. 1** Todos gozan de excelente salud. **2** *Tāwdoss góthun deh exthellénteh sullŏŏth.*

*En la ciudad*

**I am very glad. 1** Me alegro mucho. **2** *Meh ullégroh m͞ōōtchoh.*

**Please give them my kind regards. 1** Le ruego que los salude en mi nombre. **2** *Leh rwéggoh keh loss sull͞ōōdeh en me nómbreh.*

**I'm glad. Give them my best wishes. 1** Me alegro. Salúdelos en mi nombre. **2** *Meh ulléggróh. Súl͞ōōdellos en me nómbreh.*

**I certainly will. 1** Será usted complacido. **2** *Serráh oostéh cómth͞ēēdoh.*

**Have you had any sick in your house? 1** ¿Ha tenido enfermos en su casa? **2** *Ah ten͞ēēdoh enfáirmoss en soo cússer?*

**My wife and sister-in-law have been a little unwell. 1** Mi señora y mi cuñada han estado algo enfermas. **2** *Me senyórrer e me coonyárder un estárdoh úlgoh enfáirmuss.*

**I am glad to say they are well. 1** A Dios gracias ya están bien. **2** *Ah déuss grútheus yah estún byen.*

**I'm glad to have seen you. Kind regards to everybody. 1** Me alegro mucho de haberle visto. Recuerdos a todos. **2** *Meh ullégroh m͞ōōtchoh deh ubbáirleh vistoh. Reckwáirdoss ah t͞āwdos.*

**Good bye and good luck. 1** Adiós. Usted siga bien. **2** *Uddióss. Oostéh s͞ēēger byen.*

**Hello. How are you? 1** ¡Hola! ¿Cómo está usted? **2** *Óhlah; Cómmoh estár ostéh?*

**Very well. 1** Muy bien. **2** *Mooy byen.*

**I'm glad to hear it. 1** Lo celebro mucho. **2** *Loh thellébroh m͞ōōtchoh.*

**How are you Mr., Mrs., Miss...? 1** ¿Qué tal, señor, señora, señorita? **2** *Keh tull, senyórr, senyórrah, senyorr͞ēēter?*

**How are you getting on? 1** ¿Cómo le va? **2** *Cómmoh leh vár?*

**Well, and you. 1** Bien, ¿y a usted? **2** *Byén, e ah oostéh?*

**Good bye. 1** Adiós, señor, señora, señorita. **2** *Udddréss senyórr, senyórah, senyoreeter.*

**Give my regards to our friends. 1** Recuerdos a nuestros amigos. **2** *Reckwáirdoss ah nwéstross umm͞ēēgoss.*

*En la ciudad*

**Kisses for the children. 1** Besos a los niños. **2** *Béssoss ah loss nēēnyoss.*

**Until very soon. 1** Hasta muy pronto. **2** *Úster mooy próntoh.*

**Until tomorrow. 1** Hasta mañana. **2** *Úster munyúnner.*

**Until then. 1** Hasta luego. **2** *Úster lwéggoh.*

**Till next time. 1** Hasta la vista. **2** *Úster lah víster.*

**Good morning, old man. 1** Buenos días, amigo mío. **2** *Bwénnoss déarss, ummēēgoh méo.*

**Good afternoon, sir. 1** Buenas tardes, señor. **2** *Bwénnoss tárrdess, senyórr.*

**Good evening, madam. 1** Buenas tardes, señora, señorita. **2** *Bwénnoss tárrdess, senyórrah, senyorēēter.*

**How are you? 1** ¿Cómo está usted? **2** *Cómmoh estár oostéh?*

**Very well, thanks. And you? 1** Muy bien, gracias. ¿Y usted? **2** *Mooy byen, grútheus. E oostéh?*

**I don't speak French, Spanish, etc. 1** No hablo francés, español, etc. **2** *Noh úbbloh frunthéss, espanyóll, etc.*

**I speak French, Spanish, English, etc. 1** Hablo francés, español, inglés, etc. **2** *Ubbloh frunthés, espunyól, ingléss, etsétterah.*

**Excuse me. I'm in a hurry. 1** Perdóneme, que tengo prisa. **2** *Pairdónnehmeh, keh téngoh prēēser.*

**Visits**

**De visita**

**Mr. ...? 1** ¿El señor? **2** *El senyórr?*

**Is M... at home? 1** El señor..., ¿está en casa? **2** *El senyórr... estár en cússer?*

**Yes, come in please. 1** Sí, señor, pase usted. **2** *See, senyórr. Pússer oostéh.*

**Whom shall I announce? 1** ¿De parte de quién? **2** *Deh párteh deh kee.én?*

**What name, please? 1** ¿A quién he de anunciar? **2** *Ah kee.én eh deh unnōōntheárr?*

**Are you Mr...? 1** ¿Es el señor...? **2** *Ess el senyórr...*

*En la ciudad*

**Come in. 1** ¡Adelante! **2** *Úddelúnteh!*

**What a susprise! 1** ¡Qué sorpresa! **2** *Keh sorprésser!*

**I am so glad to see you. 1** ¡Cuánto celebro ver a usted! **2** *Kwúntoh théllebroh váir ah oostéh!*

**Thank you for your visit. 1** Le agradezco la visita. **2** *Leh úggredéthcoh lah vissēēter.*

**We are always very pleased to see you. 1** Siempre tenemos un gran placer en verle a usted. **2** *Syémpreh tennáimoss oon grun plutháir en váirleh ah oostéh.*

**Come along please. 1** Pase usted adelante. **2** *Pússeh oosttéh úddellúnteh.*

**Sit down. 1** Siéntese usted. **2** *Syéntusséh oostéh.*

**Take a seat. 1** Tome usted asiento. **2** *Tómmeh oostéh ussyéntoh.*

**Give Mr... a chair. 1** Dé usted una silla al señor... **2** *Déh oostéh ooner sillyer úll senyórr...*

**Won't you sit down a moment? 1** ¿No quiere sentarse un momento? **2** *Noh kyerreh sentarrseh oon mommentoh?*

**We don't see you very often. 1** Le vemos a usted muy poco. **2** *Leh vémmos ah oostéh mooy pāwcoh.*

**I came yesterday and had not the pleasure of seeing you. 1** Vine ayer y no tuve el gusto de verle. **2** *Vēēneh uhyáirr e noh tōōveh el gōōstoh deh váirleh.*

**So they said. I had just gone out. 1** Ya me lo dijeron. Acababa de salir. **2** *Yah meh loh dihháirrron. Úckerbárber deh sullēērr.*

**You will lunch with us today. 1** Hoy comerá usted con nosotros. **2** *Oy commenráh con nossótross.*

**Thank you very much. 1** Muchas gracias. **2** *Mōōtchuss grútheuss.*

**Many thanks, but I am expected. 1** Se lo agradezco mucho, pero hoy me esperan. **2** *Seh loh úggreddéthcoh mōōtchoh, péhroh roy meh esspáirrun.*

**But are you already going? 1** Pero, ¿ya se va usted? **2** *Péhroh yah seh van oostéh?*

**Stay a little longer. 1** Espere un poco más. **2** *Esspérreh oon pāwcoh múss.*

**But you have only just come. 1** ¡Pero si acaba de llegar! **2** *Péhroh see uckárber deh lyeggárr.*

*En la ciudad*

**I am in a hurry. 1** Tengo prisa. **2** *Téngoh prēēser.*
**It's late. 1** Es tarde. **2** *Ess tárrdeh.*
**You are always in a hurry. 1** Siempre va usted de prisa. **2** *Syémpreh vah oostéh deh prēēser.*
**I'm very busy. 1** Estoy muy ocupado. **2** *Esstóy mooy óccoopárdoh.*
**I have a lot to do. 1** Tengo mucho que hacer. **2** *Téngoh mōōtchoh keh utháir.*
**I'll come again tomorrow. 1** Volveré mañana. **2** *Volverráh munyúnner.*
**I'll come back another day. 1** Volveré otro día. **2** *Volverréh āwtroh déar.*
**Keep well. 1** Usted siga bien. **2** *Oostéh sēēger byén.*
**Goodbye. 1** Que usted lo pase bien. **2** *Keh oostéh loh pússeh byén.*
**Let us see more of you. 1** No sea usted tan caro de ver. **2** *Noh sáyer oostéh tun cáhroh deh váir.*
**Until next time. 1** Hasta la vista. **2** *Ússter lah víster.*
**May I introduce my wife? 1** Permítame que le presente mi mujer. **2** *Perrmēētameh keh presénteh me mooháir.*
**Pleased to meet you. 1** Mucho gusto en conocerle. **2** *Mōōtchoh gōōstoh en cónnotháirrleh.*
**My parents and my sister. 1** Les presento mis padres y mi hermana. **2** *Les presséntoh meess púddress e me airmúnner.*
**Delighted to meet you. 1** Encantado de conocerles. **2** *Encantárdoh deh connotháirless.*
**But please sit down. 1** Pero, siéntense ustedes, por favor. **2** *Pehroh syentenseh oostéddess, porr fuvvórr.*
**I see you have kept your promise. 1** Veo que ha cumplido su palabra. **2** *Váyoh keh ah cumplēēdoh soo pullárbrah.*
**I said I would come and see you. 1** Ya le dije que vendríamos a visitarles. **2** *Yah le dēēheh keh vendréamoss ah vissitárrless.*
**We are very grateful for this visit. 1** Les agradecemos mucho esta visita. **2** *Less uggrédethémmoss mōōtcho éster visseeter.*
**Come along, children, and speak to these ladies and gentlemen. 1** Niños, venid un momento.

*En la ciudad*

Saludad a los señores... 2 *Neenyoss, vennẽẽd oon momméntoh. Sullōōdud úlloss senyórress.*

**What pretty children! 1** ¡Qué niño tan hermoso, y qué niña tan guapita! 2 *Keh nẽẽnyoh tun air-mãwsoh, e keh nẽẽnyer tun gwuppẽẽter!*

**Yes, but they're very naughty. 1** Sí, pero son muy malos. 2 *See, péhroh son mooy márloss.*

**All healthy children are naughty. 1** Todos los niños sanos son traviesos. 2 *Tãwdoss los nẽẽnyoss son truvyéssoss.*

**They are both your sister's children? 1** ¿Los dos son de su hermana? 2 *Loss doss estún deh soo air-munner?*

**Exactly. 1** Efectivamente. 2 *Effeetẽẽverménteh.*

**I'm sorry my wife is away. 1** Lamento que mi esposa esté ausente. 2 *Lumméntoh keh mee esspóssoh estéh owsénteh.*

**She left on Monday and has not yet returned. 1** Salió el lunes y aún no ha regresado. 2 *Sulleóh el lōōness e ah.ōōn noh ah réggressárdoh.*

**Please give her our kind regards. 1** Tenga la bondad de saludarle en nuestro nombre. 2 *Ténger lah bondúd deh súlloodárleh en nwéstroh nómbreh.*

**With great pleasure. 1** Lo haré con mucho gusto. 2 *Loh urráy con mōōstoh.*

**Have you no children? 1** ¿Ustedes no tienen hijos? 2 *Oostéhdess noh tyénnen ẽẽhoss?*

**Yes, two, both married. The elder son has a lovely girl. 1** Sí, dos casados ya, y uno de ellos, el mayor, con una niña preciosa. 2 *See, doss cussárdoss yah, e oonoh deh éllyoss, el mahyórr, con ooner nẽẽnyer prétheóser.*

**So you are already grandparents? 1** Así, ¿son ustedes ya abuelos? 2 *Ussẽẽ, son oostéddess yah ubbwélloss.*

**Congratulationns. May it be for many years to come. 1** Enhorabuena, y que lo sean durante muchos años. 2 *En.óra.bwénner, e , keh loh súyun doorúnteh mōōtchoss únnyoss.*

**Thank you ...very much 1** Muchas gracias. 2 *Mō⁻otchuss grútheus.*

**I hope we shall see each other more often. 1**

*En la ciudad*

Esperamos que nos veamos más frecuentemente.
**2** *Esperrármoss keh noss váyermoss mús frekwén-taménteh.*

**It's your turn to visit us now. 1** Ahora les toca a ustedes venir a visitarnos. **2** *Uh.orá less tócker ah oostéddess vonéerr ah visótárrnos.*

**When our brother is back we shall be glad to come one day. 1** Cuando regrese mi hermano nos permitiremos ir un día. **2** *Kwúndoh reggrésseh me áirrmúnnoh noss páirmittirráimoss éarr oon déar.*

**When you like, but please let us know the day before, so that we shall not be out. 1** A su comodidad, con tal de que nos avisen el día antes para no movernos de casa. **2** *Ah soo commóddidúd, con tull keh noss uvvíssen el dear úntess prrer noh movváirrnoss deh cússer.*

**We will. 1** Así lo haremos. **2** *Ussée loh urráimoss.*

**Until then. Kind regards to... 1** Hasta pronto. Recuerdos a... **2** *Ússer próntoh. Rekwáirdoss ah...*

**Thanks. The same to you... 1** Muchas gracias, igualmente. Adiós. **2** *Móotchuss grútheus, iggwullmenteh. Úddy.óss.*

---

| | |
|---|---|
| **Visiting the museums, monuments, and other places, of interest** | **Visita a museos, monumentos, lugares típicos, etcétera** |

**What museums, monuments, noteworthy buildings, parks, are there in the town? 1** ¿Qué museos, monumentos, edificios notables, parques, hay en la ciudad? **2** *Keh Moosáyoss, mónnoomóntoss, éddyfethe-os nottúbless, párrkess i enlah théoodúd?*

*En la ciudad*

**There are several well worth visiting. 1** Hay varios dignos de ser visitados. **2** *I vúrreoss dígnoss deh sairr vísitárdoss.*

**The most important is... of great artistic value. 1** El más importante es... de un gran valor artístico. **2** *El múss importúnteh es... deh oon grun vullórr arrtísticoh.*

**The... museum, St... Church, the Town Hall, the Cathedral, the... building, the... monument, are specially interesting for tourists. 1** Tiene un especial interés turístico el museo..., la iglesia de..., el Ayuntamiento, la catedral, el edificio de..., el monumento de... **2** *Tyénneh oon esspéthiúl interréss tooríssticoh el moosáyoh..., lah iggléssiah deh..., el ah.yŏŏntermyéntoh, lah cútteddrúll, el éddyfēētheo deh, el monooméntoh de...*

**Is the Museum far? 1** ¿Está muy lejos el museo de...? **2** *Estár mooy léhhoss el moosáyoh deh...?*

**What can I take to get to...? 1** ¿Qué medio de locomoción hay para ir a...? **2** *Keh méddioh deh loccomóthéon i púrrar éarr ah...*

**What typical spots are there in the town, please? 1** ¿Haría el favor de decirme qué lugares típicos hay en la ciudad? **2** *Urréar el fuvvórr deh dethēērrmeh keh loogárress típicós i en la thēēudúd?*

**There are several. I would recommend you to visit the... district. 1** Existen varios. Le recomiendo visite el barrio... **2** *Existen vúrreoss. Leh récommyéndoh vissēēteh el búrreo...*

**I should like to visit some park garden, zoo, etc. 1** Desearía visitar algún parque, jardín, parque zoológico, etc. **2** *Déssayarréar vissitárr ulgŏŏn párrkeh, harrdēēn, párrkeh zóohlóggihho, etc.*

**I think you would like the... Park, the largest in the town. 1** Creo le gustará ver el parque de... el más grande de la ciudad. **2** *Créoh leh goosterréar váirr el párrkeh deh..., el múss gründeh deh lah théudud.*

**It's a lovely Park arranged in very good taste. 1** Es un parque precioso, acondicionado con mucho gusto. **2** *Ess oon párrkeh prétheóssoh, úckondithionárdoh con mŏŏtchoh gŏŏstoh.*

*En la ciudad*

**I should like to visit the Fine Arts Museum.** 1 Desearía visitar el museo de Bellas Artes. 2 *Déssayarréar vissitárr el moossáyoh deh béllyooss árrtess.*

**A gallery of old masters.** 1 Un museo de Arte Antiguo. 2 *Oon moosáyoh deh Árrteh Untíggwoh.*

**A gallery of modern art.** 1 Un museo de Arte Moderno. 2 *Oon moosáyoh deh árrteh modáirnoh.*

**A Contemporary Art Gallery.** 1 Un museo de Arte Contemporáneo. 2 *Oon moosáyoh deh árrteh contémporránneoh.*

**Of decorative art.** 1 De Artes Decorativas. 2 *Deh árrtes décoratéévas.*

**Of natural sciences.** 1 De Ciencias Naturales. 2 *Deh thee.éntheus nútturrúlless.*

**Of archeology.** 1 De Arqueología. 2 *Deh árrkióllohéer.*

**Naval.** 1 Naval. 2 *Nuvvúll.*

**Aviation.** 1 De Aviación. 2 *Deh úvvyótheón.*

**The monument to...** 1 El monumento de... 2 *El mónooméntoh deh...*

**Could you tell me on what days and at what time it is open? .** 1 ¿Podría indicarme los días y horas de visita? 2 *Poddréar indicármeh loss déarss e óruss deh visééter?*

**A guide, please.** 1 Un guía, por favor. 2 *Oon gééar, porr fuvvórr.*

**In what style is this building, this church?** 1 ¿Qué estilo tiene este edificio, esta iglesia? 2 *Keh estééloh tyénneh éssteh éddyféétheo, ésster igglésssiah?*

**It's Arabic, Gothic, Roman, Renaissance.** 1 Es de estilo árabe, gótico, románico, Renacimiento. 2 *Ess deh estééloh úrrerbeh, gótticoh, romúnnicoh, rennúthimyéntoh.*

## Means of transport

## Medios de locomoción

### In the taxi
### El taxi

**Taxi! Taxi! 1** ¡Taxi, taxi! **2** *Tucksy! Tucksy!*

**Are you free? 1** ¿Está libre? **2** *Estár lёёbreh?*

**We are going to have a drive through the main streets. 1** Vamos a dar un paseo por las avenidas principales. **2** *Vármoss ah darr con pussáyoh porr luss úvvenёёdus printhipúlless.*

**Take me to... street, No... 1** Lléveme a la calle..., número... **2** *Llévummehallah cúlyeh..., nōōmeroh...*

**How far is it to street? 1** ¿Qué distancia hay de aquí a la calle...? **2** *Keh distunthear i deh ukkée ah lah cúllyeh.*

**Take the shortest route. 1** Vaya por el camino más corto. **2** *Vý.ver porr el cummёёnoh múss córrtoh.*

**Go faster. 1** Vaya usted más de prisa. **2** *Vý.ver oostéh múss deh pёёser.*

**Go slowly, quickly. 1** Vaya usted despacio, deprisa. **2** *Vý.ver oostéh múss despúthio, deprёёser.*

**Driver, stop. 1** Chófer, pare usted. **2** *Choffeur, púrreh oostéh.*

**Stop at the next tobacconist's. 1** Cuando vea un estanco, pare usted. **2** *Kwúndoh vayer oon estúncoh, purréh oostéh.*

**To the station. 1** A la estación. **2** *A lah estútheón.*

**How much do I owe you? 1** ¿Cuánto le debo? **2** *Kwúntoh leh débboh?*

**What does the meter say? 1** ¿Cuánto marca el taxímetro? **2** *Kwúntoh márrca tacsímmetroh?*

**Here you are. 1** Tome usted. **2** *Tómeh oostéh.*

**Thank you very much. 1** Muchas gracias. **2** *Mō¯otchuss grútheus.*

*En la ciudad*

## The bus, the trolley bus, the tram, the subway

### El autobús, el trolebús, el tranvía, el metro

---

**Where does this bus go to? 1** ¿A dónde va este autobús? **2** *Ah dóndeh var oosteh ōwtobōōss?*

**Where are you going? 1** ¿A dónde va usted? **2** *Ah dóndeh var oostéh?*

**To... street, avenue, square. 1** A la calle, avenida, plaza... **2** *Ah la cúllyeh, uvvenēēder, plúther.*

**Take the one behind. 1** Tome usted el que sigue. **2** *Tómmeh oostéh el keh sēēgeh.*

**How much is the fare? 1** ¿Cuánto vale el trayecto? **2** *Kwúntoh várle el traryéctoh?*

**Stop at the first stop. 1** Pare usted en la primera parada. **2** *Púrreh oostéh en lah primáirer purráder.*

**Where does No... bus, tram pass? 1** Por dónde pasa el autobús..., el tranvía número...? **2** *Porr dóndeh pússer el ōwtobōōss..., el trunvéar nōōmeroh...?*

**Along that street. 1** Por aquella calle. **2** *Porr ukéllyer cúllyeh.*

**Conductor, does this tram go to the port? 1** Cobrador, ¿este tranvía va al puerto? **2** *Cóbrradórr, éste trunveár var ull pwáirtoh?*

**Yes, sir. No, sir but it drops you very near to it. 1** Sí, señor. No, señor, pero le dejará muy cerca. **2** *See, senyórr. Noh, senyórr, pénhroh leh déhhurráh mooy tháircker.*

**Will you tell me when we get there? 1** ¿Hará el favor de avisarme cuando lleguemos? **2** *Húrrah el fuvvórr deh uvvissármeh kwúndoh lyeggémmos?*

**Three tickets. How much is it? 1** Déme tres billetes. ¿Cuánto es? **2** *Démmeh tress billyéttess. Kwúntoh ess?*

**What is the best way to go to....? 1** Para ir a.. ¿qué medio de locomoción me aconseja? **2** *Púrrer éar ah... keh méddioh deh lóccomothión meh úconséhher?*

**The underground is the fastest, and it leaves you very near. 1** El metro es muy rápido y le deja cerca.

*En la ciudad*

**2** *El métthoh ess mooy rúppidoh e leh déhher tháircker.*

**Where do I take it? 1** ¿Dónde se coge? **2** *Dóndeh seh cóggeh?*

**At the first corner you will see the way in. 1** En la primera esquina encontrará la entrada. **2** *En lah primáirer eskēēner encóntrarrar lah entrárder.*

**At what station do I get out? 1** ¿En qué estación he de bajar? **2** *En keh estútheón eh deh buhhárr?*

**Please give me a ticket to... 1** Haga el favor de darme un billete para... **2** *Árger el fuvvórr deh dárrmeh oon billyétteh púrrer...*

**Is it far? At what station must I get out? 1** ¿Está lejos? ¿En qué estación he de apearme? **2** *Estar lehhoss? En keh estúthion eh deh úppayármeh?*

**It's near. The third station. 1** Está cerca. Es la tercera estación. **2** *Estar tháircker. Ess lah airtháir estúthion.*

---

## In the bar                              En el bar

**The counter, the bar. 1** El mostrador, la barra. **2** *El móstruddórr, lah búrrer.*
**The stool. 1** El taburete. **2** *El túbboorétteh.*
**The waiter. 1** El camarero. **2** *El cúmmerráirroh.*
**The aperitif. 1** El aperitivo. **2** *El uppérrratēēvoh.*

**The snacks. 1** Las tapas. **2** *Luss túppuss.*
**The refreshment. 1** El refresco. **2** *El refréscoh.*
**The liqueurs. 1** Los licores. **2** *Los lickórress.*
**The tray. 1** La bandeja. **2** *Lah bundéhher.*
**The bottle of water. 1** La botella de agua. **2** *Lah bottélyer deh úgwer.*
**The glass. 1** El vaso. **2** *El vússoh.*
**The wine glass. The liqueur glass. 1** La copa, la copita. **2** *Lah cópper, lah coppēēter.*
**The cup. 1** La taza. **2** *Lah túther.*
**The tea spoon. 1** La cucharilla. **2** *Lah ōōtcherríllyer.*

*En la ciudad*

**The sugar. 1** El azúcar. **2** *El uthŭcker.*
**The express coffee pot. 1** La cafetera exprés. **2** *Lah cúffettáirer expréss.*
**The jug, the pint, the half pint of beer. 1** La jarra, el doble, la caña de cerveza. **2** *Lah húrrer, el dóbbléh lan cúnyer den tháirrvéther.*
**The straws, the tooth picks. 1** Los palillos, los mondadientes. **2** *Loss pullilyoss, loss mónderdyéntess.*
**The ice cream. 1** El helado. **2** *El ellérdoh.*
**The telephone. 1** El teléfono. **2** *El telléfonoh.*
**The lavatory. 1** El lavabo. **2** *El luvvárboh.*
**The cocktail shaker. 1** La coctelera. **2** *Lah cóctelláirer.*
**I'm thirsty. Lets go to the bar. 1** Tengo sed, entremos en el bar. **2** *Téngoh seth, entrárrmoss en el barr.*
**Waiter, get me a drink. 1** Camarero, póngame un refresco. **2** *Cummerráirroh, póngerme oon refréscoh.*
**I want a glass of beer. 1** Yo quiero una caña de cerveza. **2** *Yoh kyáiroh onner cunnyer deh thairrvéther.*
**It's hot inside. Let's sit outside. 1** Dentro hace calor, sentémonos afuera. **2** *Déntroh útheh cullórr, sentáimonnoss ufwáirer.*
**What will you have? 1** ¿Qué tomará usted? **2** *Keh tommeráh oostéh?*
**I'll have an express coffee. 1** Yo tomaré un café exprés. **2** *Yoh tommeréh oon cúffeh expréss.*
**I'd rather have an orangade, an horchata, very fresh, natural. 1** Yo prefiero una naranjada, una horchata, bien fresca, natural. **2** *Yoh preffáirroh ooner núrrunhárder, ooner orrtchútter, byén frésker, nuterrúll.*
**Waiter, a vermouth and soda. 1** ¡Camarero!, un vermut con soda. **2** *Cummerráiroh! Oon vairrmŏŏt con säwder.*
**What snacks would you like? 1** ¿Qué desea de tapas? **2** *Keh dessáyer deh túpperss?*
**Give me some mussels, potato chips, prawns, olives, anchovy, salted almonds, tuna, etc. 1** Póngame almejas, patatas fritas, gambas, aceitunas, anchoas, ensaladilla, atún, etc. **2** *Póngermeh ullméhhuss, puttútterss frēētuss, gúmbuss, úthayŏŏonerss, untchóuss, ensúllur.díller, uttŏŏn, etc.*
**Give me a glass of anis. 1** Póngame una copita de anís. **2** *Póngermeh ooner cuppēēter deh unníss.*

*En la ciudad*

**Cognac. 1** Coñac. **2** *Connyúch.*
**Gin. 1** Ginebra. **2** *Hinnébbrer.*
**Rum. 1** Ron. **2** *Ron.*
**A mixer, a cocktail. 1** Un combinado, un cóctel. **2** *Oon combinárdoh, oon cóctell...*
**Ice. 1** Hielo. **2** *Yélloh.*
**A cup of chocolate. 1** Una taza de chocolate. **2** *Ooner túther deh choccolárteh.*
**A lemonade. 1** Una limonada. **2** *Ooner limmonárder.*
**Orange juice with water, with soda. 1** Zumo de naranja con agua, con soda. **2** *Thŏŏmoh deh nurrúnher con úggwer, con sǟwder.*
**Fruit juice. 1** Zumo de fruta. **2** *Thŏŏmoh deh frŏŏter.*
**Give me tea for one, tea with milk, a complete tea.** **1** Sírvame un té solo, té con leche, té completo. **2** *Sǟērvummeh oon teh sǟwloh, teh con létchet, teh comöléttoh.*
**And what would you like, sir? 1** ¿Y usted, señor, qué desea? **2** *E oostéh, senyórr, keh dessáyer?*
**An orange drink. 1** Un refresco de naranja. **2** *Oon refréscoh deh nurrónher.*
**Do you want coffee with milk? 1** ¿Quiere usted café con leche? **2** *Kyérreh oostéh cúffeh con létcheh?*
**Yes, very hot, please. 1** Sí, que esté bien caliente. **2** *See, keh estéh byén cullvénteh.*
**No, black coffee. 1** No, café solo. **2** *Noh, cúffeh sǟwloh.*
**No, just coffee. 1** No, solo. **2** *Noh, sǟwloh.*
**How do you like this coffee? 1** ¿Qué le parece este café? **2** *Keh leh purrétheh ésteh cúffeh?*
**Its quite good. 1** Es muy aceptable. **2** *Es mooy utheptárbleh.*
**Its pure mocca. 1** Es moka puro. **2** *Ess mócker pŏŏroh.*
**This cup is dirty. 1** Este vaso está sucio. **2** *Ésteh vússoh estár sóotheoh.*
**Give me a little more sugar. 1** Déme un poco más de azúcar. **2** *Démmeh oon pǟwcoh múss deh uthŏŏcker.*
**Give me a bottle of water. 1** Déme una botella de agua. **2** *Démmeh ooner bottéllyer deh úgwer.*
**Could you give me a newspaper, please? 1** ¿Tendrá usted la bondad de darme un periódico? **2** *Tendrár oosteh lah bondúd deh dárrmeh oon perriód-dicoh.*

*En la ciudad*

**Any news? 1** ¿Hay algo nuevo? **2** *I úlgoh nwévvoh?*
**Nothing special today. 1** Hoy no trae nada interesante. **2** *Oy noh trúhyeh nárder interessúnteh.*
**Where is the telephone and the lavatory? 1** ¿Dónde está la cabina del teléfono, el lavabo? **2** *Dóndeh estár lah cubbēēner del telléffonnoh, el luvvárboh?*
**Waiter, my bill please. 1** Camarero, ¿cuánto le debo? **2** *Cummerráiroh, kwúntoh leh débboh?*
**Here you are. Keep the change. 1** Tenga usted, y quédese el resto. **2** *Ténger oosteh, e kédderseh con el réstoh.*
**Thank you, very much. 1** Muchas gracias. **2** *Mō̄ otchuss grútheus.*
**Please bring me the list of ice creams. 1** ¿Hace el favor de traer la lista de helados? **2** *Úttheh el fuvvórr deh trah.áirr lah líster deh ellárdoss?*
**Yes, sir. Here it is. 1** Sí, señor, tenga usted. **2** *See, senyórr, ténger oostéh.*
**Bring me a vanilla, chocolate, strawberry, cream, ice. 1** Traiga un helado de vainilla, de chocolate, de fresa, de nata. **2** *Trýger oon ellárdoh deh vunnēē-lyer, deh chocolárteh, deh frésser, deh nútter.*
**And for me an iced lemonade. 1** Y a mí, un granizado de limón. **2** *E ah me, oon grunnithárdoh deh limmón.*

---

| **The post and telegraph office** | **En correos y telégrafos** |
| --- | --- |

**The revolving doors. 1** Las puertas giratorias. **2** *Las pwáirtus hirratórriuss.*
**The hall. 1** El vestíbulo. **2** *El vestibbooloh.*
**The letter boxes. 1** Los buzones. **2** *Loss boothónness.*
**The commissionaire. 1** El ordenanza. **2** *El orden-núnther.*

*En la ciudad*

**The post office clerk. 1** El oficial de Correos. **2** *El offitheúll deh corráyoss.*

**The postman. 1** El cartero. **2** *El carrtáiroh.*

**The telegraph boy. 1** El repartidor de telégrafos. **2** *El repártiddórr deh tellégruffoss.*

**The letter. 1** La carta. **2** *Lah cárrter.*

**The envelope. 1** El sobre. **2** *El sóbbreh.*

**The postage stamps. 1** Los sellos para franqueo. **2** *Loss séllyoss púrrer frunkáyoh.*

**The ordinary, urgent, registered, air mail letter. 1** La carta ordinaria, urgente, certificada, por avión. **2** *Lah cárrter ordinárriah, oorhénteh, tháirtifficárder, porr uvvión.*

**Declared value. 1** Valores declarados. **2** *Vullórress declarrárdoss.*

**The post card. 1** La tarjeta postal. **2** *Lah tarrhétter postull.*

**Business papers. 1** Papeles de negocio. **2** *Puppélless deh negótheoss.*

**Printed matter. 1** Impresos. **2** *Impréssoss.*

**The parcel. 1** El paquete postal. **2** *El puckétteh postúll.*

**The postal, telegraphic order. 1** El giro postal, telegráfico. **2** *El héroh postúll, tellegrúfficoh.*

**Sealing wax. 1** El lacre. **2** *El lúcreh.*

**The poste restante. 1** La lista de Correos, de Telégrafos. **2** *Lah líster de corráyoss, deh tellégruffoss?*

**Ordinary, urgent letter, telegram. 1** El telegrama ordinario, urgente, telegrama-carta. **2** *El tellegrummmer orrdinárrioh, oorhénteh, tellégrummer - cárrter.*

**Which is the way to the Post Office, please? 1** ¿Para ir a Correos, por favor? **2** *Púrrer éarr ah corráyoss, porr fuvvórr?*

**Is it very far? 1** ¿Está muy lejos? **2** *Estár mooy léhhoss?*

**Thank you. 1** Muchas gracias. **2** *Mō̄tchuss grúttheuss.*

**What's the postage to...? 1** ¿Cuánto es el franqueo de una carta para...? **2** *Kwúntoh ess el frunkáyoh deh ooner cárrter púrrer...?*

**By ordinary post or by air mail? 1** ¿Por correo ordinario o por avión? **2** *Porr corráyoh orrdinárrioh oh porr uvvión?*

**And a post card?** **1** ¿Y una tarjeta postal? **2** *E ooner tarrhétter posstúll?*

**And an urgent letter?** **1** ¿Y una carta urgente? **2** *E oiner cárrter oorrhénteh?*

**It's an urgent registered letter.** **1** Es una carta urgente certificada. **2** *E ooner cárrter oorrhénteh tháirtificárder.*

**Where do they sell postage stamps?** **1** ¿Dónde venden los sellos para el franqueo? **2** *Dóndeh vénden loss séllyoss púrrer el frunkáyoh?*

**At window number... They are sold at all post offices and, in Spain, at the tobacco shops.** **1** En la ventanilla número.. También los venden en las estafetas, y, en España, en los estancos. **2** *En lah véntunníllyer nöömeroh... Tumbyén vénden en luss ésstuffétters, e, en Espúnnyer, en loss estúncoss.*

**This is an ordinary letter.** **1** Esta carta va por correo ordinario. **2** *Éster cárrter vah porr corráyoh ordinárrioh.*

**You need not have come here. You could post it in any pillar box.** **1** No hacía falta que hubiera venido. Podía echarla en cualquier buzón de alcance. **2** *Noh uthéar fúlter keh oobyérrer venëëdoh. Poddéer etchárrlah en kwullkáirr boothón de ulcúnteh.*

**What identity papers do I need to get a parcel out?** **1** ¿Qué documentos de identidad necesito para retirar un paquete postal? **2** *Keh dóckooméntoss deh iddéntidud néthessëëtoh púrrer rettirrárr oon puckétteh postúll?*

**To send a money order?** **1** ¿Para imponer un giro? **2** *Púrrer imponnáirr oon hëëroh?*

**Postal or telegraphic?** **1** ¿Postal o telegráfico? **2** *Postúll oh telligrúfficoh?*

**You must fill in this form and hand it in at window No...** **1** Ha de llenar este impreso y dirigirse a la ventanilla número.. **2** *Ah deh lyennárr ésteh impréssoh e dirrihéérrseh ah lah ventunnillyerr nöömairroh...*

**We cannot accept money orders for abroad.** **1** No se admiten giros para el extranjero. **2** *Noh seh udmëëten hëëross púrrer el extrunháiroh.*

*En la ciudad*

**I should like to ask if there are any letters for me.**
  1 Quisiera preguntar si hay alguna carta para mí.
  2 *Kissáirrer pregoontárr see i ulgōōner cárrter púrrer me.*

**You must ask at the poste restante.** 1 Ha de dirigirse a la Lista de Correos. 2 *Ah deh dirrihēērrseh ah lah líster deh corráyoss.*

**Where is it?** 1 ¿Dónde está? 2 *Dóndeh estár?*

**At the bottom, at that window.** 1 Al fondo, en aquella ventanilla. 2 *Ull fóndoh, en uckéllyer ventunníl-yer.*

**Is there any letter for...?** 1 ¿Hay alguna carta para..? 2 *I ulgōōner cárrter púrrer...?*

**Have you anything to identify you?** 1 ¿Tiene usted algún documento de identidad? 2 *Tyénneh oostéh ulgōōn dóckoométoh deh iddéntidúd?*

**I have my passport.** 1 Tengo el pasaporte. 2 *Téngoh me pússerpórrteh,*

**That's more than sufficient.** 1 Es más que suficiente. 2 *Es muss keh sooffithiénteh.*

**Where's the letter box?** 1 ¿Dónde está el buzón? 2 *Dóndeh estar el boothón?*

**Have you got your letters yet?** 1 ¿Han recogido ya las cartas? 2 *Un reccohhēēdoh yah luss cárrtuss?*

**Is the office open on Bank Holidays?** 1 ¿Hay servicio los días festivos? 2 *I sairrvēētheo loss déarss festēēvoss?*

**Only in the morning.** 1 Solamente por la mañana. 2 *Sollerménte porr lah munyúnner.*

**There's only one delivery on holidays.** 1 Los carteros sólo hacen un reparto los días de fiesta. 2 *Loss carrtáirross sāwloh úthen oom reppárrtho loss déus deh fyéster.*

**Please register this letter and give me the receipt.**
  1 Haga el favor de certificarme esta carta y tráigame el recibo. 2 *Úgger el fuvvórr deh tháirrtifficárrmeh éster cárrter e trýgermey el rethēēboh.*

**I want to send a telegram to Madrid.** 1 Deseo enviar un telegrama a Madrid. 2 *Dessáyoh enviárr oon tellégrummer ah Muddrid.*

**All right. Fill in a form and bring it to the window.**
  1 Muy bien. Tome usted un impreso, llénelo y

*En la ciudad*

preséntelo en la ventanilla. 2 *Mooy byen. Tómmeh oostéh oon impréssoh, lyénnellóh e presséntellóh en lah ventunníllyer.*

**Must I write it in French, English, Spanish?** 1 ¿He de redactarlo en francés, inglés, español...? 2 *Ah deh reductárrloh en frunthéss, ingléss, espunyolw?*

**As you like.** 1 Como usted quiera. 2 *Cómmoh oostéh kyáirrer.*

**How much is it a word?** 1 ¿Cuánto cobran por palabra? 2 *Kwúntoh cóbrun porr pullárbrer?*

**It depends on whether it is urgent or ordinary, and the country it's for.** 1 Depende de si lo quiere urgente u ordinario y el país de destino. 2 *Dépendeh deh see loh kyáirreh oorhénteh oh orrdinárrio e el pahíss deh destēenoh.*

**How much is this telegram?** 1 ¿Cuánto vale este telegrama? 2 *Kwúntoh várleh ésteh tellégrummer?*

**Where is the poste restante for telegrams?** 1 ¿Dónde está la Lista de Telégrafos? 2 *Dóndeh estár lah líster deh tellégruffoss?*

**At the side window.** 1 En la ventanilla de al lado. 2 *En lah ventunníllyer deh ull lárdoh.*

---

## At the theater, at the cinema

## En el teatro, en el cine

---

**The booking office.** 1 La taquilla. 2 *Lah tukkillver.*
**The porter.** 1 El portero. 2 *El porrtáirroh.*
**The hall.** 1 El vestíbulo. 2 *El vestíbboolloh.*
**The bar.** 1 El bar. 2 *El barr.*
**The auditorium.** 1 La sala. 2 *Lah súller.*
**The lavatory.** 1 El lavabo. 2 *El luvvárboh.*
**The cloak room.** 1 El guardarropa. 2 *El gwárrder.rāpuss.*
**The attendant.** 1 El acomodador. 2 *El uccómmodderdór.*
**The aisle.** 1 El pasillo. 2 *El pussílloh.*
**The stage.** 1 El escenario. 2 *El esthénnárrio.*
**The curtain.** 1 El telón. 2 *El tellón.*

*En la ciudad*

**The scenery. 1** Las decoraciones. **2** *Luss déccorrutheónes.*

**The prompt box. 1** Los bastidores. **2** *Loss bustidórress.*

**The wings. 1** La concha del apuntador. **2** *Lah cóntcher del uppöönterdórr.*

**The stalls. 1** Los palcos. **2** *Loss púlcoss.*

**The orchestra stalls. 1** Los palcos proscenios. **2** *Loss púllcoss prosthénneóss.*

**The conductor. 1** El director de orquesta. **2** *El diréctorr deh orrkéster.*

**The musicians. 1** Los músicos. **2** *Loss möösicoss.*

**The orchestra. 1** La orquesta. **2** *Lah orrkéster.*

**Seats on the ground floor. 1** Las butacas de platea. **2** *Luss bootúckuss.*

**The dress circle seats. 1** Las butacas del primer piso. **2** *Luss bootúckers del primáirr pëësoh.*

**The gallery. 1** El anfiteatro. **2** *El únfitayártroh.*

**The pit, the gods. 1** General, el paraíso. **2** *Hénnrerrúll, el púrrer.ëësoh.*

**The tickets. 1** Las localidades, las entradas, los billetes. **2** *Luss locúllidárdes, luss entrárduss, loss bilyéttess.*

**The prompter. 1** El apuntador. **2** *El uppööntadórr.*

**The actor. 1** El actor. **2** *El ucktórr.*

**The actress. 1** La actriz. **2** *Lah ucktrëëfh.*

**The chorus. 1** El coro. **2** *El cäwroh.*

**The dancer. 1** La bailarina. **2** *Lah býlerrëëner.*

**The tenor. 1** El tenor. **2** *El tennórr.*

**The baritone. 1** El barítono. **2** *El burríttonnoh.*

**The comedian. 1** El cómico. **2** *El cómmicoh.*

**The soprano. 1** La tiple. **2** *Lah típleh.*

**A comedy. 1** Una comedia. **2** *Ooner commáydia.*

**A melodrama. 1** Un melodrama. **2** *Oon méllohdrármer.*

**A comedietta. 1** Un juguete. **2** *Oon hoogétty.*

**An opera. 1** Una ópera. **2** *Ooner ópperrer.*

**An operetta. 1** Una opereta. **2** *Ooner opperrétter.*

**A musical comedy. 1** Una zarzuela. **2** *Ooner thárrthoo.éller.*

**An act. 1** Un acto. **2** *Oon úcktoh.*

**An interval. 1** Un entreacto. **2** *Oon éntreh.úcktoh.*

**Half time. 1** La media parte. **2** *Lah méddier párrteh.*

*En la ciudad*

**Applause. 1** Aplausos. **2** *Upplówsuss.*
**Whistling. 1** Silbidos. **2** *Silbĕ̄edoss.*
**The sound cinema. 1** El cine sonoro. **2** *El thínneh sonnórroh.*
**The screen. 1** La pantalla. **2** *Lah puntúllyer.*
**The panoramic screen (large). 1** La pantalla panorámica (grande). **2** *Lah puntúllyer púnnerrúmmica (grundeh).*
**The three dimensional screen. 1** La pantalla tridimensional. **2** *Lah puntúllyer trĕ̄edimménseonúll.*
**The cinascope. 1** Cinemascope. **2** *Sínnema.scóppeh.*
**Documentary. 1** Documental. **2** *Dóckoomentúll.*
**Technicolour film. 1** Película en tecnicolor. **2** *Pelliccoler en técknicolórr.*
**Stereoscopic film. 1** Película en relieve. **2** *Pellícooler en rel yévveh.*
**I should like go to the theatre this evening. 1** Me gustaría ir al teatro esta noche. **2** *Meh goostaéar érrar úll tayártroh éster nótcheh.*
**Could you tell me where there in something good?** **1** ¿Podría usted decirme dónde hacen buen programa? **2** *Poddréar oostéh dethéarrmeh dódeh úthen byén prográmmer?*
**Let's look at the list of theatres in the newspaper.** **1** Veamos la cartelera, los anuncios del periódico. **2** *Váyermoss lah cártellairer, loss unnŏ̄ontheoss del perriódicoh.*
**They have a complete list in the office. 1** En la conserjería del hotel disponen de una cartelera completa. **2** *En lah conséhherréar del awtél dispónnen deh ooner cárrtelláirrer complétter.*
**There's a great programme at the cinema. 1** En el cine... hacen un programa estupendo. **2** *En el thinneh... úthen oon progrummer ésstoopéndoh.*
**Can you tell me whether children are admitted?** **1** ¿Puede decirme si es apto para menores? **2** *Pwéddeh dethéarme see ess úptoh púrrer mennórress?*
**They are replaying an old film. 1** Hacen una película de estreno, de reestreno. **2** *Úthen ooner pellícooler deh esstrénnoh, deh réh.estrénnoh.*

*En la ciudad*

**I prefer a continuous perfomance, and a film with some local colour.** 1 Prefiero un cine que hagan sesión continua y alguna película de ambiente del país. 2 *Prefyáirroh oon thínne keh úggun sesseón contínnooer e ulgōōner pellícooler deh umbyénteh del pah.íss.*

**When does the program start, please?** 1 ¿Hace el favor de indicarme a qué hora empieza la sesión? 2 *Utheh el fuvvórr deh indicárrmeh ah keh óra empyéther lah sesséón?*

**How long does the film last?** 1 ¿Cuánto dura la película? 2 *Kwúntoh dōōrer lah pellícooler?*

**There's a good show at the theatre.** 1 En el teatro... hacen una buena función. 2 *En el teh.úttroh... úthen ooner bwénner foontheón.*

**There's a three act comedy.** 1 Hacen una comedia en tres actos. 2 *Úthen ooner comméddia en tress úctoss.*

**Go and see the opera...** 1 Vaya usted a ver la ópera. 2 *Vah yer ah váirr lah óppera.*

**The famous... are acting.** 1 Trabajan los famosos artistas... 2 *Trubbúhhan loss fummóssoss arrtístuss...*

**Is it far from here?** 1 ¿Está lejos de aquí? 2 *Estár léhhoss deh uckee?*

**Two tickets for this evening, please.** 1 Haga el favor de dos localidades para la función de esta noche. 2 *Úgger el fuvvórr deh doss locúllidárdess púrrer lah foontheón deh éster nótcheh.*

**What seats do you want?** 1 ¿Qué localidades desea? 2 *Keh locúllidárress dessáyer?*

**Stalls, gallery, dress circle.** 1 De platea, anfiteatro, delantera del primer piso... 2 *Deh pluttáyer, únfitayúttroh, delluntáirer del primáirr pēeseh.*

**In row twenty. Will that do?** 1 ¿Le va bien la fila veinte? 2 *Leh vah byén lah fēēler vénteh.*

**It's too far. I should like something nearer. From the fifth to the tenth row.** 1 Demasiado lejos. Me interesaría que fuera más cerca. De la cinco a la diez. 2 *Demmússiárdoh léhhoss. Meh interréssarrear keh fwáirer muss tsáirra. Deh lah thinkoh úlluss de.uth.*

*En la ciudad*

**Against the centre gangway. 1** Tocando al pasillo central. **2** *Torkúndoh úll pussíllyoh thentrúl.*

**I'll take these. How much are they? 1** Me quedo éstas. ¿Cuánto es? **2** *Meh kéddoh éstuss. Kwúntoh ess?*

**I should like to go to the cloak room. 1** Quisiera ir al guardarropa. **2** *Kissáirrer éarr ull gwarrdarrópper*

**It's in the entrance, on the right. 1** Lo encontrará a la derecha del vestíbulo. **2** *Loh encóntrarráh ah lah derrétcher del vestíbbooloh.*

**A program, please. 1** Portero, ¿haría el favor de un programa? **2** *Porrtáiroh, urréar el fuvvórr deh oon progrúmmer?*

**At what time does it begin? 1** ¿A qué hora empiezan? **2** *Ah keh óra empyéthyetum?*

**Does it last very long? 1** ¿Dura mucho la función? **2** *Döörer möötchoh lah foontheón?*

**An attendant is coming now. 1** Ahora vendrá un acomodador. **2** *Un.or vendráh oon uccómoduddórr.*

**How many intervals are there? 1** ¿Cuántos entreactos hay? **2** *Kwúntoss éntreh.úcktoss i?*

**How long are the intervals? 1** ¿Cuánto dura cada entreacto? **2** *Kwútoh minöörer cárther éntre.úcktoh?*

**Fifteen minutes, sir. 1** Quince minutos, señor. **2** *Kíntheh minöötoss, senyórr.*

**Who is the author? 1** ¿Quién es el autor? **2** *Kyén ess el owtórr?*

**Where's the bar, the lavatory? 1** ¿Dónde está el bar, el lavabo? **2** *Dóndeh estár el barr, el luvvárboh.*

**There are a lot of people. 1** Hay muchísima gente. **2** *I mootchíssimer hénteh.*

**At what time does it finish? 1** ¿A qué hora termina? **2** *Ah ken óra tairrmééner?*

**The curtain is going up. 1** Va a levantarse el telón. **2** *Vah ah levvuntárrseh el tellón.*

**Bell boy, get me a taxi. 1** Botones, búsqueme un taxi. **2** *Bottónness, bööskermeh oon túcksi.*

**Thank you very much. 1** Muchas gracias. **2** *Möötchuss grútheus.*

## At the bull fight                 En los toros

**The arena, the bull ring. 1** La plaza de toros. **2** *Lah plúther deh tãwross.*
**The parade. 1** El ruedo. **2** *El rooéddoh.*
**The barrier. 1** La barrera. **2** *Lah burráirrer.*
**The counter barrier. 1** La contrabarrera. **2** *Lah cóntraburráirer.*
**The row of seats. 1** El tendido. **2** *El tendẽẽdoh.*
**The gradins or rows. 1** Las gradas. **2** *Luss grárduss.*
**The grand stand. 1** La andanada. **2** *Lah úndernárder.*
**The box. 1** El palco. **2** *El púlcoh.*
**The gangway. 1** El callejón. **2** *El cúllyeh.hón.*
**The band, the fanfare. 1** La banda de música, la charanga. **2** *Lah búnder deh mõõsicker, lah churrúnger.*
**The safety door. 1** El burladero. **2** *El bõõrrluddáirroh.*
**The pen for the bulls. 1** El toril, el chiquero. **2** *El torríll, el tchickáiroh.*
**The president's chair. 1** La presidencia. **2** *Lah presidénthea.*
**The assistants. 1** La cuadrilla. **2** *La kwuddrílyer.*
**The bull fighters. 1** Los toreros. **2** *Loss torráirross.*
**The matador. 1** El matador. **2** *El mutterdórr.*
**The dart. 1** El banderillero. **2** *El búndairrillyáiroh.*
**The men. 1** El peón. **2** *El payón.*
**The swordsman. 1** El mozo de estoque. **2** *El mãwthoh deh estockeh.*
**The picador. 1** El picador. **2** *El pikerdórr.*
**The «trained monkey». 1** El monosabio. **2** *El mónnoh.sárbeo.*
**The horse. 1** El caballo. **2** *El cubbúllyoh.*
**The bull. 1** El toro. **2** *El tãwroh.*
**The cloak. 1** El capote de paseo. **2** *El cuppótteh deh pussáyoh.*
**The working cloak. 1** El capote de faena. **2** *El cuppótteh deh fahyénner.*
**The red flag. 1** La muleta. **2** *Lah moollétter.*
**The sword. 1** El estoque, la espada. **2** *El estóckeh, lah espárder.*
**The killing sword. 1** El estoque de descabello. **2** *El estóckeh deh désscubbúllyoh.*

*En la ciudad*

**The finish.** 1 La puntilla. 2 *Lah poontíllyer.*
**The darts.** 1 Las banderillas. 2 *Luss búndairrílyuss.*
**The goad.** 1 La puya, la pica. 2 *Lah pōōyah, lah pēē-ker.*
**The badge.** 1 La divisa. 2 *Lah divēēser.*
**Applause.** 1 Aplausos. 2 *Upplówsuss.*
**Whistling. («The bird»).** 1 Pitos. 2 *Pēētoss.*
**Give me two good places.** 1 Déme dos entradas buenas. 2 *Démmeh doss entrárduss bwénnuss.*
**Do you want barrier, counterbarrier, chairs, the stand, sun or shade?** 1 ¿Las quiere de contrabarrera, de tendido, de andanada, de sol, de sombra? 2 *Luss kyáirreh deh cóntraburráirrer, deh tendēēdoh, deh úndunnárder, deh sol, deh sómbrer.*
**At what time does the fight begin?** 1 ¿A qué hora empieza la corrida? 2 *Ah keh óra empyether lah corrēēder?*
**The bull fighter and his staff will soon come out.** 1 Pronto saldrá la cuadrilla. 2 *Próntoh suldrár lah kwuddríllyer.*
**What is the «cuadrilla»?** 1 ¿Qué es la cuadrilla? 2 *Keh ess lah kwuddrillyer?*
**It's all the fighters with their staffs of dart placers and men.** 1 Es el conjunto de matadores con sus correspondientes compañías de banderilleros y peones. 2 *Ess el conhōōtoh deh mutterdórress con soos córrespondyéntess compunnéars deh bunderríllyes e payónes.*
**Who is that horseman in front or the «cuadrilla»?** 1 ¿Quién es ese caballista que va al frente de la cuadrilla? 2 *Kyén ess ésteh cubbullyíster keh vah ull frénteh deh lah kwuddríllyer?*
**The orderly.** 1 El alguacil. 2 *Él úlgwuh.thíl.*
**What's his job?** 1 ¿Qué misión tiene? 2 *Keh misseón tyénneh?*
**To receive the keys of the bull pens from the president, so that the fight may begin.** 1 Recibir del presidente las llaves del toril para que empiece la lidia. 2 *Rethibēērr del préssidénteh luss lyárvess del torrill púrrer keh empyétheh lah líddear.*
**And those others on horseback?** 1 ¿Y esos otros caballistas? 2 *E éssos âwtross cubbullyístuss?*

*En la ciudad*

**They are the «picadores».** 1 Son los picadores.
2 *Son loss píckerdórress.*

**Those at the side, in red blouses, are called
«monosabios».** 1 Los que van al lado con la blusa
encarnada, se les llama monosabios. 2 *Loss keh
vun al lardoh con lah bloosser encarrnader, seh
less lyármer mónnosárbeoss.*

**And what do they do?** 1 ¿Y qué hacen? 2 *El keh
úthen?*

**They are the grooms for the picador's horse.** 1 Son
los mozos que se cuidan del caballo del picador.
2 *Son loss móthōōs keh seh kwēēdun del cubbúllyoh
del píckerdórr.*

**When will the bull come out?** 1 ¿Cuándo saldrá el
toro? 2 *Kwundoh suldráh el tãwroh?*

**At once. When the fanfare sounds.** 1 En seguida.
Cuando suene el clarín. 2 *En seggēēder. Kwúndoh
swénneh el clurrēēn.*

**What's that ribbon on the bull's back?** 1 ¿Qué es
esa cinta que lleva el toro en el lomo? 2 *Keh ess
ésser thínter keh lyévver el tãwroh en el lómmoh?*

**The badge, to show what ranch he comes from.**
1 La divisa, para distinguir a qué ganadería perte-
nece. 2 *Lah divvēēser, púrrer distingēērrleh ah keh
gúnnerderría pairtennétheh.*

**Only the matadores and the swordsmen are left in
the ring.** 1 En la plaza han quedado sólo los matadores o espadas y los peones. 2 *En lah plúther un
keddárdoh sólloh loss múfferdórress oh espúdders
e loss peóhness.*

**Is that the matador?** 1 ¿Ése es el torero? 2 *Ésseh es
el torrerroh?*

**No, it's one of the assistants. He his making his
first tentative moves.** 1 No, uno de los peones.
Está dando los primeros lances de tanteo. 2 *Noh,
oonoh deh loss payónness. Estár dúndoh loss
primmáirros lúnthess deh tuntéoh.*

**What does that mean?** 1 ¿Qué quiere decir eso?
2 *Keh kyáirreh dethēērr éssoh?*

**It's an invitation to the bull to charge, and the
matador studies its way of charging.** 1 Es la invitación que se hace al toro para que éste embista y

*En la ciudad*

el matador vea la forma que tiene de embestir. **2** *Es slah invitútheón keh seh útheh ull tāwroh púrrer keh ésteh embíster e el mútterdórr váyer lah fórrmer keh tyénneh deh embistēerr.*

**That is, he studies the the bull's technique, doesn't he? 1** O sea, que hace un estudio de cómo arremete el toro. ¿Verdad? **2** *Oh sáyer, keh úthheh oon estōōdioh deh cómmoh urremmétthe el tāwrroh. Váirrdud?*

**That's right, and so he knows what tactics to use. 1** Eso es, y así sabe cómo debe torearlo. **2** *Éssoh ess, e ussēē sárbeh cómmoh débben toreárrloh.*

**Is this the matador coming out now? 1** ¿Ése que sale ahora es el torero? **2** *Éssteh keh sárleh uh.óra es el torrerroh?*

**Yes, now he will work with the cape, or he will make his moves. 1** Sí, ahora toreará con el capote, o dará sus lances. **2** *See, uh.óra tórrairráh con el cuppótteh, oh durráh soos lúnthess.*

**Are there many kinds of moves? 1** ¿Hay muchas clases de lances? **2** *I mōōtchuss clússess deh lúnthess?*

**Yes, the best known are the veronicas, the faroles, frontal and rear, the chicuelinas, the raboleras, and the half veronicas. 1** Sí, los más oídos son: Las verónicas, los faroles, de frente por detrás, las chicuelinas, las raboleras y las medias verónicas. **2** *See, loss muss oh.ēēdoss son: Luss verónicuss, loss furrólless, deh frénteh porr dettrúss, luss chíckwellēēnes, luss rubbolláiruss e luss méddier verónicuss.*

**What's the music for now? 1** ¿Por qué suena ahora la música? **2** *Por kéh swénner uh.óra lah mōōsicker?*

**Because of the endless, enthusiastic applause for the bull fighter's work. 1** Porque el público aplaude ininterrumpidamente, entusiasmado por el trabajo del torero. **2** *Pórkeh el pōōblicoh upplawdeh in.interrompeeder.menteh, entōōsiúsmárdoh porr el trubáhhoh del torrérroh.*

**And whats the fanfare for now? 1** ¿Y ahora por qué toca el clarín? **2** *E uh.óra porrhéh tócker el clurēēn?*

*En la ciudad*

**For the picadors to come out. 1** Para que salgan los picadores. **2** *Púrrer keh súlgun loss pickerdórress.*

**Now he is manoeuvering the bull «de varas». 1** Ahora está poniendo el matador al toro en suerte de varas. **2** *Uh.óra estár ponyéndoh el mutterdórr ull tãwroh en swáirteh deh vúrruss.*

**What does that mean? 1** ¿Qué significa eso? **2** *Keh sígniffééker éssoh?*

**That he is bringing the bull in front of the horse, so that the picador may goad him. 1** Que está poniendo al toro frente al caballo, para que el picador pueda clavarle la puya. **2** *Keh estár pnnyéndoh ull tãwroh frénteh ull cubbúllyoh, púrrer keh el pickerdórr pwéddeh cluvvárrleh lah põõyer.*

**And why do they torment the bull with the goad? 1** ¿Y por qué castigan al toro con la puya? **2** *E por kéh custéégun ull towroh con lah pooyer?*

**To weaken him before placing the darts and working with the red flag. 1** Para restarle fuerza, antes de ponerle las banderillas y de hacer la faena de muleta. **2** *Púrrer restárrleh fwáirther úntess deh ponnáirrleh luss búnderrílyus e deh utháir lah fah.yénner deh moolétter.*

**They generally prick him with the goad three times. 1** Generalmente le clavan tres veces la puya. **2** *Hennerulménteh leh clárvun tree véthess lah põõyer.*

**Why are the people shouting now? 1** ¿Por qué grita ahora el público? **2** *Por kéh grééter ah.óra el põõblicoh?*

**Because they dont want the bull to be goaded any more. 1** Porque no quiere que le claven más veces la puya al toro. **2** *Pórrkeh noh kyáireh keh clárven muss véthess lah põõyer ull tãwroh.*

**The matador is now going to do the «quite», i. e. to draw the bull from the horse. 1** Ahora va el torero a efectuar el quite, o sea que va a separar el toro del caballo. **2** *Ah.óra vah el torrerroh ah efféctooárr el kééteh, oh sáyer keh vah ah sepperrárr el tãwroh del cubbúllyoh.*

**He has made a magnificent «quite». 1** Ha hecho un quite magnífico. **2** *Ah étchoh oon kééteh muhnífficoh.*

*En la ciudad*

**What are those toreros doing there? 1** ¿Qué hacen
allí aquellos toreros? **2** *Keh úthen uckée ukkéllyoss
torráirross?*

**They are the matador's men, who are there for the
«quite». 1** Son los peones del torero, que están al
quite. **2** *Son loss peh.ónness del torrerroh, keh
estún úll kéeteh.*

**What does that mean? 1** ¿Qué quiere decir eso?
**2** *Keh kyáirreh dethéerr éssoh?*

**That they are ready to go, if necessary, to the help
of the toreador. 1** Que están preparados para ir,
si es necesario, en ayuda del que está toreando.
**2** *Keh estún prépurrárdoss púrrer éarr, see ess net-
hessárrioh, en ah.yóoder del keh estar tórrayúndoh.*

**To save him from possible danger from the bull's
onslaught? 1** ¿Para librarle de un posible peligro
por la acometida del toro? **2** *Púrrer librárrleh deh
oon posséebleh pelligroh porr lah uccómmettéedoh
del táwroh.*

**That's right. I see you are beginning to understand.
1** Eso es. Veo que lo va entendiendo. **2** *Éssoh ess.
Váyoh keh loh vah éntendyéndoh.*

**There goes the fanfare again. 1** Ahora vuelve a
sonar el clarín. **2** *Uh.éra vwélveh ah sonnárr el
clurréen.*

**It's the signal to change the kind of darts. 1** Es la
señal para cambiar la suerte en banderillas. **2** *Ess
el sennyúll púrrer cumbeárr lah swáirrteh en bun-
derrllyers.*

**How many darts will they place? 1** ¿Cuántas banderillas le pondrán? **2** *Kwúnteuss bunderrillyuss le
pondrún?*

**It's generally three pairs, and four if the public
demands it insistantly. 1** Acostumbra a ser tres
pares, y cuatro si el público lo pide con insistencia.
**2** *Uccostóombrer ah sár tres párress, e kwúttroh
see el póoblicoh loh péedeh con insisténthea.*

**Why are they placing explosive darts now? 1** ¿Por
qué ponen ahora banderillas explosivas? **2** *Porr
kéh pónnen ah.óra bunderríllyuss exploséevuss?*

**They're called fire dart. They are used when they
think the bull is not fierce enough. 1** Se llaman

banderillas de fuego. Las ponen cuando conside-
ran que el toro no es fiero. **2** *Seh lyármun bunderrillyuss deh fwéggoh. Luss pónnen kwúndoh con-
siddáirrun keh el tãwroh non es es fyáiroh.*

**That is, to make it attack more? 1** ¿O sea para que
embista más? **2** *Oh sáyer keh embíssteh muss.*

**That's it. 1** Así es. **2** *Ussãã ess.*

**Now the fanfare is souding for the toreador to
make the passes with the red flag and kill the
bull. 1** Ahora toca el clarín para que se haga la faena de muleta y para que se mate al toro. **2** *Ah.óra
tócca el clurãẽn púrrer keh seh úgger lah fah.yén-
ner deh mullétter e púrrer keh seh mútteh ul tãwroh.*

**What's the matador doing now? 1** ¿Qué está
haciendo ahora el matador? **2** *Keh estár uthyéndoh
ah.óra el mutterdórr?*

**He's taking his sword and the red flag from his
attandant. 1** Está recibiendo del mozo el estoque y
la muleta. **2** *Estár rethibyéndoh del mótoh el estóckeh e lah moolétter.*

**Is he saluting now? 1** ¿Ahora está saludando?
**2** *Ah.óra estárr sulloodúndoh?*

**He is offering the bull. 1** Está brindando el toro.
**2** *Estár bridúndoh el tãwroh.*

**What is «saluting the bull»? 1** ¿Qué significa brin-
dar el toro? **2** *Keh signifẽẽker brindárr el tãwroh?*

**He is offering the sacrifice of the bull to someone.
1** Que ofrece el sacrificio del toro a alguna persona.
**2** *Keh offrétheh el sucrifẽẽthio del tãwroh ah ulgõõ-
ner pairsónner.*

**He has saluted and has thrown his cap into the
middle of the crowd. 1** Ha saludado y ha tirado la
montera en el centro del ruedo. **2** *Ah sulloodárdoh e
ah tirrárdoh lah montáirer en el théntroh del rwéddoh.*

**That means he has dedicated the bull to the
public. 1** Eso significa que ha brindado el toro al
público. **2** *Éssoh signifẽẽker keh ah brindárdoh el
torrroh ul põõblico.*

**He has thrown his cap to the president's box. 1** Ha
tirado la montera a la presidencia. **2** *Ah tirrárdoh lah
montáirer a lah pressidénthia.*

*En la ciudad*

**Because he offers the bull to the president. 1** Porque le ofrece el toro al presidente. **2** *Porrkeh leh ofrétheh el tãwroh ul pressidénteh?*

**Now he is making passes. 1** Ahora está haciendo los pases de muleta. **2** *Ah.óra estár uthyényoh loss pússess deh mõõlétter.*

**What are the most usual? 1** ¿Cuáles son los más corrientes? **2** *Kwúlless son loss muss corryéntess?*

**The natural passes, which are used to give the finishing stroke in the breast, the round passes, the stationary ones, upwards, standing or kneeling, afarolados, change behind the back, manoletinas, molinetes, frontal and side. 1** Los pases naturales, que se acostumbran a rematar de pecho, los pases en redondo, estatuarios, por alto, de pie o rodillas, afarolados, de cambios por la espalda, manoletinas, molinetes, de la firma, de costadillo. **2** *Loss pússes nuttoorúlless, keh seh uccóstõ ombrun ah remmuttárr deh pétchoh, loss pússes en reddóndoh, estúttõõárioss, porr últoh, deh pyéh oh roddíllyuss, uffúrrollárdoss, deh cúmbioss porr lah espúlda, múnolltẽẽnerss, móllinéttess, deh lah féarremr, deh cóstuddíllyoh.*

**Now he's getting the bull in position for the kill. 1** Ahora está poniendo el toro en suerte de matar. **2** *Ah.óra estár ponnyéndoh el tórroh en swáirteh deh muttárr.*

**That is, he is getting him in the right position to kill him. 1** O sea, que lo está poniendo bien para matarlo. ¿Verdad? **2** *Oh sáyer, keh loh estár ponnyéndoh byén púrrer muttárrloh, váirud?*

**He has already pierced him with his sword, but he has not killed him. 1** Ya le ha clavado el estoque pero no lo ha matado. **2** *Yah leh ah cluvvárdoh el estóckeh, péhroh noh loh ah muttárdoh.*

**It was a good thrust. Now he will finish him off with the killing sword. 1** Ha sido una buena estocada. Ahora lo rematarán con la puntilla o con el estoque de descabello. **2** *Ah sẽẽdoh ooner bwenner estockárda. Ah.óra loh remmútterrún con lah poontíllyer oh con el estóckeh deh déscubellyoh.*

**I see they are going to do the «descabello». 1** Veo

que van a hacer el descabello. **2** *Váyoh keh vun ah utháirr el déscubbéllyoh.*

**What is the «descabello»? 1** ¿Qué significa el descabello? **2** *Keh signifiēēker el déscubbéllyoh?*

**That they will kill him at once by stabbing his nape of the neck with the point of the sword. 1** Que lo matarán instantáneamente hiriéndole en la cerviz con la punta del estoque. **2** *Keh loh mutterrún instuntúnneaménteh irriéndoleh en el thairvēēth con lah pōōnter del estóckeh.*

**The bull has already fallen dead. 1** Ya ha caído el toro muerto. **2** *Yah ah ky.íddoh el tónroh mwáirrtoh.*

**The people are aplauding a lot. Why are they waving their handkerchiefs so much? 1** El público aplaude mucho. ¿Por qué agitan tanto los pañuelos? **2** *El pōōblico upplōwdeh mōōtcho. Porrkéh uh.híttun túntoh loss púnnyooélloss?*

**They are asking for the ear, as a reward for the matador's good work. 1** Porque piden la oreja, como premio a la buena actuación del matador. **2** *Pórrkeh pēēdun lah orréhher cómmoh prénmmio ah la bwénner úctooutheón del mútterdórr.*

**What prizes do they give? 1** ¿Qué premios se conceden? **2** *Keh prémmioss seh conthédden?*

**The prizes, from the lowest upwards are: 1** El orden de premios, de menor a mayor importancia, es. **2** *El órrden deh prémmioss deh mennórr ah my.yórr imporrtúnthea,es:*

**The ear. 1** La oreja. **2** *Lah oréhher.*

**The two ears. 1** Las dos orejas. **2** *Luss doss oréhhus.*

**The two ears and the tail. 1** Las dos orejas y el rabo. **2** *Luss doss oréhhus e el rárboh.*

**Both ears, the tail and the foot. 1** Las dos orejas, el rabo y la pata. **2** *Luss doss urréhhuss, el rárboh e lah pútter.*

**The president decides what prize shall be given him. 1** El presidente es quien decide sobre el premio que se le otorga. **2** *El pressidéntch ess kyén dethēēdeh sobreh el prémmio keh seh leh uttórrger.*

**Why is the bullfighter running now? 1** ¿Por qué corre ahora el torero? **2** *Porrkéh córreh ah.óra el torérroh?*

*De compras*

**He's running round the ring to thank the people for their applause. 1** Está dando la vuelta al ruedo para corresponder a los aplausos. **2** *Estár dúndoh lah vwélter ull rwéddoh púrrer correspondáirr ah los upplōwsoss.*

**He salutes from the half-way, the third and the middle of the ring. 1** Saluda desde los medios, tercio, desde el centro de la plaza. **2** *Sullōōder désdeh loss méddios, táirtheo, désdeh el théntroh déller plúther.*

**And what are those horses doing? 1** ¿Y aquellos caballos qué hacen? **2** *E uckélyos cubbúllyos, kah úthen?*

**They are the mules that drag the dead bull out. 1** Son las mulillas. Es el arrastre que se lleva el toro muerto. **2** *Son loss mōōlíllyuss. Es el urrústreh keh seh lyévver el tórroh mwáirtoh.*

**It's been a good bull fight. 1** Ha sido una buena corrida. **2** *Ah sēēdoh ooner bwénner corrēēder.*

# Shopping
# De compras

---

**The stores**  **En los almacenes**

---

**Ground floor. 1** Planta baja. **2** *Plóntah búhher.*

**First, second, third floor. 1** Primer, segundo, tercer piso. **2** *Primáirr, segōōndoh, tairrtháirr pēēsoh.*

**The lift. 1** El ascensor. **2** *El ústhensórr.*

**The stairs. 1** Las escaleras. **2** *Luss ésculláirerss.*

**The departments. 1** Las secciones. **2** *Luss séctheeóness.*

**The head of the department. 1** El encargado de sección. **2** *El éncarrgárdoh deller secktheón.*

*De compras*

**The assistant.** 1 El dependiente, la dependienta. 2 *El deppendyénteh, lan deppendyénter.*
**The bell boy.** 1 El botones. 2 *El ottónness.*
**The counter.** 1 El mostrador. 2 *El móstruddórr.*
**The shop windows.** 1 Las vitrinas. 2 *Luss vittrēēners.*
**The chairs.** 1 Las sillas. 2 *Luss sílyuss.*
**The cash desk.** 1 La caja. 2 *Lah cúhher.*
**The cashier.** 1 La cajera. 2 *Lah cuhháirer.*

---

## Clothing                          Prendas de vestir

**Men's**

**Para hombres**

---

**Overcoat.** 1 Abrigo. 2 *Ubbrēēgoh.*
**Jacket.** 1 Americana. 2 *Umméricúnner.*
**Stick.** 1 Bastón. 2 *Bustón.*
**Dressing gown.** 1 Batín. 2 *Buttēēn.*
**Beret.** 1 Boina. 2 *Bóyner.*
**Boots.** 1 Botas. 2 *Bóttuss.*
**Scarf.** 1 Bufanda. 2 *Booffúnder.*
**Socks.** 1 Calcetines. 2 *Cúlthettēēness.*
**Pants.** 1 Calzoncillos. 2 *Cúlthonthíllyoss.*
**Shirt.** 1 Camisa. 2 *Cummēēser.*
**Vest.** 1 Camiseta. 2 *Cúmmissétter.*
**Belt.** 1 Cinturón. 2 *Thíntoorón.*
**Tie.** 1 Corbata. 2 *Corrbútter.*
**Collars.** 1 Cuellos. 2 *Kwéllyoss.*
**Waistcoat.** 1 Chaleco. 2 *Tchulléckoh.*
**Jacket.** 1 Chaqué. 2 *Tchuskéh.*
**Evening dress coat.** 1 Frac. 2 *Fruc.*
**Trench coat.** 1 Gabardina. 2 *Gúbbarrdēēner.*
**Binoculars.** 1 Gemelos. 2 *Hemmélloss.*
**Cap.** 1 Gorra. 2 *Górrer.*
**Gloves.** 1 Guantes. 2 *Gwúntess.*
**Rain coat.** 1 Impermeable. 2 *Impáirmeárbleh.*
**Jersey.** 1 Jersey. 2 *Jáirrseh.*
**Sock suspenders.** 1 Ligas. 2 *Lēēguss.*
**Trousers.** 1 Pantalón. 2 *Púntullón.*

*De compras*

**Sports trousers. 1** Pantalón de deporte. **2** *Puntullón deh deppórrteh.*
**Riding breeches. 1** Pantalón de montar. **2** *Puntullón de montarr.*
**Skiing trousers. 1** Pantalón de esquís. **2** *Puntullón deh eskiss (eskḗḗss).*
**Pocket handkerchiefs. 1** Pañuelos de bolsillo. **2** *Punyooélyoss deh bolsíllyoh.*
**Neckerchief. 1** Pañuelo para el cuello. **2** *Punyooélyoh p;rrer el kwélyoh.*
**Umbrella. 1** Paraguas. **2** *Purrúgwuss.*
**Pyjama. 1** Pijama. **2** *Pihhúmmer.*
**Smoking jacket. 1** Smoking. **2** *Smócking.*
**Felt hat. 1** Sombrero de fieltro. **2** *Sombráirroh deh fyéltroh.*
**Bowler hat. 1** Sombrero de copa. **2** *Sombráirrroh deh cópper.*
**Braces. 1** Tirantes. **2** *Tirrúntess.*
**Slippers. 1** Zapatillas. **2** *Thúppertilyoss.*
**Black, brown, two.colour shoes. 1** Zapatos negros, marrón, combinados. **2** *Thuppártoss néggross, murrón, combinárdoss.*

## Women's

## Para la mujer

**Fan. 1** Abanico. **2** *Úbbunníckoh.*
**Overcoat. 1** Abrigo. **2** *Ubbrḗḗgoh.*
**Dressing gown. 1** Bata. **2** *Butter.*
**Blouse. 1** Blusa. **2** *Blṓṓsser.*
**Bag. 1** Bolso. **2** *Bólsoh.*
**Drawers. Nickers. 1** Bragas. **2** *Brúgguss.*
**Night gown. 1** Camisón. **2** *Cúmmissón.*
**Evening cloak. 1** Capa de noche. **2** *Cúpper deh nótcheh.*
**Pocket book. 1** Cartera. **2** *Carrtáirrer.*
**Belt. 1** Cinturón. **2** *Thintoorón.*
**Combinations. 1** Combinación. **2** *Combinutheón.*
**Fur collar. 1** Cuello de piel. **2** *Kwélyoh deh pyél.*
**Shawl. 1** Chal. **2** *Tchull.*

*De compras*

**Jacket. 1** Chaquetón. **2** *Tchúckttón.*
**Sash. 1** Faja. **2** *Fúhher.*
**Skirt. 1** Falda. **2** *Fúllder.*
**Open skirt. 1** Falda abierta. **2** *Fúllder ubyáirrter.*
**Narrow waisted skirt. 1** Falda ceñida. **2** *Fúllder thenyééder.*
**Pleated skirt. 1** Falda plisada. **2** *Fúllder plissárder.*
**Rain coat. 1** Gabardina. **2** *Gúbberdééner.*
**Gloves. 1** Guantes. **2** *Gwúntess.*
**Jersey. 1** Jersey. **2** *Jáirrseh.*
**Garters. 1** Ligas. **2** *Leeguss.*
**Mantilla. 1** Mantilla. **2** *Muntílyer.*
**Nylon stockings. 1** Medias de nylon. **2** *Méddiuss deh nillón.*
**Purse. 1** Monedero. **2** *Mónneddáirroh.*
**Coton handkerchiefs. 1** Pañuelos de algodón. **2** *Punnyuélloss deh úlgoddón.*
**Batiste handkerchiefs. 1** Pañuelos batista. **2** *Punnyuélloss deh buttíster.*
**Linen handkerchiefs. 1** Pañuelos de hilo. **2** *Punnyuélloss deh ééloh.*
**Nylon handkerchiefs. 1** Pañuelos de nylon. **2** *Punnyuélloss deh nilón.*
**Umbrella. 1** Paraguas. **2** *Purrúgwuss.*
**Ornamental comb. 1** Peineta. **2** *Paynétter.*
**Pyjamas. 1** Pijama. **2** *Pihhúmmer.*
**Suspenders. 1** Portaligas. **2** *Pórrterléégers.*
**Cardigan. 1** Rebeca. **2** *Rebécca.*
**Dressing gown. 1** Bata. **2** *Súlltoh deh cúmmer.*
**Artificial silk. 1** Seda artificial. **2** *Sédder arrtifíthíull.*
**Natural silk. 1** Seda natural. **2** *Sédder nútterrúll.*
**Hat. 1** Sombrero. **2** *Sombráirroh.*
**Brassiere. 1** Sostén. **2** *Sostén.*
**Tailor made costume. 1** Traje sastre. **2** *Thúhheh sstreh.*
**Night dress. 1** Traje de noche. **2** *Trúheh deh nótcheh.*
**Suede shoes. 1** Zapatos de ante. **2** *Thuppúttoss deh únteh.*
**Patent leather shoes. 1** Zapatos de charol. **2** *Thuppúttoss deh churróll.*
**Black, brown, two-coloured shoes. 1** Zapatos marrón, negro, combinados. **2** *Thuppúttoss murrón, neggroh, cómbinárdoss.*

*De compras*

**Haberdashery**
**Camisería y otras secciones**

The shirt department, please? 1 ¿La sección de
camisería, por favor? 2 *Lah sectheón deh cummis-
sarréar, porr fuvvórr?*
I want two white shirts and two coloured ones.
1 Deseo dos camisas blancas y otras dos de color.
2 *Dessáyoh doss cummäësuss blúncuss e äwtruss
doss deh collórr.*
I will show you what we have. 1 Le enseñaré el surtido que tenemos. 2 *Leh ensényurréh el soortëëdoh
keh tennémmoss.*
I don't like this sort. I want finer ones. 1 Esta clase
no me gusta. Las quiero más finas. 2 *Éster clússeh
noh meh göoster.*
Do you want them in linen or nylon? 1 ¿Las quiere
de hilo, de nylón...? 2 *Luss kyáirreh deh ëëloh, deh
nillón?*
This cloth is very fine. Is it linen? 1 Esta tela es muy
fina. ¿Es de hilo? 2 *Éster téller es mooy fëëner. Ess
deh ëëloh?*
No, its poplin. 1 No, de popelina. 2 *Noh, deh popp-
lëëner.*
Is this my size? 1 ¿Me irá bien esta medida? 2 *Meh
ëërrahh byen éster muddëëder?*
The collar is a little tight. 1 El cuello me va un poco
justo. 2 *El kwéllyoh meh vah oon pówcoh hööstoh.*
We'll try a larger size. 1 Probaremos una talla mayor.
2 *Proburráimos ooner túllyer myórr.*
I'll take these four. 1 Me quedo estas cuatro. 2 *Meh
kéddoh éstuss kwúttroh.*
I want a rather typical shirt, as a souvenir. 1 Quisiera una camisa algo típica, como recuerdo. 2 *Kis-
sváirer ooner cummëëser úlgoh tipicoh, commoh
reckwáirdoh.*
Give me half a dozen vests, too, please. 1 Póngame también media docena de camisetas. 2 *Póngermeh tumbyén méddier dothénner deh cúmmis-
séttuss.*
Do you want them with or without sleeves? 1 ¿Las

*De compras*

quiere con mangas o sin mangas? **2** *Luss kyáireh con múngess oh sin múnguss?*

**For summer or for winter? 1** ¿De verano o de invierno? **2** *Deh verrárnoh oh deh inváirnoh?*

**Please show me the ties. 1** Hágame el favor de enseñarme las corbatas. **2** *Árgermeh el fuvvórr deh ensenyármeh luss corbútters.*

**We have a very large choice. 1** Tenemos un surtido muy extenso. **2** *Tennémoss oon soortēēdoh mooy exténsoh.*

**I should like to see those that are being worn this spring. 1** Quiero ver los modelos que se llevan esta primavera. **2** *Kyáiroh váirr loss modélloss keh seh lyévvun éster prēēmerváirer.*

**Do you want natural silk, artificial silk, uncrasable...? 1** ¿Cómo las quiere, de seda natural, seda artificial, inarrugables...? **2** *Cómmoh luss kyáireh, deh sédder nútterrúll, sédder árrtifitheúll, ínurroogárbless...?*

**I think they're rather loud. 1** Las encuentro un poco chillonas. **2** *Luss enkwéntroh oon pāwcoh chillyónness.*

**These are quieter and finer. 1** Estas otras son más serias y muy finas. **2** *Éstuss āwtruss son muss sáirious e mooy fēēnuss.*

**Give me these three. 1** Déme estas tres. **2** *Démmeh éstuss tress.*

**Do you want anything else? 1** ¿Desea algo más? **2** *Dessáyer úlgoh muss?*

**Yes, some handkerchiefs. 1** Sí, pañuelos de bolsillo. **2** *See, púnnyoo.élloss deh bolsíllyoh.*

**White or coloured? 1** ¿Blancos o de color? **2** *Blúncoss oh deh colórr?*

**Half a dozen of each, but fine ones. 1** Media docena de cada clase, pero que sean finos. **2** *Méddear dothénner deh cárder clússeh, péhroh keh sayún fēēnoss.*

**Do you want linen ones? 1** ¿Los quiere de hilo? **2** *Loss kyáirireh deh ēēloh?*

**No, nylon. 1** No, de nylón. **2** *Nóh, deh neelón.*

**I should like to see some raincoats and umbrellas. 1** Quisiera ver las gabardinas y paraguas. **2** *Kissáirer váirr luss gúbberdēēnerss e purrúgwuss.*

*De compras*

**Please come to the other department. This young man will go with you. 1** Haga el favor de pasar a la sección correspondiente. Este joven le acompañará. **2** *Úgger el fuvvórr deh pussárr ah lah sectheón córrespondyénteh. Éste hóvven leh uccompúnngggerréar.*

**How much it this umbrella? 1** ¿Cuánto vale este paraguas? **2** *Kwúntoh várleh ésteh purrúgwuss?*

**I want a cheaper one. 1** Lo deseo más barato. **2** *Loh dessáyoh múss burrártoh?*

**And this one? 1** ¿Y este otro? **2** *E ésteh āwtroh?*

**Where are the gloves? 1** ¿Para comprar unos guantes? **2** *Púrrer comprárrō ōōnoss gwúntess.*

**Come with me, please. 1** Haga el favor de acompañarme. **2** *Úgger el fuvvórr deh uccompúnnyárrmeh.*

**Do you want leather, coton, wool or suede? 1** ¿Los quiere de piel, de lana, de algodón, de ante...? **2** *Loss kyáireh deh pyéll, deh lúnner, deh úlgoddón, deh únteh...?*

**Light brown leather. 1** De piel y color marrón claro. **2** *Deh pyél e collór murrón clároh.*

**I'll take these. 1** Me quedo con éstos. **2** *Meh kéddoh con éstoss.*

**Now I want to buy a jersey. 1** Ahora quisiera comprar un jersey. **2** *Un.óra keesáirer comprárr oon jáirseh.*

**Please go to the first floor. 1** Haga el favor de ir al primer piso. **2** *Úgger el fuvvórr deh éarr ull primmáirr pēēsoh.*

**Do you want it open, closed, with sleeves or without, coarse or fine knited? 1** ¿Lo quiere abierto, cerrado, con mangas, sin mangas, de punto grueso, de punto delgado? **2** *Loh kyáireh ubbyáirrtoh, con múnguss, sin múnguss, deh pōōntoh grooéssoh, deh pōōntoh delgárdoh?*

**I will show you what we have. 1** Le enseñaré el surtido de que disponemos. **2** *Leh ensényarréh el sorttēēdoh deh keh dispongármoss.*

**I want a dark grey one. 1** Lo deseo de un gris obscuro. **2** *Loh dessáyoh deh oon grēēce obscōōroh.*

**I like this one. 1** Éste me gusta. **2** *Ésteh meh gōōster.*

**How much is that all together? 1** ¿Cuánto importa todo? **2** *Kwúntoh impórrter tāwdoh?*

**Where do I pay?** 1 ¿Dónde debo pagar? 2 *Dóndeh dóbboh puggárr?*

**At the cash desk. I'll go with you.** 1 En la caja. Ya le acompañaré. 2 *En lah cúhher. Yeh leh uccompúnyerreh.*

**Could you have them sent to the... Hotel?** 1 ¿Podrían llevármelo al Hotel...? 2 *Podréun lyevvárr mehloh úll awtél...?*

**When shall I get them?** 1 ¿Cuándo lo recibiré? 2 *Kwúndoh loh rethíbberréh?*

**This afternoon.** 1 Esta misma tarde. 2 *Éster mísmer tárrdeh.*

---

## At the dressmaker's    En la casa de modas

**I want to buy a ready made dress.** 1 Quisiera comprar un vestido confeccionado. 2 *Kissáirer comprárr oon vestēēdoh confestionnárdoh.*

**Of what material, Madame?** 1 ¿De qué tejido lo desea? 2 *Deh keh tehhē̄edoh loh dessáir?*

**Cotton.** 1 Algodón. 2 *Ulgoddón.*

**Natural silk.** 1 Seda natural. 2 *Sédder núttoorúll.*

**Wool.** 1 Lana. 2 *Lúnner.*

**Worsted.** 1 Estambre. 2 *Estúmbreh.*

**Linen.** 1 Hilo. 2 *Éeloh.*

**Velvet.** 1 Terciopelo. 2 *Táirthiopélloh.*

**Nylon.** 1 Nylón. 2 *Nilón.*

**Knitted.** 1 De punto. 2 *Deh pōōnth.*

**What colour?** 1 ¿De qué color? . 2 *Deh keh collórr?*

**I like this light grey one.** 1 Éste de gris claro me gusta. 2 *Ester deh greece clórros meh gōōter.*

**How much is it?** 1 ¿Cuánto vale? 2 *Kwuth várleh?*

**I'll try it on.** 1 Me lo probaré. 2 *Meh loh probburréh.*

**Will you come with me, please?** 1 ¿Quiere hacer

*De compras*

el favor de acompañarme? . **2** *Kyáirreh utháir el fuvvór deh uccómpunyárrmeh?*

**It's rather long for me, and a bit wide in the hips.** **1** Me está un poco largo y ancho de caderas. **2** *Meh estár oon páweoh lárrgoh e úntchoh deh cuddáirers.*

**It makes a crease here. 1** Me hace una arruga aquí. **2** *Meh útheh ooner urróoger uckēe.*

**We will put that right, sir, and you will have it tomorrow. 1** Se lo arreglaremos y mañana se lo entregaremos. **2** *Seh loh urréglurráimoss e munyúnner seh loh entréggurráimoss.*

**I want an overcoat, too. 1** Deseo también un abrigo. **2** *Dessáyoh tumbyen oon ubrēegoh.*

**Woolen? 1** ¿De lana? . **2** *Deh lúnner?*

**No, cheviot. 1** No, de cheviot. **2** *No, deh chevviót.*

**Flannel. 1** Franela. **2** *Frunnéller.*

**Tweed. 1** «Tweed». **2** *Tweed.*

**Sports. 1** Sport. **2** *Sporrt.*

**Half season. 1** Entretiempo. **2** *Éntretyémpoh.*

**Winter. 1** Invierno. **2** *Invayáirrnoh.*

**Dress. 1** De vestir. **2** *Deh vestēer.*

**I want a morning suit, dress. 1** Desearía un conjunto de mañana. **2** *Dessairréar oon conhōōntoh deh munyúnner.*

**What kind do you prefer? 1** ¿Cuál es su preferencia? **2** *Kwulless soo préfferrénthea?*

**White blouse, black pleated skirt and a jacket with a red pattern. 1** Blusa blanca, falda negra plisada y chaquetón a base de encarnado. **2** *Blōōser blúinker, fullder néggrer, plissárder e tchuckettón ah bússeh deh encarnárdoh.*

**Must the blouse be silk. 1** ¿La blusa ha de ser de seda? **2** *Lah blōōsser ah deh sáyer deh sédder?*

**No, nylon. 1** No, de nylón. **2** *Noh, deh nillón.*

**Do you want a flannel skirt? 1** ¿La falda ha de ser de franela? **2** *Lah fúllder ahdeh sáir deh frunnéller?*

**No, a woolen one. 1** No, de lana. **2** *Noh, deh lúnner.*

**This jacket is what is being worn this year. 1** Este chaquetón es la moda que se lleva este año. **2** *Ésteh tchúckettón (chuck in on) ess lah māwder keh seh lyévver ésteh únyoh.*

*De compras*

**It's plain. I should like one with a patern. 1** Es liso; me gustaría con algún dibujo. **2** *Ess léesoh deh kwúddross.*

**A check? 1** ¿A base de cuadros? **2** *Ar básseh deh kwódross?*

**Show me the patterns you have. 1** Enséñenme los dibujos que tienen. **2** *Ensényermeh loss dibbúhhoss keh tyénnen.*

**I like this one. 1** Éste me gusta. **2** *Ésteh meh gōōster.*

**Please come to the fitting room. 1** Haga el favor de pasar al probador. **2** *Úgger el fuvvórr deh pussárr ull próbbuddorr.*

**It fits me well. 1** Me viene bien. **2** *Meh vyénneh byén.*

**How much is that altogether? 1** ¿Cuánto sube todo? **2** *Kwúntoh sōōbeh tããwdoh?*

**Come to the cash desk, please. 1** Haga el favor de pasar a la caja. **2** *Úgger el fuvvórr deh pussárr ah lah cúhher.*

**Can you tell me when there will be a dress show? 1** ¿Podrían indicarme cuándo harán exhibición de modelos? **2** *Podréan indicárrmeh kwúndoh úrrun exhibitheón deh moddélloss?*

**If you have no samples, could you show me some models? 1** Si no pasan ustedes colección ¿podrían enseñarme modelos? **2** *See noh pússun oosteddes collectheón, podréan enseyárrmeh modélloss?*

**I should like a tailor made dress. 1** Desearía un traje sastre. **2** *Dessayurréar oon trúhheh deh sústreh.*

**I will show you our exclusive models for this season. 1** Le enseñaré los géneros que tenemos en exclusiva para esta temporada. **2** *Leh ensényurréh loss hénnerross keh tennémoss en exclosēever púrrer éstah temporrúdder.*

**I like this stuff and the dress, too. 1** Esta ropa me gusta y el modelo también. **2** *Ester rawper meh gooster e el modelloh tumbhén.*

**This is one of the latest models from Paris. 1** Este modelo es de los últimos que han venido de París. **2** *Ésteh modéllo ess deh loss ōōltimos keh un venēēdoh déh purrēēs.*

*De compras*

**It has exotic lines. 1** Tiene una línea exótica. **2** *Tyénneh ooner línnea exótica.*

**This material makes the whole dress very elegant.**
**1** Con este otro género resulta de un conjunto muy elegante. **2** *Con ésteh āwtróh hénnerroh ressöölter deh oon conhööntoy mooy elegúnteh.*

**What will a tailor made cost in this cloth? 1** ¿Cuánto cuesta un traje sastre con esta tela? **2** *Kwúntoh kwéster oon trúhheh sústreh con éstah téller?*

**Will you show me that evening dress? 1** Haga el favor de enseñarme aquel vestido de noche. **2** *Úgger el fuvvórr deh ensenyárrmeh uckéll vestēēdoh deh nótcheh.*

**What is its price? 1** ¿Qué precio tiene? **2** *Keh préthio tyénneh?*

**In what other cloth could you make this model?**
**1** ¿Ese otro modelo, en qué otra tela se puede confeccionar? **2** *Ésseh āwtroh modélloh, en keh āwtroh téllah seh pwéddeh conféctheonárr?*

**In cloth or in gauze. 1** En tela o gasa. **2** *En téller oh gússer.*

**Velvet. 1** Terciopelo. **2** *Táirtheopélloh.*

**Silk. 1** Seda. **2** *Sédder.*

**Brocade. 1** Brocado. **2** *Broccárdoh.*

**Nylon. 1** Nylón. **2** *Nillón.*

**Haye yon any other model? 1** ¿Tiene algún otro modelo? **2** *Tynneh úlgöön āwtroh modélloh?*

**I will show you another one that comes very cheap. 1** Le enseñaré otro que resulta más económico. **2** *Leh ensenyurréh awtroh keh resöölter múss éconómmicoh.*

**It's the fashion in Paris, Turin, England, America.**
**1** Es moda de París, Turín, Inglaterra, americana. **2** *Ess máwder deh purrees, toorín, inglatérreur, ummerricúnner.*

**I find it rather extreme. 1** Lo encuentro algo extremado. **2** *Loh enkwéntroh úlgoh extremmárder.*

**What cloth is this? 1** ¿Qué género es éste? **2** *Keh hénnerroh ess ésteh?*

**Organdine. 1** Organdí. **2** *Orrgundēē.*

**Organza. 1** Organza. **2** *Orgúnther.*

**Nylon. 1** Nylón. **2** *Nillón.*

*De compras*

**Guipure. 1** Guipur. **2** *Gippöör.*
**Can you show me some sketches? 1** ¿Puede enseñarme algún croquis o dibujo? **2** *Pwéddeh ensenyárrmeh úlgöön crockiss oh dibbúhhoh?*
**I should like a black velvet dress. 1** Desearía un vestido en terciopelo negro. **2** *Déssayerréar oon vestéédoh en táirtheopélloh néggroh.*
**I like this one in black guipure. 1** Éste de guipur blanco me gusta. **2** *Esteh deh gippöör blúnckoh meh gööster.*
**This looks very atractive. 1** Éste lo encuentro muy atractivo. **2** *Ésteh loh enkwéntroh mooy úttruttéévoh.*
**This model would suit you very well in glacé or in fay. 1** Este modelo le quedaría muy bien en glasé o faya. **2** *Ésteh modélloh leh keddurréar mooy byén en glusséh oh fáryer (fire).*
**It's a print. 1** En una tela estampada. **2** *Ess ooner téller estumpárder.*
**With blond lace. 1** Con encaje de blonda. **2** *Con encúhheh deh blonder.*
**Is the belt in the same material? 1** ¿El cinturón es de la misma tela? **2** *El thíntoorón ess deh lah míssmer téller?*
**I like the skirt rather long and narrow waisted. 1** Me gusta la falda un poco larga y ceñida. **2** *Meh gööster lah fulder oon pāwcoh lárrger e thennééder.*
**I will have this model. 1** Me haré este modelo. **2** *Meh urréh ésteh moddélloh.*
**Please come to the fitting room to be measured. 1** Haga el favor de pasar al probador para tomarle medidas. **2** *Úgger el fuvvórr deh pússarr ull próbberdórr púrrer tommárrleh meddééderss.*
**The dress maker will come now. 1** Ahora vendrá el modisto. **2** *Uh.óra vendrár el moddistoh.*
**When can I come for the first fitting? 1** ¿Cuándo he de venir a hacerme la primera prueba. **2** *Kwúndoh eh deh vennéérr ah utháirrmeh lah primáirrer prwébber?*
**I am in a great hurry. I am starting on a journey on Monday. 1** Me corre muchísima prisa. El lunes salgo de viaje. **2** *Meh córreh mootchíssimoh prééser. El lööness súlgoh deh ve.úhheh.*

*De compras*

**Then we will try the three fittings at once. 1** Entonces le haremos las tres pruebas en seguida. **2** *Entónthess leh urrémmoss luss tress prwébbuss en seggëëder.*

**The first fitting tomorrow, the second the day after tomorrow, and the third the next day. 1** La primera prueba mañana, la segunda pasado mañana y la tercera al siguiente. **2** *Lah primáirer prwébber munyúnner, lah segoónder pussárdoh munyúnner e lah tairrtháirer úll sigyénteh.*

**So when could you let me have the dress? 1** ¿Así cuándo podrán entregarme el vestido? **2** *Ussëë, kwúndoh porún entregárrmeh el vestëëdoh?*

**In five days' time. 1** Dentro de cinco días. **2** *Déntroh deh thínkoh déuss.*

**Could you send it to the hotel for me? 1** ¿Podrán enviármelo al Hotel...? **2** *Podrún enviármellóh ull awtél?*

**Here is my name and the number of my room. 1** He aquí mi nombre y habitación en que me hospedo. **2** *Eh uckëë me nómbren e úbbitútheón en keh meh ospéddoh.*

**Can you show me some models of tailor made costumes? 1** ¿Pueden enseñarme modelos de traje sastre? **2** *Pwédden ensenyárrmeh modélloss deh trúhheh sústreh?*

**Fancy. 1** Chaqueta sastre. **2** *Tchuckétter sústreh.*

**Tailor made jacket. 1** De fantasía. **2** *Deh funtússier.*

**Printed silk. 1** Seda estampada. **2** *Sédder estumpárder.*

**The hat department? 1** ¿La sección de sombreros? **2** *Lah sectheón deh sombráirross?*

**Will you come with me, please? 1** Tenga la bondad de acompañarme. **2** *Ténger lah bondúd deh uccómpunyárrmeh.*

**What kind do you want? 1** ¿Cómo lo desea? **2** *Cómmoh loh dessáir?*

**Do you fancy any of these models? 1** ¿Le gusta alguno de estos modelos? **2** *Leh gööster ulgöönoh deh éstoss modéllos?*

**Do you want a small one? 1** ¿Lo desea pequeño? **2** *Loh dessáyoh peckényoh?*

**Not a large one with a brim. 1** No, grande, de alas.
**2** *Noh, gründeh, deh úlluss.*
**Straw. 1** De paja. **2** *Deh púhher.*
**Felt. 1** De fieltro. **2** *Deh fyéltroh.*
**How much is this one? 1** ¿Qué vale éste? **2** *Keh vúlleh ésteh?*

---

## The tailor's Sastrería

**I want a spring suit.**
**1** Desearía un traje de entretiempo. **2** *Déssairéar oon trúhheh deh éntrethyémpoh.*

**To measure? 1** ¿A medida? **2** *Ah meddéeder?*
**Ready made. 1** De confección. **2** *Deh conféctheón.*
**Light or dark? 1** ¿Claro u obscuro? **2** *Claroh oo os.oóorroh?*
**Navy blue, gray, brown. 1** Azul marino, gris, marrón.
**2** *Uthóol murréenoh, greece, murrón.*
**Come this way, please. I'll show you our models.**
**1** Haga el favor de venir. Le enseñaré los modelos que tenemos. **2** *Úgger el fuvvórr deh venéarr. Leh ensényurréh loss modélloss keh tennemmoss.*
**What's the fashion this year? 1** ¿Cuál es la moda de este año? **2** *Kwull ess lah mäwder de ésteh únyoh?*
**The jacket is worn long. 1** Se lleva la americana larga. **2** *Seh lyévver lah ummérricúnner lárrgoh.*
**Choose the one you like best. 1** Elija usted el que más le guste. **2** *Ellééheh oostéh el keh múss leh góoster.*
**This is the one I like best. 1** Éste es el que más me gusta. **2** *Esteh ess el keh muss me góoster.*
**Let's try it on. 1** Lo probaremos. **2** *Loh próbburráimoss.*

*De compras*

**It's too small. 1** Me viene pequeño. **2** *Meh vyénneh peckénnyoh.*

**I think this measure will fit you. 1** Esta otra medida me parece que le sentará bien. **2** *Ester áwtrer meddëëder meh purrétheh keh leh séntirráh byen.*

**Yes, that's better, but there's a wrinkle on the shoulder. 1** Sí, éste me viene mejor, pero hace una arruga en el hombro. **2** *See, ésteh me vyénneh mehhórr, péhroh útthhey ooner urrööger en el ómbroh.*

**That's nothing. We'll soon put that right and send it to you today. 1** No tiene importancia. Lo arreglaremos en seguida y se lo mandaremos hoy mismo. **2** *Noh tyénneh imporrtúntheer. Loh urrégglarrémmos en seggëëder e seh loh múnduerrémmos oy mísmoh.*

**Coat. 1** Americana. **2** *Ummérricúnner.*

**Waistcoat. 1** Chaleco. **2** *Tchulléccoh.*

**Trousers. 1** Pantalón. **2** *Púnterlón.*

**I don't care much for the lining. 1** El forro no acaba de gustarme. **2** *El fórroh noh uccárber deh goostármeh.*

**How much is it? 1** ¿Cuánto vale? **2** *Kwntoh várley?*

**What else would you like? 1** ¿Qué más desea usted? **2** *Keh múss dessáyer oostéh?*

**I want to have a suit made. 1** Deseo hacerme un traje. **2** *Dessáyoh utháirmeh oon trúhheh.*

**Have you decided on the colour. 1** ¿Ha pensado ya en un color determinado? **2** *Ah pensárdoh yah en oon collórr dettérrminnardoh?*

**Yes, brown or perhaps grey. 1** Sí, marrón, o tal vez gris. **2** *See, murrón oh tull veth greece.*

**We have a large assortment of these colours. 1** De estos colores hay un gran surtido. **2** *Deh éstoss collóres i oon grun soorttëëdoh.*

**Plain, striped or check? 1** ¿Liso, de rayas, de cuadros...? **2** *Lëësoh, deh rýuss, deb kwúddross.*

**Summer, spring or winter? 1** ¿De verano, de entretiempo, de invierno? **2** *Deh verrárnoh, deh éntreh.tyémpoh, deh invyáirrnoh.*

**I will show you the samples of our sorts, colours**

**and patterns. 1** Le enseñaré los diversos muestrarios de clases, colores y dibujos. **2** *Leh ensényurréh loss divváirsoss mwúestruss deh clússess, collórress e dibbōohoss.*

**ThIs striped one is most fashionable this year. 1** Éste de rayas será la moda de este año. **2** *Ésteh deh rýus serráh lah māwder deh ésteh únnyoh.*

**Have you the same pattern in grey? 1** ¿Tienen este mismo dibujo en gris? **2** *Tyénnen ésteh mísmoh dibbúhhoh en greeces?*

**Yes, sir. I will show you the cloth. You will like it better. 1** Sí, señor. Le enseñaré la pieza y le gustará más. **2** *See, senyórr, leh ensénnyurréh lah pyether e leh goostrrah múss.*

**What sort of material is it? 1** ¿Qué clase de género es? **2** *Keh clússeh deh hénnerroh ess?*

**Worsted, sir. 1** Estambre, señor. **2** *Estúmbreh, senyórr.*

**What will a suit of this quality cost? 1** ¿Qué cuesta un traje de esta calidad? **2** *Keh kwéster oon trúhheh deh éster sullidúd?*

**With or without waistcoat? 1** ¿Completo o sin chaleco? **2** *Compléttoh oh sin tchulléccoh?*

**I will take your measurements now. 1** Ahora tomaré las medidas. **2** *Uhóra tommurréh luss medáēeders.*

**Will you go to the fitting room? 1** ¿Tiene la bondad de pasar al probador? **2** *Tyénneh lah bondúd deh pussárr úll próbberdórr?*

**Do you want a single or double breasted coat? 1** ¿Cómo lo quiere, abierto o cruzado? **2** *Cómmoh loh kyáirreh, ubbyáirtoh oh croothárdoh?*

**Have you got a model? 1** ¿Tiene algún figurín? **2** *Tyénneh ulgōōn figgurrēēn?*

**I should like to have it made at once. 1** Me interesaría que me lo hicieran en seguida. **2** *Meh ínterréssurréar keh meh loh itháirrun en segēēder.*

**We'll try it on tomorrow, and then the day after, and you will have it the next day. 1** Mañana haremos la primera prueba. Pasado mañana la segunda y al siguiente se lo entregaremos. **2** *Munyúnner urráimuss lah primāirrer prwébber. Pusssárder*

*De compras*

*munyúnner lah seggöönder e ull siggyénteh seh loh entrégurráimuss.*

**Do I pay in advance or when it is ready. 1** ¿Se paga por adelantado o a su entrega? **2** *Seh púgger porr úddelónnteh oh ah soo entráiger?*

**Have you any good cloth for an an overcoat? 1** ¿Tienen buenos paños para abrigos? **2** *Tyénnen biénnoss púnnyoss púrrer ubbrēēgoss?*

**We have the very best quality, sir. 1** Los tenemos de calidad inmejorable, señor. **2** *Loss tennáimoss deh cullidád inméhhorúbbleh, senyórr.*

**Will you have a look at this cloth? 1** Tenga la bondad de examinar estas piezas. **2** *Ténger lah bondúd deh exuminárr éstuss pyéthuss.*

**What's the price of an overcoat made to measure. 1** ¿Qué vale un abrigo a medida? **2** *Keh várleh oon ubbrēēgoh ah medēēder?*

**Of this cloth, which is the best quality... 1** De esta calidad, que es la mejor... **2** *Deh éster cullídud, keh ess lah mehhórr...*

**Have you got anything of a slightly inferior quality, but good? 1** ¿No tiene una clase inferior a ésta, pero buena? **2** *No tyénneh ooner clússeh inferriórr ah ésteh, péhroh byénnoh?*

**Yes sir. I can recommend this cloth. 1** Sí, señor. Le recomiendo esta otra calidad. **2** *See, senyórr. Leh réccommyéndoh éster āwtroh cullidúd.*

**What is the price? 1** ¿Cuánto vale? **2** *Kwúntoh várleh?*

**I will have this colour. 1** Me quedo con este color. **2** *Meh kéddoh con ésteh collórr.*

**Well take the measurements. 1** Tomaremos medidas. **2** *Tommurráimoss meddēēduss.*

**I like it fairly full. 1** Me gusta un poco ancho. **2** *Meh gööster con pāwcoh úntchoh.*

**Double or single breasted? 1** Abierto, cerrado. **2** *Ubyáirrtoh, therrárdoh.*

**With or withour belt. 1** Con cinturón, sin cinturón. **2** *Con thintoorón, sin thinturrón.*

**Broad lapel. 1** Solapa ancha. **2** *Sollúpper úntcher.*

**When will it be ready? 1** ¿Cuándo estará? **2** *Kwúndoh esturrár?*

**You can have it the day after tomorrow. 1** Pasado mañana se lo entregaremos. **2** *Pussárdoh munyún-ner seh loh entréggurrémmoss.*

---

## The shoe shop                    Zapatería

**I want a pair of shoes.**
**1** Deseo un par de zapatos.
**2** *Dessáyoh oon parr deh thuppártoss.*

**What kind do you want?**
   **1** ¿Cómo los quiere?
   **2** *Cómmoh loss kyáireh?*

**Brown, black, two colou-red. 1** De color marrón, negros, combinados. **2** *Deh collórr murrón, nég-gross, combinutheón.*

**Double sole. 1** De suela doble. **2** *Deh swéller dóbbleh.*

**Leather, suede. 1** De piel, de ante. **2** *Deh pyél, deh únteh.*

**Rubber heels. 1** Con tacón de goma. **2** *Con tuckón deh gómmer.*

**With leather, rubber soles. 1** Con suela de piel, de goma. **2** *Con swéller deh pyel, deh gómmer.*

**What is your size? 1** ¿Qué número calza? **2** *Keh nõõmmairoh cúlther?*

**I dont know. I'll try them on. 1** No sé. Vamos a pro-bar. **2** *Noh seh. Vármoss ah próbarr.*

**Do those fit you? 1** ¿Le va bien este par? **2** *Leh vah byén ésteh parr?*

**They're a little tight. 1** Me aprietan un poco. **2** *Meh uppryéttun oon pãwcoh.*

**They are a little too large. 1** Me son un poco gran-des. **2** *Meh son oon pãwcoh grúndess.*

**My feet are very delicate. 1** Tengo los pies muy deli-cados. **2** *Téngoh loss pyéss mooy déllicárdoss.*

**We'll try a larger size. 1** Buscaremos un número mayor. **2** *Booscurráimoss oon nõõmairroh mahyór.*

**Will you please show me the pair that is in the**

*De compras*

window? No... **1** Haga el favor de enseñarme el
modelo que está en el escaparate con el número... **2** *Úgger el fuvvórr deh ensenyárrmeh el
moddélloh keh estar en el escúpperrárteh con el
nōōmairroh...*
**How much are they? 1** ¿Cuánto es? **2** *Kwúntoh ess?*
**Can you send them to this address? 1** Podría
enviármelos a esta dirección? **2** *Podréar enviárr-
mehloss ah éster dirréctheón?*

---

## Jewellery                                  Joyas

**Tie pin. 1** Alfiler de corbata. **2** *Úllfilláirr deh corrbútter.*
**Bracelet. 1** Brazalete. **2** *Brútherlétter.*
**Diamonds. 1** Brillantes. **2** *Brillúntess.*
**Collar. Necklace. 1** Collar. **2** *Collyárr.*
**Diamonds. 1** Diamantes. **2** *Dearmúnntess.*
**Emerald. 1** Esmeralda. **2** *Ésmerrúllder.*
**Cuff links. 1** Gemelos. **2** *Hemmélloss.*
**Safety pin. 1** Imperdible. **2** *Impairdēēbleh.*
**Gold. 1** Oro. **2** *Óroh.*
**Ear rings. 1** Pendientes. **2** *Pendyéntess.*
**Pearls. 1** Perlas. **2** *Páirrluss.*
**Silver. 1** Plata. **2** *Plútter.*
**Platinum. 1** Platino. **2** *Pluttēēnoh.*
**Wrist. 1** Pulsera. **2** *Poolsáirrer.*
**Watch. 1** Reloj. **2** *Rellóhh.*
**Ruby. 1** Rubí. **2** *Roobēē.*
**Solitaire (diamond). 1** Solitario. **2** *Sollitárrioh.*
**Ring. 1** Sortija. **2** *Sorrtíhher.*

---

## At the watchmaker's                         Relojería

**Wrist watch. 1** Reloj de pulsera. **2** *Relóh deh pulsáirer.*
**Pocket watch. 1** Reloj de bolsillo. **2** *Relóh deh bolsíll-
yoh.*
**Clock. 1** Reloj de pared. **2** *Relóh deh purréd.*
**Tower clock. 1** Reloj de torre.
**Sundial. 1** Reloj de sol. **2** *Relóh deh sol.*

*De compras*

**Pendulum clock. 1** Reloj de péndola. **2** *Relóh deh péndooler.*

**Cuckoo clock. 1** Reloj de cuclillo. **2** *Relóh deh cooklíllyoh.*

**Alarm clock. 1** Despertador. **2** *Dess páirterdórr.*

**The hands. 1** Las agujas, saetillas, manecillas. **2** *Luss uggōōhuss, súhettillyuss, múnnithillyus.*

**The minute hands. 1** Las minuteras. **2** *Luss minotáirerss.*

**The dial. 1** Esfera. **2** *Esfáirer.*

**Automatic. 1** Automático. **2** *Owtommútticoh.*

**Antimagnetic. 1** Antimagnético. **2** *Únteh mugnétticoh.*

**Stop watch. 1** Cronógrafo. **2** *Cronnógruffoh.*

**Chronometer. 1** Cronómetro. **2** *Cronnómmetroh.*

**Rubies. 1** Rubíes. **2** *Roobéuss.*

**Chain. 1** Cadena. **2** *Cuddénner.*

**Strap. 1** Correa. **2** *Corráyer.*

**Unbreakable glass. 1** Cristal irrompible. **2** *Cristúll irrompēēbleh.*

**Please show me some wrist watches. 1** Hágame el favor de enseñarme relojes de pulsera. **2** *Úggermeh el fuvvórr deh ensenyármeh relóhhess deh poolsáirer.*

**Ladies' or gentlemen's? 1** ¿Para señora o caballero? **2** *Púrrer senyórrer oh cúbbelyáiroh?*

**Gentlemen's. 1** Para caballero. **2** *Púrrer cúbbelyáirer.*

**Do you want a gold one or a stainless steel one? 1** ¿Lo quiere de oro o de acero inoxidable? **2** *Loh kyáireh deh óroh oh deh utháiroh inoxidárbleh.*

**Steel, but a good make. 1** De acero, pero que sea de buena marca. **2** *Deh utháiroh, péhroh keh sáyer deh bwénner máárcer.*

**Well, all these are guaranteed. 1** Vea, señor, todos estos son garantizados. **2** *Váyer, senyórr, tāwdoss éstoss son gúrruntithardoss.*

**What's the price of this one? 1** ¿Qué vale éste? **2** *Keh várleh ésteh?*

**And this one? 1** ¿Y ése otro? **2** *E ésseh āwtroh?*

**I think it's quite dear. 1** Lo encuentro algo caro. **2** *Loh enkwéntroh úlgoh cárroh.*

*De compras*

**We have cheaper ones. 1** Los hay más baratos. **2** *Loss i muss burrártoss.*

**Will it take long to mend this watch? 1** ¿Tardarían muchos días en arreglarme este reloj? **2** *Tárrdurréun mõõtchos déarss en úrreglárrmeh ésteh relóh?*

**I gave it quite a hard knock and it has stopped. 1** Le he dado un golpe algo fuerte y se ha parado. **2** *Le eh dárdoh oon gólpeh úllgoh fyáirrteh e seh ar purrárdoh.*

**May I see it a moment? 1** ¿Me permite examinarlo un momento? **2** *Meh los pairmítteh exúmminárr oon mommén toh?*

**The spring is broken. 1** Tiene la cuerda rota. **2** *Tyénneh lah kwáirder róttah.*

**It will be ready in three days. 1** Estará reparado dentro de tres días. **2** *Esturráh reppurrárdoh déntroh deh tres déarss.*

**I cant leave it. I'm starting on a journey the day after tomorrow. 1** Me es imposible dejarlo. Salgo de viaje pasado mañana. **2** *Meh es imposséébleh dehárrlo. Súlgoh deh ve.úhheh pussárder munnyúnner.*

**In the morning or in the afternoon? 1** ¿Por la mañana o por la tarde? **2** *Porr lah munnyúnner oh porr lah tárrdeh?*

**In the afternoon. 1** Por la tarde. **2** *Porr lah tárdeh.*

**In that case I will try to have it ready before you go. 1** Siendo así haré un esfuerzo para tenerlo listo antes de su marcha. **2** *Syéndoh ussée u rréh esfwáirrthoh púrrer tennáirloh listoh úntes deh soo márrtcher.*

**Can you come and get it the day after tomorrow in the morning? 1** Puede usted pasarlo a recoger pasado mañana por la mañana. **2** *Pwéddeh oostéh pussárrloh ah reccohháir munyúnner por lah munnyúnner.*

**Could you send it to... Hotel...? I will tell the porter. 1** ¿Podría enviármelo al Hotel...? El conserje tendrá instrucciones. **2** *Podrear enveárrmelloh ull awtél... El consáirheh tendráh instrúctheóness.*

**With pleasure. 1** Con mucho gusto. **2** *Cin mõõtchoh gõõstoh.*

*De compras*

**How much will it cost? 1** ¿Cuánto importará la reparación? **2** *Kwúntoh impórrturrár lah réppurrútheón?*

**Please change the strap. 1** Cámbieme la correa de paso. **2** *Cúmbbearmeh lah corráyer deh pússoh.*

**Which of these do you like? 1** ¿Cuál de éstas le gusta? **2** *Kwúll deh éstuss leh g̅o̅o̅ster?*

**How much is that? 1** ¿Qué vale ésta? **2** *Keh várleh éster?*

**Put it on for me, please. 1** Póngamela. **2** *Póngermehlóh.*

**I have the voucher. 1** Tenga el resguardo. **2** *Ténger el regwárrdoh.*

**Thanks. 1** Gracias. **2** *Grútheus.*

---

## At the hardressers      En la peluquería

**The hairdresser, the barber. 1** El peluquero, el barbero. **2** *El pellookáiroh.*

**The apprentice. 1** El aprendiz. **2** *El upprendéeth.*

**The armchair. 1** El sillón. **2** *El sillyón.*

**The hatstand. 1** La percha. **2** *Lah páirtcher.*

**The wrapper. 1** El peinador. **2** *El páynerdórr.*

**The comb. 1** El peine. **2** *El páineh.*

**The thick comb. 1** La lendrera, el peine espeso. **2** *Lah lendráirrer, el páineh espéssoh.*

**The scissors. 1** Las tijeras. **2** *Luss tihháirrerss.*

**The brush. 1** El cepillo. **2** *El theppílyo.*

**The razor. 1** La navaja. **2** *Lah nuvvúhher.*

**The shaving brush. 1** La brocha. **2** *Lah brótcher.*

**The soap. 1** El jabón. **2** *El hubbón.*

**The dryer. 1** El secador. **2** *El seckerdórr.*

**The hair-cutting machine. 1** La maquinilla de cortar el pelo. **2** *Lah múckiuníllyer deh corrtárr el pélloh.*

**Bottles of scent, lotion, shampoo. 1** Los frascos de colonia, loción, masaje. **2** *Loss frúscoss deh collónnear, lotheón, mussúhheh.*

**The sprayer, vaporizer. 1** El pulverizador, vaporizador. **2** *El p̅o̅o̅lverrithuddórr, vúpporr̅e̅e̅thuddórr.*

**The towel. 1** La toalla. **2** *Lah twúlyer.*

*De compras*

**I want a shave. 1** Deseo afeitarme. **2** *Dessáyoh uffaitárrmeh.*

**Am I hurting you? 1** ¿Le hago daño? **2** *Lah árgoh dúnnyoh?*

**No, the razor goes very well. 1** No, esta navaja va muy bien. **2** *Noh, éster nuvvúhher va mooy byén.*

**Yes, a bit. 1** Sí, un poco. **2** *See, oon póccoh.*

**Excuse me, I will change the razor. 1** Perdone, cambiaré la navaja. **2** *Pairrdónneh, cumbearréh lah nuvvúhher.*

**Don't shave against the grain. 1** No me afeite a contrapelo. **2** *Noh meh uffáiteh ah contrapélloh.*

**Will you go over it again, please. 1** Vuélvame a pasar otra vez la navaja. **2** *Vwélvermeh ah pussárr ottrer veth lah nuvvúhher.*

**Put some powder on, to dry it. 1** Póngame polvos para secarme. **2** *Póngermeh pólvoss púrrer seckárrmeh.*

**Give me a massage, please. 1** Hágame masaje. **2** *Úggermeh mussúhheh.*

**Hair cut, please. 1** Córteme el pelo. **2** *Córrtermeh el pélloh.*

**Trim my hair, please. 1** Arrégleme el pelo. **2** *Urréglummeh el pélloh.*

**Leave it in the same style. 1** Déjemelo en la misma forma. **2** *Déhhermellóh en lah mísmer fórrmer.*

**I want it quite short. 1** Lo deseo un poco corto. **2** *Loh dessáyoh oon pólco córrtoh.*

**Just trim the back of the neck and the sides. 1** Arrégleme sólo el cuello y las pulseras. **2** *Urréglarmeh sólloh el kwéllyoh e luss poolsáirerss.*

**Please bring me a paper. 1** Haga el favor de traerme una revista. **2** *Úgger el fuvvór deh trah.áirrmeh ooner revvíster.*

**Do you want the moustache trimming? 1** ¿Le arreglo también el bigote? **2** *Leh urréglo tumbyén el biggótteh?*

**Yes, trim it a bit. 1** Sí, perfílelo. **2** *See, pairfē̄elehlóh.*

**How does that look, sir? 1** ¿Hace el favor de mirar? **2** *Útheh el fuvvórr deh mirrár?*

**All right. 1** Perfectamente. **2** *Pairrféctaménteh.*

**Shall I wash your hair? 1** ¿Desea lavarse la cabeza? **2** *Dessáyer luvvárrseh lah cubbéther?*

**Not necessary. 1** No es necesario. **2** *Noh ess nethessárreo.*

**Comb it as it was before. 1** Péineme tal como estaba antes. **2** *Páinermeh tull cómmoh estúbber úntess.*

**Do you want a lotion? 1** ¿Desea una loción? **2** *Dessáyer ooner lotheón?*

**Yes, give me a friction with quina, eau de cologne. 1** Sí, déme una fricción de quina, de colonia. **2** *See, démmeh ooner fríctheón de kēēner, deh collónnear.*

**Don't put any brilliantine, fixer. 1** No me ponga brillantina, fijador. **2** *Noh meh pónger bríllyuntēēner, fíhherdórr.*

**Do you take a tip? 1** ¿Cuánto es el servicio? **2** *Kwúntoh ess el sairvítheo?*

**I want a manicure. 1** Deseo me hagan la manicura. **2** *Dessáyoh meh úggun lah múnnicōōrer.*

---

## At the perfumery      En la perfumería

---

### The dressing table
### Tocador

---

**The dressing table 1** Tocador **2** *Tóccuddórr*

**Tanning oil. 1** Aceite bronceador. **2** *Utháiteh bróntheadórr.*

**Cleansing oil. 1** Aceite de limpieza. **2** *Utháiteh deh límpyéhther.*

**Scent. 1** Colonia. **2** *Collónnia.*

**Compact. 1** Colorete compacto. **2** *Collerrétth compúctoh.*

**Colouring cream. 1** Colorete crema. **2** *Collerrétteh cráimer.*

**Rimmel cosmetic. 1** Cosmético Rimmel. **2** *Cossmétticoh rímmel.*

**Shaving cream. 1** Crema para afeitar. **2** *Crémmer púrrer uffaitárr.*

*De compras*

**Antisun cream.** 1 Crema antisolar. 2 *Crémmer úntehsollárr.*

**Cleansing cream.** 1 Crema limpiadora. 2 *Crémmer limpy.uddórrer.*

**Massage cream.** 1 Crema para masaje. 2 *Cremmer púrrer mussúhheh.*

**Feeding cream.** 1 Crema nutritiva. 2 *Crémmer nōōtruttēēver.*

**Vanishing cream.** 1 Crema volátil. 2 *Crémmer vollúttil.*

**Razor blades.** 1 Hojas de afeitar. 2 *Óhhuhs deh uffaitárr.*

**Shaving soap.** 1 Jabón para afeitar. 2 *Hubbón púrrer uffaitárr.*

**Scented soap.** 1 Jabón perfumado. 2 *Hubbón páirfoomárdoh.*

**Eyebrow pencil.** 1 Lápiz para las cejas. 2 *Lúppith púrrer luss théckers.*

**Lipstick.** 1 Lápiz para los labios. 2 *Lúppith púrrer loss lúbbeoss.*

**Beauty milk.** 1 Leche de belleza. 2 *Letcheh deh bellyéhther.*

**Lotion.** 1 Loción. 2 *Lotheón.*

**Make up compact.** 1 Maquillaje compacto. 2 *Muhhilyúhheh compúctoh.*

**Make up cream.** 1 Maquillaje crema. 2 *Muhhilyóhheh crémner.*

**Make up powder.** 1 Maquillaje en polvo. 2 *Muhhilyóhheh en pólvoh.*

**Lip outliner.** 1 Perfilador para los labios. 2 *Pairfilladórr púrrer loss lúbbeoss.*

**Scent.** 1 Perfume. 2 *Pairfōōmeh.*

**Face powders.** 1 Polvos faciales. 2 *Pólvoss fúthiúlles.*

**Pulveriser. Spray.** 1 Pulverizador. 2 *Pōōlvurríthadórr.*

**Regenerator.** 1 Regenerador. 2 *Rehhénneradórr.*

**Bay rum.** 1 Ron quina. 2 *Ron keener.*

**Instantaneous colourer.** 1 Tintura instantánea. 2 *Tintōōrer instuntúnnear.*

**Gradual colouring.** 1 Tintura progresiva. 2 *Tintōōrer prógressēēver.*

*De compras*

**Face tonic. 1** Tónico facial. **2** *Tónicoh fútheúl.*
**Astringent tonic. 1** Tónico astringente. **2** *Tónicoh ústrinhénteh.*

**Toilet articles**
**Artículos para higiene**

**Hair brush. 1** Cepillo cabello. **2** *Theppílyoh cubbéll-yoh.*
**Tooth brush. 1** Cepillo para dientes. **2** *Theppílyoh púrrer dyéntess.*
**Hair removing wax. 1** Depilatorio en cera. **2** *Depillatérioh en tháirer.*
**Hair removing cream. 1** Depilatorio en crema. **2** *Depiúatórioh en crémmer.*
**Hair removing powder. 1** Depilatorio en polvo. **2** *Depillatório en pólvoh.*
**Liquid hair remover. 1** Depilatorio líquido. **2** *Depillatório líkkiddon.*
**Deodorant. 1** Desodorante. **2** *Des-sōōderrúnteh.*
**Tooth elixer. 1** Elixir dentífrico. **2** *Elixeer dentíffricoh.*
**Tooth paste. 1** Pasta dentrífica. **2** *Pússter dentífriker.*
**Comb. 1** Peine. **2** *Páyneh.*
**Hair removing tweezers. 1** Pinzas depiladoras. **2** *Pínthuss depillatóriuss.*
**Talcum powder. 1** Polvos de talco. **2** *Pólvoss deh túlcoh.*

**Articles for manucure**
**Artículos manicura**

**Nail clippers. 1** Alicates para las uñas. **2** *Ullicártess púrrer luss ōōnyuss.*
**Skin clippers. 1** Alicates para las pieles. **2** *Ullicártess púrrer luss pyélles.*
**Skin reducers. 1** Bajapieles. **2** *Búhherpyélless.*

*De compras*

**Nail brush. 1** Cepillo para las uñas. **2** *Theppílyoh púrrer luss ōōyuss.*
**Enamel dissolver. 1** Disolvente quita esmalte. **2** *Dissolvénteh kitter esmúlteh.*
**Enamel. 1** Esmalte. **2** *Esmúlteh.*
**Emery file. 1** Lima esmeril. **2** *Lēēmer esmerríll.*
**Metal file. 1** Lima metal. **2** *Lēēmer méttúll.*
**Nail polisher. 1** Pulidor de uñas. **2** *Poollidórr deh ōōyuss.*
**Shin scissors. 1** Tijeras para las pieles. **2** *Tihháiruss púrrer luss pyélless.*
**Nail scissors. 1** Tijeras para las uñas. **2** *Tihháiruss púrrer luss ōōnyuss.*

---

| The kiosk | El quiosco de periódicos |

**The newsman. 1** El quiosquero. **2** *El kioskáiroh.*
**The newspapers. 1** Los periódicos, los diarios. **2** *Loss perrióddicoss, los diúrrios.*
**The magazines. 1** Las revistas. **2** *Luss revvístuss.*
**Children's weeklies. 1** Los semanarios infantiles. **2** *Loss semenúlless infuntēēless.*
**Sporting papers. 1** Los periódicos deportivos. **2** *Loss perriódicoss depporrtēēvoss.*
**Postcards. 1** Tarjetas postales. **2** *Tarrhéttuss postúlless.*
**Collections of photos. 1** Colecciones de fotografías. **2** *Collectheóness deh fóttogrúffeárs.*
**Give me a morning, evening paper. 1** Déme un periódico de la mañana, de la tarde. **2** *Démmeh oon perriódicoh deh lah munyúnner, déller tárrdeh.*
**Have you any English, French, Spanish, German, Portuguese papers? 1** ¿Tiene diarios ingleses, franceses, españoles, alemanes, portugueses...? **2** *Tyénneh diúrrioss inglésses, frunthéssess, espunyólless, ullemúnness, pórrtoogéssess...?*

*De compras*

**And American magazines? 1** ¿Y revistas americanas? **2** *E revvístuss ummerricúnnus?*

**I want a childrens, a sporting paper. 1** Deseo una revista infantil, deportiva... **2** *Dessáyoh ooner revvíster infuntõõl, depporrtõõver.*

**Have you any plans of the town, road maps of the country? 1** ¿Tiene guías de la ciudad, de carreteras del país? **2** *Tyénneh gẽẽuss deh lah théoodúd, deh currettáirrers del pah.íss?*

**I want some postcards with views of the town. 1** Desearía tarjetas postales de la ciudad. **2** *Déssayurréar tarrhéttuss postúlless deh lah théoodúd.*

**Give me these photos of the town. 1** Déme esas fotografías de vistas de la ciudad. **2** *Démmeh éssus fóttogrufféarss deh vístuss deh lah théoodúd.*

**How much is that? 1** ¿Cuánto es? **2** *Kwúntoh ess?*

---

## Photography                          La fotografía

**The camera. 1** El aparato fotográfico.
**2** *El upperrártoh fottogrúfficoh.*
**The lense. 1** Objetivo. **2** *Obhettẽẽvoh.*
**The diaphragm. 1** Diafragma. **2** *Dearfrúgmer.*
**The diaphragm scale. 1** Graduación del diafragma. **2** *Grúddoo.utheón d el dearfrúgmer.*
**The winde. 1** Botón para bobinar.
**2** *Bottón púrrer bobbinnárr.*
**The realease. 1** Disparador. **2** *Dispúrrer.dórr.*
**The counter. 1** Contador. **2** *Cónterdórr.*
**Tre view finder. 1** Visor. **2** *Vissórr.*
**The film-winder. 1** Botón de rebobinar. **2** *Bottón deh rebóbbinárr.*
**The distance scale. 1** Escala de distancias. **2** *Escúller deh distúntheuss.*
**The tripod. 1** El trípode. **2** *El tríppodeh.*
**The case. 1** La funda. **2** *Lah foonder.*
**The range finder. 1** El telémetro. **2** *El tellémettroh.*

*De compras*

**The automatic release. 1** El disparador automático.
**2** *El dispúrrerdórr owtomútticoh.*
**The sunshade. 1** El parasol. **2** *El púrrersól.*
**The exposure meter. 1** El exposímetro. **2** *El*
*expossímmetroh.*
**The photograph. The photo. 1** La fotografía. **2** *Lah*
*fóttohgrufféar.*
**The enlargement. 1** La ampliación. **2** *Lah úmpliút-*
*heón.*
**Film, reel. 1** Película, carrete. **2** *Pellícooler, currétteh.*
**Films: infra-red, panchromatic, supersensitive to**
**red, orthochromatic. 1** Películas: infrarroja, pan-
cromática, supersensible al rojo, ortocromática.
**2** *Pellícoolers: ínfrahóhher, púncrommútticker, pún-*
*crommutticker sōoper.senséēbleh ull róhhoh, órrto-*
*crummútticker.*
**Filters: light blue, orange, light yellow, medium**
**and dark, ultraviolet. 1** Filtros: azul claro; anaranjado; amarillo claro, medio y obscuro; rojo claro y
obscuro; ultravioleta. **2** *Fíltross: uthōōl clárroh;*
*unnúrrunhárdoh; ummerrílyoh clárroh, méddioh e*
*osoōōrroh; róhhoh clárroh e osoōōroh; ōōltrah véolét-*
*ter.*
**Is there a shop for protographic material near**
**here? 1** ¿Hay cerca de aquí una tienda de material
fotográfico? **2** *I tháirca deh ukkēē ooner tyénder deh*
*mutterréul fótogrúffickoh?*
**Yes, sir. In the second street on the left. 1** Sí, señor,
en la segunda travesía a la izquierda. **2** *See,*
*senyórr, en lah segōōnder trúvvairrséar ah lah ith-*
*káirrder.*
**Please give me three reels of film. 1** Haga el favor
de darme tres rollos (carretes) de película. **2** *Úgger*
*el fuvvórr deh dárrmeh tres rólyoss (curréttess) deh*
*pellíckooler.*
**Colour film. 1** Película en colores. **2** *Pellíckooler en*
*collórress.*
**Do you want any particular make? 1** ¿Desea alguna marca determinada? **2** *Dessáyer ulgōōner márr-*
*ker dettáirminárder?*
**Have you...? 1** ¿Tienen de la marca...? **2** *Tyénnen*
*deh lah márrker...?*

*De compras*

**No, we have just sold the last. 1** No, precisamente se nos acaban de terminar. **2** *Noh, prethēēsaménte seh noss uccárbun deh táirminnárr.*

**Well give me another good make. 1** Pues déme de otra marca que sea buena. **2** *Pwess démmeh deh ̄ awtrer márrker keh sáyer wénner.*

**This make is as good as the one you wanted.** **1** Esta otra marca es tan buena como la que deseaba. **2** *Ester āwtrer márrker ess tun bwénner commoh lah keh dessayárber.*

**Yes, I know it, too. 1** Sí, también la conozco. **2** *See tumbyén lah connóthcoh.*

**How much will that be? 1** ¿Cuánto le debo? **2** *Kwúntoh lah débboh?*

**Please develop, this reel and make a copy of each photo. 1** Haga el favor de revelar este rollo y sacar una copia de cada fotografía. **2** *Ugger el fuvvorr deh revvellarr esteh rolyoh e suckarr ooner cóppier deh cúdder fóttogrufféar.*

**It's a colour film. 1** Es un film en color. **2** *Ess oon film en collórr.*

**What size do you want the prints? 1** ¿A qué tamaño han de ser las copias? **2** *Ah keh tummúnyoh un deh sáyer luss cóppyuss?*

**Six by nine. 1** A seis por nueve. **2** *Ah sáviss porr nwevveh.*

**When will they be ready? 1** ¿Cuándo estará? **2** *Kwúndoh esturrár?*

**Couldn't you make it, sooner? 1** ¿No podría hacérmelo más rápido? **2** *Noh poddréar utháirrmeloh muss rúppidoh?*

**I should like to have them by tomorrow, as we are going away. 1** Me interesaría para mañana, porque salimos de viaje. **2** *Meh ínterrésserréar púrrer munyúnner, pórrkeh sulēēmoss de véyúhheh.*

**Come for them tomorrow evening. Here is the receipt. 1** Pase a recogerlo mañana a última hora de la tarde. Tenga el resguardo. **2** *Písseh ah réccohháirrloh ah ōltimer óra deh lah tárrdeh. Ténger el resgwárrdoh.*

**Could you send them to... Hotel? I will leave word**

*De compras*

**with the porter. 1** Podrían enviarlo al Hotel...? Dejaré instrucciones al conserje. **2** *Podréun enveárrloh ull awtél...? Déhherréh ínstrooctheónes ull consáirrheh.*

**Can you tell me the price of this camera? 1** ¿Me puede decir el precio de este aparato fotográfico? **2** *Meh pwéddeh dethéarr el prétheo deh ésteh upperrártoh fotogrúffikoh?*

**And of the tripod? 1** ¿Y el del trípode? **2** *E el del tríppoddeh?*

**Does it take rolls of twenty-six photos? 1** ¿Admite rollos de treinta y seis fotografías? **2** *Udmítteh rólyoss deh trénter e sáyiss fótogrufféars?*

**Has it a telemeter? 1** ¿No lleva telémetro? **2** *Noh lyévver tellémmettroh?*

**How much is all that? 1** ¿Cuánto es todo? **2** *Kwúntoh ess tóddoh?*

**Are there no instructions for the use of the diaphram, speed and focus? 1** ¿No tiene instrucciones para el uso del diafragma, velocidad y enfoque? **2** *Noh tyénneh instrōōctheóness púrrer el ōōsoh del déarfrúgmer, velóthidúd e enfócken?*

**Have you any filters? 1** ¿Tienen ustedes filtros? **2** *Tyénneh oostédess filtross?*

**Is a red filter all right for bringing out the clouds and cutting out mist? 1** ¿Para destacar las nubes y eliminar la neblina, el filtro rojo va bien? **2** *Púrrer destuckárr luss nōōbess e ellímminnárr lah nebblēēner, el fíltroh róhhoh vah byén?*

**I would rather advise an orange one. 1** Le aconsejo mejor el anaranjado. **2** *Les uckonséhhos mehhórr el unnúrrumhárdoh.*

**Red is for transforming the bright sunshine into moonlight effects. 1** El rojo es para transformar los resplandores del Sol en efectos de Luna. **2** *El róhhorh ess púrrer trunsforrmárr loss resplundórres del sol en efféctoss deh lōōner.*

## Presents and souvenirs

## Objetos de regalo
## Recuerdos del país

**I want to buy a basket, but something original.**
1 Deseo comprar un cesto que sea original. 2 *Dessáyoh comprárr oon théstoh keh sáyer orígginnull.*

**These are typical of the country, hand made or peasant work.** 1 Éstos que le muestro son típicos del país y de fabricación manual, o sea de artesanía. 2 *Éstoss keh leh mwestroh son típicoss del pah.íss e deh fúbriccutheón múnnooúll, oh sáyer deh árrtisunnéar.*

**Have you none with the name of this town on them?** 1 ¿No tiene alguno con el nombre de esta ciudad? 2 *Noh tyénneh ulgōōnoh con el nómbre deh éster théudúd?*

**We will put it on at once.** 1 En un momento se lo ponemos. 2 *En oon moméntoh seh loh ponném-moss.*

**Meanwhile, I'll look for something I like as a souvenir.** 1 Entre tanto miraré si encuentro algo que me guste para llevármelo como recuerdo. 2 *Éntreh túntoh mirrurréh see enkwéntroh úlgoh keh meh goosteh púrrer lyevvárrmehlóh cómmoh reckwáirdoh.*

**How much is this smoker's set?** 1 ¿Qué precio tiene este juego de fumador? 2 *Keh prétheo tyénneh ésteh hwéggoh deh foomerdórr?*

**And this ashtray, cigarette holder, pocket book, purse, handkerchief?** 1 ¿Y este cenicero, pitillera, cartera, billetero, bolso, pañuelo...? 2 *E esteh thennitháiron, pittilyáiroh, carrtáirer, bilyettáiroh, bólsoh, punyooélloh?*

**This set is of hand carved wood.** 1 Este juego es de madera labrada a mano. 2 *Ésteh hwéggoh ess deh muddáirrer lubbrárdoh ah múnnoh.*

**This ashtray has a carving of Mount... at the seaside resort.** 1 Este cenicero tiene grabada una vista del monte..., de la playa de... 2 *Ésteh thennitháirroh tyénneh grubbáardoh ooner víster del mónteh..., deh lah plý.er deh...*

*De compras*

**This pocket book is embossed leather. 1** Esta cartera es de cuero repujado. **2** *Éster carrtáirer ess deh kwáirroh reppoojárdoh.*

**I'll take it, but I want my initials put on it. 1** Me quedo con ella, pero deseo que pongan mis iniciales. **2** *Meh kéddoh con éllyer, péhroh keh póngún meess inithiúlless.*

**In which department can I find a musical instrument typical of this place? 1** ¿En qué sección podré encontrar un instrumento musical típico de aquí? **2** *En keh sectheón poddréh encontrár oon ínstrooméntoh moosicúll típpicoh deh uck͞ee͞?*

**That's not what I want. I want a model in miniature. 1** No es esto lo que deseo, sino alguna reproducción en miniatura. **2** *Noh ess éstoh loh keh dessáyoh, seenoh ulg͞oo͞ner repprodooctheón en míniat͞oo͞rer.*

**This musical box, perhaps. Besides being filigrane, it plays a sardana, folk music. 1** Tal vez esta cajita de música. Aparte de ser un trabajo de filigrana toca una sardana, música folklórica.. **2** *Tull veth éster cuhh͞ee͞ter deh m͞oo͞sica. Uppárrteh deh sáyer oon trubbúhhoh deh fílligrúnner, tócker ooner sarrdúnner, m͞oo͞sica folklórrica.*

**I'll take it. It'll be a nice souvenir. Whenever I hear this music I shall remember this lovely country. 1** Me quedo con ella. Será un buen recuerdo, cada vez que oiga esta música me acordaré de este hermoso país. **2** *Meh kéddoh con élyer. Serráh oon byén reckwáirdoh, cúdder veth keh óyger éster m͞oo͞sicker meh uccórrderréh deh ésteh airmóssoh pah.íss.*

**I must buy light things, not to exceed the weight allowed in the plane. 1** Me conviene comprar cosas de poco peso, para no exceder del que autorizan en el avión. **2** *Meh convyénneh comprárr cóssus deh póccoh péssoh, púrrer noh exthedáirr del keh owtorr͞ee͞thun en el uvveón.*

## At the florist's                    En la floristería

**The lily (arum). 1** La azucena.
   **2** *Lah uthoothénner.*
**The cactus. 1** Los cactos.
   **2** *Loss cúctooss.*
**The camelias. 1** Las camelias.
   **2** *Luss cumméllyuss.*
**The bluebells. 1** Las campani-
   llas. **2** *Luss cumpunníllyuss.*
**The pinks. 1** Los claveles.
   **2** *Loss cluvvélless.*

**The carnations. 1** Las clavelli-
   nas. **2** *Luss cluvvelléēnerss.*
**The chrisanthemums. 1** Los crisantemos. **2** *Luss
   kríssúntaymoss.*
**The dahlias. 1** Las dalias. **2** *Luss dúlleass.*
**The gardenias. 1** Las gardenias. **2** *Luss garrdénn-
   yuss.*
**The geraniums. 1** Los geranios. **2** *Loss herrárneoss.*
**The hortensias. 1** Las hortensias. **2** *Luss orténsiuss.*
**The hyacinths. 1** Los jacintos. **2** *Loss huthíntoss.*
**The jasmin. 1** El jazmín. **2** *El huthmēē.*
**The lilac. 1** Las lilas. **2** *Luss lílluss.*
**The lilies. 1** Los lirios. **2** *Loss lírrioss.*
**The magnolias. 1** Las magnolias. **2** *Luss mugnóll-
   yuss.*
**The margarites. 1** Las margaritas. **2** *Luss márrgur-
   rēētuss.*
**The mimosa. 1** La mimosa. **2** *Lah mimmósser.*
**The daffodil. 1** Los narcisos. **2** *Loss narthíssoss.*
**The tuberose. 1** Los nardos. **2** *Loss nárrdoss.*
**The orchids. 1** Las orquídeas. **2** *Luss órrkiddáyerss.*
**The pansies. 1** Los pensamientos. **2** *Loss pén-
   summyéntoss.*
**The peonies. 1** Las peonías. **2** *Loss payonnéuss.*
**The roses. 1** Las rosas. **2** *Lass róssuss.*
**The tulips. 1** Los tulipanes. **2** *Loss toolippúnness.*
**The violets. 1** Las violetas. **2** *Luss véoléttuss.*
**The florist. 1** La florista. **2** *Lah florríster.*
**The flower-pots. 1** Las macetas. **2** *Luss muthéttuss.*

*De compras*

**Good afternoon. 1** Buenas tardes. **2** *Byénnuss tárr-dess.*

**I should like to order a bouquet. 1** Desearía encargar un ramo. **2** *Dessáyurréa encarrgarr oon rúmmoh.*

**What flowers do you prefer? 1** ¿Qué flores prefiere? **2** *Keh flórress prefyerreh?*

**They are to give to a lady on her saint's day. 1** Son para regalar a una señora por su santo. **2** *Son púrrer reggullárr ah ooner senyórra porr soo súntoh.*

**Do you want roses, or magnolias, camelias, dahlias...? 1** ¿Lo quiere de rosas, o bien de magnolias, camelias, dalias...? **2** *Loh kyáirreh deh róssuss, o byén deh mugnélleus, cumméleuss, dúlleuss.*

**Make it of roses. 1** Hágalo de rosas. **2** *Úggerloh deh róssuss.*

**Make it of the most suitable flowers. 1** Hágalo con una selección de las flores más indicadas. **2** *Úggerloh con ooner selléctheón deh luss flórress muss indicárduss.*

**Will you take it with you, sir? 1** ¿Se lo lleva usted, señor? **2** *Seh loh lyévver oostéh senyórr?*

**Are we to send it somewhere? 1** ¿Se han de llevar a algún sitio? **2** *Seh un deh lyevvárr ah úlgoon sēētioh.*

**Yes, here is my card. Send it to the address on the envelope. 1** Sí, tenga mi tarjeta y hágalo llevar a la dirección del sobre. **2** *See, ténger me tarrhétter e úggerloh lyévvarr uller dirréctheón del sóbbreh.*

**Send it before midday tomorrow. 1** Mándelo mañana por la mañana, antes de las doce. **2** *Múndehloh munyúnner porr lah munyúnner, úntess deh loss dótheh.*

**How much is it? 1** ¿Cuánto vale? **2** *Kwúntoh vúlleh?*

**I want a centre of gardenias. 1** Desearía un centro de gardenias. **2** *Déssayerréa oon théntroh deh garrdénneuss.*

**A bunch of white, red, various colours. 1** Un ramo de claveles blancos, rojos, de varios colores. **2** *Oon rúmmoh deh cluvvélless, blúncoss, róhhoss, deh vúrrios rollórress.*

**A bouquet for a bride. 1** Un ramo para novia. **2** *Oon rúmmoh púrrer nóvvia.*

**What flowers are most suitable? 1** ¿Qué flores son las más indicadas? **2** *Keh flórress son luss muss indicárduss?*

**They are generally gardenias, orange blossom and lilies. 1** Acostumbran a ser de gardenias, flores de azahar y... **2** *Uccotöömbrun ah sáyerr deh garrdénniuss, flórress deh utherhárr e lírrioss.*

**I prefer a bouquet of gardenias, arranged with tulle. 1** Lo prefiero de gardenias, en forma de ramillete y adornado con tul. **2** *Loh prefyáirroh deh garrdénniuss, en fórrmer deh rúmmilyétteh e udorrnárdo con tool.*

**Is it to be sent somewhere? 1** ¿Se ha de llevar a alguna dirección? **2** *Seh ah deh lyevvárr ah ulgöö-ner dirréctheón?*

**No, I'll call for it tomorrow. 1** No, pasaré mañana yo mismo a buscarlo. **2** *Noh, pusseréh munyúnner ah booscárrloh.*

**When can I come? 1** ¿A qué hora puedo venir? **2** *Ah keh orá pwéddoh venneerr?*

**Put me up a bunch of violets, of pansies. 1** Hágame un ramillete de violetas, de pensamientos. **2** *Úggermeh oon rummilyétteh deh veoléttuss, deh pensummyéntoss.*

**What are these flowers called? 1** ¿Cómo se llaman estas flores? **2** *Cómmoh seh lyúmmun éstuss flórress?*

**I should like a pot of white lilies. 1** Desearía esa maceta de azucenas. **2** *Déssayerréar esser muthétter deh uthoothénnuss.*

---

## At the fruit shop                    En la frutería

**The avocado. 1** Los aguacates. **2** *Loss úggwercúttess.*

**The apricots. 1** Los albaricoques. **2** *Loss ulberricóckess.*

**The cashew. 1** Los anacardos. **2** *Loss únnercárrdoss.*

**The cherries. 1** Las cerezas. **2** *Luss therréthuss.*

*De compras*

**The cider. 1** La cidra. **2** *Lah thēēdrer.*
**The plums. 1** Las ciruelas. **2** *Luss thirró.élluss.*
**The coconut. 1** Los cocos. **2** *Loss cóccoss.*
**The dates. 1** Los dátiles. **2** *Loss dúttilless.*
**The raspberries.** **1** Las frambuesas. **2** *Loss frumbwéssers.*
**The strawberries. 1** Las fresas. **2** *Luss fréssus.*
**The pomegranates. 1** Las granadas. **2** *Luss grunnár-duss.*
**The currants. 1** Las grosellas. **2** *Luss grosséllyuss.*
**The guava. 1** Las guayabas. **2** *Luss gwy.úbbuss.*
**The figs. 1** Los higos. **2** *Loss ēēgoss.*
**The prickly pears. 1** Los higos chumbos. **2** *Loss ēēgoss chōōmbos.*
**The lemons. 1** Los limones. **2** *Loss limmónness.*
**The tangerines. 1** Las mandarinas. **2** *Lun mundarrēē-rerss.*
**The apples. 1** Las manzanas. **2** *Luss munthúnnuss.*
**The peaches. 1** Los melocotones. **2** *Loss méllo-cottónness.*
**The melon. 1** El melón. **2** *El mellón.*
**The quince. 1** El membrillo. **2** *El membríllyoh.*
**The oranges. 1** Las naranjas. **2** *Luss nurrúnhus.*
**The medlars. 1** Los nísperos. **2** *Loss nísperross.*
**The pawpaws. 1** Las papayas. **2** *Luss puppýuss (puppíe.uss).*
**The pears. 1** Las peras. **2** *Luss páyeruss.*
**The pine apples. 1** Las piñas de América o ananás. **2** *Luss pēēnyuss deh ummérica oh unnunnúss.*
**The bananas. 1** Los plátanos o bananas. **2** *Los plút-tunnoss ob bunnúnnuss.*
**The water melons. 1** La sandía. **2** *Lah sundéar.*
**The grape. 1** La uva. **2** *Lah oover.*
**The muscatel grape. 1** La uva moscatel. **2** *Lah oover móscatel.*
**The sapota plum. 1** Los zapotes. **2** *Loss thuppóttess.*
**The blackberry. 1** La zarzamora. **2** *Lah thárrzummó-rrer.*
**The almonds. 1** Las almendras. **2** *Luss alméndruss.*
**The wallnuts. 1** Las nueces. **2** *Luss nwéthess.*
**The hazelnuts. 1** Las avellanas. **2** *Luss uvvelyún-ners.*

**The chestnuts. 1** Las castañas. **2** *Luss custúnyuss.*

**The monkey nuts. 1** Los cacahuetes o maníes. **2** *Loss cúccerwéttes oh munnéus.*

**Have you any dates? 1** ¿Tiene dátiles? **2** *Tyénneh dúttilless?*

**Yes, some very sweet ones. 1** Sí, por cierto muy dulces. **2** *See, porr tháirtoh mooy dóolthess.*

**How much are they? 1** ¿A cómo los vende? **2** *Ah cómmoh loss véndeh?*

**... a kilo. 1** A... el kilo. **2** *Ah... ell kéeloh.*

**Give me two kilos. 1** Póngame dos kilos. **2** *Póngermeh doss kéeloss.*

**And give me a kilo of grapes as well. 1** Déme también un kilo de uva. **2** *Démmeh tumbyén oon kéeloh deh óover.*

**Black or white? 1** ¿La quiere blanca o negra? **2** *Lah kyáirreh blúnker oh néggrah?*

**No, muscatel. 1** No, moscatel. **2** *Noh, mocatél.*

**I have some lovely pears. 1** Tengo unas peras preciosas. **2** *Téngoh óonuss péhruss prétheóssuss.*

**Give me three kilos of apples and two of oranges. 1** Póngame tres kilos de manzanas y dos de naranjas. **2** *Póngermeh tress kéeloss deh munthúnnuss e doss deh nuhrúnherss.*

**Have you any good class melons? 1** ¿Tiene melones de buena clase? **2** *Tyénneh mellónness deh bwénner clússeh?*

**These are ripe and very sweet. 1** Éstos salen muy dulces y están maduros. **2** *Éstoss súllen mooy dóothless e estún muddóoruss.*

**I want some lemons, but very juicy ones. 1** Desearía limones, pero que tengan mucho zumo. **2** *Dessairréar limmónness, péhroh keh téngun móotchoh thóomoh.*

**Give me some bananas, but not too ripe. 1** Déme plátanos, pero que no sean demasiado maduros. **2** *Démmeh plúttunnoss. péhroh keh noh sayun demmússeardoh muddóoruss.*

**These medlars are very sour? 1** ¿Estos nísperos son muy ácidos? **2** *Éstoss níssperros son mooy úthiddoss?*

*De compras*

**The water melon looks refreshing. 1** La sandía apetece como refrescante. **2** *Lah sundéar uppettéththeh cómmoh refrescúnteh.*

**What is this fruit called? 1** ¿Cómo se llama esta fruta? **2** *Cómmoh seh lyúmmer éster frŏŏter?*

**They are tangerines. A kind of small orange easy to peel. 1** Son mandarinas. Una especie de naranjas pequeñas de cáscara fácil de separar. **2** *Son múndurr̃ẽ̃nerss. Ooner espéthear deh nurrúnherss peckénnyuss deh cúscurrer fúthill deh sepperrarr.*

**Have you no peaches? 1** ¿No tienen melocotones? **2** *Noh tyénneh méllocottónness?*

**They are not yet in season. 1** No es todavía el tiempo. **2** *Noh ess todderṽẽ̃ar el tyémpoh.*

**Give me two pineapples. 1** Déme dos piñas americanas. **2** *Démmeh doss p̃ẽ̃nyers umméricúnners.*

**Can you send them home for me? 1** ¿Puede enviármelo todo a casa? **2** *Pwéddeh enveárrmehloh tóddoh ah cússer?*

**Your address, please? 1** ¿Su dirección, por favor? **2** *Soo dírréctheón porr fuvvórr?*

**My name is... n.º..., ... Street. 1** Mi nombre es... número... calle... **2** *Me nómbreh ess... nŏŏmeroh... cúllyeh...*

**I will pay now. 1** Se lo pago ahora. **2** *Seh loh púggoh ahora.*

**I will pay at home. 1** Se lo abonaré en casa. **2** *Seh loh ubbónnerréh en cússer.*

---

## Tabacco                                El tabaco

**The packet of cigarettes. 1** El paquete decigarrillos. **2** *El puckétteh deh thiggerríllyoss.*

**The box of cigars. 1** La caja de puros. **2** *Lah cúhher deh pŏŏrross.*

**The ash tray. 1** El cenicero. **2** *El thénnitháiroh.*

**The lighter. 1** El encendedor, el mechero. **2** *El enthéndidórr; el metcháiroh.*

**The matches. 1** Las cerillas, los fósforos. **2** *Luss therrílyuss, loss fósforross.*

**The cigarette holder. 1** La boquilla. **2** *Lah bockíllyer.*

**The pouch. 1** La petaca. **2** *Lah pettácker.*

**The pipe. 1** La pipa. **2** *Lah pêêper.*

**The cigarette case. 1** La pitillera. **2** *Lah pittillyáirer.*

**The cigar. 1** El cigarro puro. **2** *El thiggúrroh pôôrroh.*

**Give me a packet of cigarettes, light, dark, please.**
**1** Déme un paquete de cigarrillos de tabaco rubio, negro. **2** *Démmeh oon puckétteh deh tubbúckoh rôôbeo, néggroh.*

**And a box of matches. 1** Déme también una caja de cerillas, fósforos. **2** *Démmeh tubyén ooner cúhher deh therríllyerss, fosférross.*

**A cigar, please. 1** ¿Un cigarro puro, por favor? **2** *Oon thiggúrroh pôôrroh, porr fuvvórr.*

**What sort do you want? 1** ¿De qué marca lo desea? **2** *Deh keh márrcah loh dessáyer.*

**I don't mind, provided it's a good one. 1** Me es igual, pero que sea bueno. **2** *Meh ess iggwul, péhroh keh sáyer byénnoh.*

**D'you want a Havana or a native? 1** Lo deseo habano, del país. **2** *Loh dessáyoh ubbárnoh, del py.íss.*

**A large, a small one. 1** Que sea grande, pequeño. **2** *Keh sáyer grúndeh, peckénnyoh.*

**Please give me a box of Havana cigars. 1** Haga el favor de venderme una caja de cigarros habanos. **2** *Úgger el fuvvórr deh vendáirrmeh ooner cuhher deh thiggúrross.*

**Can you show me some pipes? 1** ¿Me puede enseñar un surtido de pipas? **2** *Meh pwéddeh ensenyárr oon soortêêdoh deh pêêpers?*

**I want a pipe cleaner. 1** Quisiera una escobilla para limpiar la pipa. **2** *Kyssyárrer oon escobbíllyoh púrrer limpyárr lah pêêper.*

**Have you any cigarette holders? 1** ¿Tiene boquillas? **2** *Tyénneh bockíllyuss?*

**For cigars or or cigarettes? 1** ¿Para cigarros o para cigarrillos? **2** *Púrrer thiggúrross oh púrrer thíggurríllyuss?*

**I want a pouch, a cigarette case. 1** Desearía una petaca, una pitillera. **2** *Dessáyerréar ooner pettúcker, ooner pettillyáirer.*

*De compras*

**Have you flints for lighters?** 1 ¿Tiene piedras para mecheros? **2** *Tyénneh pyédruus púrárr metcháiros.*
**Show me some lighters, souvenir ash trays.** 1 Enséñeme los encendedores, los ceniceros de recuerdo. **2** *Ensényummeh loss enthéndedórress, loss thénnitháirross deh rekwáirrdoh.*

---

## At the bank                    En el banco

---

The door. 1 La puerta.
2 *Lah pwáirrter.*
The porter. 1 El porte-ro. 2 *El porrtáiroh.*
The messenger. 1 El ordenanza. 2 *El ordenúnther.*
The bell boy. 1 El boto-nes. 2 *El bottónes.*

**The exchange rates.** 1 El tablero de cotizaciones de moneda. **2** *El tubláirroh deh cóttithúthiónes deh monnédder.*
**The windows.** 1 Las ventanillas. 2 *Luss véntunnílyuss. Lah véntuunilyer deh cúmbioh deh monnédder.*
**The exchange window.** 1 La ventanilla del cambio de moneda. **2** *Lah véntunníllyer deh trúnsferrénthear del extáirriór.*
**The foreign transfer window.** 1 La ventanilla de transferencia del exterior. **2**
**The clerk.** 1 El empleado. **2** *El emplayúddoh.*
**The cashier.** 1 El cajero. **2** *El cuhháirroh.*
**The bank notes.** 1 Los billetes. **2** *Loss billyéttess.*
**Small change.** 1 La moneda fraccionaria. **2** *Lah monnédder frúcthioária.*
**Travellers cheques.** 1 Cheque de viaje. **2** *Chéckeh deh ve.úhheh.*
**To pay.** 1 Pagar. **2** *Puggárr.*
**To cash.** 1 Cobrar. **2** *Cobbrárr.*
**Messenger, where's the exchange window?** 1 Oiga, ordenanza, ¿para cambiar moneda? **2** *Óyger, ordinnúnther, purrer cumbiarr munnéder?*

*De compras*

**The fourth window. 1** La cuarta ventanilla. **2** *Lah kwárter véntunníllyer.*

**Will you please change this traveller's cheque? 1** Haga el favor de cambiarme este cheque de viaje. **2** *Úgger el fuvvórr deh cumbiárrmeh esteh chéckeh deh ve.úhheh.*

**Wait a moment, please. 1** Tenga la bondad de esperar un poco. **2** *Ténger lah bondúd deh esperrárr oon pāwcoh.*

**Will I have to wait long? 1** ¿Habré de esperar mucho? **2** *Ubbráy deh esperrárr mōōtchoh?*

**I will tell you at once. 1** Le avisaré en seguida. **2** *Leh uvvisserráy en seggēēder.*

**What is the rate? 1** ¿A cuántos está el cambio? **2** *Ah kwúntoss estár el cúmbioh.*

**I want to change part of this traveller's cheque. Can you give me the difference in my own currency? 1** Deseo cambiar parte de este cheque de viaje. ¿Puede darme la diferencia en moneda de mi país? **2** *Dessáyoh cumbiárr párrteh deh ésteh chéckeh deh ve.úheh. Pwéddeh dárrmeh lah differénthiah en munnédeer deh me py.íss?*

**I'm sorry, it can't be done. You can only get the currency of your country at the Government Bank. 1** Lo siento, no es posible, las divisas de su país se entregan diariamente al Banco del Gobierno. **2** *Loh syentoh, noh ess posseebleh, luss divveesuss deh soo py.íss seh entráygun de.íraménteh ull búncoh del goobyáirnoh.*

**Can you change these notes into local currency? 1** ¿Puede cambiarme estos billetes en moneda del país? **2** *Pwéddeh cumbiárrmeh éstoss billyéttess en monnéddus del py.íss?*

**What are they? 1** ¿De cuánto son? **2** *Deh kwúntoh son?*

**Thousands. 1** De mil cada uno. **2** *Deh meel cúdder ⁻ōōnoh/or: - deh meel cárther ōōnoh.*

**Could you tell me whether you have received a transfer form... for...? 1** ¿Podrá indicarme si se ha recibido una transferencia de... a nombre de...? **2** *Podráh indicárrmeh see seh ah réthibēēdoh ooner trunsferrrénthia deh... ah nombreh deh...?*

*De compras*

**For what amount? 1** ¿Por qué importe? **2** *Porr kéh impórrteh?*

**For 3.000... from the Bank of... 1** Por 3.000... y del Banco de... **2** *Porr tress meel... e del buncoh deh...*

**No, sir, It's not arrived yet. 1** No, señor, todavía no ha llegado. **2** *Noh, senyórr. Toddervéer noh ah lyéggárdoh.*

**Yes, sir. Will you please show me your identity papers. 1** Sí, señor. ¿Hará el favor de acreditarme su personalidad? **2** *See, senyórr. Úrrer el fuvvórr deh uccrédditámeh soo páirsonnállidúd?*

**Here is my passport and my identity card. 1** Aquí tiene mi pasaporte, mi carnet de identidad. **2** *Ukke tyenneh me pússerpórrteh, me carrnét de iddéntidúd.*

**What rate have you given me? 1** ¿Qué cambio me ha cotizado. **2** *Keh cúmbeo me ah cottithárdoh?*

**You have given me a very low rate. 1** Me cotiza usted un cambio muy bajo. **2** *Me cottither oostéh oon cúmbeo mooy búhhoh.*

**It's the official rate, today's rate. 1** Es el cambio oficial, es el cambio de hoy. **2** *Es el cúmbeo ofitheúl, es el cúmbeo deh oy.*

**Please give me large, small notes. 1** Haga el favor de entregarme billetes grandes, pequeños. **2** *Úgger el fuvvórr deh entreggárme bilyéttess grúndess, peckénnyoss.*

**Do you send money by post, by telegraph to...? 1** ¿Remiten ustedes fondos a... por correo, por telégrafo? **2** *Remmitten oostéddess fóndoss ah... porr corráyoh, por tellégruffoh?*

*La salud*

# Health
## La salud

**I got up with a head ache. 1** Me he levantado con dolor de cabeza. **2** *Meh eh lévvuntárdoh con dollórr deh cubbéther.*

**A sore throat. 1** Dolor de garganta. **2** *Dollórr deh garrgúnter.*

**A stomach ache. 1** Dolor de estómago. **2** *Dollórr deh estómmuggoh.*

**A bad liver. 1** De hígado. **2** *Deh ígguddoh.*

**I want to see a doctor. 1** Quiero ver a un doctor. **2** *Kyérroh váirr ah oon doctórr.*

**Have you fever? 1** ¿Tengo fiebre? **2** *Téngoh fyébbreh?*

**How often must I take the medicine? 1** ¿Cuántas veces debo tomar la medicina? **2** *Kwúntuss véthess debboh tommárr lah medithḗḗner?*

**Before or after meals? 1** ¿Antes o después de las comidas? **2** *Úntess oh despwéss deh luss commḗḗders?*

**Shall I soon be all right? 1** ¿Me pondré pronto bue- no? **2** *Meh pondréh próntoh bwénnoh?*

**I hit my arm. 1** Me he dado un golpe en el brazo. **2** *Meh eh dárdoh oon gólpeh en el brúthoh.*

**I feel an acute pain in my kidneys. 1** Siento en los riñones un dolor muy fuerte. **2** *Syéntoh en loss rinyónness onn dollórr mooy fwáirteh.*

**I can't sleep at night. 1** Por las noches no puedo dormir. **2** *Porr luss nótchess noh pwéddoh dorrmḗḗrr.*

**Take a sedative when you go to bed. 1** Tome usted un calmante al acostarse. **2** *Tómmeh oostéh oon culmúnteh ull uccostárrseh.*

**I'll take a cup of linden tea. 1** Hoy tomaré una taza de tila. **2** *Oy tommerréh ooner túther deh tḗḗler.*

*La salud*

**I have fever. 1** Tengo fiebre. **2** *Téngoh fyébbreh.*

**I've got indigestion. 1** Tengo una indigestión. **2** *Téngoh ooner índihesteón.*

**I want a purgative. 1** Quiero purgarme. **2** *Kyérroh poorgármeh.*

**As a precaution, I shall eat very little today. 1** Como medida preventiva, hoy comeré muy poco. **2** *Cómmoh meddéeder préventéever, oy commerréh mooy póccoh.*

**I have tooth ache. 1** Me duelen las muelas. **2** *Meh dwéllen luss mwélluss.*

**My left arm hurts. 1** Me duele el brazo izquierdo. **2** *Meh dwélleh el brúthoh ithkyáirdoh.*

**My right foot hurts. 1** Me duele el pie derecho. **2** *Meh dwélleh el pyéh derrétchoh.*

**I have a pain here. 1** Siento un dolor aquí. **2** *Syéntoh oon dollórr uckée.*

**I have nothing serious. 1** Mi dolencia no es grave. **2** *Me dollénthea noh ess grárveh.*

**It will pass. 1** Es un dolor pasajero. **2** *Ess oon dollórr pússuhháiroh.*

**This pain troubles me. 1** Este dolor me molesta. **2** *Ésteh dollórr meh molléster.*

**I have diarrhoea. 1** Tengo diarrea. **2** *Téngoh déarréa.*

**I feel a burning pain in the stamach. 1** Siento ardor en el estómago. **2** *Syéntoh arrdórr en el estómmuggoh.*

**I have a pain. 1** Tengo dolor. **2** *Téngo dollórr.*

**I have no pain. 1** No tengo dolor. **2** *Noh téngoh dollórr.*

**I cough a lot. 1** Toso mucho. **2** *Tóssoh móotcho.*

**I have a bad cold. 1** Estoy muy resfriado. **2** *Estóy mooy réssfreeárdoh.*

**I have no appetite. 1** No tengo apetito. **2** *Noh téngoh uppiteetoh.*

## Sports                                **Los deportes**

**Chess. 1** El ajedrez. **2** *El úhhedréth.*

**Mountaineering. 1** El alpinismo. **2** *El ulpinísmoh.*

**Athletics. 1** El atletismo. **2** *El utlettísmoh.*

**Motoring. 1** El automovilismo. **2** *El ōwtohmóvvillísmoh.*

**Basket ball. 1** El baloncesto. **2** *El bullónthestoh.*

**Hand ball. 1** El balonmano. **2** *El búllonmúnnoh.*

**Volley ball. 1** El balonvolea. **2** *El bullón volláyoh.*

**Billiards. 1** El billar. **2** *El billyárr.*

**Boxing. 1** El boxeo. **2** *El boxáyoh.*

**Cycling. 1** El ciclismo. **2** *El thicklísmoh.*

**Skying. 1** El esquí. **2** *El esskēē.*

**Football. 1** El fútbol. **2** *El fútbol.*

**Gymnastics. 1** La gimnasia. **2** *Lah himnússia.*

**Golf. 1** El golf. **2** *El golf.*

**Riding. 1** La hípica. **2** *La íppica.*

**Roller hockey. 1** El hockey sobre patines. **2** *El hockey sóbbreh puttēēness.*

**Hockey. 1** El hockey sobre hierba. **2** *El hockey sóbbre yáirber.*

**Ice hockey. 1** El hockey sobre hielo. **2** *El hockey sóbbreh yélloh.*

**Wrestling. 1** La lucha libre. **2** *Lah lōōtcher lēēbreh.*

**Motoring. 1** El motorismo. **2** *El mottorrísmoh.*

**Swimming. 1** La natación. **2** *Lah nuttúthéon.*

**Skating. 1** El patinaje. **2** *El púttinnáhheh.*

**Baseball. 1** La pelota base. **2** *Lah pellótter bússeh.*

**Fishing. 1** La pesca. **2** *Lah pésker.*

**Rowing. 1** El remo. **2** *El rémmoh.*

**Rugby. 1** El rugby. **2** *El rōōgby.*

**Tennis. 1** El tenis. **2** *El tennis.*

**Table tennis/Ping Pong. 1** El tenis de mesa. **2** *El tennis deh mésser*

*Los deportes*

**The referee. 1** El árbitro. **2** *El árrbitroh.*
**The massuer. 1** El masajista. **2** *El músserhíster.*
**The trainer. 1** El entrenador. **2** *El entrénnerdórr.*
**The stadium. 1** El estadio. **2** *El estárdio.*
**The cycle track. 1** El velódromo. **2** *El vellódromoh.*
**The tracks. 1** Las pistas. **2** *Luss písters.*
**Is there any football, basket ball, handball, rugby, hockey, baseball, etc. match, today? 1** ¿Hay hoy algún partido de fútbol, baloncesto, balonmano, rugby, hockey, de pelota base, etc.? **2** *I oy ulgōōn partēēdoh de fōōtbol, bullónthéstoh, bullónmárnoh, roogby, hockey, deh pellótter bússeh, etc.?*
**Yes, sir. There are two first class teams playing. 1** Sí, señor, juegan dos equipos de primera categoría. **2** *See, senyórr. Hwéggun doss ekíposs deh primáirer cúttehgorría.*
**At what time does the match begin. 1** ¿A qué hora empieza el encuentro? **2** *Ah keh ora empyether el enkwentroh?*
**Where is the field, the ground? 1** ¿Dónde está el campo de juego? **2** *Dóndeh estár el cúmpoh deh hwéggoh?*
**They get very excited about football at home. Do they here? 1** El fútbol es un juego que apasiona las masas en mi país. ¿Aquí también? **2** *El footbol es oon hwéggoh keh uppússeóner luss mússers en me pahís. Uckēē tumbyén?*
**Definately. It's the king of sports. 1** Ya lo creo, es el deporte rey. **2** *Yah loh cráyoh, es el deppórrteh ray.*
**There are professional and amateur footballers. 1** Hay fútbol profesional y de aficionados. **2** *I foobol proféssionnúll e deh uffítheonárdoss.*
**What's the most popular sport after football, cycling, boxing...? 1** ¿Cuál es el deporte que arrastra más afición después del fútbol, el ciclismo, el boxeo...? **2** *Kwull es el deppórrteh urrústrer muss uffítheón despwéss del foobol, el thicklismoh, el boxáyoh...?*
**There are several, such as basketball, and hockey roller hockey. 1** Hay varios, entre ellos el baloncesto y el hockey sobre patines. **2** *I vúrrioss, éntreh ellyoss el búllonthéstoh e el hockey sóbbreh puttēēness.*

*Los deportes*

**They are both sports requiring agility and speed.**
1 Ambos son dos deportes que requieren mucha agilidad y rapidez. 2 *Úmboss son doss deppórrtes keh rekyáirren mõõtcher uhhíllidud e rúppidéth.*

**Is there much boxing, wrestling?** 1 ¿Se celebra hoy boxeo, lucha libre? 2 *Seh thellébra oy boxáyo, lõõtcher lẽẽobreh?*

**No, there's a cycling tournament.** 1 No, hay una velada de ciclismo. 2 *Noh, i ooner vellárder deh thicklísmoh.*

**Are there no swimming competitions?** 1 ¿No hay competiciones de natación? 2 *Noh i compettítheónes deh nuttútheón?*

**Yes, this evening there's a very interesting swimming meeting at...** 1 Sí, esta noche hay un encuentro de natación muy interesante en la piscina de... 2 *See, éster nótcheh i oon enkwéntroh deh nuttútheón mooy interressúnteh en lah pisthẽẽner deh...*

**There's also a water polo match.** 1 También hay un encuentro de water polo. 2 *Tumbyén i oon enkwéntroh deh water pãwloh.*

**The high diving is very spectacular.** 1 Los saltos desde el trampolín resultan muy espectaculares. 2 *Loss súltoss desdeh el trumpollẽẽn ressõõltun mooy espectúckoolárress.*

**I prefer to see a rugby match.** 1 Yo prefiero asistir a los encuentros de rugby. 2 *Yoh prefáirroh ussistẽẽ ah loss enflwéntross deh rõõgby.*

**That game has scarcely any importance here.** 1 Aquí casi no tiene importancia este deporte. 2 *Uck̄ ẽẽ cússy noh tyénneh imporrtúnthea ésteh depórrteh.*

**I also like international athletic tournaments.** 1 Los encuentros internacionales de atletismo también me gustan. 2 *Loss enkwéntross internútheonúlless deh útlettíssmoh tumbyén meh gõõstun.*

**I was an athlete in my youth.** 1 Yo fui atleta en mi juventud. 2 *Yoh fwee utlétter en me hõõventõõd.*

**I ran in flat races, obstacle races, relay races, springboard diving.** 1 Yo hacía carreras de fondo, obstáculos, relevos, saltos con trampolín. 2 *Yoh*

*Los deportes*

*úthéa curráirrerss deh fóndoh, obstúckōŏloss, rellévvoss, súltoss con trúmpollēēn.*

**My brother goes in for 200 meter hurdle races and weight throwing. 1** Mi hermano corre los 200 metros vallas y practica el lanzamiento de peso. **2** *Me airrmúnnoh córreh loss doss thyéntoss métross vúllyuss e pructēēker el lúnthummyéntoh deh péssoss.*

**This is a good country for skiing. 1** Este país reúne condiciones para el esquí. **2** *Ésteh pý.íss reh.ōōneh conditheónes púrrer el eskēē.*

**Don't you believe it. They are keener on mountaineering. 1** No lo crea. Hay más afición al alpinismo. **2** *Noh loh cráyer. I muss uffítheón ull úlpinníssmoh.*

**Are there no tennis matches? 1** ¿No hay encuentros de tenis? **2** *Noh i enkwéntross deh tenníss?*

**It's a fine sport. 1** Es un bello deporte. **2** *Ess oon bélyoh depórrteh.*

**I know there are some motor cycle races tomorrow, motor races. Can you tell me where they are held? 1** Sé que hay mañana carreras de motos, de automóviles. ¿Podría decirme dónde se celebran? **2** *Seh keh i munyúnner curráirrus deh móttoss, deh owtohmovvíulless. Podéar dechēērrmeh dóndeh seh thellébrun?*

**I advise you to go to the horse races tomorrow. 1** Le recomiendo que asista mañana al concurso de hípica. **2** *Leh recomyéndoh keh ussíster munyúnner ull conōōrrsoh deh íppica.*

**I can't. I have to time a cycle race. 1** Me es imposible. Tengo que cronometrar una carrera de bicicletas. **2** *Meh ess impossēēbleh. Téngoh keh crónnomettrárr ooner curráirrer deh bíthicléttuss.*

**Where? 1** ¿Dónde? **2** *Dóndeh?*

**At the... track. 1** En el velódromo de... **2** *En el vellódddromoh deh...*

*En la playa*

# At the beach

# En la playa

**The hotel, the casino.** 1 El hotel, el casino. 2 *El awtél, el cusséénoh.*

**The seaside resort.** 1 El balneario. 2 *El bullneárreoh.*

**The umbrella.** 1 La sombrilla. 2 *Lah sombréelyah.*

**The beach chair.** 1 La silla de playa. 2 *Lah síllyer deh ply.yer.*

**The sushade.** 1 La sombrilla. 2 *Lah sombríllyer.*

**The sand.** 1 La arena. 2 *Lah urráinner.*

**The sea.** 1 El mar. 2 *El marr.*

**The waves, the swell.** 1 Las olas, el oleaje. 2 *Luss ólluss, el olleúhhee.*

**The bathers.** 1 Los bañistas. 2 *Loss bunyísters.*

**The diving board, the spring board.** 1 La palanca, el trampolín. 2 *Lah pullúnker, el trumpolléén.*

**The fisher.** 1 El pescador. 2 *El peskerdórr.*

**The boat.** 1 La barca. 2 *Lah bárrker.*

**The float.** 1 El patín. 2 *El puttéén.*

**The ropes.** 1 Las cuerdas. 2 *Luss kwáirduss.*

**The bathing costume.** 1 El traje de baño. 2 *El trúhheh deh búnyoh.*

**The bath gown.** 1 El albornoz. 2 *El ulborrnóth.*

**You can go to the bathing establishment.** 1 Puede dirigirse al balneario. 2 *Pwéddeh dirrihéarrseh ull bulneárrioh.*

**Where can I hire a float, a boat?** 1 ¿Para alquilar un patín, una barca...? 2 *Púrrer ulkillárr oon puttéén, ooner bárrker?*

**You must ask at the...** 1 Deben dirigirse a... 2 *Débben dirrihéarrseh ah...*

**Where can we have a shower?** 1 ¿Dónde podremos ducharnos? 2 *Dóndeh podrémmoss dootchárrnoss?*

**Here, in the establishment.** 1 Aquí en el balneario. 2 *Uckéé en el búllneárrioh.*

**The showers are at the entrance to the beach.** 1 Las duchas están situadas en la salida de la pla-

*El tiempo*

ya. **2** *Luss dōōtchuss estún sittooárduss en lah sull‾ eder deh lah plýer.*

**Is there a pelota court here? 1** ¿Hay frontón en este balneario? **2** *I frontón en esteh bullniúrrioh?*

**Yes, and other amusements, such as ping-pong, bowls, etc. 1** Sí, y también otras distracciones, como tenis sobre mesa, boleras. **2** *See, e tumbyén otros distrúctheónes, cómmoh tennis sóbreh méser, bolláirruss.*

**The sea is choppy. 1** El mar está picado. **2** *El marr estár pickárdoh.*

**There is an undercurrent. 1** Hay mar de fondo. **2** *I marr deh fóndoh.*

**It's dangerous to bathe today. 1** Es peligroso bañarse hoy. **2** *Ess pelligróssoh bunyárrseh oy.*

**The water is dirty. 1** El agua está sucia. **2** *El úgwer estár sōōthea.*

**The water is crystal clear. 1** El agua está cristalina. **2** *El úgwer estár cristullēēner.*

**Is the station very far? 1** ¿Está muy lejos la estación de ferrocarril? **2** *Estár mooy léhhoss lah estutheón deh férrorcurrēēl?*

**When does the last train leave for...? 1** ¿A qué hora pasa el último tren para...? **2** *Ah keh óra pússer el ōōltimoh tren púrrer...?*

# Time

## El tiempo

**A century. 1** Un siglo. **2** *Oon sígloh.*

**A lustre. 1** Un lustro. **2** *Oon lōōstroh.*

**A year. 1** Un año. **2** *Oon únnyoh.*

**Leap year. 1** El año bisiesto. **2** *El únnyoh bissyésstoh.*

**Last year. 1** El año pasado. **2** *El únnyoh pussárdoh.*

**Next year. 1** El año próximo. **2** *El únnyoh próximoh.*

*El tiempo*

**A month. 1** Un mes. **2** *Oon mess.*
**The months. 1** Los meses. **2** *Loss méssess.*
**A term. 1** Un trimestre. **2** *Oon trimméstreh.*
**Monthly. 1** Mensual. **2** *Mensooúll.*
**A fortnight. 1** Una quincena. **2** *Ooner kinthénner.*
**Fortnightly. 1** Quincenal. **2** *Kinthennúll.*
**A week. 1** Una semana. **2** *Ooner semúnner.*
**Weekly. 1** Semanal. **2** *Sémmenúll.*
**Twice weekly. 1** Bisemanal. **2** *Bee.semmennúll.*
**Three times weekly. 1** Trisemanal. **2** *Tree.sem-mennúll.*
**The months of the year are: January, February, March, April, May, June, July, August, September, October, November, December. 1** Los meses del año son: enero, febrero, marzo, abril, mayo, junio, julio, agosto, septiembre, octubre, noviembre y diciembre. **2** *Loss méssess del únyoh son: enáirroh, febráirroh, márrthoh, ubbríll, máhyoh, hōōneo, hōōleo, uggósstoh, septyémbreh, octóbbreh, novvyémbreh, dithyémbreh.*
**The days of the week are: Monday, Tuesday, Wednesday, Thursday, Friday, Saturday, and Sunday. 1** Los días de la semana son: lunes, martes, miércoles, jueves, viernes, sábado y domingo. **2** *Loss déarss deh la semmúnner son: lōōness, márrtess, myáircolless, hwevvess, vyairness, súbberdoh e dommíngoh.*
**Good Friday. 1** Viernes Santo. **2** *Vyáirness súntoh.*
**Saturday before Easter. 1** Sábado de Gloria. **2** *Súbberdoh deh Glórria.*
**Palm Sunday. 1** Domingo de Ramos. **2** *Dommingoh deh Rummoss.*
**Christmas Day. 1** Día de Navidad. **2** *Déar deh núvvidúd.*
**A day. 1** Un día. **2** *Oon déar.*
**Daily. 1** Diario. **2** *Deúrrioh.*
**A week day. 1** Un día de trabajo. **2** *Oon déar deh trubbúhhoh.*
**A holiday. 1** Un día de fiesta. **2** *Oon déar deh fyéster.*
**Today. 1** Hoy. **2** *Oy.*
**Yesterday. 1** Ayer. **2** *Ahyáirr.*
**The day before yesterday. 1** Anteayer. **2** *Unteh uh.yáirr.*

*El tiempo*

**The eve.** 1 La víspera. 2 *Lah vísspurrer.*
**Tomorrow.** 1 Mañana. 2 *Munyúnner.*
**The day after tomorrow.** 1 Pasado mañana. 2 *Pussárdoh munyúnner.*
**This morning.** 1 Esta mañana. 2 *Éster munyúnner.*
**This evening.** 1 Esta tarde. 2 *Éster tárrdeh.*
**Early morning.** 1 Matinal. 2 *Muttinnúll.*
**Midday.** 1 El mediodía. 2 *El méddiodéar.*
**Morning.** 1 La mañana. 2 *Lah munyúnner.*
**Afternoon.** 1 La tarde. 2 *Lah tárdeh.*
**Night.** 1 La noche. 2 *Lah nótcheh.*
**Midnight.** 1 Medianoche. 2 *Méddea nótcheh.*
**This evening.** 1 Esta noche. 2 *Éster nótcheh.*
**Night.** 1 Nocturno. 2 *Noctōōrnoh.*
**An hour.** 1 Una hora. 2 *Ooner óra.*
**Half an hour.** 1 Media hora. 2 *Méddea óra.*
**A quater of an hour.** 1 Un cuarto de hora. 2 *Oon kwárrtoh deh óra.*
**An hour and a half.** 1 Hora y media. 2 *Óra e mééddia.*
**A minute.** 1 Un minuto. 2 *Oon minōōtoh.*
**A second.** 1 Un segundo. 2 *Oon segōōndoh.*
**Twilight.** 1 El crepúsculo. 2 *El creppōōscooloh.*
**Sunset.** 1 La puesta del sol. 2 *Lah pwéster del sol.*
**Sunrise.** 1 La salida del sol. 2 *Lah sulleeder del sol.*
**Weather.** 1 El tiempo. 2 *El tyémpoh.*
**Eternity.** 1 La Eternidad. 2 *Lah ettúrrnidúd.*
**The Infinite.** 1 Lo Infinito. 2 *Loh infinnēētoh.*
**The seasons are: Spring, Summer, Autumn and Winter.** 1 Las estaciones del año son: primavera, verano, otoño e invierno. 2 *Luss estutheóness del únnyoh son: primmerváirer, verrúnnoh, ottónyoh eh invyáirnoh.*
**A good season.** 1 Buena estación. 2 *Bwénner estutheón.*
**A bad season.** 1 Mala estación. 2 *Múller estutheón.*
**Rainy, damp, dry weather.** 1 Tiempo lluvioso, húmedo, seco. 2 *Tyémpoh lyooveóssoh, ōōmeddoh, séckoh.*
**Heat, cold.** 1 Calor, frío. 2 *Cullórr, frēēoh.*
**What's the weather like?** 1 ¿Qué tiempo hace? 2 *Keh tyémpoh útheh?*

*El tiempo*

**It's sunny. 1** Hace sol. **2** *Útheh sol.*
**It's dull. 1** No hace sol. **2** *Noh útheh sol.*
**It's cold. 1** Hace frío. **2** *Útheh frēēoh.*
**It's hot. 1** Hace calor. **2** *Útheh cullórr.*
**It's raining. 1** Está lloviendo. **2** *Estár lyohvyéndoh.*
**It's snowing. 1** Está nevando. **2** *Estár nevvúndoh.*
**It's freezing. 1** Está helando. **2** *Estár ellúndoh.*
**It's a splendid day. 1** Hace un tiempo magnífico.
    **2** *Útheh oon tyémpo mugnífficoh.*
**Intense cold. 1** Frío intenso. **2** *Frēēoh inténsoh.*
**Suffocating heat. 1** Calor sofocante. **2** *Cullórr sof-focúnteh.*

---

## The time                                    La hora

**What time is it? 1** ¿Qué hora es? **2** *Keh óra ess?*
**Please tell me the time. 1** Hágame el favor de decirme qué hora es. **2** *Úggermeh el fuvvórr deh dethēērmeh keh óra ess.*
**It is exactly two o'clock. 1** Son las dos en punto. **2** *Son luss doss en poontoh.*

**Five past two. 1** Las dos y cinco minutos. **2** *Son luss doss e thíncoh minnōōtoss.*
**Ten past two. 1** Las dos y diez. **2** *Luss doss e déuth.*
**A quarter past two, two fifteen. 1** Las dos y quince, las dos y cuarto. **2** *Luss doss e kíntheh, luss doss e kwárrtoh.*
**Twenty past two. 1** Las dos y veinte. **2** *Luss doss e vénteh.*
**Twenty-five past two. 1** Las dos y veinticinco. **2** *Luss doss e vénteh thínkoh.*
**Two thirty. Half past two. 1** Las dos y treinta, las dos y media. **2** *Luss doss e trénter, luss doss e méddear.*
**Twenty-five to three. 1** Las tres menos veinticinco. **2** *Luss tress mennoss vénteh-thínkoh.*
**Twenty to three. 1** Las tres menos veinte. **2** *Luss tress ménnoss vénth.*

*El tiempo*

**A quarter to three.** 1 Las tres menos quince, las tres menos cuarto. 2 *Luss tress ménnoss kíntheh, luss tréss ménnoss kwártoh.*

**Ten to three.** 1 Las tres menos diez. 2 *Luss tréss ménnos déeth.*

**Five to three.** 1 Las tres menos cinco. 2 *Luss tréss ménnoss thínkóh.*

**It's almost three.** 1 Van a dar las tres. 2 *Vun ah darr luss tres.*

**I's three o'clock.** 1 Son las tres. 2 *Son luss tress.*

**One o'clock.** 1 La una. 2 *Lah ooner.*

**Two o'clock.** 1 Las dos. 2 *Luss doss.*

**Three o'clock.** 1 Las tres. 2 *Luss tress.*

**Four o'clock.** 1 Las cuatro. 2 *Luss kwúttroh.*

**Five o'clock.** 1 Las cinco. 2 *Luss thínkoh.*

**Six o'clock.** 1 Las seis. 2 *Luss sáyiss.*

**Seven o'clock.** 1 Las slete. 2 *Luss sẽẽ.utteh.*

**Eight o'clock.** 1 Las ocho. 2 *Luss ótchoh.*

**Nine o'clock.** 1 Las nueve. 2 *Luss nwéveh.*

**Ten o'clock.** 1 Las diez. 2 *Luss dẽẽ.eth.*

**Eleven o'clock.** 1 Las once. 2 *Luss óntheh.*

**Twelve o'clock.** 1 Las doce. 2 *Luss dótheh.*

**Midday.** 1 Mediodía. 2 *Méddea déa.*

**Midnight.** 1 Medianoche. 2 *Méddea nótcheh.*

**A quarter.** 1 El cuarto. 2 *Oon kwárrtoh.*

**Half.** 1 La media. 2 *Lah méddier.*

**A quarter to...** 1 Menos cuarto. 2 *Ménnos kwárrtoh.*

**The hands.** 1 Las agujas. 2 *Luss uggõõhuss.*

**This watch goes well, badly.** 1 Este reloj va bien, va mal. 2 *Ésteh relóh vah byén, vah mull.*

**Clock, watch, wristwatch.** 1 Reloj de pared, de bolsillo, de pulsera. 2 *Relóh deh purréd, deh bolsíllyoh, deh poolsáirrer.*

**This clock is slow, fast.** 1 Este reloj va retrasado, va adelantado. 2 *Ésteh relóh vah rettrossárdoh, vah úddeluntárdoh.*

**It has stopped.** 1 Está parado. 2 *Estár purrárdoh.*

**It's a good, a bad clock.** 1 Es buen reloj, es mal reloj. 2 *Ess byen relóh, ess mull relóh.*

**It's right. It's wrong.** 1 Es exacto. No es exacto. 2 *Ess exúctoh, noh ess exúctoh.*

*El tiempo*

## Age                                          La edad

**How old are you? 1** ¿Cuántos años tiene usted?
**2** *Kwúntoss únyoss tyénneh osstéh?*

**I shall be thirty, thirty-five, thirty-six, forty in April.**
**1** En abril cumpliré treinta, treinta y cinco, treinta y
seis, treinta y siete, cuarenta. **2** *En ubríil cumplirréh
trénter, trénter e thínkoh, trénter e sáyiss, trénter e
séutteh, kwurrénter.*

**And your father? 1** ¿Y su padre? **2** *E soo púddreh?*

**Fifty, sixty, sixty-eight, seventy. 1** Cincuenta, sesenta, sesenta y ocho, setenta. **2** *Thinkwénter, sessénter, sessénter e ótchoh, setténter.*

**And your brother? 1** ¿Y su hermano? **2** *E soo
airmúnnoh?*

**Forty-one. 1** Cuarenta y uno. **2** *Kwurrénter e ōōnoh.*

**That's a very good age. 1** Está en muy buena edad.
**2** *Estár en mooy bwénner eddúd.*

**He does not look his age. 1** No representa la edad
que tiene. **2** *Noh repressénter lah edúd keh tyénneh.*

**A quiet life makes one young. 1** La vida tranquila
rejuvenece. **2** *Lah vēēder trunkēēler rehoovenétheh.*

**That's true. On the other hand illness ages one.**
**1** Es cierto; en cambio las enfermedades envejec-
cen. **2** *Ess tháirtoh: en cúmbeoh luss enfáirmidú-
dess envehéthen.*

**How time flies! 1** Los años pasan que es un contento. **2** *Loss únnyoss pússun keh ess oon conténtoh.*

**I shall soon be twenty, twenty-five, twenty-six,
twenty-seven. 1** Pronto cumpliré veinte, veinticinco, veintiséis, veintisiete años. **2** *Próntoh ōōm-
plirréh vénth, vénteh thínkoh, vénteh sáyiss, vénteh
séatteh únyoss.*

**You are very young. 1** Es usted muy joven. **2** *Ess
oostéh mooy hóvven.*

**I thought you were older. 1** Creía que tenía usted más años. **2** *Crayēē keh tennear oostéh múss
únyoss.*

*Números*

# Numbers

# Números

**Cardinal and ordinal numbers and fractions 1** Números cardinales, ordinales y fraccionarios **2** *Noomeross cardinúlles, ordinnúlless e fructheonnárrioss*

**Cardinal numbers 1** Números cardinales **2** *Noomeross cardinúlles*

**One. 1** Uno. **2** *Oonoh.*
**Two. 1** Dos. **2** *Doss*
**Three. 1** Tres. **2** *Tress.*
**Four. 1** Cuatro. **2** *Kwúttroh.*
**Five. 1** Cinco. **2** *Thínkoh.*
**Six. 1** Seis. **2** *Sáyiss.*
**Seven. 1** Siete. **2** *Sẽẽ-etty.*
**Eight. 1** Ocho. **2** *Ótchoh.*
**Nine. 1** Nueve. **2** *Nwévveh.*
**Ten. 1** Diez. **2** *Déuth.*
**Eleven. 1** Once. **2** *Ontheh.*
**Twelve. 1** Doce. **2** *Dótheh.*
**Thirteen. 1** Trece. **2** *Trétheh.*
**Fourteen. 1** Catorce. **2** *Cuttórrtheh.*
**Fifteen. 1** Quince. **2** *Kíntheh.*
**Sixteen. 1** Dieciséis. **2** *Dyétheh.sáyiss.*
**Seventeen. 1** Diecisiete. **2** *Dyétheh.syétteh.*
**Eighteen. 1** Dieciocho. **2** *Dyétheh.ótchoh.*
**Nineteen. 1** Diecinueve. **2** *Dyétheh.nwévveh.*
**Twenty. 1** Veinte. **2** *Vénth.*
**Twenty-one. 1** Veintiuno. **2** *Vénth.õõnoh.*
**Twenty-two. 1** Veintidós. **2** *Vénteh dóss.*
**Twenty-three. 1** Veintitrés. **2** *Vénteh tress.*
**Thirty. 1** Treinta. **2** *Trénter.*
**Forty. 1** Cuarenta. **2** *Kwurrénter.*
**Fifty. 1** Cincuenta. **2** *Thinkwénter.*
**Sixty. 1** Sesenta. **2** *Sessénter.*
**Seventy. 1** Setenta. **2** *Setténter.*

*Números*

**Eighty. 1** Ochenta. **2** *Otchénter.*
**Ninety. 1** Noventa. **2** *Novénter.*
**A hundred. 1** Ciento. **2** *Thyéntoh.*
**A hundred and one. 1** Ciento uno. **2** *Thyéntoh oonoh.*
**A hundred and two. 1** Ciento dos. **2** *Thyéntoh doss.*
**Five hundred. 1** Quinientos. **2** *Kinyéntoss.*
**Six hundred. 1** Seiscientos. **2** *Sáyss thyéntos.*
**A thousand. 1** Mil. **2** *Mill.*
**Two thousand. 1** Dos mil. **2** *Doss mil.*
**A hundred thousand. 1** Cien mil. **2** *Thyén mil.*
**A million. 1** Un millón. **2** *Oon milyón.*
**Two million. 1** Dos millones. **2** *Doss milyónness.*
**Ordinal numbers 1** Números ordinales **2** *Noomerross ordinúlless*
**First. 1** Primero. **2** *Primmáiroh.*
**Second. 1** Segundo. **2** *Segóóndoh.*
**Third. 1** Tercero. **2** *Tairtháiroh.*
**Fourth. 1** Cuarto. **2** *Kwárrtoh.*
**Fifth. 1** Quinto. **2** *Kíntoh.*
**Sixth. 1** Sexto. **2** *Sextoh.*
**Seventh. 1** Séptimo. **2** *Septimoh.*
**Eighth. 1** Octavo. **2** *Octárvoh.*
**Ninth. 1** Noveno. **2** *Novénnoh.*
**Tenth. 1** Décimo. **2** *Déthimoh.*
**Eleventh. 1** Undécimo. **2** *Ōōndéthimoh.*
**Twelfth. 1** Duodécimo. **2** *Dōō.déthimoh.*
**Thirteenth. 1** Decimotercero. **2** *Déthimoh tairtháirroh.*
**Fourteenth. 1** Decimocuarto. **2** *Déthimoh kwárrtoh.*
**Fifteenth. 1** Decimoquinto. **2** *Déthimoh kíntoh.*
**Sixteenth. 1** Decimosexto. **2** *Déthimoh séxtoh.*
**Seventeenth. 1** Decimoséptimo. **2** *Déthimoh séptimoh.*
**Eighteenth. 1** Decimoctavo. **2** *Déthimoh octárvoh.*
**Nineteenth. 1** Decimonono. **2** *Déthimoh nónnoh.*
**Twentieth. 1** Vigésimo. **2** *Vihéssimoh.*
**Twenty-first. 1** Vigésimo primero. **2** *Vihéssimoh primáirroh.*
**Thirty-second. 1** Trigésimo segundo. **2** *Trihéssimoh segōōndoh.*
**Fortieth. 1** Cuadragésimo. **2** *Kwúddrahhéssimoh.*

*Los colores*

**Fractions 1** Números fraccionarios **2** *Fructheóness.*
**A fraction. 1** Una fracción. **2** *Ooner fructheón.*
**The half. 1** La mitad. **2** *Lah mittúd.*
**A third. 1** Un tercio. **2** *Oon táirtheo.*
**A quarter. 1** Un cuarto. **2** *Oon kwáirtoh.*
**A fifth. 1** Un quinto. **2** *Oon kíntoh.*
**A sixth. 1** Un sexto. **2** *Oon séxtoh.*
**Two sevenths. 1** Dos séptimos. **2** *Dos séptimoss.*
**Three eighths. 1** Tres octavos. **2** *Tress octúvvoss.*
**Three ninths. 1** Tres novenos. **2** *Tress novénnoss.*
**Three tenths. 1** Tres décimos. **2** *Tress déthimoss.*

# The colours
## Los colores

**White. 1** Blanco, blanca. **2** *Blúncoh, blúncah.*
**Black. 1** Negro, negra. **2** *Néggroh, néggrah.*
**Blue. 1** Azul. **2** *Uthöōl.*
**Sky blue. 1** Azul celeste. **2** *Uthöōl thellésteh.*
**Sea blue, navy blue. 1** Azul marino. **2** *Uthöōl murrēē-noh.*
**Green. 1** Verde. **2** *Váirrdeh.*
**Orange. 1** Naranja. **2** *Nurrúnhah.*
**Red. 1** Rojo, roja. **2** *Róhhoh, hóhhah.*
**Yellow. 1** Amarillo, amarilla. **2** *Ummerríllyoh, ummerríllyah.*
**Purple. 1** Morado. **2** *Morrárdoh.*
**Grey. 1** Gris. **2** *Greece.*
**Brown, chestnut. 1** Marrón (o castaño). **2** *Murrón (oh custúnnyoh).*
**Pink. 1** Rosa. **2** *Rósser.*
**Light. 1** Claro, clara. **2** *Clárroh, clárrah.*
**Dark. 1** Obscuro, obscura. **2** *Obsőōōroh, obsőōōrah.*
**Pale. 1** Pálido, pálida. **2** *Púlliddoh, púllidah.*

# The language
# El idioma

---

## Public notices                    Avisos públicos

---

**Look out!** 1 Atención. 2 *Uttentheón.*
**Fresh paint.** 1 Recién pintado. 2 *Rethyén pintárdóh.*
**Stop!** 1 Alto. 2 *Últoh.*
**Entrance forbidden.** 1 Prohibida la entrada. 2 *Pro-yibbēēder lah entrárdah.*
**No smoking allowed.** 1 Prohibido fumar. 2 *Proyibbē̄eder foomárr.*
**Shut the door.** 1 Cerrar la puerta. 2 *Therrárr lah pwáirter.*
**Push the door.** 1 Empujar la puerta. 2 *Empoohhárr lah pwáirter.*
**To let.** 1 Se alquila. 2 *Seh ulkēēler.*
**Free.** 1 Libre. 2 *Lēēbreh.*
**Closed.** 1 Cerrado. 2 *Therrárdoh.*
**Notice.** 1 Aviso. 2 *Uvvíssoh.*
**Forbidden to cross the line.** 1 Prohibido atravesar la vía. 2 *Proyibbēēdoh uttruyvessárr lah véa.*
**Bathing forbidden.** 1 Prohibido bañarse. 2 *Proyibēē-doh bunyárrseh.*
**Way out.** 1 Salida. 2 *Sullēēder.*
**Way in.** 1 Entrada. 2 *Entrárder.*
**Fixed price.** 1 Precio fijo. 2 *Préthioh fíhhoh.*
**Stop.** 1 Parada. 2 *Purrárder.*
**Ring the bell.** 1 Llamar. 2 *Lyummárr.*

---

## Common phrases                    Frases corrientes

---

**Good morning.** 1 Buenos días. 2 *Bwénnoss déuss.*
**Good afternoon.** 1 Buenas tardes. 2 *Bwénnuss tárrdess.*

*El idioma*

**Good evening. 1** Buenas noches. **2** *Bwénnuss nótchess.*

**How are you? 1** ¿Cómo está usted? **2** *Cómmoh estár oóstéh?*

**How are you? 1** ¿Qué tal? **2** *Keh tull?*

**Well. Very well. 1** Bien. Muy bien. **2** *Byén. Mooy byén.*

**Quite well. 1** Perfectamente. **2** *Pairféctaménteh.*

**And how are you? 1** Y usted, ¿cómo está? **2** *E oostéh, cómmoh estár?*

**And your family? 1** ¿Y su familia? **2** *E soo fummíllyer?*

**And your wife? 1** ¿Y su señora? **2** *E soo senyórrer?*

**And your father? 1** ¿Y su padre? **2** *E soo pádreh?*

**And your brother? 1** ¿Y su hermano? **2** *E soo errmúnnoh?*

**They are well. 1** Están buenos. **2** *Estún bwénnoss.*

**The same as ever. 1** Siguen sin novedad. **2** *Sēēgun sin novvidúd.*

**They are quite well. 1** Están perfectamente. **2** *Estun pairféctaménteh.*

**What did you say? 1** ¿Qué dice usted? **2** *Keh dēētheh oostéh?*

**What? 1** ¿Cómo? **2** *Cómmoh?*

**What do you think? 1** ¿Qué opina usted? **2** *Keh uppēēner oostéh?*

**You are right. 1** Tiene usted razón. **2** *Tyénneh oostéh ruthón.*

**It's true. 1** Es cierto. **2** *Ess tháirrtoh.*

**That's true. 1** Estoy seguro. **2** *Estóy seggōōrroh.*

**It's probable. 1** Es probable. **2** *Ess probúbbleh.*

**Evidently (It's evident). 1** Es evidente. **2** *Ess evidénteh.*

**You are very kind. 1** Es usted muy amable. **2** *Ess oostéh mooy ummúbbleh.*

**The certainty. 1** La certeza. **2** *Lah thairrtétecher.*

**The certainty. 1** La seguridad. **2** *Lah segōōridúd.*

**The probability. 1** La probabilidad. **2** *Lah próbbubbíllidúd.*

**It may be. Maybe. 1** Puede ser. **2** *Pwéddeh sáirr.*

**Kindness. 1** La bondad. **2** *Lah bondúd.*

*El idioma*

**Please.** 1 Haga usted el favor. 2 *Úgger oostéh el fuvvórr.*

**Don't trouble.** 1 No se moleste usted. 2 *Noh seh molléster oostéh.*

**What do you want?** 1 ¿Qué desea usted? 2 *Keh dessáyer oostéh?*

**You may rely on me.** 1 Cuente usted conmigo. 2 *Kwénteh oostéh conmḗḗgoh.*

**Thanks very much.** 1 Muchas gracias. 2 *Mō̄ōtchuss grútheuss.*

**It's nothing (No se dice).** 1 De nada. 2 *Deh nárder.*

**It's nothing (No hay contestación).** 1 No hay de qué. 2 *Noh i deh keh.*

**It'll be for another time.** 1 Otra vez será. 2 *Óttrah veth serráh.*

**With great pleasure.** 1 Con mucho gusto. 2 *Con mō̄ōtchoh gō̄ōstoh.*

**I'm at your disposal.** 1 Estoy a su disposición. 2 *Estóy ah soo disposítheón.*

**What can I do for you?** 1 ¿En qué puedo servir a usted? 2 *En keh pwéddoh sairvḗḗrr ah oostéh?*

**Excuse me.** 1 Dispense usted. 2 *Disspénseh oostéh.*

**Sorry!** 1 Dispénseme usted. 2 *Dispénsseh meh oostéh.*

**I beg your pardon.** 1 Usted perdone. 2 *Oostéh pairdónneh.*

**Pardon!** 1 Excúseme. 2 *Excō̄ōssameh.*

**Please.** 1 Se lo ruego. 2 *Seh loh rwéggoh.*

**I beg you.** 1 Se lo suplico. 2 *Seh loh soopléḗcoh.*

**What is it?** 1 ¿Qué es? 2 *Keh ess?*

**Who is calling?** 1 ¿Quién llama? 2 *Kyén lyúmmer?*

**What's that?** 1 ¿Qué es eso? 2 *Keh ess éssoh?*

**Sorry to trouble you.** 1 Siento molestar a usted. 2 *Syéntoh mollestárr ah oostéh.*

**It's no trouble at all.** 1 Usted no me molesta. 2 *Ooteh nómmeh molléster.*

**Phone me.** 1 Llámeme por teléfono. 2 *Lyúmmermah porr telléffonoh.*

**That won't do.** 1 Eso no puede ser. 2 *Éssoh noh pwéddeh sáirr.*

**It's possible.** 1 Es posible. 2 *Ess possḗḗbleh.*

*El idioma*

**What is there special about it? 1** ¿Qué tiene de particular? **2** *Keh tyénneh deh parrtícoolárr?*

**Indeed? 1** ¿De veras? **2** *Deh váirruss?*

**Are you sure? 1** ¿Está usted seguro? **2** *Estár oostéh seggŏŏrroh?*

**Quite sure. 1** Segurísimo. **2** *Séggoorríssimoh.*

**Who are you? 1** ¿Quién es usted? **2** *Kyén ess oostéh?*

**I am... 1** Yo soy... **2** *Yo soy...*

**What is your name? 1** ¿Cómo se llama usted? **2** *Cómmoh seh lyúmmer oostéh?*

**My name is... 1** Me llamo... **2** *Meh lyúmmoh.*

**Oh! Is that you? 1** ¡Ah! ¿Es usted? **2** *Ah! Ess oostéh?*

**Where do you live? 1** ¿Dónde vive? **2** *Dóndeh vēĕveh?*

**Your house? 1** ¿Su domicilio? **2** *Soo dómmithíllioh?*

**How lovely! 1** ¡Qué placer!. **2** *Keh plutháirr!*

**What a pity! 1** ¡Qué lástima!. **2** *Keh lústimmer.*

**What nonsense! 1** ¡Qué tontería!. **2** *Keh tónterréa!*

**Do you understand me? 1** ¿Me comprende usted? **2** *Meh compréndeh oostéh?*

**Have you understood. 1** ¿Ha comprendido usted? **2** *Ah comprendēĕdoh oostéh?*

**To understand. 1** Comprender. **2** *Comprendáirr.*

**I understand. 1** Comprendo. **2** *Compréndoh.*

**I have understand. 1** He comprendido. **2** *Eh cómprendēĕdoh.*

**I don't understand. 1** No le comprendo. **2** *Noh leh compréndoh*

**Listen! 1** Escúcheme usted. **2** *Escŏŏtchérmeh oostéh.*

**To listen. 1** Escuchar. **2** *Escootchárr.*

**I am listening. 1** Escucho. **2** *Escŏŏtchoh.*

**Excuse me! 1** Oiga usted. **2** *Óyger oostéh.*

**Well? 1** Oigo. **2** *Óygoh.*

**To hear. 1** Oír. **2** *Oh.yéar.*

**But... 1** Pero... **2** *Péhroh.*

**Why don't you answer. 1** ¿Por qué no contesta usted? **2** *Porrkéoh noh contéster oostéh?*

**I can't hear you. 1** No le oigo. **2** *Noh leh óygoh.*

**Please... Will you please...? 1** ¿Tiene usted la bondad? **2** *Tyénneh oostéh lah bondúd?*

**With pleasure. 1** Con mucho gusto. **2** *Con moōtchoh goōstoh.*

**If you only knew! 1** ¡Si usted supiera!. **2** *See oostéh soopyáirer.*

**It had to be! 1** Es una fatalidad. **2** *Ess ooner futtúllidúd.*

**How awful! 1** Es una cosa horrible. **2** *Ess ooner cósser orreēbleh.*

**You astonish me. 1** Me asombra usted. **2** *Meh ussómbrer oostéh.*

**Astonishment. 1** El asombro. **2** *El ussómbroh.*

**Is is possible? 1** ¿Es posible? **2** *Ess posseēbleh?*

**You are mistaken. 1** Se equivoca usted. **2** *Seh ekkivóccer oostéh.*

**I assure you... 1** Le aseguro... **2** *Leh ussegoōrroh.*

**It's natural. 1** Es natural. **2** *Ess nútterrúll.*

**Of course. 1** Desde luego. **2** *Désdeh lwéggoh.*

**Wait. 1** Espere usted. **2** *Esspérreh oostéh.*

**I'll tell you... 1** Diré a usted... **2** *Deerés ah oostéh.*

**I've got an idea. 1** ¡Se me ocurre una idea!. **2** *Seh meh ocoōrreh ooner iddáyer.*

**A very good idea. 1** Muy buena idea. **2** *Mooy bwénner iddáyer.*

**That's splendid! 1** ¡Eso es magnífico!. **2** *Éssoh ess mugnífficoh.*

**What do you think? 1** ¿Qué le parece? **2** *Keh lah purrétheh?*

**Admirable. 1** ¡Admirable!. **2** *Udmirrárbleh!*

**Delightful. 1** ¡Delicioso!. **2** *Dellítheosoh!*

**Magnificent. 1** Estupendo. **2** *Esstoopénhoh.*

**I doubt whether it's right (true). 1** Dudo que sea verdad. **2** *Doōdoh keh sáyer vairdúd.*

**Congratulations! 1** Le felicito. **2** *Leh fellitheēetoh.*

**I congratulate you. 1** Mi enhorabuena. **2** *Me enórrabwénner.*

**Happy saint's day! 1** Feliz día de su Santo. **2** *Felleēeth déar deh soo súntoh.*

**Happy birthday! Many happy returns! 1** Feliz cumpleaños. **2** *Felleēeth coompliúnnyoss.*

*El idioma*

**Merry Christmas!** 1 Felices Navidades. 2 *Felléēth núvvidudes.*

**Happy New Year!** 1 Feliz Año Nuevo. 2 *Felléēth únyoh nwévvoh.*

**It's incredible.** 1 Es increíble. 2 *Ess incrayéébleh.*

**It's very sad.** 1 Es muy triste. 2 *Ess mooy trísteh.*

**There's no doubt about it.** 1 Es indudable. 2 *Ess índoodárbleh.*

**You acted very wrongly.** 1 Ha procedido usted mal. 2 *Ah prothedéēdoh oostéh mull.*

**You have done right.** 1 Ha hecho usted bien. 2 *Ah étchoh oostéh byén.*

**May I?** 1 ¿Me permite usted? 2 *Meh pairmééteh oostéh.*

**I shall be very much obliged.** 1 Se lo agradeceré infinitamente. 2 *Sélloh úggreddétherráy ínfinééterménteh.*

**I am very grateful.** 1 Se lo agradezco. 2 *Seh loh úggredéthcoh.*

**I am very much obliged to you.** 1 Le quedo muy agradecido. 2 *Leh keddoh mooy uggrúdethéēdoh.*

**When you like.** 1 Cuando usted guste. 2 *Kwúndoh oostéh gööster.*

**As you like.** 1 Como usted quiera. 2 *Cómmoh oostéh kyáirrer.*

**It's not worth while.** 1 No vale la pena. 2 *Noh vúlleh lah pénner.*

**It's strange.** 1 ¡Es extraño!. 2 *Ess extrúnnyoh.*

**How funny!** 1 ¡Es raro!. 2 *Ess rúrroh.*

**Who would have believed it?** 1 ¿Quién lo hubiera creído? 2 *Kyen loh oobyáirrer cryaéēdoh?*

**What a shame!** 1 ¡Qué vergüenza!. 2 *Keh vairrgwénther!*

**How horrid!** 1 ¡Qué horror!. 2 *Keh orrórr!*

**How annoying!** 1 ¡Qué fastidio!. 2 *Keh fustíddioh!*

**I am glad.** 1 Estoy contento. 2 *Estóy conténtoh.*

**I'm all right.** 1 Estoy bien. 2 *Estóy byén.*

**I am happy.** 1 Soy feliz. 2 *Soy felléēth.*

**I want..** 1 Yo deseo. 2 *Yoh dessáyoh.*

**I'm afraid...** 1 Me temo (yo dudo). 2 *Meh témmoh (yo dōōdoh).*

**I'm afraid.** 1 Tengo miedo. 2 *Téngoh myéddoh.*

**I want. 1** Quiero. **2** *Kyérroh.*
**I'm surprised. 1** Me asombro. **2** *Meh ussómbroh.*
**I'm surprised. 1** Estoy sorprendido. **2** *Estóy sórrprendéédoh.*
**I wish you... 1** Deseo a usted... **2** *Dessáyoh ah oostéh...*
**I'm annoyed. 1** Estoy enfadado. **2** *Estóy enfuddárdoh.*
**I'm sorry. 1** Lo siento. **2** *Loh syéntoh.*

---

## Some adverbs | Algunos adverbios

---

**Comfortably. 1** Cómodamente. **2** *Cómmoddaménteh.*
**Intentionally. 1** Con intención. **2** *Con inténtheón.*
**Sincerely. 1** Con sinceridad. **2** *Con sinthérridúd.*
**Without knowing. 1** Sin saberlo. **2** *Sin subbáirrloh.*
**Reluctantly. 1** A disgusto. **2** *Ah dissgööstoh.*
**Well. 1** Bien. **2** *Byén.*
**Badly. 1** Mal. **2** *Mull.*
**So, thus. 1** Así. **2** *Usseé.*
**Also, too. 1** También. **2** *Tumbyén.*
**With pleasure. 1** Con gusto. **2** *Con gööstoh.*
**Rather. 1** Más bien. **2** *Muss byén.*
**Quite. 1** Del todo. **2** *Del tóddoh.*
**Jointly. 1** Juntamente. **2** *Jööntaménteh.*
**Where. 1** Donde. **2** *Dóndeh.*
**Here. 1** Aquí. **2** *Uckéé.*
**There. 1** Allí. **2** *Ullyéé.*
**Near. 1** Cerca. **2** *Tháirrker.*
**Far. 1** Lejos. **2** *Léhhoss.*
**Everywhere. 1** En todas partes. **2** *En tódduss párrtess.*
**In front. 1** Delante. **2** *Dellúnteh.*
**Behind. 1** Detrás. **2** *Dettrúss.*
**Backwards. 1** Hacia atrás. **2** *Útheer uttrúss.*
**Inside. 1** Dentro. **2** *Déntroh.*
**Outside. 1** Fuera. **2** *Fwáirer.*
**Before. 1** En frente. **2** *En frénteh.*
**On. 1** Encima. **2** *Entheémer.*

*El idioma*

**Under.** 1 Debajo. **2** *Debbúhhoh.*
**Here and there.** 1 Aquí y allá. **2** *Uckếē e ullyáh.*
**Around.** 1 Alrededor. **2** *Ulreddedórr.*
**Above.** 1 Arriba. **2** *Unếēber.*
**Below.** 1 Abajo. **2** *Ubbúhhoh.*
**Over.** 1 Por encima. **2** *Porr enthếēmer.*
**Under.** 1 Por debajo. **2** *Porr debúhhoh.*
**To the right.** 1 Por la derecha. **2** *Porr lah derrétcher.*
**To the left.** 1 Por la izquierda. **2** *Porr lah inthkya irder.*
**Onwards, Straight on.** 1 Hacia adelante. **2** *Uthea dellunteh.*
**When.** 1 Cuando. **2** *Kwundoh.*
**Then.** 1 Entonces. **2** *Entónthess.*
**Before.** 1 Antes. **2** *Úntess.*
**After.** 1 Después. **2** *Despwéss.*
**Today.** 1 Hoy. **2** *Oy.*
**Tomorrow.** 1 Mañana. **2** *Munyúnner.*
**Yesterday.** 1 Ayer. **2** *Ahyáirr.*
**Soon.** 1 Pronto. **2** *Próntoh.*
**Late.** 1 Tarde. **2** *Tárrdeh.*
**Quickly.** 1 De prisa. **2** *Deh prếēser.*
**Often.** 1 A menudo. **2** *Ah menỗōdoh.*
**Always.** 1 Siempre. **2** *Syémpreh.*
**Never.** 1 Nunca. **2** *Nỗōnker.*
**Suddenly.** 1 De repente. **2** *Deh reppénteh.*
**A long time.** 1 Largo tiempo. **2** *Lárrgoh tyémpoh.*
**Now.** 1 Ahora. **2** *Uh.óra.*
**At once.** 1 En seguida. **2** *En segếēder.*
**Enough.** 1 Bastante. **2** *Busstúnteh.*
**Little.** 1 Poco. **2** *Póccoh.*
**Much, a lot.** 1Mucho . **2** *Mỗōtchoh.*
**Hardly.** 1 Apenas. **2** *Uppénnuss.*
**More.** 1 Más. **2** *Muss.*
**Too much.** 1 Demasiado. **2** *Demmussyárdoh.*
**Less.** 1 Menos. **2** *Ménnoss.*
**Nothing.** 1 Nada. **2** *Núdder (Nárder).*
**Nearly.** 1 Casi. **2** *Cussee.*
**More and more.** 1 Cada vez más. **2** *Cúdder veth muss.*
**Little by little.** 1 Poco a poco. **2** *Póccoh ah póccoh.*
**Nothing at all.** 1 Nada absolutamente. **2** *Núdder ub-solỗōtaménteh.*

*El idioma*

**Quite. 1** Completamente. **2** *Compléttaménteh.*
**The more... 1** Cuando más. **2** *Kwúndoh muss.*
**The less... 1** Cuando menos. **2** *Kwúndoh ménnoss.*
**First of all. 1** Primeramente. **2** *Primmáiraménteh.*
**Then. 1** Luego. **2** *Lwéggoh.*
**At last. 1** En fin. **2** *En fin.*
**Quite recently. 1** Últimamente. **2** *Ōōltimmerménteh.*
**Finally. 1** Finalmente. **2** *Finnúlménteh.*
**In the first place. 1** En primer lugar. **2** *En primmáirr loogárr.*
**Before all. 1** Ante todo. **2** *Únteh táwdoh.*
**All at once. 1** A la vez. **2** *Úller veth.*
**Out of order. 1** Sin orden. **2** *Sin órrden.*
**Yes. 1** Sí. **2** *See.*
**In accordance with. 1** Conforme. **2** *Confórrmeh.*
**Also, too. 1** También. **2** *Tumbién.*
**Yes, certainly. 1** Sí, por cierto. **2** *See, porr tháirrtoh.*
**Doubtless. 1** Sin duda. **2** *Sin dooder.*
**That's right. 1** Eso es. **2** *Éssoh ess.*
**Yes, that's right. 1** Sí, es verdad. **2** *See, ess verrdúd.*
**Nothing at all. 1** Nada de eso. **2** *Nárder deh éssoh.*
**Nothing more, nothing else. 1** Nada absolutamente.
    **2** *Núdder úbbsollōōtaménteh.*
**Not even. 1** Nada más. **2** *Núdder muss.*
**Neither. 1** Ni siquiera... **2** *See sickyáirrer.*
**Neither. 1** Tampoco. **2** *Tumpóccoh.*
**Probably. 1** Probablemente. **2** *Probbúblaménteh.*
**Maybe. 1** Quizás. **2** *Keethúss.*
**Perhaps. 1** Acaso... **2** *Uccússoh.*
**By chance. 1** Por casualidad. **2** *Porr cússoo.úllidúd.*

# Models of letters and telegrams

## Modelos de cartas y telegramas

---

**Letters**                                      **Cartas**

---

**Dear Sir,**
  **Having just arrived here, I am writing to ask you to give me an interview. Kindly let me know the day and hour that it would suit you to receive me. Meanwhile.**
  **Yours faithfully,**

Muy señor mío:
  A mi llegada a ésta formulo la presente para solicitarle una entrevista.
  Le ruego me indique día y hora en que puede recibirme.
  Suyo muy afectuosamente.

---

**Dear Sir,**
  **I have been asked to greet yon on behalf of our mutual friend, Mr. X.**
  **As I shall be out of town and, therefore, unable to call personally, I must ask you to excuse my carrying out my commission in writing.**
  **Your sincerely,**

Distinguido señor:
  Tengo el encargo de saludar a Vd. en nombre de nuestro común amigo, señor...
  No siéndome posible hacerlo personalmente, por ausentarme hoy de ésta, me permito cumplir dicho encargo por medio de la presente, rogándole se sirva disculparme.
  Muy atentamente.

---

**Dear Sir,**
I was extremely sorry not to have been able to see you yesterday.
I trust to have that pleasure today, by your accepting my invitation to dine with me at my hotel, where I shall expect you at about 8 o'clock.
**Yours sincerely,**

Estimado señor:
Sentí en extremo no poder verle ayer.
Espero que hoy me proporcionará ese placer aceptando mi invitación para cenar juntos en el hotel, donde le esperaré a partir de las ocho.
Muy atentamente.

---

**Dear Sir,**
In the assurance that your many and various occupations will allow you a few hours of relaxation, I ask you to let me know whether I may have the pleasure of lunching with you this morning.
Will you please let me have your answer by phone.
**Your sincerely,**

Muy señor mío:
En la confianza de que sus diversas ocupaciones le permitirán distraer unas horas, le ruego me diga si tendré el placer de comer con usted mañana.
Espero su contestación por teléfono. Muy atentamente.

---

**Dear Sir,**
I am very sorry not to be able to accept your kind invitation. Before receiving it, I had already promised to dine with some friends.
The day after tomorrow, however, we shall have an opportunity to see each other, and shall be able to fix another day, when I shall be delighted to accept.
**Yours sincerely,**

*Modelos de cartas y telegramas*

Muy señor mío:
   Siento mucho no poder aceptar su amable invitación. Antes de recibirla había prometido a unos amigos que comería con ellos.
   No obstante, pasado mañana tendremos ocasión de vernos, y podremos quedar para otro día, en lo que tendré muchísimo gusto.
   Muy atentamente.

---

**Dear friend,**
   **When your letter arrived yesterday, I had already left the hotel, and so was unable to keep your appointment.**
   **I trust you will forgive me, and believe in my continued friendship.**
   **Yours as ever,**

Estimado amigo:
   Cuando llegó ayer su carta al hotel había salido ya del mismo.
   Por esta razón no pude asistir a la cita que me daba Vd.
   Le pido mil perdones y le ruego crea en la buena amistad de su afmo. amigo y s. s.

---

**Dear Mr. ...,**
   **I am coming to fetch you tomorrow afternoon, at about 5 o'clock, to have the pleasure of a few hours of your company. We will decide then where want to go.**
   **Until tomorrow, then,**
   **Yours,**

Muy señor mío y amigo:
   Para tener el gusto de pasar unas horas en su compañía, me permitiré ir a recogerle a su casa mañana por la tarde, a partir de las cuatro.
   Entonces decidiremos dónde podemos ir.
   Hasta mañana, pues, le saluda muy afectuosamente.

---

**Dear Sir,**
   Should you have received any letters for me I ask you to be kind enough to redirect them to me at ... Hotel, where I am at present staying.
   Thanking you for your attention,
   Yours faithfully,

Muy señor mío:
   Le agradeceré que, en el caso de que se haya recibido correspondencia a mi nombre, se sirva reexpedirla al Hotel... donde en la actualidad me hospedo.
   Con gracias anticipadas, le saluda muy atentamente.

---

**Dear G...,**
   At about X o'clock this afternoon I am going to... If you can come at that time, I shall be very glad to see you.
   Yours as ever,

Muy señor mío y amigo:
   Esta tarde, alrededor de..., iré a...
   Si puede Vd. ir a esa hora tendrá mucho gusto en saludarle su buen amigo.

---

**Dear Sir,**
   I am anxious to see you about an affair that is of great interest to us both. I earnestly ask you to let me know at what time and on what day we can meet at your convenience.
   I am staying at ... Hotel, Room No. X.
   Yours faithfully,

Muy señor mío:
   Deseo hablar con Vd. de un asunto de gran interés para los dos.
   Le ruego encarecidamente se sirva avisarme día y hora en que podemos entrevistarnos, a comodidad suya.
   Me hospedo en el Hotel... habitación núm...
   Muy afectuosamente.

---

**Dear Mr. ...,**
   I have been obliged by unforeseen circumstan-

ces to hasten my return here, for which reason I was unable to call on you, as I ought to have done, to say goodbye.

I trust you will accept my excuses and that I shall soon have the pleasure of seeing you again,
Yours sincerely,

Muy señor mío:
Circunstancias imprevistas me obligaron a precipitar mi viaje de regreso a ésta.

Esto ha sido el motivo de que no pasara por su domicilio para despedirme, como debía.

Le ruego se sirva aceptar mis excusas, y en la confianza de saludarle pronto de nuevo. Muy atentamente.

---

My dear friend.
On leaving this delightfuf spot, I must express my deep appreciation of the kindness and hospitality I received at the hands of your dear family during my stay at ...

I am anxious to be able to repay so much kindness, and trust that I shall soon have the opportunity on the occasion of a visit to this country.

Please give my kind regards to your wife and accept for yourself my very best wishes,
Your faithfully,

Mi querido amigo:
Al ausentarme de esta magnífica localidad, cumplo el deber de expresarle mi profundo agradecimiento por las atenciones y hospitalidad que he recibido de esa estimada familia durante todos los días que he permanecido en...

Estoy deseoso de poder corresponder a tantas delicadezas, y confío que se presente pronto esa oportunidad en ocasión de un viaje a este país.

Mis respetos a su señora, y le deseo lo mejor para usted. Muy afectuosamente.

## Telegrams                                    Telegramas

**Send my order ... Hotel instead of ... Hotel.**
Envíe mi pedido... Hotel en vez... Hotel.

**Objects to be sent on ... not received.**
No he recibido objetos que debía enviarme el...

**Send earliest possible ...**
**Hotel objects bought ... inst. last.**
Envíeme lo antes posible... Hotel objetos compra-
dos... del corriente, pasado.

**Send COD (c. o. d.) ... Hotel goods ordered my**
**letter ... ... inst. ult.**
Envíe contra reembolso... Hotel mercancías pedi-
das mi carta... corriente, pasado.

**Require urgently goods bought ... inst. ult.**
Urgente recibir mercancías compradas... corriente,
pasado.


# Reserving rooms

## Reservas de habitaciones


## Letters                                         Cartas

Dear Sir,
   **Please let me know by return of post the price of**
**an inner, outer room** (1).
   **Answer to ...**
   **Yours faithfully,**

---

(1)  In this letter and those phollowing, only the words in thick type that
you require should be copied.

Sr.
Señor.
   Tenga la bondad de indicarme, a vuelta de correo, el precio de una habitación interior, exterior (2).
   Sírvase contestar a...
   En espera de su contestación le saluda muy atentamente.

---

**Dear Sir,**
   **Please let me know the price of a single bedded, double bedded room with bath room.**
   **Yours faithfully,**

Sr.
Señor.
   Tenga la bondad de indicarme el precio de una habitación con una cama, dos camas, cama para matrimonio y cuarto de baño.
   Le saluda muy afectuosamente.

---

**Dear Sir,**
   **Please let me know at the earliest possible the price of a single bedded, double bedded room with bath room. It must be a room communicating with another single bedded, double bedded room.**
   **Please answer to ...**
   **Awaiting your reply,**
   **Yours faithfully,**

Sr.
Señor.
   Tenga la amabilidad de indicarme, a la mayor brevedad posible, el precio de una habitación con una cama, dos camas, cama de matrimonio y cuarto de baño. La habitación ha de tener comunicación con otra que tenga una cama, dos camas.
   Sírvase dirigir la contestación a...

---

(2)   En esta carta, y en las siguientes, cópiense únicamente las palabras en negritas que convengan.

Entre tanto recibo su contestación le saluda atentamente.

---

**Dear Sir,**
**Please let me know the price of full board for one, two persons, with a good bedroom and bath room for four, six, eight, ten, fifteen, twenty-five, thirty days, a month and a half, two months.**
**Will you please reply to ... Hotel.**
**An early answer will oblige,**
**Yours faithfully,**

Sr.
Señor.
Tenga la amabilidad de indicarme el precio de la pensión completa para una, dos personas, con una buena habitación para dormir y cuarto de baño, durante cuatro, seis, ocho, diez, quince, veinte, veinticinco, treinta días, mes y medio, dos meses.
Sírvase dirigir su respuesta al Hotel...
Le ruego una rápida contestación. Muy atentamente.

---

**Dear Sir,**
**I should like to know the price of a single bedded, double bedded room with a bath room, and the price of full board for one, two persons for a stay of four, six, eight, ten, fifteen, twenty, twenty-five, thirty days, a month and a half, two months.**
**Please reply at your earliest to...**
**Yours faithfully,**

Sr.
Señor.
Sírvase indicarme el precio de una habitación con una, dos camas, cama de matrimonio y cuarto de baño, así como el precio de la pensión completa para una, dos personas, calculando la estancia de cuatro, seis, ocho, diez, quince, veinte, veinticinco, treinta días, mes y medio, dos meses.
Sírvase contestar a...
Muy afectuosamente.

---

*Modelos de cartas y telegramas*

**Dear Sir,**
Please let me know your price for full board for two, three, four, six persons and one, two, three communicating rooms, one of them with bath room.

The room, rooms must be large and comfortable, particularly as I intend staying at your hotel for five, ten, fifteen, twenty, twenty-five, thirt days, a month and a half, two mouths.

Kindly address your reply to...

Awaiting your answer,

Yours faithfully,

Señor.
Sírvase indicarme el precio de la pensión completa para dos, tres, cuatro, seis personas, y una, dos, tres habitaciones que se comuniquen, y una de ellas con cuarto de baño.

Deseo que esta habitación, estas habitaciones sean espaciosas y cómodas, tanto más cuanto que tengo la intención de habitar en su hotel durante cinco, diez, quince, veinte, veinticinco, treinta días, mes y medio, dos meses.

Sírvase contestar a...

Queda en espera de su contestación.

Muy afectuosamente.

---

**Dear Sir,**
Please book me for the ... of this, next month an inner, outer room with bath room.

Señor.
Sírvase reservarme para el... del corriente, del mes próximo, una habitación interior, exterior, con cuarto de baño.

---

**Dear Sir,**
I regret to say that, owing to unforeseen circumstances, I shall be unable to use the room you kindly reserved for me for the ... of this, next month. It remains, therefore, at your disposal.

Yours faithfully,

Señor.
   Siento mucho comunicarle, que por motivos imprevistos no puedo utilizar la habitación que usted me ha reservado para el... del corriente, del mes próximo, y por lo tanto puede usted disponer de ella.
   Le saluda afectuosamente.

---

**Dear Sir,**
   **Owing to unexpected events, I shall not be able to use the room reserved for me until the ... this, next month. It was booked for the ... of this, next month.**
   **Please note this change that I am obliged to make, and excuse the trouble it may cause you.**
   **Yours faithfully,**

Señor.
   Por motivos inesperados no podré utilizar hasta el... del corriente, del mes próximo, la habitación que me tenía reservada para el... de este mes, del mes próximo.
   Le ruego, tome nota de esta rectificación que me veo precisado hacer, y pidiéndole disculpas por las molestias que ello le origine.
   Le saluda afectuosamente.

---

**Dear Sir,**
   **Please wire me by return if I can have, for the ... of this next month, the room that you had reserved for me for the ... of this, next month, i. e., ... days beforehand.**
   **Hoping to have your affirmative answer, for which I beg to thank you in advance.**
   **Yours faithfully,**

Señor.
   Le ruego me informe telegráficamente, a vuelta de correo, si para el... del corriente, del mes próximo, podré disponer de la habitación que usted me ha reservado para el... del corriente, del mes próximo, esto es, con días de anticipación.
   Confiando en que su respuesta será afirmativa, le anticipo gracias, y le saludo atentamente.

---

**Telegrams**                          **Telegramas**

---

**Hotel...**
**Reserve for ...** *inst, prox* **room** *one, two, double bed.*

Reserve para... *corriente, próximo* habitación *una cama, dos camas, cama de matrimonio.*

---

**Unable use before ... room booked for ...** *this, next.*

Imposible utilizar antes del... habitación solicitada para... *corriente, próximo.*

---

**Reserve for ...** *inst, prox* **room with bathroom** *one, two, double bed.*

Reserve para el... *del corriente, próximo* habitación con cuarto de baño, *una cama, dos camas, cama de matrimonio.*

---

**State by return price** *one, two, double hedded room.*

Indique vuelta correo precio habitación *una cama, dos camas, cama de matrimonio.*

---

**State by return price** *one, two, double bedded* **room with bathroom.**

Indique vuelta correo precio habitación *una cama, dos camas, cama de matrimonio* con cuarto baño.

---

**State next post price** *one, two, double bedded* **room with bathroom and** *one, two bedded* **communicating room.**

Indique próximo correo precio habitación *dos camas, cama matrimonio* con cuarto baño y habitación contigua *una cama, dos camas.*

---

**State by return price full board** *one, two* **persons.**

Indique vuelta correo precio pensión completa *una persona, dos personas.*

---

**State by return price full board** *two people, two beds, double bed,* **bathroom.**

Indique vuelta correo precio pensión completa *dos personas, dos camas, cama de matrimonio,* cuarto de baño.

---

**State by return price full board** *three, four, five, six* **persons** *two, three* **rooms communicating bath in** *one, two* **rooms.**

Indique vuelta correo precio pensión completa *tres, cuatro, cinco, seis* personas, *dos, tres* habitaciones, comunicación con cuarto de baño en *una, dos* habitaciones.

---

**Accept price yours ...** *inst, ult.* **Reserve room** *one, two, double bedded* **for ...** *inst, prox.*

Acepto su precio... *corriente, pasado.* Reserve habitación *una cama, dos camas, cama matrimonio,* para... *corriente, próximo.*

---

**Accept price yours ...** *inst, ult.* **Reserve room with bath** *one, two, double bedded* **for ...** *this, next.*

Acepto su precio... *corriente, pasado.* Reserve habitación con cuarto de baño, *una cama, dos camas, cama matrimonio,* para... *corriente, próximo.*

---

**Say by return price full board one person staying eight ... days.**

Indique a vuelta de correo precio pensión completa una persona, estancia ocho... días.

# Vocabulary

## A

**Abandon.** Abandonar *(ub-bún.donnárr)*.

**Abandoning.** Abandono *(ub-bún.dónnoh)*.

**Abbot.** Abate *(ubbútteh)*.

**Abbreviation.** Abreviatura *(ub-brévvier.tóōrer)*.

**Abdicate.** Abdicar *(úbbdic-cárr)*.

**Ability.** Habilidad *(ubbillidúd)*.

**Able.** Capaz *(cuppúth)*.

**Ablution.** Ablución *(ubblōō-theón)*.

**Abnegation.** Abnegación *(úb-negáy.theón)*.

**Abnormal.** Anormal *(únnor-rmúll)*.

**Abominable.** Abominable *(ub-bóminnárbleh)*.

**About.** Acerca de *(uctháirker deh)*.

**About.** Alrededor *(úllreddi-dórr)*.

**Above.** Arriba *(urreebúr)*.

**Abridge.** Abreviar *(ubbre-vriárr)*.

**Absence.** Ausencia *(owsént-hea)*.

**Absolute.** Absoluto *(úbbsu-llōōtoh)*.

**Absolutely.** Absolutamente *(ubbsollōōter.ménteh)*.

**Absorbent.** Absorbente *(úb-bsorbéntch)*.

**Abstain.** Abstenerse *(úbbs-tennáirrseh)*.

**Abstinense.** Abstinencia *(ub-bstinnénthea)*.

**Absurd.** Absurdo *(ubbsōōrr-doh)*.

**Abundance.** Abundancia *(ub-bundúnthea)*.

**Abundant.** Abundante *(ub-bundúnteh)*.

**Abuse.** (s.) Insulto, atropello *(insōōltoh, uttróppélyoh)*.

**Abuse.** (v.) Abusar *(ubbo-sárr)*.

**Abyss.** Abismo *(ubbísmoh)*.

**Abyss.** Sima *(sēēmer)*.

**Acacia.** Acacia *(uckússea)*.

**Academy.** Academia *(úcker.-démmea)*.

**Accelerate.** Acelerar *(uthe-llerárr)*.

**Accelerater.** Acelerado *(uthé-llerrárdoh)*.

**Accent.** Acento *(uthéntoh)*.

**Accentration.** Acentuación *(uthéntoo.uthéon)*.

**Accept.** Aceptar *(utheptárr)*.

**Accessory.** Accesorio *(úck.-thessoréoh)*.

**Acclamation.** Aclamación *(úcklúmmutheón)*.

**Aclimatise.** Aclimatar *(uck-lēēmuttárr)*.

**Acompany.** Acompañar *(uc-kómpunnyárr)*.

**According to.** Según *(se-gōōn)*.

**Acoordian.** Acordeón *(uc-kórrdeón)*.

**Account.** Cuenta *(kwénter)*.

**Accredit.** Acreditar *(uckréd-dittárr)*.

**Accumulation.** Acumulación *(uckōōmoolútheón)*.

**Accumulator.** Acumulador *(uckōōmooluddórr)*.

**Accuse.** Acusar *(úckoosárr)*.

**Accused.** Reo, acusado *(ráyoh, uckoossárdoh)*.

**Accustom.** Acostumbrar, habituar *(ukkóstoombrárr, ubbittoo.árr)*.

**Acid.** Ácido *(úthedoh)*.

**Acknowledge.** Reconocer *(reckonnotháirr)*.

**Acknowledgment.** Reconocimiento *(reckonnothimmeyéntoh)*.

**Acquire.** Adquirir *(úddkírrēēr)*.

**Acquisition.** Adquisición *(uddkizzitheón)*.

**Across.** A través *(uttruvvéss)*.

**Act.** (s.) Acta. *(úckter)*.

**Act.** (v.) Actuar *(uectooárr)*.

**Actual.** Real *(rayúll)*.

**Actuality.** Realidad, hecho *(rayúlledúd, étchoch)*.

**Active.** Activo *(ucktēēpoh)*.

**Activity.** Actividad *(ucktívvídúd)*.

**Adapt.** Adaptar *(údduptárr)*.

**Adaptation.** Adaptación *(udduptútheón)*.

**Add.** Añadir *(únyuddēēr)*.

**Addition.** Sumar *(soommárr)*.

**Address.** (s.) Dirección, señas *(dirrectheón, sényuss)*.

**Address.** (v.) Dirigir, -se *(dirrihhēēr, -seh)*.

**Addup.** Adicionar, sumar *(udditheonárr, soomárr)*.

**Adequate.** Adecuado *(uddekárdoh)*.

**Adhere.** Adherir *(údderrēēr)*.

**Adjacent.** Adyacente *(udd.huthénteh)*.

**Adjudge.** Adjudicar *(udhōō dickárr)*.

**Adjust.** Ajustar *(uh.hoostárr)*.

**Adjuster.** Ajustador *(uh.hoosterdórr)*.

**Adjutant.** Ayudante *(ah-yoodúnteh)*.

**Administer.** Administrar *(udmínistrárr)*.

**Admire.** Admirar *(údmirrárr)*.

**Admission.** Admisión *(udmisseón)*.

**Admit.** Admitir *(údmittēēr)*.

**Admonish.** Amonestar *(udmónnestárr)*.

**Adopt.** Adoptar *(úddoptárr)*.

**Adore.** Adorar *(úddawrárr)*.

**Adorn.** Engalanar, adornar *(engullunnárr, uddorrnárr)*.

**Adulterate.** Adulterar *(uddōōl.terrárr)*.

**Advance.** (s.) Anticipo *(untithíppoh)*.

**Advance.** (v.) Adelantar, avanzar *(úddelluntárr, unvunthárr)*.

**Advantage.** (s.) Ventaja *(ventúh.her)*.

**Advantage.** (v.) Aventajar *(uvventuh.hárr)*.

**Advertise.** Anunciar *(unnōōntheárr)*.

**Advertisement.** Anuncio *(unnōōtheo)*.

**Advertiser.** Anunciante *(unnōōnthe.únteh)*.

**Advice.** Consejo *(conséhhoh)*.

**Advise.** Aconsejar *(uccónsehhárr)*.

**Adze.** Azuela *(uthwéller)*.

**Aerodrome.** Aeródromo *(aháiródráwmoh)*.

**Afability.** Afabilidad *(úfferbíllidúd)*.

**Affect.** Afectar *(uffectárr)*.

**Affection.** Afición, cariño *(uffíthión, currēēnyoh)*.

**Affectionete.** Afectuoso *(ufféctoo.awsoh)*.

**Affirm.** Afirmar *(uffeermarr)*.

**Affirmation.** Afirmación *(uffeermutheón)*.

**Affinity.** Afinidad *(uffínnidad)*.

**Afflict.** Angustiar, afligir, apenar *(ungoostiárr, afflihhēērr, uppennárr)*.

**Alfray.** Refriega *(reffre.égger)*.

**Afront.** Afrontar *(uffrentárr)*.

**Afront.** Afrontar *(uffrentárr)*.

**Against.** Contra *(cóntrer)*.

**Age.** Edad *(eddúd)*.

**Aggregate.** Agregar *(uggreggárr)*.

**Agility.** Agilidad, soltura *(uhhíllidud, soltōōrer)*.

**Agitation.** Agitación *(uggitutheón)*.

**Aglutinate.** Aglutinar *(ugglōō tinarr)*.

**Agonise.** Agonizar *(uggónnithárr)*.

**Agony.** Agonía *(uggonéa)*.

**Agree.** Convenir, acordar *(convennēērr, uckorrdárr)*.

**Agricultural.** Agrícola *(uggríckoller)*.

**Agriculture.** Agriculture *(úggrikooltōōrer)*.

**Agrieve.** Agravar *(uggruvvárr)*.

**Air.** (s.) Aire *(iry)*.

**Air.** (v.) Airear *(i.ray.árr)*.

**Airport.** Aeropuerto *(aháropwáirtoh)*.

**Alive.** Vivo *(vēēvoh)*.

**All.** Todo *(tóddoh)*.

**Allege.** Aducir, alegar *(uddōōthēēr, ullegárr)*.

**Allow.** Conceder, permitir *(contheddáirr, pairmittēēr)*.

**Allusion.** Alusión *(ullōōsseón)*.

**Almond.** Almendra *(ullméndrer)*.

**Almost.** Casi *(cusee)*.

**Alms.** Limosna *(limmósner)*.

**Alone.** Solo *(sáwloh)*.

**Alphabet.** Abecedario *(úbbeh.theddárrioh)*.

**Alpinism.** Alpinismo *(úllpinníssmoh)*.

**Already.** Ya *(yah)*.

**Also.** También *(tumbyén)*.

**Altar.** Altar *(ulltarr)*.

**Alter.** Alterer *(úllterrárr)*.

**Alternate.** Alternar, turnar *(úlltaernárr, toorrnárr)*.

**Although.** Aunque *(ōwnkeh)*.

**Amalgamate.** Fusionar *(fooseonnárr)*.

**Ambassador.** Embajador *(embuhherdórr)*.

**Amber.** Ámbar *(úmberr)*.

**Ambiguous.** Ambiguo *(umbigwoh)*.

**Ambition.** Ambición *(umbitheón)*.

**Ambitious.** Ambicioso *(umbítheóso)*.

**American.** Americano *(ummericárno)*.

**Ammoniac.** Amoníaco *(ummónniúckoh)*.

**Amputate.** Amputar *(úmpootarr)*.

**Analise.** Analizar *(únnalithárr)*.

**Analogue.** Análogo *(unnálloggoh)*.

**Analysis.** Análisis *(unnúllissis)*.

**Anatomy.** Anatomía *(unnútomméa)*.

**Ancestors.** Antepasados *(úntepsuradorss)*.

**Anchor.** Ancla *(únclah)*.

**Ancient.** Antiguo *(untígwoh)*.

**Anecdote.** Anécdota *(unnécdorter)*.

**Anemia.** Anemia *(unnáymea)*.

**Anemic.** Anémico *(unnémmicoh)*.

**Anesthesia.** Anestesia *(unnestéssier)*.

**Angel.** Ángel *(únhell)*.

**Angelical.** Angelical *(unhéllicull)*.

**Anger.** Enojo, ira *(ennóhhoh, ēērer)*.

**Angle.** Ángulo *(únngōōloh)*.

**Anguish.** Angustia, zozobra, *(ungōōsteah, thothób-brer)*.

**Animal.** Animal *(únnimmúll)*.

**Animate.** Avivar *(úvvivárr)*.

**Animation.** Animación *(un-nimmátheón)*.

**Ankle.** Tobillo *(tobbílyoh)*.

**Anníhilate.** Aniquilar *(unní-dióssoh)*.

**Annoying.** Fastidioso *(fussti-dióssoh)*.

**Annul.** Anular *(únnoolárr)*.

**Annulment.** Anulación *(únnō ōlutheón)*.

**Anoint.** Untar *(oontárr)*.

**Anonymous.** Anónimo *(an-nónnimmoh)*.

**Anottier.** Otro *(óttroh)*.

**Answer.** Contestar, responder *(contestárr, respondáirr)*.

**Ant.** Hormiga *(orrmeeger)*.

**Antecedent.** Antecedente *(úntetheddénteh)*.

**Antichamber.** Antecámara *(únticúmmerah)*.

**Anticipate.** Anticipar *(unti-thippárr)*.

**Anticipation.** Anticipación *(untíthipputheón)*.

**Antipathy.** Antipatía *(úntipu-théa)*.

**Antipode.** Antípoda *(untíp-poder)*.

**Antiquated.** Anticuado *(un-tikwárdoh)*.

**Antiquity.** Antigüedad *(antig-wedúd)*.

**Antithesis.** Antítesis *(untité-siss)*.

**Anvil.** Yunque *(yōōnkeh)*.

**Anxiety.** Ansiedad *(únsear-dúd)*.

**Aperitif.** Aperitivo *(uppérrit-tēēvoh)*.

**Apogee.** Apogeo *(úppoh-há-yoh)*.

**Apostle.** Apóstol *(uppóstol)*.

**Apothecary.** Farmacéutico *(fárrmer.tháy.ootickoh)*.

**Apparatus.** Aparato *(upper-rártoh)*.

**Apparition.** Aparición *(úp-perritheón)*.

**Appear.** Aparecer *(uppúrre-tháirr)*.

**Appear.** Comparecer, parecer *(compurretháirr, purre-tháirr)*.

**Appeared.** Parecido *(purre-thēēdoh)*.

**Appease.** Sosegar *(sosseg-gárr)*.

**Appetite.** Apetito *(úppettēē-toh)*.

**Applaud.** Aplaudir *(uppláw-dēēr)*.

**Application.** Aplicación *(úp-plickútheón)*.

**Apply.** Aplicar *(upplickárr)*.

**Appoint.** Citar *(thēētárr)*.

**Apprentice.** Aprendiz *(upren-dēēth)*.

**Apprenticeship.** Aprendiza-je *(uppréndithúhheh)*.

**Approach.** Acercarse *(ut-haircárrseh)*.

**Appropriate.** Apropiar *(up-proppeárr)*.

**Approve.** Aprobar *(úppro-bbárr)*.

**April.** Abril *(ubbríll)*.

**Arbitrate.** Arbitrar *(urbitrárr)*.

**Arch.** (s.) Arco *(árrkoh)*.

**Arch.** (v.) Arquear *(árrkayárr)*.

**Architect.** Arquitecto *(arrkit-téctoh)*.

**Architecture.** Arquitectura *(árrkittectōōrer)*.

**Archive.** Archivo *(artchēēvoh)*.

**Arduous.** Arduo *(árrdoo.oh)*.

**Area.** Área *(urráyer)*.

**Argue.** (s.) Argüir *(arrgoo.-ēēr)*.

**Argue.** (v.) Argumentar, opinar, razonar, *(arrgoontentárr, oppinnárr, ruthonárr).*

**Argument.** Argumento *(arrgooméntoh).*

**Aristocracy.** Aristocracia *(úrristockrúthea).*

**Arithmetic.** Aritmética *(úrritt.métticker).*

**Arm.** (s.) Arma, brazo *(ármer, brúthoh).*

**Arm.** (v.) Armar *(arrmárr).*

**Armchair.** Sillón *(silyón).*

**Armpit.** Sobaco *(sobbúckoh).*

**Army.** Ejército *(ehháirrthittoh).*

**Around.** Alrededor *(úllreddidórr).*

**Arrange.** Arreglar *(úrreglárr).*

**Arrangement.** Arreglo *(urrégloh).*

**Arrival.** Llegada *(lyiggárder).*

**Arrive.** Llegar *(lyeggárr).*

**Arrow.** Flecha, saeta *(flétcher, sah.étter).*

**Arsenal.** Arsenal *(árrsennúll).*

**Art.** Arte *(árrteh).*

**Articulate.** Articular *(arrtickoolárr).*

**Artificial.** Artificial, postizo *(artifitheúll, postēēthoh).*

**Artist.** Artista *(arrtíster).*

**As.** Como *(cómmoh).*

**Ascend.** Ascender *(ústhendáirr).*

**Ascent.** Ascenso *(uthénsoh).*

**Ascention.** Ascensión *(usthéntheón).*

**Ash.** Ceniza *(thennēēther).*

**Ashamed, to be.** Avergonzarse *(uvváirgonthárrseh).*

**Ask.** Preguntar, pedir *(preggoontárr, peddēērr).*

**As much.** Tanto *(túntoh).*

**Aspect.** Aspecto *(usspécttoh).*

**Aspire.** Aspirar *(ússpirrárr).*

**Ass.** Asno, burro *(úsnoh, bōōrroh).*

**Assail.** Embestir *(embestēēr).*

**Assault.** Acometer, saltear *(uckómmettáirr, sulteárr).*

**Assets.** Activo, haber *(uctēēvoh, ubbáirr).*

**Assiduity.** Asiduidad *(ussidōōedúd).*

**Assiduous.** Asiduo *(ussiddoo.oh).*

**Assign.** Asignar *(ussignárr).*

**Assimilate.** Asimilar *(ussímilárr).*

**Assist.** Ayudar, secundar, presenciar *(áhyoodarr, seccoondárr, pressenthéarr).*

**Assistance.** Ayuda *(uhyōōder).*

**Associate.** Asociar *(ussóh.-theárr).*

**Association.** Asociación *(ussóhtheáytheón).*

**Assortment.** Surtido *(soorrtēēdoh).*

**Assure.** Asegurar *(usséggobrárr).*

**Asterisk.** Asterisco *(usterrískoh).*

**Astonish.** Asombrar *(ussombrárr).*

**Astonished.** Asombrado *(ussombrárdoh).*

**Astonishing.** Asombroso *(ussombróssoh).*

**Astronomy.** Astronomía *(usstronnomméa).*

**Attenuate.** Atenuar *(uttenoo.árr).*

**Atmosphere.** Atmósfera *(uttmósferrah).*

**Atom.** Átomo *(úttommoh).*

**Atrocious.** Atroz *(uttróth).*

**Atrocity.** Atrocidad *(attróssidúr).*

**Attach.** Sujetar *(soohettárr).*

**Attack.** (v.) Atacar *(úttuckárr).*

**Attack.** (s.) Ataque *(uttúckeh).*

**Attain.** Lograr *(loggrárr)*.
**Attempt.** Atentar, tentativa *(uttentár, tentuttêêver)*.
**Attend (somethg).** Asistir *(ussitêêr)*.
**Attend to.** Atender *(uttendáirr)*.
**Attract.** Atraer *(uttrráirr)*.
**Attraction.** Atracción *(uttrútheón)*.
**Attractive.** Atractivo *(úttructêêvoh)*.
**Attribute.** (v.) Atribuir *(uttribwêêrr)*.
**Attribute.** (s.) Atributo *(úttribbôôtoh)*.
**Auction.** Almoneda, subasta *(úllmonnédder, soobúster)*.
**Audacious.** Audaz *(owdúth)*.
**Audacity.** Audacia *(owdúthear)*.
**Audience.** Audiencia, auditorio *(owdyénthea, owdittórreo)*.
**Augury.** Agüero *(uggwêârroh)*.

**August.** Agosto *(uggôstoh)*.
**Aunt.** Tía *(téar)*.
**Austrian.** Austríaco *(owstriáckoh)*.
**Authentic.** Auténtico *(owténticoh)*.
**Authenticity.** Autenticidad *(owtentíthidud)*.
**Author.** Autor *(owtorr)*.
**Authorisation.** Autorización *(owtorrithutheón)*.
**Authority.** Autoridad *(owtorridúd)*.
**Authorize.** Autorizar *(owtorrithárr)*.
**Autograph.** Autógrafo *(owtóggruffoh)*.
**Automation.** Autómata *(owtómmutter)*.
**Autumn.** Otoño *(ottónyoh)*.
**Auxiliary.** (adj.) Auxiliar *(owkzillyárr)*.
**Avenge.** Vengar *(vengárr)*.
**Avoid.** Evitar *(evvittarr)*.
**Axle.** Cabria *(cubréar)*.

# B

**Bachelor.** Soltero *(soltáirroh)*.
**Bachelorship.** Bachillerato *(búlchelyerrártoh)*.
**Back.** Espalda *(espúlder)*.
**Backshop.** Trastienda *(trustyénder)*.
**Bad.** malo *(márloh)*.
**Bag.** Saco *(súckoh)*.
**Bag.** Talega *(tullégger)*.
**Bagatel.** Bagatela *(buggertéller)*.
**Baggage.** Bagaje *(buggúh.-heh)*.
**Bagpipe.** Gaita *(gáh.eeter)*.
**Baker.** Panadero *(punnerdáiroh)*.

**Bakery.** Panadería *(beiköri)*.
**Baker's.** Panadería *(punnudderréar)*.
**Balance.** Equilibrio, balance, saldo *(ékky.líbbreoh, bullúntheh, súldoh)*.
**Balcony.** Bulcón *(bullcón)*.
**Ball.** Bala, pelota *(búller, pellótter)*.
**Ball (dance).** Baile *(bý.leh)*.
**Balsam.** Bálsamo *(búllsummoh)*.
**Balustrade.** Balaustrada *(búllowstrárdeh)*.
**Ban.** Prohibición *(prohibbiseón)*.

**Banana.** Plátano *(plúttunnoh)*.

**Band.** Banda, faja *(búnder, fúhher)*.

**Bandage.** Venda *(vénder)*.

**Bandit.** Bandido *(bundēē doh)*.

**Bank.** Banca, orilla *(búnker, orríllyer)*.

**Banker.** Banquero *(buncáiroh)*.

**Banquet.** Banquete *(bunkétteh)*.

**Bar.** (v.) Atrancar *(uttruncárr)*.

**Bar.** (s.) Bar *(barr)*.

**Bargain.** Ganga *(gúnger)*.

**Bark.** Ladrar *(luddrárr)*.

**Barking.** Ladrido *(luddrēēdoh)*.

**Barley.** Cebada *(thebárder)*.

**Barter.** Trocar *(trockárr)*.

**Base.** Cimentar *(thimmentárr)*.

**Base.** Zócalo *(thóckulloh)*.

**Basin.** Palangana *(pullungúnner)*.

**Basket.** Canasta *(cunnúster)*.

**Basket (large).** Cesta *(thésster)*.

**Basket (small).** Cesto *(thésstoh)*.

**Batch.** Hornada *(orrnárder)*.

**Bathing establishment.** Balneario *(búllne.árroh)*.

**Bay.** Bahía *(by.éar)*.

**Be.** Ser, estar *(sáir, estárr)*.

**Beach.** Playa *(pláhyer)*.

**Beam.** Viga *(vēēger)*.

**Bean, broad.** Haba *(úbber)*.

**Bear.** Oso *(óssoh)*.

**Bearer.** Portador *(porrtuddórr)*.

**Beat (with a stick).** Apalear *(uppúlleárr)*.

**Beat.** Golpear, pegar *(golpay.árr, peggárr)*.

**Beautiful.** Hermoso *(airrmósso)*.

**Beautify.** Embellecer *(embéllyetháir)*.

**Beauty.** Hermosura *(airrmósóōrah)*.

**Because.** Porque *(pórrkeh)*.

**Bed.** Cama, lecho *(cúmmer, létchoh)*.

**Bedroom.** Alcoba, dormitorio *(ulcawber, dorrmittorioh)*.

**Bee.** Abeja *(ubbéhher)*.

**Beer.** Cerveza *(thaervéther)*.

**Beer house.** Cervecería *(tháirrvetherréa)*.

**Beet.** Acelga, remolacha *(uthélgger, remmolútcher)*.

**Beetle.** Escarabajo *(escúrrerbúhhoh)*.

**Before.** Delante *(delúnteh)*.

**Beg.** Suplicar *(sooplickárr)*.

**Beggar.** Mendigo *(mendēē goh)*.

**Begin.** Comenzar, empezar *(commenthárr, empethárr)*.

**Beginning.** Comienzo *(commyénthoh)*.

**Beginning.** Principio *(printhíppeoh)*.

**Behind.** Atrás, detrás *(uttrúss, detrúss)*.

**Believe.** Creer *(cray.áirr)*.

**Bell.** Campana *(cumpúnner)*.

**Bellows.** Fuelle *(fwéllyeh)*.

**Belly.** Vientre, panza *(vyéntreh, púnther)*.

**Belong.** Pertenecer *(pairrtennetháirr)*.

**Belonging.** Perteneciente *(pairrtennethyénteh)*.

**Bench.** Banco *(búncoh)*.

**Bend.** Plegar, encorvar *(pleggárr, encorrvárr)*.

**Berth.** Litera *(litterer)*.

**Beside.** Al lado de *(ull lárdoh deh)*.

**Besides.** Además *(úddimúss)*.

**Besiege.** Asediar *(usséd-deárr).*
**Bet.** Apuesta *(uppuéstah).*
**Better.** Mejor *(mehhórr).*
**Between.** Entre *(éntry).*
**Bile.** Hiel *(e.él).*
**Bill.** Cuenta, cartel *(kávénter, carrtéll).*
**Bill.** Cuenta, cartel *(kwénter, narráy).*
**Bind.** Agarrotar *(ugúrrottárr).*
**Bind.** Agarrotar, atar, ligar, encuadernar *(ugúrrottárr, uttárr, liggárr, enkwudder-nárr).*
**Binding.** Encuadernación *(enkwúddernutheón).*
**Bird.** Pájaro *(púhherroh).*
**Birth.** Nacimiento *(nu-thi.mmyéntoh).*
**Biscuit.** Galleta *(gullyétter).*
**Bishop.** Obispo *(obbíspoh).*
**Bishop's crozier.** Báculo *(búccooloh).*
**Bite.** (v.) Morder *(morrdáirr).*
**Bite.** (s.) Mordisco *(morrdis-coh).*
**Bitter.** Amargo *(ummárrgoh).*
**Black.** Negro *(néggroh).*
**Blacksmith.** Herrero *(errái-rroh).*
**Blame.** Censurar *(thenso-orárr).*
**Blanket.** Manta *(múnter).*
**Bleat.** Balar *(bullárr).*
**Bleed.** Sangrar *(sungrárr).*
**Blind.** (adj.) Ciego *(thyég-goh).*
**Blind.** (v.) Cegar *(theggárr).*
**Blindness.** Ceguera *(theggö öerer).*
**Blood.** Sangre *(súngreh).*
**Bloody.** Sangriento *(sun-griyéntoh).*
**Blow.** (s.) Golpe, porrazo, puñetazo *(gólpeh, porrút-hoh, poonyettúthoh).*

**Blow.** (v.) Soplar *(sopplárr).*
**Blue.** Azul *(uthöól).*
**Bluish.** Azulado *(uthoolár-doh).*
**Blush.** (s.) Rubor, sonrojo *(roobórr, sonróhhoh).*
**Blush.** (v.) Ruborizar, sonrojarse *(rooborrithárr, son-rohhárrseh).*
**Boar.** Jabalí *(hubbullëë).*
**Board.** Tabla, tablero, junta *(túbbler, tubláirroh, höön-ter).*
**Boast.** Jactarse, ostentar *(hucktárrseh, ostentárr).*
**Boat.** Bote *(bótteh).*
**Body.** Cuerpo *(kwáirrpoh).*
**Boil.** Hervir *(airvëërr).*
**Boldness.** Osadía *(ossud-déa).*
**Bone.** Hueso *(wéssoh).*
**Bonfire.** Hoguera *(ogháirer).*
**Bonnet.** Gorro *(górroh).*
**Book.** Libro *(lëëbroh).*
**Booking-office.** Taquilla *(tackíllyer).*
**Book-keeping.** Contabilidad *(contubbillidúd).*
**Bookshop.** Librería *(libre-rréar).*
**Bore.** Taladrar *(tulludrárr).*
**Bored.** Aburrido *(úbboorëë doh).*
**Boredom.** Aburrimiento *(ub-böörimyéntoh).*
**Borer.** Taladro *(tullúdroh).*
**Born, to be.** Nacer *(nutháirr).*
**Bosom.** Pecho, seno *(pét-choh, sénnoh).*
**Both.** Ambos *(úmboss).*
**Bottle.** Botella *(bottélyer).*
**Bottom.** Fondo *(fóndoh).*
**Boundary.** Linde *(líndeh).*
**Bow.** Lazo *(lúthoh).*
**Bowels.** Tripas *(trëëpuss).*
**Box.** Caja, palco *(cúh.her, púlcoh).*

**Boy.** Niño, muchacho *(nēē nyoh, mootchútchoh)*.
**Bracelet.** Pulsera *(poolsáirrer)*.
**Braid.** Trenzar *(trenthárr)*.
**Brain.** Cerebro, seso *(thérrebbroh, séssoh)*.
**Brake.** Freno *(frénnoh)*.
**Bramble.** Zarza *(thárrther)*.
**Bran.** Salvado *(sulvúddoh)*.
**Branch.** Rama, sucursal *(rúmmer, soockoorrsúll)*.
**Brandy.** Aguardiente *(úggwarrdyénteh)*.
**Brasier.** Brasero *(brussáirroh)*.
**Brave.** Valiente *(vullyénteh)*.
**Braveness.** Bravura *(bruvvõõrer)*.
**Bravery.** Valentía *(vullentēēr)*.
**Bravo.** Bravo *(brárvoh)*.
**Bray.** Rebuznar *(rebboothnárr)*.
**Bread.** Pan *(pun)*.
**Breadth.** Amplitud *(úmplittúd)*.
**Break.** Romper *(rompáirr)*.
**Breakfast.** Desayuno *(désser.yõõnoh)*.
**Breast-bone.** Esternón *(essternnón)*.
**Breath.** Aliento *(ullyéntoh)*.
**Breathe.** Respirar *(respirárr)*.
**Breathing.** Aspiración *(ússpirrútheón)*.
**Breeches.** Calzón *(cullthón)*.
**Breed.** Criar *(cree.árr)*.
**Brewery.** Cervería *(wairrvétherréa)*.
**Bribe.** Sobornar *(sobborrnárr)*.
**Bribery.** Cohecho *(coh.étchoh)*.
**Bridge.** Puente *(pwénteh)*.
**Bridle.** Brida *(brēēder)*.
**Briery.** Zarzal *(tharrthúl)*.

**Brigade.** Brigada *(briggárder)*.
**Brightness.** Resplandor *(resplundórr)*.
**Brilliant.** Brillante *(brilyúnteh)*.
**Bring.** Traer *(tryáirr)*.
**Bristled.** Erizado *(errithárdoh)*.
**Broken.** Roto *(róttoh)*.
**Bronze.** Bronce *(bróntheh)*.
**Broom.** Escoba, retama *(escóbber, rettummer)*.
**Brother.** Hermano *(airrmúnnoh)*.
**Brown.** Moreno *(morrénnoh)*.
**Brush.** (s.) Cepillo, brocha *(theppíllyoh, brótcher)*.
**Brush.** (v.) Accpillar *(uthéppillyárr)*.
**Brutal.** Brutal *(brootúll)*.
**Brutality.** Brutalidad *(brootúllidúd)*.
**Bride.** Novia *(nóvvear)*.
**Build.** Edificar *(eddifficárr)*.
**Builder.** Edificador *(eddifficadórr)*.
**Building.** Edificio *(eddiffitheo)*.
**Bulky.** Voluminoso *(volloominosoh)*.
**Bull.** Toro *(tāwroh)*.
**Bull (papal).** Bula *(bõõler)*.
**Bullet.** Bala *(búller)*.
**Bullfighter.** Torero *(torráirroh)*.
**Bullfighting.** Tauromaquia *(towrommuckēēr)*.
**Bunch.** Manojo *(munnóhhoh)*.
**Bunch of grapes.** Racimo *(rúthimmoh)*.
**Bundle.** Bulto *(bõõltoh)*.
**Bundle.** Lío *(léoh)*.
**Buoy.** Boya *(bóy.yer)*.
**Burial.** Entierro *(entyérroh)*.
**Bury.** Enterrar *(enterrárr)*.
**Burin.** Buril *(boorēēl)*.
**Burn.** (v.) Abrasar, arder,

quemar *(úbbrussárr, arr-dáirr, kemmárr).*
**Burn.** (s.) Quemadura *(kem-merdŏŏrer).*
**Burst.** (s.) Estallido *(estullēē-doh).*
**Burst.** (v.) Reventar, estallar *(revventárr, estullyárr).*
**Bury.** Sepultar *(seppooltárr).*
**Bushel.** Fanega *(fúnnigger).*
**Business.** Negocio *(negó-theoh).*
**Bust.** Busto *(boostoh).*

**But.** Pero *(páirroh).*
**Butcher.** Carnicero *(carrni-tháirroh).*
**Butter.** Mantequilla *(mun-tikíllyer).*
**Button.** Botón *(bottón).*
**Button hole.** Ojal *(ohhúll).*
**Button hook.** Abrochador *(ubbrótcher.dórr).*
**Buy.** Comprar *(comprárr).*
**Buyer.** Comprador *(cómpru-ddórr).*
**By.** Por *(porr).*

# C

**Cabbage, white.** Repollo *(reppólyoh).*
**Cabin.** Cabina, cabaña, camarote *(cubbēēner, cubbú-nyer, cummerrótteh).*
**Cabinet.** Gabinete *(gubbin-nétteh).*
**Cabinet-maker.** Ebanista *(eb-bunníster).*
**Cable.** (s.) Cable *(cárbleh).*
**Cable.** (v.) Cablegrafiar *(cár-blehgrúffeárr).*
**Cage.** Jaula *(hŏwler).*
**Cake.** Torta, pastel *(tórrter, pustéll).*
**Calamity.** Calamidad *(cullú-mmiddúd).*
**Calculation.** Cálculo *(cúllcoo-loh).*
**Calender.** Calendario *(cu-lledárreoh).*
**Calf.** Pantorrilla *(puntorrílyer).*
**Calf.** Becerro *(bethérroh).*
**Call.** Llamar *(lyummárr).*
**Caller.** Llamador *(lyummer-dórr).*
**Calm.** (v.) Apaciguar *(uppú-thigwárr).*

**Calm.** (s.) Calma, sosiego *(cúlmer, sossyéggoh).*
**Calm.** (adj.) Calmado *(cúll-mudoh).*
**Calumniate.** Calumniar *(cu-lloomneárr).*
**Camel.** Camello *(cummél-yoh).*
**Camomile.** Manzanilla *(mun-thuníllyer).*
**Camp.** (s.) Campamento *(cumper.méntoh).*
**Camp.** (v.) Acampar *(uc-kumpárr).*
**Camphor.** Alcanfor *(úll-cunfórr).*
**Canal.** Canal *(cunnúll).*
**Canary.** Canario *(cunárreoh).*
**Cancer.** Cáncer *(cúnther).*
**Candelabra.** Candelabro *(cundellárbroh).*
**Candidate.** Candidato *(cún-didártoh).*
**Candle.** Bujía *(boo.héar).*
**Candle.** Vejiga *(vehhēēger).*
**Candlestick.** Palmatoria, candelero *(pullmuttórrea, cun-delláirroh).*

**Candlewood.** Tea *(táyer)*.
**Cane.** Caña *(cúnnyer)*.
**Cannon.** Cañón *(cunnyón)*.
**Cannon (bilyds).** Carambola *(currumbóhler)*.
**Canteen.** Cantina *(cuntēēner)*.
**Canvas.** Lona *(lónner)*.
**Cap.** Gorra *(górrer)*.
**Capacity.** Capacidad *(cupputhidúd)*.
**Cape.** Cabo *(cárbo)*.
**Capital.** Capital, caudal *(cuppittúll, cowdúll)*.
**Capitalise.** Capitalizar *(cúppittullithárr)*.
**Capitalist.** Capitalista *(cúppittullíster)*.
**Captain.** Capitán *(cuppittún)*.
**Captivate.** Cautivar *(cowtivvárr)*.
**Captura.** Presa *(présser)*.
**Capture.** Captura *(cuptōōrer)*.
**Car.** Carro, coche *(cúrroh, cótcheh)*.
**Caravan.** Caravana *(currer.-vúnner)*.
**Carbine.** Carabina *(cúrrer.-bēēner)*.
**Card.** Tarjeta *(tarrhétter)*.
**Cardboard.** Cartón *(carrtón)*.
**Care.** (s.) Cuidado *(quiddárdoh)*.
**Care.** (v.) Cuidar *(quiddárr)*.
**Carelessness.** Descuido *(deskwēēdoh)*.
**Caress.** (v.) Acariciar *(uckúrri.theárr)*.
**Caress.** (s.) Caricia *(curríthear)*.
**Caricature.** Caricatura *(cúrricuttōōrer)*.
**Carman.** Carretero *(currettáiroh)*.
**Carnival.** Carnaval *(carrnervúll)*.
**Carpenter.** Carpintero *(carpintáiroh)*.

**Carpenter's shop.** Carpintería *(carpinterréar)*.
**Carpet.** Alfombra *(ullfómbrer)*.
**Carry.** Acarrear, llevar *(uckúrreárr, lyervárr)*.
**Carry off.** Arrebatar *(úrrebbuttárr)*.
**Cartridge.** Cartucho *(carrtōō tchoh)*.
**Cartridge-box.** Canana *(cunnúnner)*.
**Carve.** Trinchar *(trintchárr)*.
**Case.** Caso, estuche, funda *(cussoh, estōōtcheh, fōōnder)*.
**Cash.** Cobrar *(cobbrárr)*.
**Casino.** Casino *(cussēēnoh)*.
**Cask.** Casco, tonel, cuba *(cúscoh, tonnéll, cōōber)*.
**Cast.** Lance *(lúntheh)*.
**Caste.** Casta *(cúster)*.
**Castle.** Castillo *(custíllyoh)*.
**Casual.** Casual *(cússoo.úl)*.
**Casualty.** Casualidad *(cússoo.úllidúd)*.
**Cat.** Gato *(gúttoh)*.
**Catahr.** Catarro *(cuttárroh)*.
**Catastrophe.** Catástrofe *(cuttústroffeh)*.
**Catch.** Coger *(coh.háirr)*.
**Catch a cold.** Constiparse *(constippárrseh)*.
**Catch a cold.** Resfriarse *(résfreárrseh)*.
**Catch.** Atrapar *(uttruppárr)*.
**Category.** Categoría *(cútteggorréah)*.
**Cattle.** Ganado *(gunnárdoh)*.
**Cause.** (s.) Causa *(cówser)*.
**Cause.** (v.) Causar *(cowsárr)*.
**Cavalier.** Jinete *(hinnétthe)*.
**Cavalry.** Caballería *(cúbbullerréar)*.
**Cease.** Cesar *(thessárr)*.
**Ceiling.** Techo *(tétchoh)*.

**Celebrated.** Afamado *(uffermárdoh).*

**Celebrated.** Célebre *(théllebbreh).*

**Cell (prison).** Calabozo *(cullerbãwthoh).*

**Cellar.** Sótano *(sóttun-noh).*

**Cement.** Cemento *(thimméntoh).*

**Centigrade.** Centígrado *(thentígruddoh).*

**Centime.** Céntimo *(théntimmoh).*

**Centimeter.** Centímetro *(thenlerbãwthok).*

**Central.** Céntrico *(théntrickoh).*

**Centre.** Centro *(théntroh).*

**Century.** Siglo *(síggloh).*

**Ceremony.** Ceremonia *(thérremmonnéah).*

**Certain.** Cierto *(thyáirtoh).*

**Certainly.** Efectivamente *(effecteeverménteh).*

**Chain.** Cadena *(cuddénner).*

**Chair.** Silla *(sílyer).*

**Chalk.** Tizón, yeso *(tithón, yéssoh).*

**Challenge.** (s.) Desafío *(déssufféoh).*

**Challenge.** (v.) Retar *(rettárr).*

**Chamber.** Cámara *(cúmmerrer).*

**Chance.** Suerte, azar *(swáirrteh, uther.hárr).*

**Change.** (s.) Cambio, muda *(cúmbeoh, mõõder).*

**Change.** (v.) Cambiar *(cumbeárr).*

**Character.** Carácter *(curruck.tairr).*

**Charcoal.** Carbón *(carrbón).*

**Charge.** (v.) Cargar, gravar, encargar *(carrgárr, gruvvárr, encarrgárr).*

**Charge.** (s.) Cargo, grava-

men *(cárrgoh, gruvvahmen).*

**Charity.** Caridad *(carridúd).*

**Charm.** Encantar *(encuntárr).*

**Charmer.** Encantador *(encunterdórr).*

**Chat.** (v.) Charlar *(charrlárr).*

**Chat.** (s.) Charla *(chárrler).*

**Cheat.** Tramposo *(trumpóssoh).*

**Check.** Comprobar *(comprobbárr).*

**Cheek.** Mejilla *(mehhíllyer).*

**Cheekbone.** Pómulo *(pómmooloh).*

**Cheer.** Animar *(unnimárr).*

**Cheese.** Queso *(késsoh).*

**Chemist.** Boticario *(botticárreo).*

**Chemist's.** Farmacia *(farmúthea).*

**Chemistry.** Química *(kimmicker).*

**Cherry.** Cereza *(therréther).*

**Cherry tree.** Cerezo *(therréthoh).*

**Chess.** Ajedrez *(uh.heddréth).*

**Chest.** Pecho *(pétchoh).*

**Chestnut.** Castaña *(cusstúnnyer).*

**Chew.** Mascar *(muscarr).*

**Chicken.** Pollo *(póllyoh).*

**Chief.** Jefe *(héffeh).*

**Chiefly.** Principalmente *(printhippulménteh).*

**Chignon.** Moño *(mónyoh).*

**Chilblain.** Sabañón *(subbunyón).*

**Child.** Niño *(nẽẽnyoh).*

**Child-birth.** Parto *(párrtoh).*

**Childhood.** Niñez *(nẽẽnyeth).*

**Childish.** Infantil *(infuntíll).*

**Chime.** Repicar *(reppickárr).*

**Chimney.** Chimenea *(chimmennáyer).*

**Chip.** Astilla *(usstíllyer).*

**Chisel.** Cincel, formón (thinthél, forrmón).

**Chocolate.** Chocolate (chockolárteh).

**Cholera.** Cólera (cóllerrah).

**Choose.** Escoger (escohháirr).

**Chop.** Costilla (costíllyer).

**Chorus.** Coro (cãwroh).

**Christmas.** Navidad (nuvvidúd).

**Christmas Eve.** Nochebuena (nótchehbwénner).

**Chronic.** Crónico (crónickoh).

**Chronicle.** Crónica (crónnicker).

**Chruch.** Iglesia (iggléssea).

**Cider.** Sidra (síddrer).

**Cigar.** Cigarro (thiggárroh).

**Cigarcase.** Petaca (pettúcker).

**Cigarette.** Cigarríllo (thiggarríllyoh).

**Cipher.** Cifra (thíffrer).

**Circle.** Aro, círculo (árroh, thēērcooloh).

**Circular.** Circular (thēērcoolárr).

**Circulation.** Circulación (théercoolutheón).

**Circumference.** Circunferencia (theercoonferrénthear).

**Citizen.** Ciudadano (thēē.ooduddúnnoh).

**City.** Ciudad (thēē.oodúd).

**Civil.** Civil (thívvil).

**Civility.** Urbanidad (oorrbunniddúd).

**Civilization.** Civilización (thívvillithutheón).

**Civilize.** Civilizar (thivvillithárr).

**Claim.** Reclamación (recklummutheón).

**Clarity.** Claridad (clurridúd).

**Class.** Clase (clússeh).

**Classic.** Clássico (clússicoh).

**Classify.** Clasificar (clussifficárr).

**Claw.** Garra, zarcillo (gúrrer, tharrthílyoh).

**Clay.** Arcilla (arthíllyer).

**Clean. (adj.).** Limpio (límpeoh).

**Clean. (v.)** Limpiar (limpeárr).

**Cleanness.** Limpieza (limpyéther).

**Clerk.** Escribiente (escribbyénteh).

**Cleverly.** Hábilmente (ubbillménteh).

**Clew.** Ovillo (ovvíllyoh).

**Climate.** Clima (clēēmer).

**Climb.** Trepar (treppárr).

**Cloak.** Capa (cúpper).

**Clog.** Zueco (thwéckoh).

**Closing.** Cláusula (clōwsooler).

**Cloth.** Lienzo, paño, tela (lyénthoh, púnnyoh, téller).

**Clothing.** Ropa (rópper).

**Cloud.** Nube (nōbeh).

**Cloudy.** Nublado (nooblárdoh).

**Coach.** Autocar (ōwtoccarr).

**Coach.** Coche (cótcheh).

**Coal.** Carbón (carrbón).

**Coalyard.** Carbonería (carrbonnerréar).

**Coarse.** Grosero (grossáirroh).

**Coast. (s.)** Costa (cóster).

**Coast. (v.)** Costear (costeh.árr).

**Coat of Arms.** Escudo (escō ōdoh).

**Cod.** Abadejo, bacalao (ubberdehoh, buckerlōw).

**Code.** Código (códdigoh).

**Coffee.** Café (cufféh).

**Coffin.** Féretro (férretroh).

**Coin.** Moneda (monnédder).

**Coincide.** Coincidir (coh.inthiddéarr).

**Coincidence.** Coincidencia *(cóh.inthiddénthea)*.
**Coining.** Acuñación *(uckoonyútheón)*.
**Colander.** Colador *(collerdórr)*.
**Cold.** Frío, resfriado *(frēēoh, resfreúddoh)*.
**Coldness.** Frialdad *(freuldúd)*.
**Colic.** Cólico *(cóllicoh)*.
**Collar.** Collar *(colyárr)*.
**Colleague.** Colega *(collégger)*.
**Collect.** Coleccionar *(collecktheonnárr)*.
**Collecting.** Recaudación *(reckowdutheón)*.
**Collection.** Colección *(collécktheón)*.
**College.** Colegio *(colléh.-eoh)*.
**Collision.** Choque *(tchóckeh)*.
**Colour.** Color *(collórr)*.
**Colt.** Potro *(póttroh)*.
**Column.** Columna *(collōōmner)*.
**Comb.** (s.) Peine *(páyneh)*.
**Comb.** (v.) Peinar *(paynárr)*.
**Combination.** Combinación *(combinnútheón)*.
**Combine.** Combinar *(combinárr)*.
**Come.** Venir *(vennēērr)*.
**Come down.** Bajar *(buh.-hárr)*.
**Come out.** Salir *(sullēērr)*.
**Come up.** Subir *(soobéar)*.
**Comfort.** Comodidad *(commodidúd)*.
**Commandment.** Mandamiento *(mundermyéntoh)*.
**Comment.** Comentar *(commentárr)*.
**Commerce.** (s.) Comercio *(commérrtheo)*.
**Commerce.** (v.) Comerciar *(commáirtheárr)*.

**Commission.** Comisión *(comisseón)*.
**Commissionist.** Comisionista *(commisseoníster)*.
**Commit.** Cometer *(commettáirr)*.
**Common.** Común *(commōōn)*.
**Communicate.** Comunicar *(commoonicárr)*.
**Communication.** Comunicación *(commōōnicútheón)*.
**Community.** Comunidad *(commoonidúd)*.
**Companion.** Compañero, acompañante *(cómpunyáiroh, uckompunnyúnteh)*.
**Company.** Compañía, sociedad *(kómpuunyéar, sótheardúd)*.
**Compare.** Comparar *(compurrárr)*.
**Comparison.** Comparación *(cómpurrútheón)*.
**Compass.** Compás, brújula *(compúss, brōōhhaller)*.
**Compensate.** Compensar *(compensárr)*.
**Competence.** Competencia *(competténthear)*.
**Competent.** Competente *(competténteh)*.
**Compile.** Recopilar *(recoppillárr)*.
**Complacence.** Complacencia *(cómpluthénthear)*.
**Complain.** Quejarse *(kehhárrseh)*.
**Complaint.** Queja *(kéhher)*.
**Complete** (v.) Completar *(cómplettáirr)*.
**Complete.** (adj.) Completo *(compléttoh)*.
**Compliment.** Cumplido *(coomplēēdoh)*.
**Compose.** Componer *(componnáirr)*.

**Composed.** Compuesto *(compuéstoh).*

**Composition.** Composición *(compositheón).*

**Compositor.** Cajista *(cuh.híster).*

**Compress.** Apretar, comprimir *(upprettárr, comprimméarr).*

**Compromise.** Compromiso, transigir *(compromíssoh, trunsihhēērr).*

**Comrade.** Camarada *(cumerrárder).*

**Concavity.** Concavidad *(concúvvydúd).*

**Conceive.** Concebir *(conthebēēr).*

**Concentrate.** Concentrar *(conthentrárr).*

**Concern.** Concernir *(cónthairrnēēr).*

**Concert.** Concierto *(contháirrtoh).*

**Concision.** Concisión *(conthisseón).*

**Conclude.** Concluir *(concloo.ēēr).*

**Conclusion.** Conclusión *(conclooseón).*

**Concourse.** Concurso *(concōōrrsoh).*

**Concrete.** Concreto, hormigón *(concréttoh, orrmiggón).*

**Concude.** Ultramar *(ooltrermárr).*

**Concurrence.** Concurrencia *(concurrénthea).*

**Condemn.** Condenar *(condenárr).*

**Condemnation.** Condena *(condénner).*

**Condense.** Condensar *(condensárr).*

**Condition.** Condición *(conditheón).*

**Conduct.** Conducta *(condōōcter).*

**Confection.** Confección *(confectheón).*

**Confectioner's.** Confitería *(confitterréar).*

**Conference.** Conferencia *(conferrénthear).*

**Confess.** Confesar *(confessárr).*

**Confession.** Confesión *(confesseón).*

**Confidence.** Confidencia *(cónfee.únther).*

**Confirm.** Confirmar *(confurmárr).*

**Conflict.** Conflicto *(conflictoh).*

**Conformable.** Conforme *(confórmeh).*

**Conformity.** Conformidad *(conformidúd).*

**Confound.** Confundir *(confoondēēr).*

**Confused.** Confuso *(confōō ssoh).*

**Confusion.** Confusión *(confoosseón).*

**Congregate.** Reunirse *(reh.oonēērrseh).*

**Congress.** Congreso *(congréssoh).*

**Conjugate.** Conjugar *(conhoogár).*

**Conjugation.** Conjugación *(conhoogutheón).*

**Conjunction.** Conjunción *(conhoontheón).*

**Conjuror.** Prestidigitador *(prestidihhituddórr).*

**Connect.** Enlazar *(enluthárr).*

**Connection.** Enlace, relación *(enlútheh, rellutheón).*

**Conscience.** Conciencia *(conthyénthear).*

**Consecrate.** Consagrar *(consugrárr).*

**Consent.** Consentir *(consentēērr).*

**Consequence.** Consecuencia *(consekwénthear)*.

**Consider.** Considerar *(considderrárr)*.

**Consideration.** Consideración *(considderrútheon)*.

**Consignee.** Consignatario *(conséggnuttórioh)*.

**Consist.** Consistir *(conssitēēr)*.

**Console.** Consolar *(consollár)*.

**Consolidate.** Consolidar *(consollidárr)*.

**Conspiration.** Conspiración *(conspirrutheón)*.

**Conspire.** Conspirar *(conspirrárr)*.

**Constance.** Constancia *(constúnthea)*.

**Constituent.** Constituente *(constitooyénteh)*.

**Constitute.** Constituir *(constitoo.ēēr)*.

**Constitution.** Constitución *(constitootheón)*.

**Construct.** Construir *(constroo.ēērr)*.

**Construction.** Construcción *(constitootheón)*.

**Constructor.** Constructor *(constroocktórr)*.

**Consult.** Consultar *(consooltárr)*.

**Consultation.** Consultación *(consooltutheón)*.

**Consume.** Consumir *(consoomēērr)*.

**Consumption.** Consumo *(consõõmoh)*.

**Contain.** Contener *(contennáirr)*.

**Contemporary.** Contemporáneo *(contemporrúnneo)*.

**Contempt.** Desprecio *(desprétheoh)*.

**Contemptible.** Despreciable *(despréteh.úbbleh)*.

**Contend.** Altercar, porfiar *(úlltaircárr, porrfeárr)*.

**Content.** Contentar *(contentarr)*.

**Contest.** Contienda *(contyénder)*.

**Continual.** Continuo *(contínnoo.oh)*.

**Continuation.** Continuación *(contíunoo.útheón)*.

**Continue.** Continuar *(contínnoo.ár)*.

**Contraband.** Contrabando *(cóntrerbúndoh)*.

**Contract.** (v.) Contratar *(contruttárr)*.

**Contract.** (s.) Contrato *(contrúttoh)*.

**Contradict.** Contrariar *(contrúrreárr)*.

**Contradiction.** Contradicción *(cóntrerdictheón)*.

**Contrary.** Contrario *(contrárreoh)*.

**Contrast.** Contraste *(constrússteh)*.

**Contribute.** Contribuir *(contribboo.éer)*.

**Contribution.** Contribución *(contribbootheón)*.

**Contrive.** Ingeniar *(inhenneárr)*.

**Convenience.** Comodidad, conveniencia *(commóddidúd, convennyénthea)*.

**Convenient.** Cómodo, conveniente, oportuno *(commodoh, convennyénteh, opportõõnoh)*.

**Convenient.** Oportuno *(opportõõnoh)*.

**Conversation.** Conversación *(convairrsutheón)*.

**Converse.** Conversar *(convairrsárr)*.

**Convert.** Convertir *(convairrtēērr)*.

**Conveyance.** Conducción *(conductheón).*

**Convict.** Presidiario *(pressiddiúrreoh).*

**Convince.** Convencer *(conventháirr).*

**Convoke.** Convocar *(convoccárr).*

**Cook.** (s.) Cocinero *(cothinnáirroh).*

**Cook.** (v.) Cocer, guisar *(cotháirr, ghissárr).*

**Cool.** Enfriar *(enfree.árr).*

**Co-operate.** Coadyuvar, cooperar *(coh.údyoovárr, coh.-opperárr).*

**Co-ordinate.** Coordenar *(cohorrdinárr).*

**Copper.** Cobre *(cóbreh).*

**Copper-coloured.** Cobrizo *(cobrẽẽthoh).*

**Copy** (v.) Copiar *(coppeárr).*

**Copy.** (s.) Copia *(cóppea).*

**Copybook.** Cuaderno *(kwoddáirrnoh).*

**Cord.** Cordón *(corrdón).*

**Corduroy.** Pana *(púnner).*

**Cork.** Tapón, corcho *(tuppón, córrtcher).*

**Corkscrew.** Sacacorchos *(suckercórtchuss).*

**Corn.** Grano, cereal *(grárnoh, therreúl).*

**Corn (foot).** Callo *(cúllyoh).*

**Cornea.** Córnea *(córrnear).*

**Corner.** (s.) Esquina, rincón *(eskẽẽner, rincón).*

**Corner.** (v.) Arrinconar *(urrínconnárr).*

**Cornice.** Cornisa *(cormísser).*

**Corporal.** Cabo *(cárboh).*

**Corporation.** Corporación *(corrporrútheón).*

**Corpse.** Cadáver *(cuddúvverr).*

**Correct.** Enmendar, corregir *(enmendarr, corrihhẽẽr).*

**Correspondant.** Corresponsal *(corresponsúll).*

**Correspondence.** Correspondencia *(correspondénthear).*

**Corridor.** Corredor *(correddórr).*

**Corrupt.** Corromper *(corromper).*

**Cost.** Costar *(costárr).*

**Cotton.** Algodón *(ullgoddón).*

**Cough.** (s.) Tos *(toss).*

**Cough.** (v.) Toser *(tossáirr).*

**Council.** Consejo *(conséhhoh).*

**Count.** Contar *(contárr).*

**Counter.** Mostrador *(mostruddórr).*

**Countermand.** Contraorden *(cóntrerórrden).*

**Counterpane.** Colchón *(coltchón).*

**Country.** País *(pahyíss).*

**Countryman.** Compatriota *(computtriótter).*

**County.** Comarca *(commárker).*

**Couple.** Pareja *(purréhher).*

**Couplet.** Copla *(cópler).*

**Courage.** Ánimo *(únnimmoh).*

**Course.** Rumbo *(rõõmboh).*

**Court.** Galantear *(gullunteárr).*

**Cover.** Cubrir, tapar *(coobrẽẽr, tuppárr).*

**Cow.** Vaca *(vúcker).*

**Coward.** Cobarde *(cobbárrdeh).*

**Cowardice.** Cobardía *(cóbbarrdéar).*

**Crack.** (s.) Grieta *(gree.étter).*

**Crack.** (v.) Agrietar, chasquear *(uggree.ettárr, chuskeh.árr).*

**Cradle.** Cuna *(cõõner).*

**Crane.** Grúa *(grõõer).*

**Creak.** Rechinar *(retchiunárr)*.
**Cream.** Nata *(nútter)*.
**Create.** Crear *(crayár)*.
**Creature.** Criatura *(creatōō-rer)*.
**Credit.** Crédito *(créddittoh)*.
**Crevice.** Grieta, hendidura *(gryétter, endidōōrer)*.
**Crib.** Pesebre *(pessébreh)*.
**Crime.** Delito, crimen *(dellēē toh, crēēmen)*.
**Criminal.** Criminal *(criminúll)*.
**Cristalisation.** Cristalización *(cristullíthutheón)*.
**Cristalize.** Cristalizar *(cristallithárr)*.
**Criterium.** Criterio *(crittái-rreoh)*.
**Critic.** Crítico *(critticoh)*.
**Criticise.** Criticar *(critticárr)*.
**Cry.** (v.) Llorar, gritar *(lyorrárr, greetárr)*.
**Cry.** (s.) Grito *(grēētoh)*.
**Croak.** Graznido *(gruthnēē doh)*.
**Crockery.** Loza *(lóther)*.
**Crop.** Cosecha *(cossétcher)*.
**Cross.** (s.) Cruz *(crooth)*.
**Cross.** (v.) Cruzar, atravesar *(croothárr, úttruvvessárr)*.
**Crossing.** Travesía *(truv-vessēēr)*.
**Crossway.** Encrucijada *(en-crōōthihhárder)*.
**Crowd.** (v.) Agolparse, apretar *(uggolpárrseh, úpprettárr)*.
**Crowd.** (s.) Muchedumbre, multitud *(mōōtcheddōōm-breh, mōōltitúd)*.
**Crown.** (s.) Corona *(corrón-ner)*.
**Crown.** (v.) Coronar *(corro-nárr)*.
**Cruel.** Cruel *(croo.él)*.
**Cruelty.** Crueldad *(croo.el-dúd)*.

**Cruiser.** Crucero *(croothái-roh)*.
**Crumble.** Triturar, desmenuzar *(trittoorárr, desmeno-othárr)*.
**Crush.** Aplastar, machacar *(upplusstárr, mutchuccárr)*.
**Cry.** Llorar, vocear *(lyorrárr, votheárr)*.
**Crystal.** Cristal *(cristúll)*.
**Cuban.** Cubano *(coobúnnoh)*.
**Cudgelling.** Paliza *(pullsēē ther)*.
**Culminating.** Culminante *(coolminnúnteh)*.
**Cultivation.** Cultivo *(cooltēē voh)*.
**Culture.** Cultura *(cooltōōrer)*.
**Cunning.** (adj.) Astuto *(ustōō toh)*.
**Cunning.** (s.) Astucia *(usstō ōthea)*.
**Cup.** Taza, copa *(túther, cóp-per)*.
**Cupidity.** Codicia *(coddíthea)*.
**Cure.** (s.) Cura *(cōōrer)*.
**Cure.** (v.) Curar *(coorárr)*.
**Curiosity.** Curiosidad *(coo-ríóssidúd)*.
**Curt.** Rizo *(rēēthoh)*.
**Current.** Corriente *(corryén-teh)*.
**Curse.** (v.) Maldecir *(mul-dethēēr)*.
**Curse.** (s.) Maldición *(mull-dítheón)*.
**Cursed.** Maldito *(muldēē toh)*.
**Curtain.** Cortina, telón *(corr-tēēner, tellón)*.
**Cushion.** Cojín *(coh.ēēn)*.
**Custard.** Flan *(flunn)*.
**Custom.** Costumbre *(costōō mbreh)*.
**Customer.** Cliente *(clee.énteh)*.
**Customs-house.** Aduana *(uddoo.únner)*.

**Cut.** (v.) Cortar, recortar *(corrtárr, reckorrtárr).*
**Curt.** (s.) Tajo *(túhhoh).*

**Cutting.** Retazo *(rettúthoh).*
**Cyclone.** Ciclón *(thicklón).*
**Cylinder.** Cilindro *(thillíndroh).*

# D

**Dagger.** Puñal *(poonyúll).*
**Daily paper.** Diario *(de.úrreoh).*
**Dam.** Dique *(dēēkeh).*
**Damage.** Daño, avería *(dúnnyoh, uvverreer).*
**Damp.** Húmedo *(ōōmeddoh).*
**Dampness.** Humedad *(ōō meddúd).*
**Dance.** Bailar *(by.lárr).*
**Danger.** Peligro *(pellígroh).*
**Dangerous.** Peligroso *(pelligróssoh).*
**Dare.** Atrever *(uttrevuáirr).*
**Daring.** (adj.) Atrevido *(uttrevvēēdoh).*
**Daring.** Atrevimiento, desahogo *(uttrúvvimyéntoh, désser.óggoh).*
**Dark.** Obscuro *(obscōōroh).*
**Darkness.** Tinieblas *(tinnyébluss).*
**Darn.** Zurcir *(thoorthēērr).*
**Date.** Fecha *(fétcher).*
**Datum.** Dato *(dártoh).*
**Daughter.** Hija *(íhher).*
**Dawn.** (s.) Alba, madrugada *(úllber, mudroogárder).*
**Dawn.** (v.) Amanecer, alborear *(úmmer.nethairr, ullborreárr).*
**Day.** Día *(déar).*
**Day beforé yesterday.** Anteayer *(unteh.i.yairr).*
**Dazzle.** Deslumbrar *(deslombrárr).*
**Dead.** Muerto *(mwáirrtoh).*

**Deaf.** Sordo *(sórrdoh).*
**Deafness.** Sordera *(sorrdáirrer).*
**Deal.** Traficar *(truffickárr).*
**Dealer.** Negociante *(neggótheúnteh).*
**Dear.** Caro *(cároh).*
**Death.** Muerte, defunción *(mwáirrteh, defoontheón).*
**Debt.** Deuda *(déh.ooder).*
**Debtor.** Deudor *(deh.oodórr).*
**Decadence.** Decadencia *(déckuddénthea).*
**Decay.** Decaer, menguar *(deckah.airr, mengwárr).*
**Deceive.** Engañar *(engunnyárr).*
**Decence.** Decencia *(dethéntheár).*
**Decide.** Decidir *(dethiddéear).*
**Decigramme.** Decigramo *(dethiggrummoh).*
**Decilitre.** Decilitro *(dethillēētroh).*
**Decimeter.** Decímetro *(dethímmettroh).*
**Decision.** Decisión *(dethisseón).*
**Decisive.** Decisivo *(dethissēēvoh).*
**Declaration.** Declaración *(declurrutheón).*
**Declare.** Declarar *(deeklurrárr).*
**Decorate.** Decorar *(decorrárr).*

**Decorum.** Decoro *(deccórroh)*.

**Decree.** (v.) Decretar *(decrettárr)*.

**Decree.** (s.) Decreto, auto *(decréttoh, ōwtoh)*.

**Dedicate.** Dedicar *(dedicárr)*.

**Deduct.** Deducir *(deddoothéerr)*.

**Deduction.** Deducción *(deddooctheón)*.

**Deep.** Profundo, hondo *(proffōōndoh, óndoh)*.

**Deepley.** Hondamente *(onderménteh)*.

**Defalcation.** Desfalco *(desfúlcoh)*.

**Defamation.** Difamación *(diffummútheón)*.

**Defect.** Defecto *(deféctoh)*.

**Defective.** Defectuoso *(deféctoo.óssoh)*.

**Defence.** Defensa *(deffénser)*.

**Defend.** Defender *(deffendáirr)*.

**Defender.** Defensor *(deffensórr)*.

**Defer.** Retrasar *(rettrussárr)*.

**Deference.** Deferencia *(defferrénthear)*.

**Deferment.** Prórroga *(prórrogger)*.

**Deficiency.** Deficiencia *(déffithyénthear)*.

**Define.** Definir *(deffinnēērr)*.

**Definitely.** Definitivamente *(deffinnittēēverménteh)*.

**Definition.** Definición *(deffinitheón)*.

**Definitive.** Definitivo *(deffinnittēēvoh)*.

**Deform.** Deformar, afear *(deforrmárr, uffay.árr)*.

**Deformed.** Deforme *(defförrmeh)*.

**Deformity.** Deformidad *(defformidúd)*.

**Defraud.** Defraudar *(defrowdárr)*.

**Degenerate.** Degenerar *(dehennerrárr)*.

**Degeneration.** Degeneración *(dehénnerrútheón)*.

**Degrade.** Degradar *(degruddárr)*.

**Deign.** Dignarse *(dignárrseh)*.

**Delay.** Tardar *(tarrdárr)*.

**Delegate.** (v.) Delegar *(dellegárr)*.

**Delegate.** (s.) Delegado *(dellegárdoh)*.

**Deliberately.** Deliberadamente *(dillíberrárderménteh)*.

**Delicious.** Delicioso *(dellitheóssoh)*.

**Delight.** (v.) Deleitar *(delláyittárr)*.

**Delight.** (s.) Deleite *(delláy.itteh)*.

**Delirium.** Delirio *(dellírreoh)*.

**Deliver.** Entregar *(entreggárr)*.

**Demolish.** Derribar, demoler *(derribárr, demmolláirr)*.

**Demon.** Demonio *(demmónneoh)*.

**Demonstrate.** Demostrar *(demmostrárr)*.

**Demoralize.** Desmoralizar *(des.moralithárr)*.

**Den.** Guarida *(gwurrēērr)*.

**Denominate.** Denominar *(dennómminnárr)*.

**Denote.** Denotar *(dennottárr)*.

**Density.** Densidad *(densiddúd)*.

**Dentist.** Dentista *(dentíster)*.

**Denunciation.** Denuncia *(dennōōnthea)*.

**Deny.** Negar *(neggárr)*.

**Depart.** Partir *(parrtēērr)*.

**Department.** Departamento *(depárrterménteh)*.

**Departure.** Partida *(parrtēē der)*.

**Depend.** Depender *(deppendáirr)*.

**Dependence.** Dependencia *(deppendénthear)*.

**Deplorable.** Deplorable *(déplorrúbbleh)*.

**Deplore.** Deplorar *(deplorrárr)*.

**Depopulate.** Despoblar *(despoblárr)*.

**Deposit.** (v.) Depositar *(deppóssitárr)*.

**Deposit.** (s.) Depósito *(deppóssittoh)*.

**Depth.** Profundidad *(proffoondiddúd)*.

**Deputation.** Diputación *(dippuotaytheón)*.

**Deputy.** Diputado *(dippootárdoh)*.

**Derive.** Derivar *(derrivárr)*.

**Desert.** Desierto *(dessyáirtoh)*.

**Deserve.** Merecer *(merretháirr)*.

**Design.** Designio *(dessígneoh)*.

**Desire.** Gana *(gúnner)*.

**Desirous.** Deseoso *(dessay.óssoh)*.

**Desist.** Desistir *(dessistēēr)*.

**Desolation.** Desolación *(déssollutheón)*.

**Despair.** (s.) Desesperación *(dessesperrútheón)*.

**Despair.** (v.) Desesperar *(déssesperrárr)*.

**Despise.** Despreciar *(despretheárr)*.

**Despoil.** Despojar *(despoh.hárr)*.

**Dessert.** Postre *(póstreh)*.

**Destination.** Destino *(destēēnoh)*.

**Destine.** Destinar *(destinárr)*.

**Destiny.** Destino *(destēēnoh)*.

**Destroy.** Destrozar, destruir *(destrothárr, destroo.ēēr)*.

**Destruction.** Destrucción *(desstrōōck.theón)*.

**Defail.** Detalle, pormenor *(detúllyeh, porrmennorr)*.

**Detention.** Detención *(dettentheón)*.

**Determination.** Determinación *(dettáirrmiunútheón)*.

**Determine.** Determinar *(dettáirrminnár)*.

**Determined.** Determinado *(dettáirrminnárdoh)*.

**Detestable.** Detestable *(dettestúbbleh)*.

**Development.** Desarrollo *(déssurrólyoh)*.

**Deviate.** Desviar *(desvee.-árr)*.

**Deviation.** Extravío *(extrúvvioh)*.

**Devil.** Diablo *(dyúbloh)*.

**Devolution.** Devolución *(dévvollootheón)*.

**Devour.** Devorar *(dévvorrár)*.

**Dew.** Rocío *(rothéoh)*.

**Diagram.** Diagrama *(deargrúmmer)*.

**Dial.** Cuadrante *(kwudrúnteh)*.

**Dialect.** Dialecto *(dearléctoh)*.

**Dialogue.** Diálogo *(de.úllagoh)*.

**Diameter.** Diámetro *(de.úmmetroh)*.

**Dictate.** Dictar *(dictárr)*.

**Dictionary.** Diccionario *(díctheonnárreoh)*.

**Die.** (s.) Cuño *(cōōnyoh)*.

**Die.** (v.) Fallecer, morir *(fullyetháirr, morrēērr)*.

**Difference.** Diferencia *(differénthear)*.

**Difficult.** Difícil *(diffēēthill).*

**Difficulty.** Dificultad *(difficooltúd).*

**Diffuse.** Difundir *(diffondēēr).*

**Difussion.** Difusión *(diffoosseón).*

**Dig.** Cavar *(cuvvárr).*

**Digest.** Digerir *(dihherrēēr).*

**Dignity.** Dignidad *(digniddúd).*

**Dilatation.** Dilatación *(dillutútheón).*

**Dilate.** Dilatar *(dilluttárr).*

**Dilation.** Dilación *(dillutheón).*

**Diligence.** Diligencia *(dillihhénthea).*

**Diligent.** Diligente *(díllihhénteh).*

**Dimention.** Dimensión *(dimménseón).*

**Diminish.** Disminuir *(dismínnoo.ēēr).*

**Dine.** Comer *(commáirr).*

**Diplomacy.** Diplomacia *(diplommúthea).*

**Diptych.** Díptico *(díptickoh).*

**Direct.** (adj.) Directo *(dirréctoh).*

**Direct.** (v.) Dirigir *(dirrehhēēr).*

**Direction.** Dirección *(dirrectheón).*

**Director.** Director *(dirrectórr).*

**Directress.** Directriz *(dirrectrēēth).*

**Dirty.** (adj.) Sucio *(sōōtheoh).*

**Dirty.** (v.) Ensuciar *(ensootehárr).*

**Disadvantage.** Desventaja *(desventúh.her).*

**Disagreable.** Desagradable *(déssuggrudúbbleh).*

**Disagreement.** Desacuerdo *(désser.quáredoh).*

**Disappear.** Desaparecer *(déssuppúrretháirr).*

**Disarrange.** Desarreglar *(déssurreglárr).*

**Disaster.** Desastre *(dessústreh).*

**Disastrous.** Desastroso *(dissustróssoh).*

**Discharge.** Despedir *(despeddēērr).*

**Disciple.** Discípulo *(disthíppooloh).*

**Discipline.** Disciplina *(disthipplēēner).*

**Discourage.** Desanimar *(dessunnimárr).*

**Discouragement.** Desaliento *(déssullyéntoh).*

**Discourse.** Discurso *(discōōrrsoh).*

**Discrect.** Discreto *(discréttoh).*

**Discretion.** Discreción *(discretheón).*

**Discuss.** Discutir *(discootēēr).*

**Disease.** Dolencia *(dollénthea).*

**Disentangle.** Desenredar *(déssenreddárr).*

**Disfigure.** Desfigurar *(desfiggoorárr).*

**Disguise.** Disfraz *(disfrúth).*

**Disgust.** (v.) Disgustar, dar asco *(disgoostárr, darr úskoh).*

**Disgust.** (s.) Disgusto, asco *(disgōōstoh, úscoh).*

**Disgusting.** Asqueroso *(uskerróssoh).*

**Dish cloth.** Estropajo *(estroppúhhoh).*

**Dishearten.** Desanimar *(déssunnimárr).*

**Dishonour.** (v.) Deshonrar *(dessonrárr).*

**Dishonour.** (s.) Deshonra *(dessónrah).*

**Disimulate.** Disimular *(dissimmoolárr).*
**Disimulation.** Disimulación *(dissimmoolutheón).*
**Disinter.** Desenterrar *(dessenterrárr).*
**Disinterestedness.** Desinterés *(dessinterréss).*
**Disk.** Disco *(dískoh).*
**Disloyal.** Desleal *(deslay.-úll).*
**Dismal.** Funesto *(foonéstoh).*
**Dismantle.** Arrasar *(urrussárr).*
**Dismount.** Apear *(úppeh.árr).*
**Disobey.** Desobedecer *(désobbéddetháirr).*
**Disolved.** Disuelto *(diswéltoh).*
**Disorder.** (v.) Desordenar *(dessorrdenárr).*
**Disorder.** (s.) Desorden *(dessórrden).*
**Disorient.** Desorientar *(déssórientárr).*
**Dispatch.** Despachar, expedir *(desputchárr, eckspeddéérr).*
**Dispel.** Disipar *(dissippárr).*
**Displease.** Desagradar *(déssugruddárr).*
**Dispose.** Disponer *(díspornáir).*
**Disposition.** Dispasición *(disspossitheón).*
**Disregard.** Desairar *(déssah.irrárr).*
**Disrespect.** Desaire *(dessáheereh).*
**Distance.** Distancia *(distúnthea).*
**Distant.** Lejano *(lehhúnnoh).*
**Distinct.** Distinto *(distíntoh).*
**Distinction.** Distinción *(distintheón).*
**Distinctive.** Distintivo *(distintēēvoh).*

**Distinguish.** Distinguir *(distinghēēr).*
**Distract.** Distraer *(distrah.-áirr).*
**Distraction.** Distracción *(distrúctheón).*
**Distribute.** Distribuir repartir *(distriboo.ēērr, reparrtēēr).*
**Distribution.** Distribución *(distribbotheón).*
**Disturb.** Estorbar, molestar, incomodar, perturbar, turbar *(esstorrbárr, mollestárr, incommoddárr, pairrtoorbárr, toorbárr).*
**Ditch.** Zanja *(thúnher).*
**Diver.** Buzo *(bōōthoh).*
**Diversion.** Diversión *(divváirrsee.ón).*
**Diversity.** Diversidad *(divváirrsiddúd).*
**Divide.** Dividir *(divvidēērr).*
**Divinity.** Divinidad *(divvinnidúd).*
**Division.** División *(divvisseón).*
**Do.** Hacer *(utháirr).*
**Doctor.** Doctor *(doctórr).*
**Doctrine.** Doctrina *(doctrēēner).*
**Document.** Documento *(dockooaméntoh).*
**Dog.** Perro *(pérroh).*
**Domestic.** Doméstico *(dommésticoh).*
**Domicile.** Domicilio *(dommithíllioh).*
**Dominical.** Dominical *(domminnicúll).*
**Dominion.** Dominio *(dommínnioh).*
**Done.** Hecho *(étchoh).*
**Donkey.** Borrico *(borrēēékoh).*
**Door.** Puerta *(pwáirrter).*
**Dose.** Dosis *(dóssiss).*
**Double.** Doblar, redoblar *(dobblárr, reddoblárr).*

**Doubt.** (s.) Duda *(dõõder).*
**Doubt.** (v.) Dudar *(doodárr).*
**Dove.** Paloma, tórtola *(pullómmer, tórrtoller).*
**Downfail.** Hundimiento *(oondimyéntoh).*
**Dozen.** Docena *(dothénner).*
**Draft, rough copy.** Borrador *(borrerdórr).*
**Drag.** Arrastrar *(urrustrárr).*
**Drama.** Drama *(drármer).*
**Draw.** (s.) Cajón *(cuh.hón).*
**Draw.** (v.) Dibujar *(dibbõõhhárr).*
**Drawing.** Dibujo *(dibbõõhhoh).*
**Draw lots.** Sortear *(sorrteh.-árr).*
**Dream.** Soñar *(sonyárr).*
**Drench.** Empapar *(empuppárr).*
**Dress.** (s.) Vestido *(vestēdoh).*
**Dress.** (v.) Enderezar *(endérrithárr).*
**Drinkable.** Potable *(pottúbbleh).*
**Drive.** Conducir *(condoothéar).*
**Drivel.** (s.) Baba *(báber).*
**Drivel.** Babear *(bubbeárr).*

**Driver** **(tram).** Maquinista *(muckinníster).*
**Drop.** Gota *(gótter).*
**Dross.** Escoria *(escórrear).*
**Drown.** Ahogar *(uh.oggár).*
**Drug.** Droga *(drãwger).*
**Drum.** Tambor *(tumbórr).*
**Drunk.** Borracho *(borrútchoh).*
**Drunkennes.** Borrachera *(borrútcháirrer).*
**Dry.** (adj.) Seco *(séckoh).*
**Dry.** (v.) Secar *(seckárr).*
**Duel.** Duelo *(doo.élloh).*
**Dull.** Sombrío *(sombréoh).*
**Dullness.** Torpeza *(torrpéther).*
**Dumb.** Mudo *(mõõdoh).*
**Durable.** Duradero *(dõõrer.-dáirroh).*
**Duration.** Duración *(docrutheón).*
**Dust.** Polvo *(pólvoh).*
**Dust cloud.** Polvareda *(polvurrédder).*
**Duty.** Deber *(debbáirr).*
**Dwelling.** Vivienda *(vivyénder).*
**Dye.** Teñir *(tenyẽarr).*
**Dyer.** Tintorero *(tintorráirroh).*
**Dyer's.** Tintorería *(tintorrerrẽẽr).*

# E

**Eagerness.** Afán *(uffún).*
**Ear.** Oreja *(orréhher).*
**Ear (corn).** Espiga *(espẽẽgher).*
**Early.** Temprano *(temprúnnoh).*
**Earth.** Tierra *(tyáirrer).*
**Earthly.** Terreno *(terrénnoh).*
**Earthquake.** Terremoto *(terrehmóttoh).*
**Easily.** Fácilmente *(fúthilménteh).*

**East.** Este *(ésteh).*
**Easter.** Pascua *(púskwer).*
**Easy.** Fácil *(fútheel).*
**Eat.** Comer *(commáirr).*
**Ebony.** Ébano *(ébunnoh).*
**Ebullition.** Ebullición *(ebboolitheón).*
**Eclipsar.** Eclipsar *(ecklipsárr).*
**Economical.** Económico *(eckonnómmicoh).*
**Economy.** Economía *(eckonnomméa).*

**Ecstasy.** Éxtasis *(éckstussis).*

**Edge.** Filo, borde *(fēēloh bórrdeh).*

**Editing office.** Redacción *(reddutheón).*

**Edition.** Edición *(edditheón).*

**Education.** Educación *(eddoocutheón).*

**Effective.** Eficaz *(efficúth).*

**Effectiveness.** Eficacia *(efficúthea).*

**Effort.** Esfuerzo *(esfwáirrthoh).*

**Egg.** Huevo *(wévvoh).*

**Eight.** Ocho *(ótchoh).*

**Eighth.** Octavo *(octárvoh).*

**Eighty.** Ochenta *(otchénter).*

**Elect.** Elegir *(ellihēērr).*

**Electricity.** Electricidad *(electrithidúd).*

**Electromotor.** Electromotor *(ellectrommotórr).*

**Elegance.** Elegancia *(ellegúnthea).*

**Elephant.** Elefante *(elleffúnteh).*

**Elevate.** Elevar *(ellevárr).*

**Elevation.** Elevación *(ellevutheón).*

**Eleven.** Once *(óntheh).*

**Eleventh.** Undécimo *(oondéthimmoh).*

**Eliminate.** Eliminar *(elimminnárr).*

**Emancipate.** Emancipar *(emmunthippárr).*

**Embalm.** Embalsamar *(embúlsummárr).*

**Embaress.** Embarazar *(embúrrerthárr).*

**Embark.** Embarcar *(embarrcárr).*

**Embellish.** Embellecer *(embélletháirr).*

**Embrace.** (v.) Abrazar *(úhbruthárr).*

**Embrace.** (s.) Abrazo *(ubbrúthoh).*

**Embryo.** Embrión *(embreón).*

**Emerald.** Esmeralda *(esmerrúlder).*

**Emetic.** Vomitivo *(vommittēēvoh).*

**Emigrant.** Emigrante *(emmigrúnteh).*

**Emigrate.** Emigrar *(emmígrárr).*

**Eminence.** Eminencia *(emminnénthea).*

**Eminent.** Eminente *(emminnénteh).*

**Emissary.** Emisario *(emmissárreoh).*

**Employ.** Emplear *(emplayárr).*

**Employment.** Empleo *(empláyoh).*

**Empty.** (adj.) Vacío *(vuthéoh).*

**Empty.** (v.) Vaciar *(vuthiárr).*

**Enable.** Habilitar *(ubbillitárr).*

**Enamel.** Esmalte *(esmúlteh).*

**Enchant.** Encantar *(encuntárr).*

**Encourage.** Alentar *(ullentárr).*

**Encyclopaedia.** Enciclopedia *(entheecloppéddea).*

**End.** Fin *(fin).*

**Endorse.** Endosar *(endossárr).*

**Endorsement.** Endoso *(endóssoh).*

**Enemy.** Enemigo *(ennimēēgoh).*

**Energy.** Energía *(ennerrhéar).*

**Engage.** Comprometer *(cómprommettáirr).*

**Engagement.** Compromiso *(comprommíssoh).*

**English.** Inglés *(ingléss).*

**Engrave.** Grabar *(grubbárr).*

**Engraver.** Grabador *(grúbberdórr).*

**Engraving.** Grabado *(grub-bárdoh).*

**Enigma.** Enigma *(enigma).*

**Enigmatic.** Enigmático *(enig-mútticoh).*

**Enjoy.** Disfrutar, gozar *(dis-frootárr, gothárr).*

**Enjoyment.** Gozo, goce *(gó-thoh, gótheh).*

**Enlarge.** Agrandar *(uggrun-dárr).*

**Enlist.** Alistar *(ullistárr).*

**Enmity.** Enemistad *(enne-mistúd).*

**Ennunciate.** Enunciar *(en-noutheárr).*

**Enormity.** Enormidad *(ennórr-midúd).*

**Enormous.** Enorme *(ennórr-meh).*

**Enrich.** Enriquecer *(enric-ketháirr).*

**Enslave.** Esclavizar *(esluv-vithárr).*

**Entangle.** Embrollar, enredar *(embrolyárr, enreddárr).*

**Entanglement.** Enredo *(en-réddoh).*

**Enter.** Entrar *(entrárr).*

**Entertain.** Entretener *(éntre-tenáairr).*

**Enthusiasm.** Entusiasmo *(entoosiúsmoh).*

**Entire.** Íntegro *(ínteggroh).*

**Entrance.** Entrada *(entrár-der).*

**Entrench.** Atrincherar *(uttrín-cherárr).*

**Enumeration.** Enumeración *(ennoomerrutheón).*

**Envelope.** Sobre *(sóbbreh).*

**Epidemic.** Epidemia *(éppi-ddémmea).*

**Epigram.** Epigrama *(eppí-grummer).*

**Epigraph.** Epígrafe *(eppí-gruffeh).*

**Epilogue.** Epílogo *(eppíllo-gooh).*

**Episode.** Episodio *(eppis-sóddio).*

**Epistle.** Epístola *(eppístoller).*

**Epoch.** Época *(éppocker).*

**Equal.** Igual *(iggwúll).*

**Equality.** Igualdad *(igwull-dúd).*

**Equation.** Ecuación *(eckwu-theón).*

**Equator.** Ecuador *(eckwud-dórr).*

**Equatorial.** Ecuatorial *(eck-wuttoriúll).*

**Equilibrium.** Equilibrío *(ek-killíbreoh).*

**Equitable.** Equitativo *(ékkit-tuteêêvoh).*

**Equivalent.** Equivalente *(ekkí-vvullénteh).*

**Era.** Era *(áirer).*

**Err.** Errar *(errárr).*

**Escape.** (v.) Escapar *(es-cuppárr).*

**Escape.** (s.) Escape *(escúp-peh).*

**Essence.** Esencia *(essén-thear).*

**Establishment.** Establecimiento *(estúblethimyéntoh).*

**Estale.** Hacienda, finca *(uthyénder, fínker).*

**Esteem.** Estimar *(estim-márr).*

**Estimable.** Estimable *(es-timmúbbleh).*

**Estimate.** Presupuesto *(pre-ssoopwéstoh).*

**Eternal.** Eterno *(ettáirrmoh).*

**Eternity.** Eternidad *(ettáirr-niddúd).*

**Ether.** Éter *(éttairr).*

**Etiquette.** Etiqueta *(ettikét-ter).*

**Evaporation.** Evaporación *(evvúpporrútheón).*

**Eve.** Víspera *(víssperreer)*.

**Evening's entertainment.** Velada *(vellúdder)*.

**Evenness.** Llaneza *(lyunnéther)*.

**Event.** Acontecimiento, suceso *(uckontéthemyéntoh, soothéssoh)*.

**Eventual.** Eventual *(evvéntooúll)*.

**Eventuality.** Eventualidad *(evvéntoo.ullidúd)*.

**Everything.** Todo *(tóddoh)*.

**Evidence.** Evidencia *(evviddénthea)*.

**Evident.** Evidente *(evviddénteh)*.

**Evil.** Mal *(mull)*.

**Exact.** (v.) Exhibir *(exihbēēr)*.

**Exact.** (adj.) Exacto, cabal *(exúctoh, cubbúll)*.

**Exactitude.** Exactitud *(eckzúcktitōōd)*.

**Exagerate.** Exagerar *(exúhhairrárr)*.

**Exageration.** Exageración *(exúhhairrrútheón)*.

**Examination.** Examen *(exumen)*.

**Examine.** Examinar *(exummennárr)*.

**Example.** Ejemplo *(ehhémploh)*.

**Exceed.** Sobrar *(sobbrárr)*.

**Excellent.** Excelente, sobresaliente *(exthellénteh, sobbrehsullyénteh)*.

**Except.** (v.) Exceptuar *(exthéptoo.árr)*.

**Except.** (prep.) Excepto *(exthéptoh)*.

**Exception.** Excepción *(exthéptheón)*.

**Excess.** Exceso *(exthéssoh)*.

**Excessive.** Excesivo *(exthesēēvoh)*.

**Excite.** Excitar *(exthettárr)*.

**Exclaim.** Exclamar *(exclummárr)*.

**Exclusive.** Exclusivo *(exclosēēvoh)*.

**Exclusively.** Exclusivamente *(excloosēēverménteh)*.

**Excursion.** Excursión *(excoorrseón)*.

**Excuse.** (v.) Disculpar, dispensar *(discoolpárr, dispensárr)*.

**Excuse.** (s.) Disculpa *(discōōlper)*.

**Execute.** Ajusticiar, ejecutar *(uh.hoostitheárr, éh.heckootárr)*.

**Execution.** Ejecución *(ehhehcootheón)*.

**Executioner.** Verdugo *(vairrdōōgoh)*.

**Exercise.** Ejercicio *(ehherthē ētheoh)*.

**Exhalation.** Exhalación *(exullútheón)*.

**Exhale.** Exhalar *(exullárr)*.

**Exhaust.** Agotar *(uggottarr)*.

**Exhibit.** Exponer, exhibir *(exponnáirr, exibbēēr)*.

**Exhibition.** Exposición *(exspossitheón)*.

**Exigence.** Exigencia *(exihhénthea)*.

**Exile.** Desterrar *(desterrárr)*.

**Exorbitant.** Exorbitante *(exorrbittúnteh)*.

**Exotic.** Exótico *(exótticoh)*.

**Expansion.** Expansión *(eckspunseón)*.

**Expedition.** Expedición *(éckspeddítheón)*.

**Expel.** Expulsar *(expoolsárr)*.

**Expense.** Gasto *(gústoh)*.

**Experience.** Experiencia *(ecksperriénthea)*.

**Experiment.** (v.) Experimentar *(eckspérrimentárr)*.

**Experiment.** (s.) Experimento *(ecksperriméntoh)*.
**Expert.** Experto, perito *(expáirrtoh, perríttoh)*.
**Expiation.** Expiación *(eckspiútheón)*.
**Expire.** Expiar *(expeárr)*.
**Explain.** Explicar *(explicárr)*.
**Explanation.** Explicación, aclaración *(explicútheón, úclurrutheón)*.
**Exploit.** Hazaña *(uthúnnyer)*.
**Exploitation.** Explotación *(explottutheón)*.
**Explosion.** Explosión *(explosseón)*.
**Explosive.** Explosivo *(plosséēvoh)*.
**Export.** Exportar *(exporrtárr)*.
**Exportation.** Exportación *(exporrtutheón)*.
**Expose.** Exponer *(exponnáirr)*.
**Express.** Expresar, exprimir *(expressarr, exprimmēērr)*.
**Expression.** Expresión *(expresseón)*.
**Expropriate.** Expropiar *(exproppeárr)*.

**Exquisite.** Exquisito *(exkisséētoh)*.
**Extend.** Extender *(extendáirr)*.
**Extension.** Extensión *(extenseón)*.
**Exterior.** Exterior *(exterreórr)*.
**Exterminate.** Exterminar *(ekstairrminnárr)*.
**Extermination.** Exterminio *(eckstairrmínneo)*.
**External.** Externo *(eckstáirrnoh)*.
**Extirpate.** Extirpar *(exteerpárr)*.
**Extract.** (v.) Extractar, extraer *(extructárr, extruhyáirr)*.
**Extract.** (s.) Extracto *(extrúctoh)*.
**Extraction.** Extracción *(extructheón)*.
**Extraordinary.** Extraordinario *(éxtra.orrdinnárreoh)*.
**Extreme.** Extremo *(extrémmoh)*.
**Eye.** Ojo *(óhhoh)*.
**Eyeball.** Pupila *(poopíller)*.
**Eyelash.** Pestaña *(pestúnnyer)*.
**Eyelid.** Párpado *(párrpuddoh)*.

# F

**Fable.** Fábula *(fúbbooler)*.
**Fabrication.** Fabricación *(fubbricutheón)*.
**Face.** Cara, rostro, semblante *(cúrrer, róstroh, semblúnteh)*.
**Facet.** Faceta *(fussétter)*.
**Facilitate.** Facilitar *(futhíllitárr)*.
**Facility.** Facilidad *(futhíllidúd)*.
**Factor.** Factor *(fuctórr)*.

**Factory.** (s.) Fábrica *(fúbbricker)*.
**Factory.** (adj.) Fabril *(fubbrēēl)*.
**Faculty.** Facultad *(fuckooltúd)*.
**Fad.** Capricho *(cupprēētch-ch)*.
**Fade.** Ajar *(uh.hárr)*.
**Fagot.** Haz *(uth)*.
**Fail.** Fracasar *(fruckussárr)*.

**Failure.** Fracaso *(fruckússoh).*

**Faint.** (v.) Desmayarse *(desmah.yárseh).*

**Faint, fainting.** Desfallecimiento *(dessfúllyethimyéntoh).*

**Fair.** (s.) Feria *(férrear).*

**Fair.** (adj.) Rubio *(rõõbeoh).*

**Faith.** Fe *(feh).*

**Faithful.** Fiel *(fyéll).*

**Faithfulness.** Fidelidad *(fiddéllidúd).*

**Fall.** (v.) Caerr *(kah.áirr).*

**Fall.** (s.) Caída *(kah.ēéder).*

**False.** Falso *(fúllsoh).*

**Falsehood.** Mentira *(mentēē rer).*

**Falseness.** Falsedad *(fullseddúd).*

**Falsification.** Falsificación *(fullsifficutheón).*

**Falsity.** Falsificar *(fullsifficárr).*

**Fame.** Fama *(fúmmer).*

**Familiarity.** Roce *(rótheh).*

**Family.** Familia *(fummíllyer).*

**Famous.** Famoso *(fummóssoh).*

**Fan.** Abanico *(ubbunnēēkoh).*

**Fanciful.** Caprichoso *(cappritchóssoh).*

**Fancy.** Capricho *(cuprēētchoh).*

**Fantastic.** Fantástico *(funtústickoh).*

**Far.** Lejos *(léhhoss).*

**Farce.** Sainete *(sah.innétteh).*

**Farm.** Granja *(grúnher).*

**Farse.** Farsa *(fárrser).*

**Fashion.** (v.) Amoldar *(úmmolldárr).*

**Fashion.** (s.) Moda, hochura *(mawder, etchõõrer).*

**Fat.** (adj.) Gordo *(górrdoh).*

**Fat.** (s.) Grasa *(grússer).*

**Fatten.** Engordar *(engorrdárr).*

**Fatal.** Fatal *(futtúll).*

**Fatality.** Fatalidad *(futtúllidúd).*

**Father.** Padre *(púddreh).*

**Father-en-law.** Suegro *(swèggroh).*

**Fatherland.** Patria *(púttrear).*

**Fatigue.** Fatiga *(futtēēgger).*

**Fault.** Tacha *(tútcher).*

**Favour.** (v.) Agraciar *(uggrútheárr).*

**Favour.** (s.) Favor *(fuvvór).*

**Favourable.** Favorable *(fuvvorrúbbleh).*

**Fear.** (s.) Miedo *(myéddoh).*

**Fear.** (v.) Temer *(temmáirr).*

**Fearful.** Temible *(temmēē bleh).*

**Feast.** (s.) Festejo *(festéhhoh).*

**Feast.** (v.) Festejar *(festehhárr).*

**February.** Febrero *(febbráirroh).*

**Fee.** Honorario *(onnorrúrreo).*

**Feeble.** Débil *(débbil).*

**Feed.** Alimentar *(úllimentárr).*

**Feeding.** Alimenticio *(úllimentítheo).*

**Feel.** Sentir *(sentēērr).*

**Feign.** Fingir *(finhēērr).*

**Fell (tress).** Talar *(tullárr).*

**Female.** Hembra *(émbrer).*

**Feminine.** Femenino *(femmennēēnoh).*

**Fence.** Seto, vallado *(séttoh, vullyúddoh).*

**Ferocity.** Ferocidad *(ferróthidúd).*

**Fertile.** Fértil *(fáirrtill).*

**Festival.** Festival *(festivvúl).*

**Festivity.** Festividad *(festivvidúd).*

**Fever.** Fiebre, calentura *(fyébbreh, cullentōōrrer)*.

**Fibre.** Fibra, hebra *(fēēbrer, ebbrer)*.

**Fiction.** Ficción *(ficktheón)*.

**Fictitious.** Ficticio *(ficktēētheo)*.

**Fidelity.** Fidelidad *(fiddellidúd)*.

**Figure.** (s.) Figura *(figōōrer)*.

**Figure.** (v.) Figurar *(figgoorárr)*.

**Field.** Campo *(cúmpoh)*.

**Fiery.** Fogoso *(foggóssoh)*.

**Fifteen.** Quince *(kíntheh)*.

**Fifth.** Quinto *(kíntoh)*.

**Fifty.** Cincuenta *(thinkwénter)*.

**Fight.** Combatir, pelear *(combuttēēr, pelleárr)*.

**File.** (s.) Lima *(lēēmer)*.

**File.** (v.) Limar *(leemárr)*.

**Filiation.** Filiación *(filliutheón)*.

**Filigree.** Filigrana *(filligrúnner)*.

**Fill.** Llenar *(lyennárr)*.

**Fill up.** Colmar, rellenar *(colmárr, relynnárr)*.

**Filter.** (v.) Colar *(collár)*.

**Filter.** (s.) Filtro *(filltroh)*.

**Filth.** Porquería, suciedad *(porrkerréar, sōōtheerdúd)*.

**Final.** Final *(finnúll)*.

**Finally.** Finalmente *(finnulménteh)*.

**Find.** Encontrar, hallar *(encontrárr, ullyárr)*.

**Finding.** Hallazgo *(ullyúthgoh)*.

**Fine.** (adj.) Fino *(fēēnoh)*.

**Fine.** (s.) Multa *(mōōlter)*.

**Finger.** Dedo *(déddoh)*.

**Finish.** Acabar, finalizar, rematar, terminar *(uckerbárr, finnullithárr, remmuttárr, tairminnárr)*.

**Fir.** Abeto *(ubbéttoh)*.

**Fire.** Incendio, fuego *(inthéndeoh, fwéggoh)*.

**Fireman.** Bombero, fogonero *(bombáirroh, faggonnáiroh)*.

**Firewood.** Leña *(lényer)*.

**Firm.** (s.) Firma *(fēērrmer)*.

**Firm.** (adj.) Firme *(fēērrmeh)*.

**Firmament.** Firmamento *(fēērrmumméntoh)*.

**First.** Primero *(primmáirroh)*.

**Firstborn.** Primogénito *(primmohhénittoh)*.

**First performance.** Estreno *(estrénnoh)*.

**First performance (to give).** Estrenar *(estrennárr)*.

**Fish.** (s.) Pescado, pez *(pesscúddoh, peth)*.

**Fish.** (v.) Pescar *(pescárr)*.

**Fishing-line.** Sedal *(seddúll)*.

**Fist.** Puño *(poōnyoh)*.

**Fitting.** Idóneo *(iddónneoh)*.

**Five.** Cinco *(thínkoh)*.

**Fivehundred.** Quinientos *(kiuyéntoss)*.

**Fix.** Fijar *(fihhárr)*.

**Fixed.** Fijo *(fēēhoh)*.

**Flag.** Bandera *(bundáirer)*.

**Flagrant.** Flagrante *(fluggrúnteh)*.

**Flame.** Llama *(lyúmmer)*.

**Flank.** Flanco *(flúnkoh)*.

**Flat.** Llano *(lyúnnoh)*.

**Flat.** Piso *(pēēssoh)*.

**Flatter.** Adular, halagar *(uddoolárr, ullergárr)*.

**Flaterry.** Lisonja, zalamería *(lissónher, thullermerréar)*.

**Flee.** Huir *(oo.éarr)*.

**Fleet.** Flota *(flótter)*.

**Flexibility.** Flexibilidad *(flexibilidúd)*.

**Flight.** Vuelo *(uwélloh)*.

**Float.** Flotar *(flottáirr)*.

**Floating.** Flotante *(flottúnteh)*.

**Flog.** Azotar *(úthottárr).*

**Floor.** Suelo *(swélloh).*

**Florist.** Florista *(florríster).*

**Flour.** Harina *(urriēēner).*

**Flourishing.** Floreciente *(florrithyénteh).*

**Floury.** Harinoso *(urrinnóssoh).*

**Flow.** Afluir *(uffloo.ēērr).*

**Flower.** Flor *(florr).*

**Flowerpot.** Maceta *(muthétter).*

**Fluctuate.** Fluctuar *(floocktoo.árr).*

**Fluctuation.** Vaivén *(vy.ivén).*

**Fluid.** Fluido *(flōōiddoh).*

**Flute.** Flauta *(flōwter).*

**Fly.** (s.) Mosca *(mósker).*

**Fly.** (v.) Volar *(vollárr).*

**Fly wheel.** Volante *(vollúnteh).*

**Foam.** Espuma *(espōōmer).*

**Focus.** Foco *(fāwcoh).*

**Foetus.** Feto *(féttoh).*

**Fog.** Niebla *(nyébbler).*

**Fold.** Plegar *(pleggárr).*

**Folder.** Plegadura *(plégger.-dōōrer).*

**Folio.** Folio *(fóllioh).*

**Follow.** Seguir *(seggēērr).*

**Following.** Siguiente *(sigwénteh).*

**Food.** Alimento *(úlliméntoh).*

**Fool.** Necio *(nétheoh).*

**Foot.** Pie *(pyéh).*

**Footstep.** Pisada *(pissárder).*

**For.** Para, por *(púrrer, porr).*

**Forbid.** Prohibir, vedar *(prohhibbēērr, veddárr).*

**Forced.** Forzado *(forrthárdoh).*

**Forcibly.** Forzosamente *(forrthósserménteh).*

**Ford.** Vado *(vúddoh).*

**Forefather.** Antecesor *(únteh.théssorr).*

**Forehead.** Frente *(frénteh).*

**Foreigner.** Extranjero *(extrunháirroh).*

**Forest.** Bosque, floresta, selva *(bóskeh, forréster, sélver).*

**Forestbred.** Selvático *(selvútticoh).*

**Foretell.** Adivinar *(uddivvinárr).*

**Forge.** (v.) Forjar *(forrhárr).*

**Forge.** (s.) Fragua *(frúgwer).*

**Forget.** Olvidar *(olviddárr).*

**Forgetfulness.** Olvido *(olvēēdoh).*

**Fork.** Tenedor, horquilla *(tennedórr, orkíllyer).*

**Form.** (s) Forma *(fórrmer).*

**Form.** (v.) Formar *(forrmárr).*

**Formal.** Formal *(forrmúll).*

**Formality.** Formalidad *(forrmúllidúd).*

**Formalize.** Formalizar *(forrmúllithárr).*

**Forman.** Capataz *(cuppertúth).*

**Formula.** Fórmula *(fórrmooler).*

**Formulate.** Formular *(forrmoolárr).*

**Forseer.** Previsor *(previssórr).*

**Fort.** Fuerte *(fwáirrteh).*

**Fortnight.** Quicena *(kinthénner).*

**Fortune.** Fortuna *(forrtōōner).*

**Found.** Fundar *(foondárr).*

**Foundation.** Fundamento *(fōōnderméntoh).*

**Foundry.** Fundición *(foonditheón).*

**Fountain.** Fuente, surtidor *(fwénteh, soorrtidórr).*

**Four.** Cuatro *(kwúttroh).*

**Fourteen.** Catorce *(cuttórrteh).*

**Fox.** Zorro *(thórroh)*.
**Fraction.** Fracción *(fructheón)*.
**Fragile.** Frágil *(frúghill)*.
**Fragment.** Fragmento *(frugméntoh)*.
**Frank.** (v.) Franquear *(frunkay.árr)*.
**Frank.** (adj.) Franco *(frúncoh)*.
**Frankly.** Francamente *(frúnkerménteh)*.
**Frankness.** Franqueza *(frunkéther)*.
**Fraternise.** Fraternizar *(fruttáirnithárr)*.
**Fraternity.** Fraternidad *(fruttáirnidúd)*.
**Fraud.** Fraude, timo *(frõõ deh, tẽẽmoh)*.
**Free.** Gratis *(grúttiss)*.
**Freely.** Libremente *(libbrerménteh)*.
**Freeze.** Helar *(ellárr)*.
**Freight.** Flete *(flétteh)*.
**French.** Francés *(frunthéss)*.
**Frenzy.** Frenesí *(frennussẽẽ)*.
**Frequency.** Frecuencia *(freckwénthea)*.
**Frequently.** Frecuentemente *(freckwéntemménteh)*.
**Fresh.** Fresco *(fréscoh)*.
**Fresheness.** Frescura *(frescõõrer)*.
**Friction.** Rozadura *(rotherdõ õrer)*.
**Friday.** Viernes *(vyáirrness)*.
**Friend.** Amigo *(ummẽẽgoh)*.
**Friendship.** Amistad *(úmmistúd)*.
**Fright.** Susto *(sõõstoh)*.
**Frightened.** Asustado *(assoostárdoh)*.
**Frightful.** Espantoso *(espuntóssoh)*.

**Fringe.** Fleco *(fléckoh)*.
**Frisk.** Retorzar *(rettothárr)*.
**Frivolity.** Frivolidad *(frivvóllidúd)*.
**Frog.** Rana *(rúnner)*.
**Front.** Delante, fachada, frente *(delúnteh, futchárder, frénteh)*.
**Frontier.** Frontera *(frontáirrer)*.
**Fruitful.** Fructuoso *(frooktoo.óssoh)*.
**Fruit.** Fruto, fruta *(frõõtoh, frõõter)*.
**Fruit (preserved).** Almíbar *(úllmibárr)*.
**Fruitful.** Fecundo, fructífero *(feckõõndoh, frooktífferroh)*.
**Frustrate.** Frustrar *(froostrárr)*.
**Fry.** Freir *(frayẽẽrr)*.
**Frying pan.** Sartén *(sarrtén)*.
**Fulfill.** Cumplir *(coomplẽẽrr)*.
**Fun.** Alegría, broma *(ullegrẽ ẽr, braumer)*.
**Function.** Función *(foontheón)*.
**Furious.** Furioso *(foorrióssoh)*.
**Furnish.** Amueblar, proporcionar *(úmmerblárr, propporrtheonnárr)*.
**Furnish.** Proporcionar *(propporrtheonnárr)*.
**Furnish.** Suministrar *(soominnistrarr)*.
**Furniture.** Muebles, mobiliario *(myébbless, mobbilliáreoh)*.
**Furrow.** (v.) Surcar *(soorrcárr)*.
**Furrow. (s).** Surco *(sõõrkoh)*.
**Fury.** Furia *(fõõrrea)*.
**Fusion.** Fusión *(foosseón)*.
**Future.** Porvenir, futuro *(porrvennẽẽr, footõõroh)*.

# G

**Gag.** Mordaza *(morrdúther)*.
**Gain.** (s.) Ganancia *(gunnúnthea)*.
**Gain.** (v.) Ganar *(gunnárr)*.
**Gallant.** Galante *(gullúnthe)*.
**Gallery.** Galería *(gullerréar)*.
**Gallicism.** Galicismo *(gullithísmoh)*.
**Gallon.** Galón *(gullón)*.
**Gallop.** (v.) Galopar *(gulloppár)*.
**Gallop.** (s.) Galope *(gullóppeh)*.
**Gallows.** Horca *(órrker)*.
**Game.** Juego, partido *(hwéggoh, parrtēēdoh)*.
**Garden.** Jardín *(harrdēēn)*.
**Gardener.** Jardinero *(hardinnáirroh)*.
**Garnish.** Guarnecer *(gwarrnetháirr)*.
**Gas.** Gas *(guss)*.
**Gaseous.** Gaseoso *(gussióssoh)*.
**Gasometer.** Gasómetro *(gussómmettroh)*.
**Gate.** Reja *(réh.her)*.
**Gather.** Recoger *(recoh.-háirr)*.
**Gaul.** Galo *(gúlloh)*.
**Gazzette.** Gaceta *(guthétter)*.
**Gender.** Género *(hénneroh)*.
**General.** General *(hennerrúll)*.
**Generalize.** Generalizar *(hennerrallithárr)*.
**Generally.** Generalmente *(hennerrulménteh)*.
**Generation.** Generación *(hennerutheón)*.
**Generosity.** Generosidad *(hennerrossidúd)*.

**Generous.** Generoso *(hennerróssoh)*.
**Generously.** Generosamente *(hennerrósserménteh)*.
**Genial.** Genial *(henniúl)*.
**Genteel.** Gentil *(henteel)*.
**Gentle.** Dócil *(dóthill)*.
**Gentleman.** Caballero *(cúbbullyáirroh)*.
**Geography.** Geografía *(háyoggrafféar)*.
**Geometry.** Geometría *(háyommetréar)*.
**Germ.** Germen *(háirrmen)*.
**Gestation.** Gestación *(hestutheón)*.
**Gesture.** Ademán, gesto *(úddemún, héstoh)*.
**Get.** Conseguir, llegar *(consseggēēr, lyeggárr)*.
**Giant.** Gigante *(higgúnteh)*.
**Giddiness.** Aturdimiento, vértigo *(uttõõrrdimmyéntoh, váirrtiggoh)*.
**Gift.** Don, regalo *(don, reggúlloh)*.
**Gigantic.** Gigantesco *(higguntéscoh)*.
**Gild.** Dorar *(dorrár)*.
**Girdle.** (v.) Ceñir *(thenyéarr)*.
**Girdle.** (s.) Cincha, cinturón *(thíntcher, thintoórn)*.
**Girl.** Niña, muchacha *(nēēnyer, mootchútcher)*.
**Give.** Dar *(darr)*.
**Give up.** Abandonar *(ubbúndonhárr)*.
**Give way.** Ceder *(theddáirr)*.
**Giver.** Dador *(dárdorr)*.
**Glacial.** Glacial *(glusseúll)*.
**Glance.** Ojeada *(ohheh.údder)*.

**Glass.** Vaso *(vássoh)*.
**Gleam.** Lucir *(loothéēr)*.
**Globe.** Globo *(glóbboh)*.
**Glorious.** Glorioso *(glorriós-soh)*.
**Glory.** Gloria *(glórrea)*.
**Gloss.** Lustre *(lōōstreh)*.
**Glove.** Guante *(gwúntek)*.
**Glover's.** Guantería *(gwunterréar)*.
**Glutton.** Glotón *(glottón)*.
**Gnaw.** Roer *(raw.áirr)*.
**Go.** Andar, ir *(undárr, eer)*.
**Go down.** Bajar *(buh.hárr)*.
**Go out.** Salir *(sulléērr)*.
**Go up.** Subir *(soobéēr)*.
**Goat.** Cabra *(cúbbrer)*.
**God.** Dios *(dēē.oss)*.
**Goddess.** Diosa *(dee.ós-ser)*.
**Godfather.** Padrino *(puddrēēnoh)*.
**God-mother.** Madrina *(muddrēēner)*.
**Going.** Ida *(ēēder)*.
**Gold.** Oro *(áwroh)*.
**Good.** Bueno *(bwénnoh)*.
**Goodness.** Bondad *(bondúd)*.
**Goods.** Mercancía *(maircunthēēr)*.
**Gospel.** Evangelio *(evvunhélleoh)*.
**Govern.** Gobernar *(gobbairnárr)*.
**Government.** Gobierno *(gobyérrnoh)*.
**Governor.** Gobernador *(gobbairnuddór)*.
**Gracious.** Gracioso *(gruthióssoh)*.
**Grade.** Grado *(grárdoh)*.
**Graduate.** Graduar *(gruddoo.árr)*.
**Grammar.** Gramática *(grummútticah)*.
**Grammatical.** Gramatical *(grummutticúll)*.

**Gramme.** Gramo *(grúmmoh)*.
**Grand.** Grandioso *(grundiós-soh)*.
**Grandfather.** Abuelo *(ubbwé-lloh)*.
**Grandmother.** Abuela *(ub-bwéller)*.
**Grant.** Otorgar *(ottorrgárr)*.
**Grape.** Uva *(ōōver)*.
**Graphic.** Gráfico *(grúfficoh)*.
**Grapple.** Aferrar *(ufferrárr)*.
**Grasp.** Agarrar *(ugurrárr)*.
**Grasshopper.** Saltamontes *(sultermóntess)*.
**Grate.** (s.) Fogón, verja *(fogón, vairrher)*.
**Grate.** (v.) Rallar *(rullyárr)*.
**Gratitude.** Gratitud *(gruttitōōd)*.
**Gratuitous.** Gratuito *(grut-too.íttoh)*.
**Grave.** Grave *(grárveh)*.
**Gravity.** Gravedad *(grúv-vedúd)*.
**Gray.** Pardo *(párrdoh)*.
**Graze.** Apacentar *(uppú-thentárr)*.
**Great.** Gran, grande *(grun, grúndeh)*.
**Great-great-grandfather.** Tatarabuela *(tuttarrerbwéller)*.
**Great-great-grandson.** Tataranieto *(tuttarrernyéttoh)*.
**Greatness.** Grandeza, *(gruudéther)*.
**Greek.** Griego *(gri.éh.goh)*.
**Gridiron.** Parrillas *(purrílyuss)*.
**Grief.** Dolor, pena *(dollórr, pénner)*.
**Grievous.** Gravoso *(gruvvóssoh)*.
**Grind.** Moler *(molláirr)*.
**Groan.** Gemir *(hemmēēr)*.
**Groin.** Ingle *(íngleh)*.
**Group.** Grupa *(grōōpper)*.
**Group, grouping.** (s.) Agrupación *(uggroopútheón)*.

**Group.** (v.) Agrupar, -se *(úg-groopárr, -seh).*
**Gross.** Gruesa *(groo.ésser).*
**Grotesque.** Grotesco *(gro-ttéscoh).*
**Grotto.** Gruta *(grõõter).*
**Group.** Grupo *(grõõpoh).*
**Grove.** Alameda, soto *(uller-médder, sóttoh).*
**Grow.** Crecer *(cretháirr).*
**Grumble.** Refunfuñar *(reffo-onfoonyárr).*
**Grunt.** Gruñido *(groonyéédoh).*
**Guarantee.** Afianzar *(ufféun-thárr).*
**Guard.** (v.) Custodiar *(coos-toddeárr).*

**Guard.** (s.) Guarda, resguardo, guardia *(gwárrder, resgwárrdoh, gwárrdea).*
**Guess right.** Acertar *(ut-hairrtárr).*
**Guest.** Huésped *(wésped).*
**Guide.** (s.) Guía *(gheer).*
**Guide.** (v.) Guiar, dirigir *(gheárr, dirrihhéérr).*
**Guild.** Gremio *(grémmeoh).*
**Guillotine.** Guillotina *(ghil-yottéèner).*
**Guilty.** Culpable *(coolpúb-bleh).*
**Guitar.** Guitarra *(ghittúrrer).*
**Gum.** Goma *(gómmer).*
**Gust.** Ráfaga *(rúfferger).*

# H

**Haggie.** Regatear *(reggut-teárr).*
**Hair.** Cabello, pelo *(cubbéll-yoh, pélloh).*
**Hairdresser.** Peluquero *(pe-llookáiroh).*
**Hairdressing.** Peinado *(pei-nnúddoh).*
**Half.** Mitad *(mittúd).*
**Hall.** Sala, vestíbulo *(súller, vestíbboooloh).*
**Hallucination.** Aberración *(úbberrátheón).*
**Hallucination.** Quimera *(ki-mmáirrer).*
**Halter.** Ronzal *(ronthúll).*
**Hammar.** Martillo *(marrtilyoh).*
**Hand.** Mano *(múnnoh).*
**Handful.** Puñado *(poonyár-doh).*
**Handkerchief.** Pañuelo *(pu-nyoo.élloh).*
**Handle.** Asa, mango *(árrser, mungoh).*

**Handling.** Manejo, maniobra *(munnéhhoh, munyób-brer).*
**Handsaw.** Serrucho *(serrõõt-choch).*
**Handsome.** Guapo *(gwup-poh).*
**Hang.** Colgar, suspender *(colgárr, soospendáirr).*
**Happen.** Acontecer *(uckón-teháir).*
**Happily.** Felizmente *(fellith-ménteh).*
**Happiness.** Felicidad *(felli-thidúd).*
**Happy.** Feliz *(felléèth).*
**Hard.** Duro *(dõõrroh).*
**Hardness.** Dureza *(doorré-ther).*
**Hardware.** Quincalla *(kincúll-yer).*
**Hare.** Liebre *(lyébbreh).*
**Harmless.** Inofensivo *(innof-fenséèvoh).*

**Harmonise.** Armonizar *(arrmonithárr).*
**Harmony.** Armonía *(arrmonēēr).*
**Harpoon.** Arpón *(arrpón).*
**Harrow.** Trillo *(trílyoh).*
**Harry.** Activar, darse prisa, *(úcktivárr, dárrseh prēēser).*
**Harvest.** Siega *(syégger).*
**Haste.** Prisa *(prēēsser).*
**Hasten.** Apremiar *(uppremmeárr).*
**Hat.** Sombrero *(sombráirroh).*
**Hatchet.** Hacha *(útcher).*
**Hatred.** Odio *(óddioh).*
**Havana.** Habano *(ubbúnnoh).*
**Have.** Tener, haber *(tennáirr, ubbáirr).*
**Hawker.** Revendedor *(revvendeddórr).*
**Hawksbell.** Cascabel *(cúskerbéll).*
**He.** Él *(el).*
**Head.** Cabeza *(cubbéther).*
**Headiness.** Desatino *(díssuttēēnoh).*
**Heal.** Sanar, curar *(sunnárr, coorárr).*
**Health.** Salud *(sullōōd).*
**Healthy.** Sano *(súnnoh).*
**Heap.** (v.) Amontonar *(ummóntonnárr).*
**Heap.** (s.) Colmo *(cólmoh).*
**Heap up.** Aglomerar *(ugglómmerrár).*
**Hear.** Oir *(or.ēēr).*
**Heart.** Corazón *(correrthón).*
**Heartbeat.** Latido *(luttēēdoh).*
**Heat.** Calor *(cullórr).*
**Heel.** Tacón, talón *(tuckón, tullón).*
**Height.** Altura, estatura *(ultōōrer, estattōōrer).*
**Heir.** Heredero *(erriddáiroh).*
**Helicopter.** Helicóptero *(ellicópterroh).*

**Helm.** Timón *(timmón).*
**Helmsman.** Timonel *(timmonnél).*
**Help.** (s.) Ayuda *(ah.yōō.-der).*
**Help.** (v.) Socorrer, ayudar *(soccorráirr, ahyoodárr).*
**Hem.** Ribetear *(ribbettay.árr).*
**Hemisphere.** Hemisferio *(émmisferréoh).*
**Hen.** Gallina *(gullyēēner).*
**Herb.** Hierba *(yáirrber).*
**Herculean.** Hercúleo *(áirrcōōleoh).*
**Herd.** Rebaño *(rebbúnyoh).*
**Here.** Aquí *(uckēē).*
**Hereditary.** Hereditario *(erriddittárreoh).*
**Heresy.** Herejía *(errihéar).*
**Heroic.** Heroico *(erróicoh).*
**Heroism.** Heroísmo *(erroíssmoh).*
**Hesitate.** Titubear *(tittoobay.árr).*
**Hey!** ¡Eh! *(eh).*
**Hidden.** Oculto *(occōōltoh).*
**Hide.** Esconder, ocultar *(escondáirr, occooltárr).*
**Hieroglyph.** Jeroglifico *(herrogglifficoh).*
**High.** Alto *(últoh).*
**Highwayman.** Salteador *(sulteh.uddórr).*
**Hill.** Lomo, cuesta *(lómmoh, kwéster).*
**Hill.** Monte *(monteh).*
**Hilly.** Montuoso *(montoo.ossoh).*
**Hinder.** Estorbar *(estórrbárr).*
**Hint.** Insinuar *(insinnoo.árr).*
**Hip.** Cadera *(cuddáirrer).*
**Hire.** Alquilar *(úllkilárr).*
**His.** Su, suyo *(sōō, sōōyoh).*
**Historical.** Histórico *(istórricoh).*
**History.** Historia *(istórrea).*
**Hive.** Colmene *(collménner).*

**Hold.** Aguantar *(úggwuntárr)*.

**Hole.** Agujerear *(uggōō.herreárr)*.

**Hole.** (s.) Hoyo, agujero *(óyo, uggooháiroh)*.

**Holidays.** Vacaciones *(vuckutheóness)*.

**Hollow.** (s.) Hueco *(wéckoh)*.

**Hollow.** (v.) Ahuecar *(uh.weckárr)*.

**Homage.** Homenaje *(ommenúhheh)*.

**Home.** Hogar *(oggárr)*.

**Honey.** Miel *(myél)*.

**Honey-comh.** Panal *(punnúl)*.

**Honour.** (s.) Honor, honra *(onnórr, hónrer)*.

**Honour.** (v.) Honrar *(onrárr)*.

**Hook.** Garabato *(gurrerbártoh)*.

**Hook (fish).** Anzuelo *(unthwélloh)*.

**Hook.** (s.) Gancho *(gúntchoh)*.

**Hook.** (v.) Enganchar *(enguntchárr)*.

**Hope.** (s.) Esperanza *(esperrunther)*.

**Hope.** (v.) Esperar *(esperrárr)*.

**Horizon.** Horizonte *(orrithónteh)*.

**Horizontal.** Horizontal *(orrithontúll)*.

**Horticulture.** Floricultura *(flórricooltōōrrer)*.

**Horrible.** Horrible *(orríbleh)*.

**Horror.** Horror *(orrórr)*.

**Horse.** Caballo, *(cubbúllyoh)*.

**Horseness.** Ronquera, *(ronkáirrer)*.

**Hospice.** Hospicio *(ospitheo)*.

**Hospital.** Hospital *(ospitúll)*.

**Hospitality.** Hospitalidad, hospedaje *(ospitullidúd, ospeddúheh)*.

**Host.** Anfitrion *(unfitreón)*.

**Hostel.** Posada *(possárder)*.

**Hostess (air).** Azafata *(útherfárter)*.

**Hostile.** Hostil *(óstill)*.

**Hot.** Caliente *(cullyénteh)*.

**Hotel.** Hotel, fonda *(ottéll, fónder)*.

**House.** Casa *(cússer)*.

**How much.** Cuanto *(kwúntoh)*.

**Hum.** Zumbar *(thoombúrr)*.

**Human.** Humano *(oomúnnoh)*.

**Humanity.** Humanidad *(oomúnnidúd)*.

**Humiliation.** Humillación *(oomillútheón)*.

**Humility.** Humildad *(oomildúd)*.

**Humming.** Zúmbido *(thoombēēdoh)*.

**Hundred.** (adj.) Ciento *(thyéntoh)*.

**Hundred.** (s.) Centena *(thenténner)*.

**Hundredth.** Centésimo *(then.-téssimmoh)*.

**Hung.** Suspenso *(soospénsoh)*.

**Hunger.** Hambre *(úmbreh)*.

**Hungry.** Hambriento *(umbriéntoh)*.

**Hurrah.** Bravo *(brárvoh)*.

**Hurricane.** Huracán *(oorercún)*.

**Hurry.** Apresurarse *(uppréssoorárrseh)*.

**Hurt.** (v.) Dañar *(dunyárr)*.

**Hurt.** (s.) Lesión *(lesseón)*.

**Husband.** Esposo, marido *(espóssoh, marrēēdoh)*.

**Hut.** Choza *(chāwther)*.

**Hydrophobia.** Hidrofobia *(iddroffóbbea)*.

232

**Hydrophobus.** Hidrófobo *(iddróffobõõh).*
**Hygiene.** Higiene *(ihhyénneh).*
**Hygienic.** Higiénico *(ihhyénnicoh).*
**Hymn.** Himno *(ímnoh).*

**Hyphen.** Guión *(ghión).*
**Hypocrisy.** Hipocresía *(ippócrusséah).*
**Hypocrite.** Hipócrita, santurrón *(ippócritter, suntoorrón).*

## I

**I.** Yo *(yoh).*
**Iberian.** Ibero *(ibbáirroh).*
**Ice.** Hielo *(yéllow).*
**Idea.** Idea *(iddáyer).*
**Ideal.** Ideal *(iddiúl).*
**Identify.** Identificar *(iddentifficárr).*
**Idiot.** Idiotia *(iddiótter).*
**Idiotism.** Idiotismo *(iddiottismoh).*
**Idle.** Ocioso *(othióssoh).*
**Idolatry.** Idolatría *(iddollutréar).*
**Idolize.** Idolatrar *(iddollutrárr).*
**If.** Sí *(see).*
**Ignoble.** Innoble *(innóbbleh).*
**Ignominy.** Ignominia *(ignommínnea).*
**Ignorant.** Ignorante *(ignorrúnteh).*
**Ill.** (s.) Enfermo *(enfáirrmoh).*
**Ill.** (v.) Enfermar *(enfairrmárr).*
**Illegal.** Ilegal *(illeggúll).*
**Illegality.** Ilegalidad *(illeggullidúd).*
**Illegitimate.** Ilegítimo *(illehittimoh).*
**Illicit.** Ilícito *(illílhitoh).*
**Illness.** Enfermedad *(enfáirrmeddúd).*
**Illogical.** Ilógico *(illóhhicoh).*
**Ill-timed.** Intempestivo *(intempestéēvoh).*
**Illumination.** Iluminación *(illoominútitheón).*

**Illustrate.** Ilustrar *(illoostrárr).*
**Illustrated.** Ilustrado *(illoostrárdoh).*
**Illustration.** Ilustración *(illoostrutheón).*
**Illustrious.** Ilustre *(illõõstreh).*
**Image.** Imagen *(immúhhen).*
**Imagination.** Imaginación *(immuhhinnutheón).*
**Imagine.** Imaginar *(immuhhinárr).*
**Imbecille.** Imbécil *(imbéthill).*
**Imbibe.** Embeber *(embebbáirr).*
**Imitate.** Imitar *(immittárr).*
**Imitation.** Imitación *(immittutheón).*
**Immediate.** Inmediato *(inmeddiúttoh).*
**Immediately.** Inmediatamente *(inméddi.utterménteh).*
**Immense.** Inmenso *(inménsoh).*
**Immensity.** Inmensidad *(inmensiddúd).*
**Immigrant.** Inmigrante *(inmiggrúnteh).*
**Immigrate.** Inmigrar *(inmiggrárr).*
**Immoral.** Inmoral *(inmorrúll).*
**Immortal.** Inmortal *(ínmortúll).*
**Impartial.** Imparcial *(imparrtheúll).*

**Impassable.** Intransitable (*intrunsittúbleh*).

**Impassible.** Impasible (*impussíbleh*).

**Impatience.** Impaciencia (*imputhyénthea*).

**Impede.** Impedir (*impedéẽrr*).

**Impediment.** Impedimento (*impeddiméntoh*).

**Impenetrable.** Impenetrable (*impennitrúbbleh*).

**Imperceptible.** Imperceptible (*impairrtheptíbbleh*).

**Imperfect.** Imperfecto (*impairrféctoh*).

**Imperious.** Imperioso (*impairrióssoh*).

**Impertinence.** Impertinencia (*impairrtinnénthea*).

**Impetuous.** Impetuoso (*ímpettoo.óssoh*).

**Impiety.** Impiedad (*impéeadúd*).

**Implacable.** Implacable (*impluckúbleh*).

**Import.** (v.) Importar (*importárr*).

**Importance.** Importancia (*importúncia*).

**Impose.** Imponer (*imponnáirr*).

**Impossibility.** Imposibilidad (*impossibillidúd*).

**Impossible.** Imposible (*impossíbleh*).

**Impotence.** Impotencia (*impotténthea*).

**Impoverish.** Empobrecer (*empóbbretháirr*).

**Impracticable.** Inpracticable (*impructicúbbleh*).

**Impression.** Impresión (*impresseón*).

**Imprison.** Aprisionar, encarcelar (*upprisseonárr; encarrthellár*).

**Improper.** Impropio (*impróppeoh*).

**Improve.** Mejorar (*mehhor.-rárr*).

**Imprudence.** Imprudencia (*improodénthea*).

**Impudent.** Desahogado (*désser.oggárdoh*).

**Impure.** Impuro (*impõõroh*).

**Impute.** Achacar (*útchuckárr*).

**In.** En (*en*).

**Inadmissible.** Inadmisible (*innudmissíbleh*).

**Inalterable.** Inalterable (*innulterrúbleh*).

**Inattentive.** Desatento (*dessutténtoh*).

**Inauguration.** Inauguración (*in.owgoorrutheón*).

**Incalculable.** Incalculable (*inculcoolúbbleh*).

**Incapacity.** Incapacidad (*incupputhedúd*).

**Incense.** Incienso (*inthyénsoh*).

**Incensory.** Incensario (*inthensúrrioh*).

**Incertitude.** Incertidumbre (*inthairrtidõõmbreh*).

**Incessant.** Incesante (*inthessúnteh*).

**Inch.** Pulgada (*poolgárder*).

**Incident.** Incidente (*inthiddénteh*).

**Incitement.** Aliciente (*alli.-thyénteh*).

**Inclemency.** Intemperie (*intemperréa*).

**Inclination.** Inclinación (*inclinnutheón*).

**Incline.** Ladear (*luddeárr*).

**Inclosed.** Incluido, incluso (*incloo.ẽẽdoh, inclõõsoh*).

**Incomparable.** Incomparable (*incomparrúbleh*).

**Incompatible.** Incompatible (*incomputtíbleh*).

**Incomplete.** Incompleto *(incompléttoh).*

**Inconceivable.** Inconcebible *(inconthebbíbleh).*

**Inconvenient.** Incómodo *(incómmoddoh).*

**Incorrect.** Incorrecto *(incorréctoh).*

**Increase.** (v.) Aumentar *(owmentárr).*

**Increase.** (s.) Aumento *(owméntoh).*

**Incredible.** Increíble *(incray.-íbbleh).*

**Inculcate.** Inculcar *(incullcárr).*

**Incur.** Incurrir *(incõõrēērr).*

**Incurable.** Incurable *(incõõrrúbleh).*

**Indefensible.** Insostenible *(insostennēēbleh).*

**Indemnification.** Indemnización *(indemnithutheón).*

**Independent.** Independiente *(independénteh).*

**Indescribable.** Indescriptible *(indescriptíbbleh).*

**Index.** Índice *(índitheh).*

**Indicate.** Indicar, designar *(indickárr, dessignárr).*

**Indication.** Indicación *(indiccutheón).*

**Indicator.** Indicador *(indickerdórr).*

**Indifference.** Indiferencia *(indifferrénthea).*

**Indigestion.** Indigestión *(indihhesteón).*

**Indignation.** Indignación *(indignutheón).*

**Indispensable.** Indispensable, imprescindible *(indispensúbbleh, impresthindibbleh).*

**Individual.** (s.) Individuo *(individdõõ.oh).*

**Individual.** (adj.) Individual *(indivvidõõ.úll).*

**Industry.** Industria *(indõõstria).*

**Inebriate.** Embriagar *(embréuggárr).*

**Inestimable.** Inestimable *(inestimmúbleh).*

**Inevitable.** Ineludible *(inelõõdíbbleh).*

**Inexhaustible.** Inagotable *(innuggottúbleh).*

**Inexplicable.** Inexplicable *(inexplicúbbleh).*

**Inexpressible.** Indecible *(indethíbbleh).*

**Infamous.** Infame *(infúmmeh).*

**Infamy.** Infamia *(infúmmea).*

**Infancy.** Infancia *(infúnthia).*

**Infect.** Contagiar *(contúhhee.árr).*

**Infectious.** Contagioso *(contahhuggióssoh).*

**Inferior.** Inferior *(inferriórr).*

**Inferiority.** Inferioridad *(inferriorridúd).*

**Infernal.** Infernal *(infurrnúll).*

**Infinitely.** Infinitamente *(infinnitterménteh).*

**Infinity.** Infinidad *(infinnidúd).*

**Infirmary.** Enfermería *(enfáïrmerrēēr).*

**Inflamation.** Inflamación *(inflummutheón).*

**Inflict.** Infligir *(inflihhēērr).*

**Influence.** (s.) Influencia *(inflõõ.énthia).*

**Infuence.** (v.) Influir *(inflooēērr).*

**Inform.** Informar *(inforrmárr).*

**Information.** Información *(informutheón).*

**Ingenious.** Ingenioso *(inhennióssoh).*

**Ingratitude.** Ingratitud *(ingruttitõõd).*

**Inhabit.** Habitar *(ubbittárr).*

**Inherit.** Heredar *(erriddárr).*

**Inheritance.** Herencia *(errénthea)*.

**Inhospitable.** Inhospitalario *(inospittul.lárioh)*.

**Inhuman.** Inhumano *(in.oomúnnoh)*.

**Iniquity.** Iniquidad *(innikkiddúd)*.

**Initial.** Inicial *(innitheúll)*.

**Initiate.** Iniciar *(innitheárr)*.

**Injury.** Perjuicio *(pairrhwithioh)*.

**Injustice.** Injusticia *(inhōōstithia)*.

**Ink.** Tints *(tínter)*.

**Inkstand.** Tintero *(tintáirroh)*.

**Inlay.** Embutido *(embootēēdoh)*.

**Inn.** Hostería, mesón, parador *(osterréa, messón, purrurdórr)*.

**Inn-keeper.** Hostelero *(ostelláiroh)*.

**Innocence.** Inocencia *(innothénthea)*.

**Innocent.** Inocente *(innothénteh)*.

**Innundate.** Inundar *(innundárr)*.

**Inquire.** Averiguar *(uvvérrigwárr)*.

**Inquiry.** Pesquisa *(peskēēsser)*.

**Insane.** Demente, loco *(demménteh, lóccoh)*.

**Insatiable.** Insaciable *(insuthiúbbleh)*.

**Insensate.** Insensato *(insensúttoh)*.

**Insensible.** Insensible *(insensíbbleh)*.

**Inseparable.** Inseparable *(insepparrúbbleh)*.

**Insipid.** Soso *(sóssoh)*.

**Insist.** Insistir *(insistēērr)*.

**Insistence.** Insistencia *(insisténthea)*.

**Insolence.** Insolencia *(insollénthea)*.

**Insolent.** Insolente *(insollénteh)*.

**Inspection.** Inspección *(inspectheón)*.

**Inspector.** Inspector *(inspectórr)*.

**Inspiration.** Inspiración *(inspirruthéon)*.

**Instal.** Instalar *(instullárr)*.

**Installation.** Instalación *(instullutheón)*.

**Instance.** Instancia *(instúnthea)*.

**Instant.** Instante *(instúnteh)*.

**Instinct.** Instinto *(instíntoh)*.

**Institute.** Instituto *(instittōōtoh)*.

**Institution.** Institución *(instittōōtheón)*.

**Instruct.** Instruir *(instroo.ēērr)*.

**Instruction.** Instrucción *(instroocktheón)*.

**Instrument.** Instrumento *(instroomméntoh)*.

**Insult.** (v.) Insultar *(insōōltárr)*.

**Insult.** (s) Insulto, atropello *(insōōltoh, uttroppéllyoh)*.

**Insupportable.** Insoportable *(insopporrtúbbleh)*.

**Insurrection.** Sublevación *(sōōblevvutheón)*.

**Intact.** Intacto *(intúcktoh)*.

**Intellectual.** Intelectual *(intellectoo.úll)*.

**Intelligence.** Inteligencia *(intellihénthea)*.

**Intelligent.** Inteligente *(intellihénteh)*.

**Intensity.** Intensidad *(intensiddúd)*.

**Intention.** Intención *(intentheón)*.

**Intercalate.** Intercalar *(intairrcullár)*.

**Intercede.** Interceder *(intairrtheddáirr).*
**Intercept.** Interceptar *(interrtheptárr).*
**Interest.** (s.) Interés *(interrés).*
**Interest.** (v.) Interesar *(interressárr).*
**Interested.** Interesado *(interressárdoh).*
**Interesting.** Interesante *(interressúnteh).*
**Interior.** Interior *(interriórr).*
**Interlocutor.** Interlocutor *(interrlockõõtórr).*
**Intermediary.** Intermediario *(interrméddiarioh).*
**Interminable.** Interminable *(inttairrminnúbbleh).*
**Internal.** Interno *(intáirrnoh).*
**Interpret.** Interpretar *(intáirrprettárr).*
**Interpreter.** Intérprete *(intáirrpretteh).*
**Interrogate.** Interrogar *(interrroggárr).*
**Interrupt.** Interrumpir *(interrõõmpêêrr).*
**Interval.** Intervalo *(intáirrvulloh).*
**Intervene.** Intervenir *(interrvenêêrr).*
**Intervention.** Intervención *(interrventheón).*
**Interview.** Entrevista *(éntrevvister).*
**Intestine.** Intestino *(intestêênoh).*
**Intimate.** Íntimo *(íntimmoh).*
**Intolerable.** Intolerable, inaguantable *(intollerúbleh, inuggwuntúbleh).*
**Intractable.** Intratable *(intruttúbbleh).*
**Intrepid.** Intrépido *(intréppiddoh).*
**Intrepidity.** Intrepidez *(intreppidaíth).*

**Intrigue.** (s.) Intriga *(intrêêger).*
**Intrigue.** (v.) Intrigar *(intriggárr).*
**Introduce.** Introducir *(introdõõthêêrr).*
**Introduction.** Introducción *(introddõõktheón).*
**Inundation.** Inundación *(inõõndutheón).*
**Invade.** Invadir *(invuddêêrr).*
**Invalid.** Impedido *(impeddêêdoh).*
**Invariable.** Invariable *(invurriúbble).*
**Invent.** Inventar *(inventárr).*
**Invention.** Invento, invención *(invéntoh, inventheón).*
**Inventor.** Inventor *(inventórr).*
**Inventory.** Inventario *(inventúrrioh).*
**Invest.** Invertir *(invairrtêêrr).*
**Investigate.** Investigar *(investiggárr).*
**Investigation.** Investigación *(investiggutheón).*
**Invincible.** Invencible *(inventhêêbleh).*
**Invisible.** Invisible *(invissêêbleh).*
**Invite.** Convidar, invitar *(conviddárr; invitárr).*
**Invoice.** (s.) Factura *(fuctõõrer).*
**Invoice.** (v.) Facturar *(fuctoorárr).*
**Invoke.** Invocar *(invockárr).*
**Involuntary.** Involuntario *(involluntárioh).*
**Invulnerable.** Invulnerable *(invullnerrúbleh).*
**Iris.** Iris *(iriss).*
**Iron.** (s.) Hierro *(yérro).*
**Iron.** (v.) Planchar *(pluntchárr).*
**Ironclad.** Acorazado *(uckórruthárdoh).*
**Irony.** Ironía *(irrónnea).*

**Irradiate.** Irradiar *(irrardeárr)*.
**Irrational.** Irracional *(irruthionúll)*.
**Irregation.** Riego *(re.éggoh)*.
**Irregular.** Irregular *(irrégōōlárr)*.
**Irremediable.** Irremediable *(irremméddeúbleh)*.
**Irremissible.** Irremisible *(irremmissíbleh)*.
**Irresistible.** Irresistible *(irresssistíbleh)*.

**Irresponsable.** Irresponsable *(irrisponsúbbleh)*.
**Irrevocable.** Irrevocable *(irrevocúbbleh)*.
**Islander.** Isleño *(islénnyoh)*.
**Isle.** Isla *(ísler)*.
**Islet.** Islote *(islótteh)*.
**Isolate.** Aislar *(ice.lárr)*.
**Itch.** Sarna *(sárrner)*.
**Itinerary.** Itinerario *(ittinerráreoh)*.
**Ivory.** Marfil *(marrfēēl)*.

# J

**Jailer.** Carcelero *(carrthelláirroh)*.
**January.** Enero *(ennáirroh)*.
**Japanese.** Japonés *(hupponnéss)*.
**Jaw.** Quijada *(kihhúdder)*.
**Jaw-bone.** Mandíbula *(mundíbbooler)*.
**Jester.** Truhán *(trōōhún)*.
**Jet.** Chorro *(tchórroh)*.
**Jewel.** Joya *(hóyer)*.
**Jeweller's.** Joyería *(hoyerréar)*.
**Join.** Juntar *(hōōntárr)*.
**Joke.** (s.) Broma, chiste *(bróumer, chísteh)*.
**Joke.** (v.) Bromear, embromar *(bróumeárr, embrommárr)*.
**Journalist.** Periodista *(perrioddíster)*.

**Journey.** Viaje *(vēē.úhheh)*.
**Journeyman.** Jornalero *(horrnulláiroh)*.
**Joy.** Júbilo *(hōōbilloh)*.
**Judge.** (s.) Juez *(hweth)*.
**Judge.** (v.) Juzgar *(hōōthgárr)*.
**Judgement.** Juicio *(hwítheoh)*.
**Juice.** Jugo, zumo *(hōōgoh, thōōmoh)*.
**July.** Julio *(hōōleoh)*.
**Jump.** (v.) Saltar *(sultárr)*.
**Jump.** (s.) Salto *(súltoh)*.
**June.** Junio *(hōōneoh)*.
**Just.** Justo *(hōōstoh)*.
**Justice.** Justicia *(hōōstíthea)*.
**Justify.** Justificar *(hōōstiffikárr)*.
**Justly.** Justamente *(hōōster.ménteh)*.

# K

**Keep.** Guardar *(gwarrdárr)*.
**Key.** Clave, llave, *(clárveh, lyárveh)*.

**Kick.** Cocear *(cotheárr)*.
**Kidney.** Riñón *(rinyón)*.
**Kill.** Matar *(muttárr)*.

**Kilogramme.** Kilogramo (ki-
llogrúmmoh).
**Kilolitre.** Kilolitro (killoléētroh).
**Kilometer.** Kilómetro (killóm-
metroh).
**Kilowat.** Kilovatio (killovú-
theoh).
**Kind.** Bueno, amable (buén-
noh, ummúbleh).
**Kindness.** Bondad, amabili-
dad (bondúd, úmmerbilli-
dúd).
**King.** Rey (réh.ēē).
**Kingdom.** Reino (ráy.innoh).
**Kiosk.** Kiosco (kēē.óscoh).
**Kirie.** Kirie (kírrieh).
**Kitchen.** Cocina (cothēēner).
**Kitchen-garden.** Huerta (wér-
ter).

**Knead.** Amasar (úmmus-
sárr).
**Knee.** Rodilla (roddílyer).
**Kneel.** Arrodillarse (urródi-
lyárrseh).
**Knife.** Cuchillo (cootchillyoh).
**Knife/sword.** Sable (súb-
bleh).
**Knock down.** Aporrear (up-
porreárr).
**Knot.** (v.) Anudar (unnōōdárr).
**Knot.** (s.) Nudo (nōōdoh).
**Know.** Saber, conocer (sub-
báirr, connotháirr).
**Knowledge.** Conocimiento
(connotheruyéntoh).
**Known.** Conocido (conno-
thēēdoh).
**Kodak.** Kodak (kódduk).

# L

**Laborious.** Laborioso (lub-
borrióssoh).
**Labour.** Labor (lubbórr).
**Labourer.** Obrero (obráirroh).
**Labourer (land).** Labrador
(lubbrerdórr).
**Lack.** Carecer (curretháirr).
**Lactation.** Lactancia (luck-
túnthea).
**Ladder.** Escala (escúller).
**Lagoon.** Laguna (luggōōner).
**Lamb.** Cordero (corrdáiroh).
**Lame.** Cojo (cóhhoh).
**Lamentable.** Lamentable (lú-
mmentúbleh).
**Lamp.** Lámpara (lúmpurrer).
**Lance.** Lanza (lúnther).
**Landing.** Meseta (messétter).
**Landlord.** Propietario, case-
ro (propréaturreoh, cussái-
rroh).
**Language.** Lengua, idioma
(léngwer, iddiómer).

**Lantern.** Farol, linterna (fur-
ról, lintáirner).
**Lapel.** Solapa (sollúpper).
**Larger.** Mayor (mahyórr).
**Lash.** Azote (uthótteh).
**Last.** Último (ōōltimmoh).
**Last night.** Anoche (unnót-
cheh).
**Late.** Tarde (tárrdeh).
**Lateness.** Tardanza (tarrdún-
ther).
**Lathe.** Torno (tórrnoh).
**Laugh.** Reír (reh.ēērr).
**Laughter.** Risa (rēēsser).
**Launch.** (v.) Botar, lanzar
(bottárr, lunthárr).
**Launch.** (s.) Lancha (lún-
cher).
**Laundrette.** Lavandera (luv-
vundáirrer).
**Laurel.** Laurel (lowrél).
**Lavatory.** Lavabo (luvvúb-
boh).

**Lavatory.** Lavatorio *(luvvertório)*.
**Law.** Ley *(láyee)*.
**Lawn.** Césped *(thésped)*.
**Lawyer.** Abogado *(ubbogárdoh)*.
**Lawyer's office.** Bufete *(booffétteh)*.
**Lay down.** Acostar *(uckostárr)*.
**Laziness.** Pereza *(perréther)*.
**Lazy.** Holgazán, perezoso *(olguthún, perrethóssoh)*.
**Lead.** (v.) Capitanear *(cappitúneh-árr)*.
**Lead.** (s.) Plomo *(plómmoh)*.
**League.** Legua *(légwer)*.
**Leaf.** Hoja *(óhher)*.
**Lean.** Apoyar, -se *(uppoyarr, -seh)*.
**Learn.** Aprender, enterarse *(apprendáirr, enterrárrseh)*.
**Learned.** Docto, sabio *(dóctoh, súbbeoh)*.
**Learning.** Sabiduría *(subbiddoorrëēr)*.
**Lease rent.** Arrendamiento *(urrénder.myéntoh)*.
**Leather.** Cuero *(kwáirroh)*.
**Leave.** Dejar *(dehárr)*.
**Leech.** Sanguijuela *(súnghihhwéller)*.
**Left.** Izquierda *(ithkyáirrder)*.
**Leg.** Pierna, pata *(pyáirner, pútter)*.
**Legacy.** Legado *(leggárdoh)*.
**Legality.** Legalidad *(leggullidúd)*.
**Legalize.** Legalizar *(leggullithár)*.
**Legally.** Legalmente *(leggulménteh)*.
**Legate.** Legado *(leggárdoh)*.
**Legend.** Leyenda *(layénder)*.
**Legendary.** Legendario *(lehendúrreo)*.

**Legging.** Polaina *(polláh.inner)*.
**Legion.** Legión *(lehheón)*.
**Legitimate.** Legítimo *(lehíttimoh)*.
**Leisure.** Ocio *(ótheoh)*.
**Lemon.** Limón *(limmón)*.
**Lemon-coloured.** Cetrino *(thittrēēnoh)*.
**Lend.** Prestar *(prestárr)*.
**Length.** Largura *(larrgōōrer)*.
**Lengther.** Alargar *(ullarr.gárr)*.
**Lens.** Lente *(lénteh)*.
**Less.** Menos *(ménnoss)*.
**Lessen.** Escatimar, achicar *(escuttimjmárr, útchickárr)*.
**Lesson.** Lección *(lektheón)*.
**Lethargy.** Letargo *(lettárrgoh)*.
**Letter.** Carta, letra *(cárrter, léttrer)*.
**Level.** (v.) Allanar *(úllyunnárr)*.
**Level.** (s.) Nivel *(nivvéll)*.
**Lever.** Palanca *(pullúncker)*.
**Liar.** Embustero, mentiroso *(emboostáirroh, mentirróssoh)*.
**Liberal.** Liberal *(libberrúl)*.
**Liberty.** Libertad *(libberrtúd)*.
**Fickle.** Liviano *(livviúnnoh)*.
**Library.** Biblioteca *(bibliotécker)*.
**Licit.** Lícito *(lithítoh)*.
**Lid.** Cubierto, tapa *(coobyáirrtoh, túpper)*.
**Lie.** (s.) Mentira *(mentēērer)*.
**Lie.** (v.) Mentir *(mentēēr)*.
**Lieutenant.** Teniente *(tenyénteh)*.
**Life.** Vida *(vēēder)*.
**Lifebouy.** Salvavidas *(sulvervēēdus)*.
**Lifelong.** Vitalicio *(vittúlitheoh)*.
**Lift.** (v.) Alzar *(ullthárr)*.
**Lift.** (s.) Ascensor *(ústhensórr)*.
**Light.** (v.) Alumbrar, encen-

der *(úlloombrárr, enthendárr)*.
**Light.** (s.) Luz *(looth)*.
**Light.** (adj.) Ligero *(lihhároh)*.
**Lighten.** Esclarecer, aligerar *(esclurrithárr, alli.herrarr)*.
**Lighter.** Mechero *(metchárroh)*.
**Lightly.** Ligeramente *(lihárrrumménteh)*.
**Lightning.** Relámpago, rayo *(rellúmpuggoh, ráhyoh)*.
**Lightning-rod.** Pararrayo *(purrer.ráhyoss)*.
**Like.** Semejante *(semmehhúnteh)*.
**Likeness.** Semejanza *(semmehhúnther)*.
**Lily.** Lirio *(lírreoh)*.
**Lime.** Cal *(cull)*.
**Limit.** (s.) Límite *(límmiteh)*.
**Limit.** (adj.) Limitar *(limmittárr)*.
**Limited.** Limitado *(limmittárdoh)*.
**Limp.** Cojear *(cohheárr)*.
**Linden.** Tila *(tééler)*.
**Line.** (v.) Forrar *(forrárr)*.
**Line.** (s.) Línea *(linnear)*.
**Line up.** Alinear *(ullinneár)*.
**Lineal.** Lineal *(linneúll)*.
**Lined.** Forrado *(forrárdoh)*.
**Lining.** Forro *(fórroh)*.
**Linnet.** Jilguero *(hilgáirroh)*.
**Lion.** León *(layón)*.
**Lip.** Labio *(lúbbeoh)*.
**Liquid.** Líquido *(líkkiddoh)*.
**Liquidate.** Liquidar *(likkiddárr)*.
**Liquidation.** Liquidación *(likkidduthéon)*.
**Liquor.** Licor *(lickórr)*.
**List.** Lista *(líster)*.
**Literary.** Literario *(litterrário)*.
**Literature.** Literatura *(litterráttõõrer)*.

**Lithography.** Litografía *(littogrúffia)*.
**Litigation.** Litigio, pleito *(littíhheoh, pláyittoh)*.
**Litre.** Litro *(léétroh)*.
**Little.** Poco *(póckoh)*.
**Littoral.** Litoral *(littorrúl)*.
**Live.** Vivir *(vivvéérr)*.
**Liver.** Hígado *(ígguddoh)*.
**Lividness.** Lividez *(livviddéth)*.
**Lizard.** Lagarto *(luggárrtoh)*.
**Load.** Carga *(cárrger)*.
**Loan.** Préstamo *(présstummoh)*.
**Loathe.** Aborrecer *(ubbórretháirr)*.
**Lobster.** Langosta *(lungóster)*.
**Local.** Local *(lockúl)*.
**Locality.** Localidad *(locullidúd)*.
**Lock.** (v.) Cerrar *(therrárr)*.
**Lock.** (s.) Cerradura *(thérruddõõrer)*.
**Lock up.** Encerrar *(éntherrár)*.
**Locker.** Gaveta *(guvvétter)*.
**Locksmith.** Cerrajero *(thérruh.hérroh)*.
**Locomotive.** Locomotora *(lockomottórer)*.
**Locust.** Langosta *(lungóster)*.
**Lodge.** Albergar *(ullbáirgheh)*.
**Lodging.** Albergue *(ullbáirgheh)*.
**Loft.** Buhardilla *(boo.ardílyer)*.
**Logically.** Lógicamente *(lóhhickerménteh)*.
**Loin.** Lomo *(lómmoh)*.
**Loiter.** Vagar *(vuggárr)*.
**Loneliness.** Soledad *(solleddúd)*.
**Long.** (adj.) Largo *(lárrgoh)*.
**Long.** (v.) Ansiar *(unseárr)*.

**Longitude.** Longitud (lonhit-tõõd).
**Look.** (s.) Mirada (mirrár-derr).
**Look.** (v.) Mirar (meerrárr).
**Look for.** Buscar (booscárr).
**Loom.** Telar (tellárr).
**Loose.** Flojo (flóckoh).
**Loosen.** Soltar (soltárr).
**Loquacity.** Locuacidad (lok-wuthidúd).
**Lose.** Perder (pairrdáirr).
**Loss.** Pérdida (páirrdidder).
**Lot.** Lote (lótteh).
**Lottery.** Lotería (lotterréar).
**Louse.** Piojo (pyóhhoh).
**Love.** (v.) Amar, querer (um-márr, kerráirr).

**Love.** (s.) Enamorado (en-númmorrárdoh).
**Lover.** Amante (ummún-teh).
**Lowest.** Ínfimo (ínfimmoh).
**Loyal.** Leal (layúll).
**Loyally.** Lealmente (layul-ménteh).
**Lozenge.** Pastilla (pustílyer).
**Lucrative.** Lucrativo (lookru-tēēvoh).
**Luminous.** Luminoso (loomi-nóssoh).
**Lunch.** Almorzar (úllmorr-thárr).
**Lung.** Pulmón (poolmón).
**Luxury.** Lujo (lõõhoh).
**Lyric.** Lírico (lírrickoh).

# M

**Mace.** Maza (múther).
**Machine.** Máquina (múckin-ner).
**Mad.** Rabioso, loco (rub-beóssoh, lóckoh).
**Made.** Hecho (étchoh).
**Madhouse.** Manicomio (mu-nnicómmioh).
**Madness.** Locura (lockõõrer).
**Magisterial.** Magistral (muh-histrúll).
**Magistrate.** Magistrado (mu-histrárdoh).
**Magnetism.** Magnetismo (mugnettísmoh).
**Magnificent.** Magnífico (mug-nífficoh).
**Magnitude.** Magnitud (mug-nitõõd).
**Mahogany.** Caoba (cah.āw-ber).
**Maintenance.** Manutención, sustento (munootentheón, soosténtoh).

**Maize.** Maíz (mah.ēēth).
**Majestic.** Majestuoso (muh-héstoo.óssoh).
**Majesty.** Majestad (muhhes-túd).
**Make.** Hacer, confeccionar (utháirr, confecthionnárr).
**Male.** Macho, varón (mút-choh, vurrón).
**Malefactor.** Malhechor (mu-lletchórr).
**Malice.** Malicia (mullíthea).
**Malicious.** Malicioso (mulli-thióssoh).
**Malignant.** Maligno (múllíg-noh).
**Mallow.** Malva (múlver).
**Mamma.** Mamá (mummár).
**Man.** Hombre (ómbreh).
**Manage.** Manejar (munnihárr).
**Management.** Gerencia (he-rrénthear).
**Manager.** Gerente, director (herrénteh, dirrectórr).

**Mandate.** Mandato *(mundúttoh).*

**Mania.** Manía *(munnēēr).*

**Manifest.** Manifiesto *(munnifyéstoh).*

**Manifestation.** Manifestación *(munnifestutheón).*

**Manikin.** Maniquí *(munnikēē).*

**Manly.** Varonil, viril *(vurronnēēl, vírrill).*

**Manner.** Manera *(munnáirer).*

**Mansion.** Mansión *(munseón).*

**Manual.** Manual *(munooúll).*

**Manufacture.** Fabricar *(fubbrickárr).*

**Manuscript.** Manuscrito *(munooscríttoh).*

**Map.** Mapa *(múpper).*

**Marble.** Mármol *(márrmol).*

**March.** Marcha *(márrcher).*

**Mare.** Yegua *(yégwer).*

**Margin.** Margen *(márrhen).*

**Mark.** Marca *(márrker).*

**Market.** Mercado *(mairrcúddoh).*

**Marriage.** Casamiento *(cussermyéntoh).*

**Marry.** Casarse *(cussárrseh).*

**Marrow.** Médula *(méddooler).*

**Marsh.** Pantano *(puntúnnoh).*

**Martyr.** Mártir *(márrtirr).*

**Marvel.** Maravilla *(murrer.vílyer).*

**Masculine.** Masculino *(muscoolēēnoh).*

**Mask.** Careta *(currétter).*

**Mason.** Albañil *(ullbunnyill).*

**Mass.** Masa *(músser).*

**Mass.** (igl.) Misa *(mēēser).*

**Massive.** Macizo *(muthēēthoh).*

**Master.** (v.) Amaestrar *(ummáh.estrárr).*

**Master.** (s.) Amo, patrono,

dueño, maestro *(úmmoh, puttrónnoh, dwényoh, mah.éstroh).*

**Mat.** Estera *(estáirrer).*

**Match.** Cerilla, fósforo *(therrílyer, fóssforroh).*

**Matchbox.** Cerillera *(thérrillyáirrer).*

**Material.** Material *(muttáireul).*

**Maternal.** Maternal *(muttairrnúl).*

**Mathematics.** Matemáticas *(muttimútticuss).*

**Matrice.** Matriz *(muttrēēth).*

**Matrimonial.** Matrimonial *(muttrimonneúl).*

**Matrimony.** Matrimonio *(muttrimmónneoh).*

**Matter.** (s.) Asunto, materia *(ussōōntoh, muttáirreah).*

**Maturity.** Sazón *(suthón).*

**Maxim.** Máxima *(múcksimmer).*

**Maximum.** Máximo *(múcksimmoh).*

**May.** Mayo *(máhyoh).*

**Mayor.** Alcalde *(ullcúlldeh).*

**Mayor's office.** Alcaldía *(ullculldéar).*

**Me.** Me *(meh).*

**Meadow.** Prado *(prárdoh).*

**Mean.** Mezquino *(methkēēnoh).*

**Mean.** (v.) Significar *(signifficárr).*

**Mean.** (s.) Ruin, tacaño, villano *(rooēēn, tuckúnyoh, vilyúnnoh).*

**Meanness.** Mezquindad, vileza *(methkinnidúd, villether).*

**Meannig.** Significado *(signifficúddoh).*

**Means.** Medio *(méddioh).*

**Meanwhile.** Entretanto *(entritúntoh).*

**Measure.** (s.) Medida *(meddēēder).*

**Measure.** (v.) Medir *(meddéar)*.

**Meat.** Carne *(cárrneh)*.

**Mechanically.** Maquinalmente *(muckinnulménteh)*.

**Mechanics.** Mecánica *(meckúnniker)*.

**Mechanism.** Mecanismo *(meckunnísmoh)*.

**Medal.** Medalla *(medúlyer)*.

**Mediation.** Mediación *(meddiutheón)*.

**Medicine.** Medicina *(meddithēēner)*.

**Meditate.** Meditar *(meddittárr)*.

**Meet.** Encontrar *(encontrárr)*.

**Meeting.** Encuentro, reunión *(enkwéntroh, reh.ooneón)*.

**Molodious.** Melodioso *(melloddióssoh)*.

**Melody.** Melodía *(mellóddear)*.

**Melt.** Derretir, fundir *(derritēērr, foondēērr)*.

**Melted.** Fundido *(foondēēdoh)*.

**Member.** Miembro *(myémbroh)*.

**Membrane.** Membrana *(membrúnner)*.

**Memorial.** Memorial *(memmorriúl)*.

**Memory.** Memoria, recuerdo *(memmórria, reckwáirrdoh)*.

**Mend.** Remendar *(remmendár)*.

**Mention.** Mencionar *(mentheonárr)*.

**Mercantile.** Mercantil *(mairrcuntíll)*.

**Mercy.** Misericordia *(misserricórdia)*.

**Meridian.** Meridiano *(merriddeúnno)*.

**Meridional.** Meridional *(merriddeonnúl)*.

**Merit.** Mérito *(mérrittoh)*.

**Merriment.** Alegría *(ullegréar)*.

**Merry.** Alegre *(alléggreh)*.

**Message.** Mensaje, recado *(mensúhheh, reccúddoh)*.

**Messenger.** Mensajero *(mensuhháirroh)*.

**Metal.** Metal *(mettúl)*.

**Metallic.** Metálico *(mettúllicoh)*.

**Meter.** Metro *(méttroh)*.

**Method.** Método *(méttoddoh)*.

**Mexican.** Mejicano *(mehhickúnnoh)*.

**Microscope.** Microscopio *(microscóppeoh)*.

**Middling.** Mediano *(meddi.ùnnoh)*.

**Midnight.** Medianoche *(méddiernótcheh)*.

**Milk.** Leche *(létche)*.

**Mill.** Molino *(mollēēnoh)*.

**Milligramme.** Miligramo *(milligrúmmoh)*.

**Millimeter.** Milímetro *(millímmetroh)*.

**Million.** Millón *(milyón)*.

**Millionth.** Millonésimo *(milyonéssimoh)*.

**Mine.** Mina *(mēēner)*.

**Mine.** Mío *(mēēoh)*.

**Miner.** Minero *(minnáiroh)*.

**Mineral.** Mineral *(minnerrúl)*.

**Minimum.** Mínimo *(mínnimmoh)*.

**Minor.** Menor *(mennórr)*.

**Minute.** Minuto *(minnōōtoh)*.

**Miracle.** Milagro *(millúgroh)*.

**Miraculous.** Milagroso *(millugróssoh)*.

**Mire.** Fango *(fúngoh)*.

**Miriameter.** Miriámetro *(mirriúmmetro)*.

**Mirror.** Espejo *(espéhhoh)*.

**Miscarry.** Abortar *(ubborrtárr)*.

**Miserable.** Miserable *(misserrúbleh)*.
**Misery.** Miseria *(missáirrear)*.
**Misfortune.** Desgracia, infortunio, percance *(desgrúthear, inforrtõõneoh, pairrcúntheh)*.
**Mislead.** Extraviar *(extruvveár)*.
**Mission.** Misión *(misseón)*.
**Misspend.** Malbaratar *(múlburrestárr)*.
**Mistake.** Equivocación, error *(ekkivvocutheón, errórr)*.
**Mister.** Señor *(senyórr)*.
**Mistress.** Ama *(úmmer)*.
**Mitigate.** Amortiguar *(ummórrtígwárr)*.
**Mix.** Mezclar *(methclar)*.
**Mixed.** Mixto *(míxtoh)*.
**Mixture.** Mezcla *(méthcler)*.
**Mockery.** Burla, mofa *(bõõrrlah, móffer)*.
**Mode.** Modo *(móddoh)*.
**Model.** Modelo *(moddélloh)*.
**Moderate.** (v.) Moderar *(modderárr)*.
**Moderate.** (adj.) Módico *(móddiccoh)*.
**Modern.** Moderno *(moddáirnoh)*.
**Modesty.** Modestia *(moddestéar)*.
**Modify.** Modificar *(moddiffickárr)*.
**Molar.** Muela *(mwéller)*.
**Mole.** Lunar *(loonárr)*.
**Molestation.** Molestia *(molléstea)*.
**Moment.** Momento *(mommméntoh)*.
**Monarchy.** Monarquía *(monnarkẽẽrr)*.
**Monday.** Lunes *(lõõness)*.
**Money.** Dinero *(dinnáirroh)*.
**Monologue.** Monólogo *(monnóllogoh)*.

**Monomania.** Monomanía *(monnomunnẽẽr)*.
**Monopoly.** Monopolio *(monnopóllioh)*.
**Monosyllable.** Monosílabo *(monnosíllubboh)*.
**Monster.** Monstruo *(mónstroo.oh)*.
**Monstrosity.** Monstruosidad *(monstroo.óssidúd)*.
**Monstrous.** Monstruoso *(monstroo.ósooh)*.
**Month.** Mes *(mess)*.
**Monthly.** Mensual *(mensoo.-úl)*.
**Monument.** Monumento *(monnooméntoh)*.
**Moon.** Luna *(lõõner)*.
**Moor.** (v.) Atracar *(uttruckárr)*.
**Moor.** (s.) Moro *(mórroh)*.
**Moral.** Moral *(morrúll)*.
**Morally.** Moralmente *(morrulménteh)*.
**More.** Más *(muss)*.
**Morning star.** Lucero *(lootháiroh)*.
**Mortal.** Mortal *(morrtúll)*.
**Mortify.** Mortificar *(morrtifficárr)*.
**Mosaic.** Mosaico *(mossáh.-iccoh)*.
**Mosquito net.** Mosquitero *(mosskittáiroh)*.
**Moth.** Polilla *(pollílyer)*.
**Mother.** Madre *(múddreh)*.
**Mother-in-law.** Suegra *(swéggrah)*.
**Motive.** Motivo *(mottẽẽvoh)*.
**Motive force.** Motriz *(mottrẽẽth)*.
**Motor.** Motor *(mottórr)*.
**Motor bus.** Autobús *(owtohbõõs)*.
**Motor car.** Automóvil *(owtohmóvvil)*.
**Motorist.** Automovilista *(owtommóvvellíster)*.

**Motorway/highway.** Autopista *(owtoppíster)*.
**Motto.** Lema *(lémmer)*.
**Mould.** Molde *(móldeh)*.
**Moulding.** Moldura *(moldõõrer)*.
**Mount.** Montar *(montárr)*.
**Mountain.** Montaña *(montúnyer)*.
**Mounter.** Montador *(montuddórr)*.
**Mournful.** Lúgubre *(lõõgoobreh)*.
**Mourning.** Luto *(lõõtoh)*.
**Mouse.** Ratón *(ruttón)*.
**Move.** (v.) Mover, conmover *(movváir, conmovváirr)*.
**Move.** (s.) Traslado *(truslúddoh)*.
**Move house.** Trasladar *(trusluddárr)*.
**Movement.** Movimiento *(movvimyéntoh)*.
**Much.** Mucho *(mõõtchoh)*.
**Mud.** Barro, fango *(búrroh, fúngoh)*.
**Muddy.** Turbio *(tõõrrbioh)*.
**Mule.** Mula *(mõõler)*.
**Multiplication.** Multiplicación *(mooltiplícutheión)*.
**Multiply.** Multiplicar *(mooltiplíccárr)*.

**Multitude.** Multitud *(mooltitõõd)*.
**Municipal Corporation.** Ayuntamiento *(ahyõõntermyéntoh)*.
**Murder.** (v.) Asesinar *(ussessinárr)*.
**Murder.** (s.) Homicidio *(ommethíddeo)*.
**Murderer.** Asesino *(ussessēēnoh)*.
**Murmur.** (v.) Murmurar *(moorrmoorrárr)*.
**Murmur.** (s.) Murmullo *(moorrmõõlyoh)*.
**Muscatel.** Moscatel *(mosscuttéll)*.
**Muscle.** Músculo *(mõõscooloh)*.
**Muscular.** Musculoso *(mooscoolóssoh)*.
**Museum.** Museo *(moossáyoh)*.
**Mushroom.** Seta *(sétter)*.
**Music.** Música *(mõõsicker)*.
**Muting.** Motín *(mottēēn)*.
**Mutton.** Carnero *(carrnáirroh)*.
**Mutual.** Mutuo *(mõõttoo.oh)*.
**Muzzle.** Bozal *(bothúll)*.
**My.** Mi *(me)*.
**Mystery.** Misterio *(mistáirreoh)*.

# N

**Nacre.** Nácar *(núcker)*.
**Nail.** (s.) Clavo *(clárvov.)*.
**Nail.** (v.) Clavar *(cluvvárr)*.
**Naked.** Desnudo *(desnõõdoh)*.
**Name.** (v.) Nombrar *(nombráirr)*.
**Name.** (s.) Nombre *(nómbreh)*.

**Name.** Nombre *(nómbreh)*.
**Nap.** Siesta *(syéster)*.
**Napkin.** Servilleta *(sairrvilyétter)*.
**Narcissus.** Narciso *(narrthissoh)*.
**Narrate.** Relatar, explicar *(relluttár, explickárr)*.

**Narration.** Relato *(rellúttoh)*.
**Narrow.** Estrecho *(estrétchoh)*.
**Nation.** Nación *(nutheón)*.
**Nativity.** Natividad *(nuttivvidúd)*.
**Natural.** Natural *(nuttoorúll)*.
**Naturalness.** Naturalidad *(nuttoorrullidúd)*.
**Nature.** Naturaleza, índole *(nuttoorrulléther, índolleh)*.
**Naughty.** Travieso *(truvvyésoh)*.
**Navel.** Ombligo *(omblēēgoh)*.
**Navigate.** Navegar *(nuvvegárr)*.
**Navigation.** Navegación *(núvvegútheón)*.
**Navy.** Armada, marina *(urmárder, murrēēner)*.
**Near.** (adv.) Cerca *(tháirrker)*.
**Near.** (adj.) Cercano *(thirrcúnnoh)*.
**Necessary.** Menester *(mennéstáir)*.
**Necessity.** Forzoso *(forrthósoh)*.
**Neck.** Cuello *(kwéllyoh)*.
**Need.** (v.) Necesitar *(nethesitár)*.
**Need.** (s.) Necesidad *(nethessidúd)*.
**Needle.** Aguja *(uggōōher)*.
**Negation.** Negación *(neggutheón)*.
**Negative.** Negativa *(neggutēēver)*.
**Negligence.** Negligencia *(neglihéntheur)*.
**Negotiate.** Agenciar, negociar *(uhhénthearr, neggotheárr)*.
**Neigh.** Relinchar *(relintchárr)*.
**Neighbour.** Próximo, vecino *(próximoh, vethēēnoh)*.
**Neighbourhood.** Vecindad *(vethindúd)*.

**Neither.** Tampoco, ni *(tumpócco, nee)*.
**Nephew.** Sobrino *(sobrēēnoh)*.
**Nerve.** Nervio *(náirrveoh)*.
**Nervous.** Nervioso *(nairrveóssoh)*.
**Nest.** (s.) Nido *(nēēdoh)*.
**Nest.** (v.) Anidar *(unneedárr)*.
**Net.** Red *(red)*.
**Neuter.** Neutro *(náyootroh)*.
**Neutral.** Neutral *(nayootrúll)*.
**Never.** Nunca, jamás *(nōō nker, hummús)*.
**New.** Nuevo *(nwévvoh)*.
**Newspaper.** Periódico *(Perrióddicoh)*.
**Nice.** Simpático *(simputticoh)*.
**Nickel.** Níquel *(nickéll)*.
**Nicotine.** Nicotina *(nickotēēner)*.
**Niece.** Sobrina *(sobrēēner)*.
**Night.** Noche *(nótcheh)*.
**Night out.** Trasnochar *(trusnotchárr)*.
**Nine.** Nueve *(nwévveh)*.
**Ninety.** Noventa *(novvénter)*.
**Ninth.** Novena *(novvéner)*.
**No.** No *(noh)*.
**Nobility.** Hidalguía, nobleza *(iddulgéar, nobléther)*.
**Noble.** Noble *(nóbbleh)*.
**Nobody.** Nadie *(núddi.eh)*.
**Noise.** Ruido, estrépito *(roo.-ēēdoh, estréppitoh)*.
**Noisy.** Ruidoso *(roo.iddósoh)*.
**Nominal.** Nominal *(nomminnúl)*.
**Nomination.** Nombramiento *(nombrummyéntoh)*.
**None.** Ningún *(ningōōn)*.
**Nonsense.** Disparate, tontería *(dispurrárrteh, tonterréar)*.
**Noon.** Mediodía *(méddioh.déar)*.
**Nor.** Ni *(nee)*.
**Normal.** Normal *(norrmúll)*.

**Normality.** Normalidad *(norr-mullidúd)*.
**North.** Norte *(nórrteh)*.
**Northeast.** Nordeste *(norr-déssteh)*.
**Nose.** Nariz *(nurrëëth)*.
**Notability.** Notabilidad *(not-tubbullidúd)*.
**Notary.** Notario *(nottárreoh)*.
**Notary's office.** Escribanía *(escríbbunnéar)*.
**Notch.** Mellar *(mellyárr)*.
**Note.** (v.) Anotar *(únnotárr)*.
**Note.** (s.) Nota *(nótter)*.
**Nothing.** Nada *(nárder)*.
**Notice.** Noticia, aviso *(not-tëëthea, uvvëësoh)*.
**Novel.** Novela *(novvéller)*.
**Novelty.** Novedad *(novved-dúd)*.
**November.** Noviembre *(no-vvyémbreh)*.

**Novice.** Novicio *(novvítheo)*.
**Novitiate.** Noviciado *(novvi-thiúddoh)*.
**Noxious.** Nocivo *(nothëëvoh)*.
**Nudity.** Desnudez *(desnoo-déth)*.
**Null.** Nulo *(nõõloh)*.
**Number.** Número *(nõõmai-roh)*.
**Numerous.** Numeroso *(noo-mairróssoh)*.
**Nuptials.** Nupcias *(nõõpt-heus)*.
**Nurse.** (v.) Amamantar *(um-múmmuntárr)*.
**Nurse.** (s.) Aya, nodriza *(ár-yer, nozdrëëther)*.
**Nursery garden.** Plantel *(pluntél)*.
**Nut.** Tuerca *(twáirker)*.
**Nutrition.** Nutrición *(nootri-theón)*.

# O

**Oak.** Roble, encina *(róbbleh, enthëëner)*.
**Oar.** Remo *(rémmoh)*.
**Oath.** Juramento *(hoorer.-méntoh)*.
**Obedience.** Obediencia *(ob-bedyénthia)*.
**Obedient.** Obediente *(obbe-ddyénteh)*.
**Obey.** Obedecer *(obbedde-tháirr)*.
**Object.** Objeto *(obhéttoh)*.
**Objection.** Objeción *(obye-thión)*.
**Obligation.** Obligación *(obli-gutheón)*.
**Obligatory.** Obligatorio *(obli-gguttórioh)*.
**Oblige.** Obligar *(obligárr)*.
**Oblique.** Oblicuo *(oblíquoh)*.

**Observance.** Observancia *(obsairrvúnthea)*.
**Observation.** Observación *(obsairrvutheón)*.
**Observatory.** Observatorio *(obsairrvuttórioh)*.
**Observe.** Observar *(obsáirr-várr)*.
**Obstacle.** Obstáculo *(obstú-ckooloh)*.
**Obstinacy.** Porfía, terquedad *(porrféar, tairrkeddúd)*.
**Obstinate.** Obstinado, terco *(obstinnúddoh, táirrcoh)*.
**Obstinately.** Tercamente *(tairrcumménteh)*.
**Obstination.** Obstinación *(obstinnutheón)*.
**Obstruct.** Obstruir *(obstroo-ëërr)*.

**Obstruction.** Estorbo *(estórrboh).*
**Obtain.** Obtener *(obtennáirr).*
**Occasion.** Ocasión *(occusseón).*
**Occidente.** Occidente *(octhiddénteh).*
**Occidental.** Occidental *(octhiddentúll).*
**Occupation.** Ocupación *(occoopucheón).*
**Occupy.** Ocupar *(occoopárr).*
**Occur.** Ocurrir *(occooréēr).*
**Occurrence.** Ocurrencia *(occoorrénthea).*
**Ocean.** Océano *(otháy.unnoh).*
**October.** Octubre *(octōōbreh).*
**Odd.** Impar *(ímparr).*
**Odious.** Odioso *(oddióssoh).*
**Offence.** Ofensa *(offénser).*
**Offend.** Agraviar, ofender *(uggruvveárr, offendáirr).*
**Offer.** (v.) Ofrecer *(offretháirr).*
**Offer.** (s.) Oferta *(offáirrter).*
**Offering.** Donativo, ofrecimiento *(donnertēēvoh, ofréthimyéntoh).*
**Office.** Despacho, oficina *(despútchoh, offithēēner).*
**Often.** A menudo *(ummennō ōdoh).*
**Oh!** Oh! *(oh).*
**Oil.** Aceite *(utháyteh).*
**Oil can.** Aceitera *(uthéyittáyrer).*
**Ointment.** Ungüento *(oongwéntoh).*
**Old.** Viejo, anciano *(vyéh.-hoh, úntheúnnoh).*
**Old age.** Vejez *(vehhéth).*
**Olive.** Aceituna *(úthettōōner).*
**Omelet.** Tortilla *(torttílyer).*
**Omit.** Omitir *(ommittēērr).*
**Ommission.** Omisión *(ommisseón).*

**Omnibus.** Ómnibus *(ómnibooss).*
**Omoplate.** Omóplato *(ommópluttoh).*
**On.** Sobre, encima de *(sóbreh, enthēēmer deh).*
**Once.** Una vez *(ōōner véth).*
**One.** Uno, una *(ōōnoh, ōōner).*
**One-eyed.** Tuerto *(twáirrtoh).*
**One-handed.** Manco *(múncoh).*
**Onion.** Cebolla *(thebbóllyer).*
**Only.** Solamente *(sollerménteh).*
**Opaque.** Opaco *(oppúckoh).*
**Open.** (adj.) Abierto *(ubbyáirtoh).*
**Open.** (v.) Abrir *(ubbrēērr).*
**Opera.** Ópera *(ópperrah).*
**Operate.** Operar *(opperrárr).*
**Operation.** Operación *(opperrutheón).*
**Opinion.** Opinión, dictamen *(oppinneón, dictármen).*
**Opportunity.** Oportunidad *(opportoonidúd).*
**Opposite.** Opuesto *(opwéstoh).*
**Opposition.** Oposición *(oppossitheón).*
**Oppression.** Opresión *(opresseón).*
**Oppressor.** Abrumador *(ubbrōōmer.dórr).*
**Opulence.** Opulencia *(oppoolénthea).*
**Opulent.** Opulento *(oppoolléntoh).*
**Orange.** Naranja *(nurrúnker).*
**Orange blossom.** Azahar *(úther.hárr).*
**Orang-outang.** Orangután *(orrungootún).*
**Oratory.** Oratorio *(orruttórrioh).*
**Orbit.** Órbita *(órrbitter).*

**Orchestra.** Orquesta *(orr-késster)*.
**Order.** (s.) Orden, encargo, consigna *(órrden, encárrgoh, consíggner)*.
**Order.** (v.) Ordenar *(orrden-nárr)*.
**Ordinary.** Ordinario *(orrdin-núrrioh)*.
**Ordination.** Ordenanza *(orr-dinnúnther)*.
**Organ.** Órgano *(órgunnoh)*.
**Organisation.** Organización *(orrgunnithútheón)*.
**Organism.** Organismo *(orr-gunnísmoh)*.
**Orient.** Oriente *(orriénteh)*.
**Oriental.** Oriental *(orrien-túll)*.
**Orientation.** Orientación *(or-rientutheón)*.
**Original.** Original *(orriggin-núl)*.
**Orphan.** Huérfano *(wérfun-noh)*.
**Orthography.** Ortografía *(or-toggrufféa)*.

**Oscillation.** Oscilación *(ossi-llutheón)*.
**Ostentation.** Alarde *(úllárr-deh)*.
**Ostentation.** Ostentación *(os-tentutheón)*.
**Ounce.** Onza *(ónther)*.
**Our, ours.** Nuestro *(nwés-troh)*.
**Out.** Fuera *(fwáirrer)*.
**Oven.** Horno *(órrnoh)*.
**Overcoat.** Abrigo *(ubbrēēgoh)*.
**Overcome.** Vencer, sobrevenir *(ventháirr, sobbreh.ven-nēērr)*.
**Overfloat.** Sobrenadar *(sob-brehnuddárr)*.
**Overflow.** Rebosar *(rebbos-sárr)*.
**Overheat.** Achicharrar *(utchí-tchurrárr)*.
**Overseer.** Capataz *(cupper-túth)*.
**Owl.** Búho *(bōō.oh)*.
**Ox.** Buey *(bwáy)*.
**Oxygen.** Oxígeno *(oxíhhen-noh)*.

# P

**Pacific.** Pacífico *(puthífficoh)*.
**Pacify.** Pacificar *(pussifficárr)*.
**Pack.** Embalar *(embullárr)*.
**Padlock.** Candado *(cundár-doh)*.
**Page.** Página *(púhhinner)*.
**Pain.** (s.) Pena *(pénner)*.
**Pain.** (v.) Penar *(pennárr)*.
**Painful.** Penoso *(pennóssoh)*.
**Paint-brush.** Brocha, pincel *(brótcher, pinsél)*.
**Painter.** Pintor *(pintórr)*.
**Painting.** Pintura *(pintōōrer)*.
**Pair.** Pareja, par *(purréhher, parr)*.

**Palace.** Palacio *(pullútheoh)*.
**Palate.** Paladar *(pulluddárr)*.
**Pale.** Pálido *(púlliddoh)*.
**Paleness.** Palidez *(pulliddéh)*.
**Palette.** Paleta *(pullétter)*.
**Palisade.** Empalizada *(em-pullithárder)*.
**Palm.** Palma *(púllmer)*.
**Palm-tree.** Palmera *(pullmái-rrer)*.
**Palpable.** Palpable *(pulpú-bleh)*.
**Palpitate.** Palpitar *(pulpittárr)*.
**Palpitating.** Palpitante *(pul-pittúnteh)*.

250

**Palpitation.** Palpitación *(pul-pittutheón).*
**Pampa.** Pampa *(púmper).*
**Pamphlet.** Folleto *(foyllét-toh).*
**Pan.** Cazuela *(cuthwéller).*
**Panic.** Pánico *(púnnicoh).*
**Panorama.** Panorama *(pun-norrúmmer).*
**Pantheon.** Panteón *(pun-teón).*
**Panther.** Pantera *(puntáir-rer).*
**Paper.** Papel *(puppél).*
**Paper *(a sheet).*** Pliego *(plyéggoh).*
**Parade.** Desfilar *(desfillárr).*
**Paradise.** Paraíso *(purrer.ís-soh).*
**Paralize.** Paralizar *(purrer.li-thárr).*
**Parallel.** Paralelo *(purrerlé-lloh).*
**Paralyse.** Entorpecer, parali-zar *(entórpetháirr, púrrulli-tharr).*
**Parapet.** Parapeto *(purrer.-pettoh).*
**Parasol.** Sombrilla *(sombríl-yer).*
**Parcel.** Paquete *(pukkétteh).*
**Parchment.** Pergamino *(pairr-gummēēnoh).*
**Pardon.** Indulto, perdón *(in-dōltoh, pairrdón).*
**Parenthesis.** Paréntesis *(purréntessíss).*
**Parish.** Parroquia *(purróc-keer).*
**Parliament.** Parlamento *(parr-lumméntoh).*
**Parlour.** Locutorio *(lockootó-rreoh).*
**Parody.** (s.) Parodia *(purród-dear).*
**Parody.** (v.) Parodiar *(pa-rroddeár).*

**Parricida.** Parricida parrici-dio *(purrithēēder, purrithíd-deoh).*
**Parrot.** Papagayo *(pupper-gáhyoh).*
**Part.** Parte *(párrteh).*
**Partial.** Parcial *(parrtheúl).*
**Particular.** Particular *(parrti-coolárr).*
**Particularidad.** Particulari-dad *(particoolurridúd).*
**Partition.** Tabique *(tubbēē-keh).*
**Partner.** Socio *(sótheoh).*
**Pass.** Pasar *(pussárr).*
**Passage.** Pasaje *(pussúh-heh).*
**Passenger.** Pasajero *(pus-ser.hárrow).*
**Passerby.** Transeúnte *(trun-say.ōōnteh).*
**Passion.** Pasión *(pusseón).*
**Passive.** Pasivo *(pussēē-voh).*
**Passport.** Pasaporte *(pus-serpórrteh).*
**Pasta.** Pasta *(pússter).*
**Pasture.** Pasto *(pústoh).*
**Patch.** Parche, remiendo *(párrtcheh, remmyéndoh).*
**Patent.** Patente *(putténteh).*
**Patent leather.** Charol *(chu-rról).*
**Paternal.** Paternal *(puttáirr-núl).*
**Paternity.** Paternidad *(put-tairrniddúd).*
**Path.** Senda, sendero *(sén-der, sendáirroh).*
**Patience.** Paciencia *(pu-thyénthea).*
**Patio.** Patio *(pútteoh).*
**Patrimony.** Patrimonio *(put-trimónnioh).*
**Patriotism.** Patriotismo *(put-triotíssmoh).*
**Pattern.** Patrón *(puttrón).*

**Pause.** Pausa *(pôwser)*.

**Pave.** Adoquinar *(uddócki-nárr)*.

**Pavement.** Acera, empedrado, pavimento *(utháirer, empedrárdoh, puvviméntoh)*.

**Pavillion.** Pabellón *(pubbelyón)*.

**Pawn.** Empeñar *(empenyárr)*.

**Pay.** Pagar *(puggárr)*.

**Pay duty.** Adeudar *(uddáyoodárr)*.

**Payment.** Pago *(púggoh)*.

**Peace.** Paz *(púth)*.

**Peartree.** Peral *(perrúll)*.

**Pebble.** Guijarro *(ghihhúrroh)*.

**Peculiar.** Peculiar *(peckooleárr)*.

**Pedal.** Pedal *(peddúll)*.

**Pedant.** Pedante *(peddúnteh)*.

**Pedestrian.** Pedestre *(peddéstreh)*.

**Peel.** (s.) Cáscara *(cússkurrer)*.

**Peel.** (v.) Mondar, pelar *(mondárr, pellárr)*.

**Peep.** Asomar *(ussohmárr)*.

**Peg.** Tarugo *(turrôõgoh)*.

**Pen.** Pluma *(plôõmer)*.

**Pencil.** Lápiz *(luppith)*.

**Pendent.** Pendiente *(pendyéntteh)*.

**Penetrate.** Penetrar *(pennettrár)*.

**Peninsula.** Península *(pennínsooler)*.

**Pension.** Pensión *(pensión)*.

**Pentence.** Penitencia *(pennitténthea)*.

**Penultimate.** Penúltimo *(pennôõltimmoh)*.

**People.** (s.) Gente, pueblo *(hénteh, pwébloh)*.

**People.** (v.) Poblar *(poblárr)*.

**Pepper.** Pimiento *(pimmyéntoh)*.

**Perceive.** Apercibir *(uppáirthebbéêr)*.

**Perch.** Percha *(páirrtcher)*.

**Perfect.** Perfecto *(pairrféctoh)*.

**Perfectly.** Perfectamente *(pairrfecterménteh)*.

**Perfidy.** Perfidia *(pairrfíddea)*.

**Perforate.** Perforar, acribillar *(páirforrárr, uckríbbilyárr)*.

**Perform.** Funcionar *(foontheonnárr)*.

**Perfume.** (s.) Perfume *(pairrfôõmeh)*.

**Perfume.** (v.) Sahumar *(sah.oomárr)*.

**Perfumer's.** Perfumería *(pairrfoomerréar)*.

**Perhaps.** Acaso, quizá *(uckússoh, kheethárr)*.

**Period.** Período *(perrêê.oddoh)*.

**Perish.** Perecer *(perritháirr)*.

**Permanent.** Permanente *(pairrrmunnénteh)*.

**Permit.** Permitir *(pairrmittéêr)*.

**Perpendicular.** Perpendicular *(pairrpendícoolúr)*.

**Perpetual.** Perpetuo *(pairrpéttoo.oh)*.

**Persecute.** Perseguir *(pairrseggéêrr)*.

**Persecution.** Persecución *(páirrseckootheón)*.

**Persist.** Persistir *(pairrsistéêr)*.

**Person.** Persona *(pairrsónner)*.

**Personage.** Personaje *(pairrsonnúhheh)*.

**Personality.** Personalidad *(pairrsonnullidúd)*.

**Personally.** Personalmente *(pairsonnulménteh)*.

**Perspicacions.** Perspicaz *(pairrspicúth)*.

**Persuade.** Persuadir *(pairrswuddéêr)*.

**Pervert.** Pervertir *(pairrvairr-tēĕr)*.
**Pest.** Peste *(pésteh)*.
**Petition.** Petición *(pettitheón)*.
**Petroleum.** Petróleo *(pettró-lleoh)*.
**Phantom.** Fantasma *(funtúss-mer)*.
**Phase.** Fase *(fússy)*.
**Phenomenon.** Fenómeno *(fennómennoh)*.
**Philosopher.** Filosofo *(fillós-soffoh)*.
**Philosophy.** Filosofía *(fillo-sofféar)*.
**Phonograph.** Fonógrafo *(fo-nnóggruffoh)*.
**Photographer.** Fotógrafo *(fo-ttógruffoh)*.
**Photography.** Fotografía *(fó-ttoggrufféar)*.
**Physician.** Médico *(méddi-coh)*.
**Physiognomy.** Fisionomía *(fi-ssonnómmea)*.
**Piano.** Piano *(peúnnoh)*.
**Pick-axe.** Azadón *(uther-dón)*.
**Pickpocket.** Ratero *(ruttáir-roh)*.
**Picture.** Cuadro *(kwúdroh)*.
**Pie.** Pastel *(pustél)*.
**Piece.** Pieza, trozo, pedazo *(pyéther, tróthoh, peddú-thoh)*.
**Piety.** Piedad *(pé.eddúd)*.
**Pig.** Cerdo, puerco *(tháirr-doh, pwáirrcoh)*.
**Pigeon-house.** Palomar *(pu-llommárr)*.
**Pigsty.** Zahurda *(thuh.õõrder)*.
**Pile.** Pila *(pēĕler)*.
**Pilgrimage.** Romería *(rom-merréarr)*.
**Pillar.** Pilar *(pillárr)*.
**Pillow (small).** Almohadilla *(úllmoher.díllyer)*.

**Pin.** Alfiler *(ullfillárr)*.
**Pincers.** Alicates *(ullicár-tess)*.
**Pinch.** (s.) Pellizco *(pellyíth-coh)*.
**Pinch.** (v.) Pinchar *(pintchárr)*.
**Pine.** Pino *(pēĕnoh)*.
**Pine-apple.** Piña *(pēĕnyer)*.
**Pine nut.** Piñón *(pinyón)*.
**Pine wood.** Pinar *(pinnárr)*.
**Pip.** Pepita *(peppēĕter)*.
**Pipe.** Pipa *(pēĕper)*.
**Pirate.** Pirata *(pirrútter)*.
**Pistol.** Pistola *(pistóller)*.
**Piston.** Pistón *(pistón)*.
**Pitcher.** Cántaro *(cúntarroh)*.
**Pitiful.** Lastimoso *(lustim-móssoh)*.
**Pity.** (v.) Compadecer *(com-púddetháirr)*.
**Pity.** (s.) Compasión, lástima *(compusseón, lústimmer)*.
**Place.** (v.) Colocar *(collo-cárr)*.
**Place.** (s.) Lugar, plaza, sitio *(loogárr, plúther, síttioh)*.
**Plagiarize.** Plagiar *(plug-geárr)*.
**Plague.** Plaga *(plúgger)*.
**Plain.** (s.) Llanura *(lyunõõ-rer)*.
**Plain.** (adj.) Plano *(plúnnoh)*.
**Plan.** Plan *(plún)*.
**Planet.** Planeta *(plunnétter)*.
**Plant.** (s.) Planta *(plúnter)*.
**Plant.** (v.) Plantar *(pluntárr)*.
**Plaster.** Yeso *(yéssoh)*.
**Plate.** (v.) Chapear *(chup-peár)*.
**Plate.** (s.) Plancha, plato, lámina *(plúntcher, plúttoh, lúmminner)*.
**Platform.** Plataforma *(plút-terfórrmer)*.
**Platinum.** Platino *(pluttēĕnoh)*.
**Play.** Jugar *(hoogárr)*.
**Plead.** Pleitear *(pláyitteár)*.

**Pleasant, pleasing.** Agradable *(úggruddúbleh)*.

**Please.** Agradar, complacer *(úggruddárr, complutháirr)*.

**Pleasure.** Placer *(plutháirr)*.

**Pledge.** Prenda *(prénder)*.

**Plenitude.** Plenitud *(plenittõõd)*.

**Plough.** Arado *(urrárdoh)*.

**Plumber.** Lampista *(lumpíster)*.

**Plunder.** Saqueo *(suckéh.oh)*.

**Plural.** Plural *(ploorúl)*.

**Pneumatic.** Neumático *(nay.-oomútticoh)*.

**Pneumonia.** Pulmonía *(poolmónnear)*.

**Pocket-book.** Cartera *(carrtáirrer)*.

**Poet.** Poeta *(poh.étter)*.

**Poetical.** Poético *(poh.étticoh)*.

**Poetry.** Poesía *(poh.esséẽr)*.

**Point.** (v.) Apuntar *(uppoontárr)*.

**Point.** (s.) Punto, punta *(põõ ntoh, põnter)*.

**Point out.** Señalar *(senyullárr)*.

**Poison.** (v.) Envenenar, atosigar *(envéninnárr, uttóssigárr)*.

**Poison.** (s.) Veneno *(vennénnoh)*.

**Poisonous.** Venenoso *(vennennóssoh)*.

**Polar.** Polar *(pollárr)*.

**Pole.** Polo *(pãwloh)*.

**Police.** Policía *(pollithéa)*.

**Polish.** Bruñir *(broonyéarr)*.

**Polite.** Cortés *(corrtés)*.

**Politeness.** Cortesía *(corrtesséar)*.

**Politics.** Política *(pollítticker)*.

**Pond.** Estanque *(estúnkeh)*.

**Ponder.** Ponderar *(ponderárr)*.

**Pontiff.** Pontífice *(pontíffitheh)*.

**Poor.** Pobre *(póbbreh)*.

**Poplar.** Álamo *(úllummoh)*.

**Popular.** Popular *(poppoolárr)*.

**Popularity.** Popularidad *(poppoolurridúd)*.

**Population.** Población *(poblutheón)*.

**Porc.** Tocino *(tothẽẽnoh)*.

**Porch.** Atrio, portal, zaguán *(úttreo, porrtúll, thuggwún)*.

**Pore.** Poro *(pãwroh)*.

**Portable.** Portátil *(porrtúttil)*.

**Porter.** Portero, mozo *(porrtáiroh, móthoh)*.

**Portion.** Porción *(porrtheón)*.

**Portmanteau.** Valija *(vullẽẽ her)*.

**Portrait.** Retrato *(rettrúttoh)*.

**Portray.** Retratar *(rettruttárr)*.

**Portuguese.** Portugués *(porrtooguéss)*.

**Position.** Posición *(possittheón)*.

**Positive.** Positivo *(possittẽẽvoh)*.

**Possess.** Poseer *(possay.áirr)*.

**Possessor.** Poseedor *(possay.iddórr)*.

**Possibility.** Posibilidad *(possibbillidúd)*.

**Possible.** Posible *(possẽẽbleh)*.

**Post.** Correo *(curráy.oh)*.

**Postman.** Cartero *(carrtáirroh)*.

**Postage.** Franqueo *(frunkayoh)*.

**Postal.** Postal *(postúll)*.

**Posterior.** Posterior *(postereórr)*.

**Posterity.** Posteridad *(posterridúd)*.

**Posthumous.** Póstumo *(pósstoomoh)*.

**Postpone.** Aplastar (*upplustárr*).

**Posture.** Postura (*postõõrer*).

**Pot.** Olla (*óllyer*).

**Pot (food).** Puchero (*pootcháirroh*).

**Potash.** Potasa (*pottússer*).

**Potatoe.** Patata (*puttútter*).

**Pottage.** Potaje (*pottúh.heh*).

**Pound.** Libra (*lēēbrer*).

**Poverty.** Pobreza (*pobréther*).

**Powder.** (s.) Polvo (*pólvoh*).

**Powder.** (v.) Empolvar (*empolvárr*).

**Power.** Poder (*poddáirr*).

**Powerful.** Poderoso, pudiente (*podderróssoh, poodyénteh*).

**Practicable.** Practicable (*pruckticúbbleh*).

**Practice.** (s.) Práctica (*prúckticker*).

**Practice.** (v.) Practicar (*pruckticárr*).

**Praise.** (s.) Alabanza, elogio (*uller.búnther, ellohheoh*).

**Praise.** (v.) Alabar (*ullerbárr*).

**Praiseworthy.** Laudable (*lowdúbleh*).

**Pray.** Orar, rezar, rogar (*orrárr, rethárr, roggárr*).

**Prayer.** Oración, súplica (*orrutheón, sõõplicker*).

**Preach.** Predicar (*preddiccárr*).

**Preamble.** Preámbulo (*preh.úmbooloh*).

**Precaution.** Precaución (*preckowtheón*).

**Precept.** Precepto (*pressséptoh*).

**Preceptor.** Preceptor (*presseptórr*).

**Precious.** Precioso (*pretheóssoh*).

**Precipice.** Precipicio (*prethippítheoh*).

**Precipitate.** Precipitar (*prethippittárr*).

**Precipitation.** Precipitación (*prethippittutheón*).

**Precise.** (v.) Precisar (*prethissárr*).

**Precise.** (adj.) Preciso (*prethēēso*).

**Precisely.** Precisamente (*prethisserménteh*).

**Precision.** Precisión (*prethisseón*).

**Predestinate.** Predestinar (*predestinnárr*).

**Predestination.** Predestinación (*preddestinnutheón*).

**Predomination.** Predominio (*preddommínneoh*).

**Preface.** Prefacio (*preffútheoh*).

**Prefer.** Preferir (*prefferrēēr*).

**Preferable.** Preferible (*prefferrēēbleh*).

**Preference.** Preferencia (*prefferrénthea*).

**Prejudice.** Perjuicio (*pairrhwítheo*).

**Prejudicial.** Perjudicial (*pairrhooditheúl*).

**Preliminary.** Preliminar (*prellimminnárr*).

**Preludia.** Preludio (*prellõõdioh*).

**Premeditation.** Premeditación (*premmedditatheón*).

**Preoccupation.** Preocupación (*preh.occooputheón*).

**Preparation.** Preparación (*preppurrutheón*).

**Preparative.** Preparativo (*preppurruttēēvoh*).

**Prepare.** Preparar (*preppurrárr*).

**Preposition.** Preposición (*preppossitheón*).

**Presage.** Presagio (*pressúhheoh*).

**Prescribe.** Recetar *(rethettárr)*.

**Prescription.** Receta *(rethétter)*.

**Presence.** Presencia *(pressénthear)*.

**Present.** (v.) Obsequiar, regalar, presentar *(obsékkyar, reggullárr, pressentárr)*.

**Present.** (s.) Regalo *(reggúlloh)*.

**Presentation.** Obsequio *(obsékkeoh)*.

**Presentiment.** Presentimiento *(pressentimyéntoh)*.

**Preservation.** Conservación *(consairrvútheón)*.

**Preserve.** Conservar, preservar *(consairrvárr, pressairrvárr)*.

**Preside.** Presidir *(pressidēēr)*.

**Presidence.** Presidencia *(pressiddénthea)*.

**President.** Presidente *(pressidénteh)*.

**Press.** (v.) Estrujar *(estroohárr)*.

**Press.** (s.) Prensa *(prénser)*.

**Pressure.** Presión *(presseón)*.

**Prestige.** Prestigio *(prestíhheoh)*.

**Presume.** Presumir *(pressoomēēr)*.

**Pretend.** Fingir *(finhēēr)*.

**Pretender.** Pretendiente *(prettendyenteh)*.

**Pretension.** Pretensión *(prettenseón)*.

**Pretext.** Pretexto *(prettéxtoh)*.

**Prevent.** Evitar, precaver *(evvitárr, preckuvváir)*.

**Prevention.** Prevención *(preventheón)*.

**Preventive.** Preventivo *(prevventēēvoh)*.

**Price.** Precio *(prétheoh)*.

**Prick.** (v.) Picar, pinchar *(piccár, pintchárr)*.

**Prick.** (s.) Picadura *(pickerdō ōrer)*.

**Pricking.** Punzante *(poonthúnteh)*.

**Pride.** Soberbia, orgullo *(sobbáirrbear, orgōōlyoh)*.

**Priest.** Sacerdote *(sutherdótteh)*.

**Prime.** Primja *(prēēmer)*.

**Primitive.** Primitivo *(primmittēēvoh)*.

**Principal.** Principal *(printhippúl)*.

**Print.** (s.) Impreso *(impréssoh)*.

**Print.** (v.) Imprimir *(imprimmēēr)*.

**Printer.** Impresor *(impressorr)*.

**Printer's error.** Errata *(errárter)*.

**Printing works.** Imprenta *(imprénter)*.

**Prison.** Cárcel, prisión *(cárrthel, prisseón)*.

**Prisoner.** Preso *(préssoh)*.

**Privilege.** Privilegio *(privvilléhheoh)*.

**Privileged.** Privilegiado *(privvillehheúddoh)*.

**Prize.** Premio *(prémmeoh)*.

**Probability.** Probabilidad *(probberbillidúd)*.

**Probable.** Probable *(probbúbbleh)*.

**Problem.** Problema *(problémmer)*.

**Process.** Proceso *(prothéssoh)*.

**Procession.** Procesión *(prothesseón)*.

**Procure.** Procurar *(prockoorárr)*.

**Prodigious.** Portentoso *(portentóssoh)*.

**Prodigy.** Prodigio portento *(prodihheo, porrténtoh).*

**Produce.** Fructificar *(frooktificárr).*

**Producer.** Productor *(proddoocktórr).*

**Product.** Producto *(proddõõcktoh).*

**Profanation.** Profanación *(proffunnutheón).*

**Profess.** Profesar *(professárr).*

**Profession.** Profesión *(professeón).*

**Professor.** Profesor *(proffessórr).*

**Profile.** Perfil *(pairrfêêl).*

**Profit.** Aprovechar *(úpprovvetchárr).*

**Profit.** Beneficio, provecho *(bénneffêêtheoh, provétcho).*

**Profitable.** Provechoso *(provetchóssoh).*

**Prognostic.** Pronóstico *(pronósticoh).*

**Program.** Programa *(progrúmmer).*

**Progress.** (v.) Progresar *(progressárr).*

**Progress.** (s.) Progreso *(progréssoh).*

**Project.** Proyecto *(proyéctoh).*

**Projectil.** Proyectil *(proyécktil).*

**Projection.** Proyección *(proyectheón).*

**Proletarian.** Proletario *(prollettárreoh).*

**Prolix.** Prolijo *(prollíhhoh).*

**Prologue.** Prólogo *(prólloggoh).*

**Prolong.** Prolongar *(prollongárr).*

**Promenade.** Rambla *(rámbler).*

**Prominence.** Realce *(ray.últheh).*

**Promise.** (v.) Prometer *(prommettáirr).*

**Promise.** (s.) Promesa *(prommésser).*

**Promissory note.** Pagaré *(puggerréh).*

**Promontory.** Promontorio *(prommonttórreoh).*

**Promote.** Promover *(prommovváirr).*

**Promptness.** Prontitud *(prontittõõd).*

**Pronoun.** Pronombre *(pronnómbreh).*

**Pronunciation.** Pronunciación *(pronnoontheuthéon).*

**Proof.** Prueba *(prwébber).*

**Propaganda.** Propaganda *(proppergúnder).*

**Propagate.** Propagar *(proppergárr).*

**Propense.** Propenso *(proppénsoh).*

**Proper.** Propio *(próppeoh).*

**Property.** Propiedad *(proppeerdúd).*

**Prophesy.** Profecía *(proffethéar).*

**Prophet.** Profeta *(proffétter).*

**Proportion.** Proporción *(propporrtheón).*

**Propose.** Proponer *(propponnáirr).*

**Proposition.** Proposición *(proppossithéon).*

**Proprieter.** Propietario *(próppi.ettúrreoh).*

**Prose.** Prosa *(prósser).*

**Prosody.** Prosodia *(prossóddea).*

**Prospectus.** Prospecto *(prospéctoh).*

**Prosper.** Prosperar *(prosperrárr).*

**Prosperity.** Prosperidad *(prosperridúd).*

**Protect.** Amparar, proteger *(úmpurrárr, prottehháirr).*
**Protection.** Protección *(protecktheón).*
**Protector.** Protector *(protecktórr).*
**Protest.** (s.) Protesta *(prottéster).*
**Protest.** (v.) Protestar *(prottestárr).*
**Protestant.** Protestante *(prottestúnteh).*
**Proud.** Soberbio, orgulloso *(sobbáirrbeoh, orgoolyóssoh).*
**Proverb.** Proverbio, refrán *(provváirrbeoh, reffrún).*
**Proverbial.** Proverbial *(provvairrbeúl).*
**Providence.** Providencia *(provviddéntheer).*
**Providential.** Providencial *(provviddentheúl).*
**Province.** Provincia *(provvinthear).*
**Provincial.** Provincial *(provvintheúl).*
**Provisional.** Provisional *(provvisseonnúl).*
**Provisions.** Víveres *(vêêveress).*
**Provocation.** Provocación *(provvockutheón).*
**Provocative.** Provocativo *(provvockuttêêvoh).*
**Provoke.** Provocar *(provvoccárr).*
**Prow.** Proa *(práwer).*
**Proximity.** Proximidad *(proximiddúd).*
**Prudence.** Prudencia *(proodénthear).*
**Prudent.** Prudente *(proodénteh).*
**Prune.** Podar *(poddárr).*
**Pruning knife.** Podadera *(podderdáirer).*

**Psalm.** Salmo *(súllmoh).*
**Public.** Público *(pôôblickoh).*
**Publication.** Publicación *(pooblicutheón).*
**Publish.** Publicar *(pooblicárr).*
**Publisher.** Editor *(eddittór).*
**Pudding (black).** Morcilla *(morrthílyer).*
**Pulley.** Polea *(polláyer).*
**Pulmonary.** Pulmonar *(poolmonnárr).*
**Pulsation.** Pulsación *(poolsutheón).*
**Pulse.** Pulso *(pôôlsoh).*
**Pulverize.** Pulverizar *(poolverrithárr).*
**Pumpkin.** Calabaza *(cúllerbúther).*
**Punch.** Ponche *(póntcheh).*
**Punctuality.** Puntualidad *(poontoo.ullidúd).*
**Punctuation.** Puntuación *(poontoo.utheón).*
**Punish.** (v.) Castigar *(custigárr).*
**Punishment.** (s.) Castigo *(cústêêgoh).*
**Pure.** Puro *(pôôrroh).*
**Purgative.** Purgante *(poorgúnteh).*
**Purge.** Purgar *(poorgárr).*
**Purity.** Pureza *(poorréther).*
**Purpose.** Propósito *(proppóssittoh).*
**Purpurine.** Purpurina *(poorrporêêner).*
**Purse.** Monedero *(monneddáiroh).*
**Pursue.** Proseguir *(prossiggêêr).*
**Pus.** Pus *(poos).*
**Push.** Empujar *(empoohhárr).*
**Pusillanimous.** Pusilánime *(poossillúnnimmeh).*
**Put.** Poner *(ponnáirr).*
**Put in.** Meter *(mettáirr).*

**Putrefaction.** Putrefacción *(pootrefffucktheón)*.
**Pyramid.** Pirámide *(pirrúmmiddeh)*.

**Pyramidal.** Piramidal *(pirrer.middúl)*.
**Pyrenean.** Pirenaico *(pirrenáh.ickoh)*.

# Q

**Quadrant.** Cuadrante *(kwudrúnteh)*.
**Qualify.** Calificar *(cullificárr)*.
**Quality.** Calidad *(cullidúd)*.
**Quantity.** Cantidad *(cuntidúd)*.
**Quarantine.** Cuarentena *(kwurrentener)*.
**Quarrel.** Reñir *(renyêêr)*.
**Quarry.** Cantera *(cuntáirrer)*.
**Quarter.** (v.) Acuartelar *(uckwártellarr)*.
**Quarter.** (s.) Cuarta parte *(kwárterpárty)*.
**Queen.** Reina *(ray.êêner)*.

**Quench.** Aplacar *(úppluckárr)*.
**Question.** Cuestión, pregunta *(kwesteón, preggôônter)*.
**Quicksilver.** Azogue *(uthóggeh)*.
**Quiet.** Tranquilo *(trunkílloh)*.
**Quietness.** Tranquilidad *(trunkillidúd)*.
**Quinine.** Quine *(kêêner)*.
**Quinsy.** Angina *(unhêêner)*.
**Quotation.** Cotización *(cottithútheón)*.
**Quote.** Cotizar *(cottithárr)*.

# R

**Rabbit (young).** Gazapo *(guthúppoh)*.
**Race.** Carrera, raza *(curráirrerrer, rúther)*.
**Radiant.** Radiante *(ruddeúnteh)*.
**Radical.** Radical *(ruddickúl)*.
**Radish.** Rábano *(rúbbunnoh)*.
**Raffle.** Rifa *(rêêfer)*.
**Raft.** Balsa *(bullser)*.
**Rag.** Andrajo, harapo, trapo *(undrúhhoh, úrruppoh, trúppoh)*.
**Rage.** (s.) Rabia *(rúbbear)*.
**Rage.** (v.) Rabiar *(rubbeárr)*.
**Ragged.** Haraposo *(urrerpóssoh)*.
**Rag-shop.** Trapería *(trupperrêêr)*.

**Railway.** Ferrocarril *(férrocurríll)*.
**Rain.** Lluvia *(lyôôvia)*.
**Raise.** Subir, levantar, alzar *(soobêêr, levvuntárr, ullthárr)*.
**Rake.** Rastrillo *(rustrílyoh)*.
**Ram.** Borrego *(borráygoh)*.
**Rancid.** Rancio *(rúntheoh)*.
**Rancorous.** Rencoroso *(rencorróssoh)*.
**Rancour.** Rencor *(rencórr)*.
**Range (mountains).** Cordillera *(cordillyáirrer)*.
**Ransack.** Saquear *(suckeárr)*.
**Ransom.** Rescate *(rescútteh)*.
**Rapid.** Rápido *(rúppiddoh)*.
**Rapidity.** Rapidez *(ruppiddéth)*.

**Rapine.** Rapiña *(ruppēēnyer)*.

**Rare.** Raro *(rárroh)*.

**Rarity.** Rareza *(rurréther)*.

**Rascal.** Granuja *(grunōōh.-her)*.

**Rasp.** Raspador *(rusperdórr)*.

**Rat.** Rata *(rútter)*.

**Ration.** Ración, cuota, *(rutheón, quórter)*.

**Rational.** Racional *(rutheonnúl)*.

**Rattle.** Estertor *(estairrtór)*.

**Ravage.** (v.) Asolar *(ússoh.-lárr)*.

**Ravage.** (s.) Estrago *(estrúggoh)*.

**Raw.** Crudo *(crōōdoh)*.

**Reach.** Alcanzar *(úllcunthárr)*.

**Read.** Leer *(layáirr)*.

**Reading.** Lectura *(lecktōōrer)*.

**Ready.** Listo *(lístoh)*.

**Real.** Real *(ray.úl)*.

**Reality.** Realidad *(ray.ullidúd)*.

**Realize.** Realizar *(ray.ullithárr)*.

**Ream.** Resma *(résmer)*.

**Reanimate.** Reanimar *(ray.-unnimárr)*.

**Reaper.** Segador *(seggudórr)*.

**Reason.** Razón *(ruthón)*.

**Reasonable.** Razonable *(ruthonúbleh)*.

**Rebel.** (s.) Rebelde *(rebbéldeh)*.

**Rebel.** (v.) Rebelarse *(rebbellárrseh)*.

**Rebound.** Resaltar, rebotar *(ressultárr, rebbottárr)*.

**Recall.** Acordarse *(uckorrdárrseh)*.

**Receipt.** Recibo *(rethēēboh)*.

**Receive.** Acoger, recibir *(úckohháirr, réthebbēēr)*.

**Recent.** Reciente *(rethyénteh)*.

**Reception.** Recepción *(retheptheón)*.

**Reception clerk.** Recepcionista *(retheptheonníster)*.

**Recharge.** (v.) Recargar *(reckárrgárr)*.

**Recharge.** (s.) Recargo *(reckárrgoh)*.

**Recipient.** Recipiente *(rethippyénteh)*.

**Reclaim.** Reclamar *(reeklummár)*.

**Recollection.** Recolección *(reckollecktheón)*.

**Recommend.** Encomendar, recomendar *(encommendárr, recommendárr)*.

**Recommendation.** Recomendación *(reckommendutheón)*.

**Record.** Acta *(úckter)*.

**Resort.** Recurso *(recōōrrsoh)*.

**Recover.** Recobrar, recuperar *(reckobbrárr, recooperrárr)*.

**Recreate.** Recrear *(reckreárr)*.

**Recriminate.** Recriminar *(reckrimminárr)*.

**Rectify.** Rectificar *(rectíffícárr)*.

**Rectitude.** Rectitud *(rectitōōd)*.

**Rector.** Rector *(réctorr)*.

**Recur.** Recurrir *(recorrēēr)*.

**Red.** Rojo *(róh.hoh)*.

**Redeem.** Redimir *(reddimmēērr)*.

**Redeemer.** Redentor *(reddentórr)*.

**Redemption.** Redención *(reddentheón)*.

**Red-hot.** Ascua *(ússkwer)*.

**Reduce.** Rebajar, reducir *(rebbuhhárr, reddoothēēr)*.

**Reduction.** Reducción, rebaja *(reddooktheón, rebbúhher)*.

**Reed.** Carrete *(currétteh)*.

**Re-enlist.** Reenganchar *(re-henguntchárr)*.

**Re-establish.** Restablecer *(restublethdáirr)*.

**Re-establishmet.** Restable-cimiento *(restublethimyén-toh)*.

**Refer.** Referir *(refferrēēr)*.

**Reference.** Referencia *(ref-ferrénthea)*.

**Reflect.** Reflejar, reflexionar *(refflehhárr, refflexionnárr)*.

**Reflector.** Reverbero *(rev-vebbáirroh)*.

**Reform.** (v.) Reformar *(ref-forrmárr)*.

**Reform.** (s.) Reforma *(reffór-rmer)*.

**Refresh.** Refrescar *(reffres-cárr)*.

**Refreshment.** Refresco *(ref-fréscoh)*.

**Regenerate.** Regenerar *(rehhennerrárr)*.

**Regeneration.** Regenera-ción *(rehhennerrutheón)*.

**Regent.** Regente *(rehhénn-teh)*.

**Regime.** Régimen *(réhhim-men)*.

**Region.** Región *(rehheón)*.

**Register.** (v.) Registrar, certifi-car *(rehhistrárr, tháirrtifficárr)*.

**Register.** (s.) Registro, ma-trícula *(rehhístroh, muttrí-cooler)*.

**Regular.** Regular *(regoolárr)*.

**Regularly.** Regularmente *(re-ggoolarrménteh)*.

**Regulate.** Reglamentar *(re-glermentárr)*.

**Regulation.** Reglamento *(re-glermyéntoh)*.

**Rehabilitate.** Rehabilitar *(re-hhubbíllittarr)*.

**Rehearsal.** Ensayo *(ensy.oh)*.

**Rehearse.** Ensayar *(ensy.árr)*.

**Reheat.** Recalentar *(recu-llentárr)*.

**Reign.** Reinar *(reh.innárr)*.

**Reigning.** Reinante *(raynún-teh)*.

**Reimburse.** Reembolsar *(re-h.embolsárr)*.

**Rein.** Rienda *(re-énder)*.

**Reinforcement.** Refuerzo *(re-ffwáirrthoh)*.

**Reiterate.** Reincidir *(reh.int-hiddēērr)*.

**Reject.** Rechazar *(retchuthárr)*.

**Rejoice.** Alegrar, -se *(ulleg-grárr, -seh)*.

**Rejoicing.** Regocijo *(reggo-h.thēēhoh)*.

**Rejuvenate.** Rejuvenecer *(rehhovennetháirr)*.

**Relapse.** Recaer *(reccah.-áirr)*.

**Relation.** Relación *(rellu-theón)*.

**Relationship.** Parentesco *(purrrentéhcoh)*.

**Relative.** (s.) Pariente *(pu-rryénteh)*.

**Relative.** (adj.) Relativo *(re-lluttēēvoh)*.

**Relic.** Reliquia *(rellih.kear)*.

**Relief.** Alivio *(ullēēvioh)*.

**Relieve.** Aliviar, relevar *(ulli-vvéarr, rellevvárr)*.

**Religion.** Religión *(rellih.-heón)*.

**Remain.** Demorar, restar, permanecer *(demmorrárr, restárr, pairrmunnetháirr)*.

**Remainder.** Resto *(réstoh)*.

**Remarkable.** Insigne *(insíg-neh)*.

**Remedy.** (v.) Remediar *(rem-meddiárr)*.

**Remedy.** (s.) Remedio *(re-mméddeoh)*.

**Remind.** Recordar *(reckorr-dárr)*.

**Remit.** Remitir *(remmittēērr).*

**Remittance.** Envío *(envéo).*

**Remorse.** Remordimiento *(remmorrdimmyéntoh).*

**Remote.** Remoto *(remmóttoh).*

**Remount.** Remontar *(remmontárr).*

**Removal.** Mudanza *(moodúnther).*

**Remove.** Mudar, quitar, sacar *(moodárr, kittárr, succárr).*

**Remunerate.** Remunerar *(remmoonerrárr).*

**Renaissance.** Renacimiento *(rennuthimmyéntoh).*

**Renew.** Renovar *(rennovvárr).*

**Renounce.** Renunciar *(rennoontheárr).*

**Renown.** Renombre *(rennómbreh).*

**Rent.** Alquiler, rasgón *(állkilláirr, rusgón).*

**Renunciation.** Renuncia *(rennōōntheer).*

**Reorganisation.** Reorganización *(reh.orrgunnithutheón).*

**Repair.** Reparar *(reppurrárr).*

**Reparation.** Reparación *(reppurrutheón).*

**Repeat.** Repetir *(reppettēērr).*

**Repent.** Arrepentirse *(úrreppentēērseh).*

**Repentance.** Arrepentimiento *(urreppéntimyéntoh).*

**Repertory.** Repertorio *(repperrtórreoh).*

**Replace.** Reemplazar, reponer *(reh.empluthárr, repponnáirr).*

**Reply.** Contestar *(contestárr).*

**Reprehend.** Reprender *(reprendáirr).*

**Reprehensible.** Reprensible *(reprensēēbleh).*

**Represent.** Representar *(repressentárr).*

**Representation.** Representación *(repressentutheón).*

**Representative.** Representante *(repressentúnteh).*

**Repress.** Reprimir *(reprimmēērr).*

**Reprimand.** Reprimenda *(reprimménder).*

**Reproach.** Reproche *(reprótcheh).*

**Reproduce.** Reproducir *(reproddoothēērr).*

**Reproduction.** Reproducción *(reproddooktheón).*

**Reptile.** Reptil *(reptēēl).*

**Republic.** República *(reppōōblicker).*

**Repugnance.** Repugnancia *(reppoognúnthear).*

**Repulsive.** Repulsivo *(reppoolsēēvoh).*

**Require.** Requerir *(reckerrēēr).*

**Research.** Investigación *(investigguthe'on).*

**Reserve.** (v.) Reservar *(ressairrvárr).*

**Reserve.** (s.) Reserva *(ressáirrver).*

**Reside.** Residir *(ressiddēērr).*

**Residence.** Residencia *(ressidénthea).*

**Residue.** Sobrante *(sobbrúnteh).*

**Resign.** Resignarse *(ressignarrseh).*

**Resignation.** Dimisión *(demmísseón).*

**Resin.** Resina *(ressēēner).*

**Resinous.** Resinoso *(ressinnóssoh).*

**Resist.** Resistir *(ressistēērr).*

**Resistence.** Resistencia *(ressisténthea).*

**Resolution.** Resolución *(ressollootheón).*

**Resolve.** Resolver *(ressolváirr).*

**Resonance.** Resonancia *(re-ssonnúnthea)*.
**Resonant.** Resonante *(re-ssonnúnteh)*.
**Resound.** Retumbar *(re-ttoombárr)*.
**Respect.** (v.) Respetar *(res-pettárr)*.
**Respect.** (s.) Respeto *(res-péttoh)*.
**Respectable.** Respetable *(respettúbleh)*.
**Respective.** Respectivo *(res-pectêêvoh)*.
**Responsability.** Responsabilidad *(responsubbillidúd)*.
**Responsable.** Responsable *(responsúbbleh)*.
**Rest.** (v.) Reposar, descansar *(reppossárr, descunsárr)*.
**Rest.** (s.) Reposo, descanso *(reppóssoh, descúnsoh)*.
**Restaurant.** Restaurante *(restowrúnteh)*.
**Restore.** Restaurar, restituir *(restowrrárr, restitoo.êêrr)*.
**Restrain.** Restringir *(res-tringgêêrr)*.
**Resucitate.** Resucitar *(res-soothitárr)*.
**Result.** (s.) Resultado *(res-sooltárdoh)*.
**Result.** (v.) Resultar *(resso-oltárr)*.
**Retain.** Retener *(rettennáirr)*.
**Retard.** Retardar *(rettarr-dárr)*.
**Retention.** Retención *(re-ttentheón)*.
**Return.** Volver *(volváirr)*.
**Retina.** Retina *(rettêêner)*.
**Retire.** Retirar *(rettirrárr)*.
**Retouch.** Retocar *(ret-tockárr)*.
**Retort.** Retorta *(retórrter)*.
**Retreat.** Retirada *(retirrár-der)*.

**Retribute.** Retribuir *(rettrib-boo.êêrr)*.
**Retrocede.** Retroceder *(rett-rotheddáirr)*.
**Retrocession.** Retroceso *(re-ttrothéssoh)*.
**Return (give back).** Devolver *(devvolváirr)*.
**Return.** (v.) Volver, regresar *(volváirr, regressárr)*.
**Return.** (s.) Regreso *(regrés-soh)*.
**Reveal.** Revelar *(revvellárr)*.
**Revelation.** Revelación *(rev-vellutheón)*.
**Revenue.** Renta *(rénter)*.
**Reverence.** Reverencia *(rev-verrénthea)*.
**Reverse.** Revés *(revvéss)*.
**Review.** Revista *(revvíster)*.
**Revise.** Revisar *(revvissárr)*.
**Revisor.** Revisor *(revvis-sórr)*.
**Revocable.** Revocable *(rev-vockúbbleh)*.
**Revoke.** Revocar *(revvo-cárr)*.
**Revolt.** Revuelta *(revwél-ter)*.
**Revolution.** Revolución *(rev-vollootheón)*.
**Revolve.** Revolver *(revolv-váirr)*.
**Reward.** (v.) Premiar, gratificar, recompensar *(prem-meárr, gruttifficárr, reckom-pensárr)*.
**Reward.** (s.) Recompensa *(reccompénser)*.
**Rheumatism.** Reumatismo *(reh.oommuttíssmoh)*.
**Rib.** Costilla *(costíllyer)*.
**Ribbon.** Cinta *(thínter)*.
**Rice.** Arroz *(urróth)*.
**Rich.** Rico *(ríckoh)*.
**Riches.** Riqueza *(rickéther)*.
**Ride.** Cabalgar *(cubbulgárr)*.

**Ridicule.** Ridículo *(riddícko-loh)*.

**Ridiculous.** Ridículo *(riddíckooloh)*.

**Rifle.** Fusil *(fóõssill)*.

**Right.** (s.) Derecho *(derrétchoh)*.

**Right.** (adj.) Derecho, derecha *(derrétchoh, derrétcher)*.

**Rigid.** Rígido *(ríggiddoh)*.

**Rigidity.** Rigidez *(riggiddéth)*.

**Rigor.** Rigor *(ríggorr)*.

**Ring.** (s.) Anillo, sortija *(unnillyoh, sorrtíhher)*.

**Ring.** (v.) Tocar (un timbre) *(tockárr)*.

**Ripe.** Maduro *(muddõõroh)*.

**Risk.** (s.) Riesgo *(re.ésgoh)*.

**Risk.** (v.) Arriesgar *(ùrre.esgárr)*.

**Rival.** Rival *(rivvúll)*.

**Rivalry.** Rivalidad *(rivvullidúd)*.

**River.** Río *(rẽẽ.oh)*.

**Rivet.** Remachar *(remmutchárr)*.

**Road.** Carretera, camino *(cúrrettáyrer, cummẽẽnoh)*.

**Roar.** (s.) Rugido *(roohẽẽdoh)*.

**Roar.** (v.) Rugir *(roo.hẽẽrr)*.

**Roaring.** Bramido *(brammẽẽdoh)*.

**Roast.** (s.) Asado *(ussárdoh)*.

**Roast.** (v.) Asar *(ussárr)*.

**Robust.** Robusto *(robbõõstoh)*.

**Robustness.** Robustez *(robboostéth)*.

**Rock.** (v.) Mecer *(metháirr)*.

**Rock.** (s.) Roca, peña *(rócker, pényer)*.

**Rod.** Vara *(várrer)*.

**Rodent.** Roedor *(roydórr)*.

**Roll.** Rodar *(roddárr)*.

**Roller.** Rodillo *(roddílyoh)*.

**Romance.** Romance *(rommúntheh)*.

**Roof.** Tejado *(tehhúddoh)*.

**Room.** Habitación *(ubbitutheón)*.

**Root.** (v.) Arraigar *(úrruy.gárr)*.

**Root.** (s.) Raíz *(rý.ith)*.

**Rope.** Maroma, cuerda, soga *(murrómma, kwáirder, sógger)*.

**Rotten.** Podrido *(podrẽẽdoh)*.

**Rose.** Rosa *(rosser)*.

**Rose tree.** Rosal *(rossúll)*.

**Rough.** Rudo, escabroso *(rõ õdoh, escubróssoh)*.

**Roulette.** Ruleta *(roolétter)*.

**Round.** (adj.) Redondo *(reddóndoh)*.

**Round.** (v.) Rodear *(roddeárr)*.

**Routine.** Rutina *(rootẽẽner)*.

**Row.** Renglón, fila *(renglón, fẽẽler)*.

**Royal.** Real *(ray.úl)*.

**Rub.** Frotar, refregar, rozar, restregar *(frottárr, reffreggárr, rothárr, restreggárr)*.

**Rub out.** Borrar *(borrárr)*.

**Rubber.** Caucho *(cõwchoh)*.

**Ruffian.** Rufián *(rooffeún)*.

**Ruin.** (v.) Arruinar *(urõõ.-inárr)*.

**Ruin.** (s.) Ruina *(rooẽẽner)*.

**Ruinous.** Ruinoso *(roo.innóssoh)*.

**Rule.** Regla *(réggler)*.

**Ruminate.** Rumiar *(roomeárr)*.

**Rumour.** Rumor *(roommórr)*.

**Run.** Correr *(corráirr)*.

**Run over.** Arrollar, recorrer *(úrrollyárr, reckorráirr)*.

**Rupture.** Ruptura *(rooptẽẽrer)*.

**Rural.** Rural *(roorrúll)*.

**Rustic.** Rústico *(rõõstickoh)*.

**Rye.** Centeno *(thenténnoh)*.

# S

**Sacrament.** Sacramento (su-ckrerméntoh).

**Sacramental.** Sacramental (suckrermentúll).

**Sacrifice.** Sacrificio (suckriffítheo).

**Sacrilege.** Sacrilegio (suckrilléh.hio).

**Sacristan.** Sacristán (suckristún).

**Sad.** Triste, aciago (tríssteh, utheárgoh).

**Sadden.** Apesadumbrar, entristecer (uppésser.doombrárr, entristethárr).

**Sadness.** Tristeza (tristéther).

**Sailor.** Marinero (murrinái-roh).

**Saint.** Santo (súntoh).

**Salary.** Salario, sueldo (sullúrrioh, swéldoh).

**Sale.** Venta (vénter).

**Salient.** Saliente (sulliyén-teh).

**Saliva.** Saliva (sullééver).

**Salmon.** Salmón (sulmón).

**Saloon.** Salón (sullón).

**Salt.** (s.) Sal (sull).

**Salt.** (v.) Salar (sullárr).

**Salt-celler.** Salero (sulláir-roh).

**Saltceller.** Salero (sulláirroh).

**Salted.** Salado (sullúddoh).

**Salute.** Saludo (sullõõdoh).

**Salvation.** Salvación (sulvutheón).

**Same.** Mismo (mísmoh).

**Sample.** Muestra (mwéstrer).

**Sanction.** Sancionar (suntheonárr).

**Sanctity.** Santidad (suntidúd).

**Sand.** Arena (urrénner).

**Sanitary.** Sanitario (sunnitárreoh).

**Sanitation.** Sanidad (sunnidúd).

**Sap.** Savia (súvveer).

**Sapper.** Zapador (thupperdórr).

**Sarcasm.** Sarcasmo (sarrcássmoh).

**Sardine.** Sardina (sarrdéé ner).

**Sarsaparrilla.** Zarzaparrilla (tharrthupperrílyer).

**Satellite.** Satélite (suttéllitteh).

**Satire.** Sátira (súttirrer).

**Satisfaction.** Satisfacción (suttisfuckseón).

**Satisfactory.** Satisfactorio (suttisfuctórrioh).

**Satisfied.** Satisfecho (suttisfétchoh).

**Satisfy.** Satisfacer (suttisfuthárr).

**Saturday.** Sábado (súbberdoh).

**Sauce.** Salsa (súlser).

**Saucepan.** Cacerola (cútherróller).

**Saucer.** Platillo (pluttílyoh).

**Sausage.** Salchicha, embutido (sullséétcher, embootéédoh).

**Savage.** Salvaje (sulvúhheh).

**Save.** Salvar, ahorrar (sullvárr, uh.orrárr).

**Savings.** Ahorro (uh.órroh).

**Saviour.** Salvador (sulverdórr).

**Savory.** Sabroso (subbróssoh).

**Saw.** (v.) Aserrar *(ússerrárr).*
**Saw.** (s.) Sierra *(syérrer).*
**Scabbard.** Vaina *(výner).*
**Scaffold.** Patíbulo *(puttíbooloh).*
**Scaffolding.** Andamio *(undúmmeoh).*
**Scale.** (s.) Escama, escala *(escúmmer, escúller).*
**Scale.** (v.) Escalar *(escullár).*
**Scales.** Balanza *(bullanther).*
**Scandal.** Escándalo *(escúndulloh).*
**Scandalous.** Escandaloso *(escúndullóssoh).*
**Scar.** Cicatriz *(thickutrēēth).*
**Scarce.** Escaso *(escússoh).*
**Scarecrow.** Espantajo *(espuntúhhoh).*
**Scene.** Escena *(esthénner).*
**School.** Escuela, colegio *(eskweller, colléh.heoh).*
**School-fellow.** Condiscipule *(condisthíppoolloh).*
**Science.** Ciencia *(thyénthea).*
**Scissors.** Tijeras *(tihháirruss).*
**Scorpion.** Alacrán *(uller.crún).*
**Scoundrel.** Bribón *(bribbón).*
**Scratch.** Arañar, rascar *(urrunnyárr, ruscárr).*
**Screen.** Pantalla *(puntúlyer).*
**Screw.** (v.) Atornillar *(uttórrnillyárr).*
**Screw.** (s.) Tornillo *(tornillyoh).*
**Screwdriver.** Destornillador *(déstorrnillyerdórr).*
**Scrub.** Fregar *(freggárr).*
**Scruple.** Escrúpulo *(escrōō poolloh).*
**Scrupulous.** Escrupuloso *(escrōōpoollóssoh).*
**Sculptor.** Escultor *(escooltórr).*
**Scythe.** Guadaña *(gwuddúnyer).*
**Semblance.** Simulacro *(simmoolúckroh).*

**Sew.** Coser *(cossáirr).*
**Sea.** Mar *(marr).*
**Seal.** (v.) Sellar *(selyárr).*
**Seal.** (s.) Sello *(sélyoh).*
**Sealed.** Sellado *(selyhúd doh).*
**Sealingwax.** Lacre *(lúccreh).*
**Seam.** Costura *(costōōrer).*
**Search.** Indagar *(induggárr).*
**Season.** (v.) Sazonar *(suthonnárr).*
**Season.** (s.) Temporada *(temporrúdder).*
**Season ticket.** Abono *(ubbonnoh).*
**Seat.** Asiento *(ussyéntoh).*
**Second.** Segundo *(seggōōndoh).*
**Secret.** Secreto *(seckróttoh).*
**Secretary.** Secretario *(seckretúrrioh).*
**Sect.** Secta *(séckter).*
**Seduce.** Seducir *(seddoo thēērr).*
**Seducer.** Seductor *(seddooktórr).*
**Seduction.** Seducción *(sed dooctheón).*
**See.** Ver *(váirr).*
**Seed.** Grano, semilla *(grúnnoh, semmíllyer).*
**Seed-time.** Siembra *(syémbrer).*
**Seize.** Embargar, prender *(embarrgárr, prendáirr).*
**Selfish.** Egoísta *(eggo.ísster).*
**Selfishness.** Egoísmo *(éggoh.íssmoh).*
**Sell.** Vender *(vendáirr).*
**Senate.** Senado *(sennúddoh).*
**Senator.** Senador *(sennud dórr).*
**Send.** Enviar *(ennveárr).*
**Senior.** Decano *(decúnnoh).*
**Sensation.** Sensación *(sensutheón).*

**Sense.** Sentido *(sentēēdoh)*.

**Sensible.** Sensato *(sensút-toh)*.

**Sensual.** Sensual *(sensoo.úll)*.

**Sensuality.** Sensualidad *(sensoo.ullidúd)*.

**Sentence.** Sentencia, frase *(senténthear, frússeh)*.

**Sentiment.** Sentimiento *(sentimyéntoh)*.

**Sentimental.** Sentimental *(sentimentúll)*.

**Sentinel.** Centinela *(thentinéller)*.

**Separable.** Separable *(sepperrúbbleh)*.

**Separate.** (adj.) Separado *(seppurrárdoh)*.

**Separate.** (v.) Separar, apartar *(sepperrárr, úpparrtárr)*.

**Separation.** Separación *(sepperutheón)*.

**September.** Septiembre *(septyémbreh)*.

**Septentrion.** Septentrión *(septentreón)*.

**Sequestrate.** Secuestrar *(sekwestrárr)*.

**Sequestration.** Secuestración *(seckwestrutheón)*.

**Serenade.** Serenata *(serrennárter)*.

**Serene.** Sereno *(serrénnoh)*.

**Series.** Serie *(sérrieh)*.

**Seriousness.** Seriedad *(serri.eddúd)*.

**Sermon.** Sermón *(sairrmón)*.

**Serpent.** Serpiente *(sairrpyénteh)*.

**Servant.** Sirviente *(sirvvyénte)*.

**Serve.** Servir *(sairrvēērr)*.

**Service.** Servicio, servidumbre *(sairrvítheoh, saírrvidōōmbreh)*.

**Session.** Sesión *(sesseón)*.

**Set.** Colocar *(collocárr)*.

**Settle.** Asentar *(ussentárr)*.

**Seven.** Siete *(syétteh)*.

**Seven hundred.** Setecientos *(sétteh.thyéntoss)*.

**Seventh.** Séptimo *(séptimmoh)*.

**Seventieth.** Septuagésimo *(septooerhéssimmoh)*.

**Seventy.** Setenta *(setténter)*.

**Severity.** Severidad *(sevverridúd)*.

**Sex.** Sexo *(sécksoh)*.

**Sexual.** Sexual *(sexooúl)*.

**Shade.** Sombra *(sómbrer)*.

**Shaking.** Sacudida *(suckoodēēder)*.

**Shame.** Vergüenza *(vairrgwénther)*.

**Share.** (v.) Participar *(parrticipárr)*.

**Share.** (s.) Porción, acción, participación, parte *(porrtheón, ucktheón, partithiputheón, párteh)*.

**Shareholdre.** Accionista *(úcktheoníster)*.

**Sharp.** Agudo *(uggōōdoh)*.

**Sharpen.** Afilar *(uffillárr)*.

**Shaper.** Fullero *(foollyáiroh)*.

**Shave.** Afeitar, afeitarse *(uffaytárr, uffaytárrseh)*.

**Shawl.** Mantón *(muntón)*.

**She.** Ella *(éllyer)*.

**Sheep.** Oreja *(oréhher)*.

**Sheet.** Sábana *(súbberner)*.

**Shelf.** Escollo *(escóllyoh)*.

**Shelter.** (s.) Abrigo *(ubbrēēgoh)*.

**Shelter.** (v.) Abrigar, refugiar *(ubbregárr, reffoohe.árr)*.

**Shepherd.** Pastor *(pustórr)*.

**Shepherd's bag.** Zurrón *(thoorrón)*.

**Sherbet.** Sorbete *(sorbétteh)*.

**Shield.** Escudo *(escōōdoh)*.

**Shin-bone.** Tibia *(tibbeer)*.

**Shine.** Brillar, relucir *(brilyárr, relloothêêr).*

**Ship.** Barco, buque *(barrcoh, bôôkeh).*

**Shipwreck.** Náufrago *(nõwfruggoh).*

**Shirt.** Camisa *(cummêêser).*

**Shocking.** Chocante *(shockúnteh).*

**Shoe.** (v.) Calzar *(cullthárr).*

**Shoe.** (s.) Zapato *(thuppúttoh).*

**Shoe horses.** Herrar *(errárr).*

**Shoemaker.** Zapatero *(thupputtáirroh).*

**Shoemaker's.** Zapatería *(thupper.terréar).*

**Shoot.** Disparar, fusilar *(disparrárr, foossillár).*

**Shop.** Tienda *(tyénder).*

**Shopkeeper.** Tendero *(tendáirroh).*

**Short.** Corto, breve *(córrtoh, brévveh).*

**Shot.** Disparo *(dispúrroh).*

**Shotgun.** Escopeta *(escoppétter).*

**Shoulder.** Hombro *(ómbroh).*

**Shovel (fire).** Badila *(buddêêler).*

**Shower.** Ducha *(dôôtcher).*

**Shrink.** Encoger *(encohháirr).*

**Shroud.** Amortajar *(ummórtuhhárr).*

**Shudder.** Estremecer *(estremmetháirr).*

**Shuddering.** Estremecimiento *(éstremméthimmyéntoh).*

**Shuttle.** Lanzadora *(lúntherdórer).*

**Shut up.** Callar *(cullyárr).*

**Shyness.** Pudor, timidez *(podórr, timmiddéth).*

**Sick.** Enfermo *(enfáirrmoh).*

**Sickly.** Achacoso *(utchuckóssoh).*

**Side.** Lado, costado *(lárdoh, costárdoh).*

**Sidewalk.** Acera *(utháirer).*

**Sigh.** Suspiro *(soospêêroh).*

**Sight.** Vista *(víster).*

**Sign.** (v.) Firmar *(fêêrrmárr).*

**Sign.** (s.) Indicio, señal, signo, rótulo *(indítheoh, senyúl, sígnoh, róttooloh).*

**Sign (writing).** Letrero *(lettráiroh).*

**Signature.** Firma *(fêêrmer).*

**Silence.** Silencio *(silléntheo).*

**Sill.** Alféizar *(ullfáithur).*

**Silly.** Necio *(nétheoh).*

**Silver.** Plata *(plútter).*

**Silverplate.** Platear *(pluteárr).*

**Silversmith.** Platero *(pluttáirroh).*

**Simple.** Simple *(símpleh).*

**Simplicity.** Sencillez, simpleza *(senthilyeth, simpléther).*

**Simplify.** Simplificar *(simplifficárr).*

**Simultaneous.** Simultáneo *(simmooltúnneoh).*

**Sin.** (s.) Pecado *(peckúddoh).*

**Sin.** (v.) Pecar *(peckárr).*

**Sincerely.** Sinceramente *(sintherrerménteh).*

**Sincerity.** Sinceridad *(sintherridúd).*

**Sing.** Cantar *(cúntarr).*

**Singular.** Singular *(singoolárr).*

**Sinister.** Siniestro *(sinyéstroh).*

**Sink.** Ahondar, -se, hundir *(uh.ondarr, -seh, oondêêr).*

**Sinnous.** Sinuoso *(sinnoo.óssoh).*

**Sip.** (v.) Sorber *(sorrbáirr).*

**Sip.** (s.) Sorbo *(sórrboh).*

**Sister.** Hermana *(airmúnner).*

**Sit down.** Sentarse *(sentárr-seh)*.

**Situation.** Situación *(sittoo.útheon)*.

**Six.** Seis *(sáy.iss)*.

**Six hundred.** Seiscientos *(sáyisthéntoss)*.

**Six months.** Semestre *(semméstreh)*.

**Sixth.** Sexto *(séckstoh)*.

**Sixtieth.** Sexagésimo *(sekserhéssimmoh)*.

**Sixty.** Sesenta *(sessénter)*.

**Size.** Talla, tamaño *(túlyer, tummúnyoh)*.

**Skein.** Madeja *(muddéhher)*.

**Sketch.** Croquis *(crockíss)*.

**Skilfull.** Diestro *(dyéstroh)*.

**Skill.** Maña, acierto *(múnyer, uthiáirtoh)*.

**Skin.** (v.) Desollar *(dessollyárr)*.

**Skin.** (s.) Piel, pellejo *(pyél, pelyéhhoh)*.

**Skirt.** Falda *(fúllder)*.

**Skull.** Cráneo *(crárrneoh)*.

**Sky.** Cielo *(thyélloh)*.

**Slap.** Abofetear *(ubbúffetehárr)*.

**Slaughter.** (v.) Degollar *(degollyárr)*.

**Slaughter.** (s.) Matanza *(muttúnther)*.

**Slaughter-house.** Matadero *(mutterdáirroh)*.

**Slave.** Esclavo *(esclúvvoh)*.

**Slavery.** Esclavitud *(esclúvvittúd)*.

**Sleep.** (s.) Sueño *(swénnyoh)*.

**Sleep.** (v.) Dormir *(dormēēr)*.

**Sleep (send to).** Adormecer *(uddórmetthháir)*.

**Sleep walker.** Somnámbulo *(somnúmbooloh)*.

**Sleeve.** Manga *(múnger)*.

**Slice.** Raja, rebanada, tajada *(rúhher, rebunnárder, tuhhúdder)*.

**Slide.** Deslizar *(deslithárr)*.

**Sling.** Honda *(ónder)*.

**Slip.** Resbalar *(resbullár)*.

**Slipper.** Babucha *(bubbōōtcher)*.

**Slippery.** Resbaladizo *(resbulluddēēthoh)*.

**Sloping.** Escote *(escótteh)*.

**Slow.** Lento *(léntoh)*.

**Slow.** Moroso *(morróssoh)*.

**Slowness.** Lentitud *(lentitōōd)*.

**Skeleton.** Esqueleto *(eskelléttoh)*.

**Small.** Pequeño, menudo *(peckényoh, menōōdoh)*.

**Smallness.** Pequeñez *(peckenyéth)*.

**Smart.** Elegante *(ellegunteh)*.

**Smartness.** Aseo *(ussáyoh)*.

**Smell.** (v.) Oler *(olláir)*.

**Smell.** (s.) Olor *(ollórr)*.

**Smile.** Sonreír *(sonray.ēērr)*.

**Smith.** Herrero *(erráirroh)*.

**Smoke.** (v.) Fumar, ahumar *(foomárr, uh.oomárr)*.

**Smoke.** (s.) Humo *(ōōmoh)*.

**Smoker.** Fumador *(foomerdórr)*.

**Smooth.** (adj.) Liso *(lēēssoh)*.

**Smooth.** (v.)·Alisar *(úllisárr)*.

**Smuggling.** Contrabando *(cóntrerbúndoh)*.

**Snail.** Caracol *(currer.cóll)*.

**Snarl.** Regañar *(reggunyárr)*.

**Sneeze.** Estornudar *(estórrnoodárr)*.

**Snore.** (v.) Roncar *(roncárr)*.

**Snore.** (s.) Ronquido *(ronkídoh)*.

**Snow.** Nieve *(nyévveh)*.

**Snowdrift.** Ventisquero *(ventiskáirroh)*.

**So.** Tan, así *(tun, ussēē)*.

**Soak.** Remojar *(remmohhárr)*.

**Soap.** Jabón *(hubbón)*.
**Soapdish.** Jabonear *(hubbonáirrer)*.
**Sob.** (s.) Llanto, sollozo *(lyúntoh, solyóthoh)*.
**Sob.** (v.) Sollozar *(solyothárr)*.
**Sober.** Sobrio *(sóbreoh)*.
**Sobriety.** Sobriedad *(sobréuddúd)*.
**Sociable.** Sociable *(sotheúbleh)*.
**Socialism.** Socialismo *(sotheullísmoh)*.
**Sock.** Calcetín *(cúllthetēēn)*.
**Sofa.** Sofá *(sofár)*.
**Soften.** Ablandar, suavizar *(ubblundárr, swuvvithárr)*.
**Softly.** Suavemente *(swuvveménteh)*.
**Solder.** Soldar *(soldárr)*.
**Soldier.** Soldado *(soldárdoh)*.
**Solemn.** Solemne *(sollémneh)*.
**Solemnity.** Solemnidad *(sollemniddúd)*.
**Solfa.** Solfear *(solfeárr)*.
**Solicit.** Solicitar *(sollissittárr)*.
**Solicitude.** Solicitud *(sollithitōōd)*.
**Solid.** Sólido *(sólliddoh)*.
**Solidity.** Solidez *(sollidéth)*.
**Solidly.** Sólidamente *(sollidder.ménteh)*.
**Some.** Algún *(ullgōōn)*.
**Somebody.** Alguien *(úllghee.n)*.
**Someone.** Alguno *(ullgōōnoh)*.
**Something.** Algo *(úllgoh)*.
**Somewhere.** Alguna parte *(ullgōner párrteh)*.
**Son.** Hijo *(íhhoh)*.
**Song.** Canción *(cuntheón)*.
**Son-in-law.** Yerno *(yáirrnoh)*.
**Sonorous.** Sonoro *(sonnórroh)*.

**Soon.** Pronto *(próntoh)*.
**Soul.** Alma *(úllmer)*.
**Sound.** (v.) Sonar, sondar *(sonnárr, sondárr)*.
**Sound.** (s.) Sonido, sonda *(sonnēēdoh, sónder)*.
**Soup.** Sopa *(sópper)*.
**Sour.** Agrio *(úggreoh)*.
**Sour, to turn.** Agriar *(uggrreárr)*.
**Source.** Manantial *(munnuntiúll)*.
**South.** Sur *(soorr)*.
**Sovereign.** Soberano *(sobberrúnnoh)*.
**Sow.** Sembrar *(sembrárr)*.
**Space.** Espacio *(espútheoh)*.
**Spade.** Pala *(púller)*.
**Spaniard.** Español *(espunyóll)*.
**Spanish.** Español *(espunyóll)*.
**Spatter.** Salpicar *(sulpickárr)*.
**Speak.** Hablar *(ubblárr)*.
**Special.** Especial *(espetheúl)*.
**Specialist.** Especialista *(espethiullister)*.
**Species.** Especie *(espéthea)*.
**Spectacle.** Espectáculo *(espectúckooloh)*.
**Spectacles.** Gafas *(gúffers)*.
**Spectre.** Espectro *(espéctroh)*.
**Speculate.** Especular *(especoolárr)*.
**Speculation.** Especulación *(espécoolutheón)*.
**Speed.** Velocidad *(vellossiddúd)*.
**Spend.** Gastar, pasar *(gustárr, pussárr)*.
**Sphere.** Esfera *(esfáirrer)*.
**Spill.** Derramar, verter *(dérrer.márr, vairrtáirr)*.
**Spin.** Hilar *(illárr)*.
**Spine.** Espinazo *(espinnúthoh)*.
**Spiral.** Espiral *(espirrúll)*.

**Spiritual.** Espiritual *(espirri-tooúll)*.
**Spit.** Escupir *(escoopēērr)*.
**Splash.** Salpicar *(sullpickárr)*.
**Splendid.** Espléndido *(espléndiddoh)*.
**Split.** Hendir *(endēēr)*.
**Spoils.** Despojo *(despóh.-hoh)*.
**Sponge.** Esponja *(espónher)*.
**Spontaneous.** Espontáneo *(espontúnneoh)*.
**Spoon.** Cuchara *(cootchúr-rer)*.
**Spot.** Borrón *(borrón)*.
**Spring.** (v.) Manar *(mun-nárr)*.
**Spring.** (s.) Resorte, muelle, primavera *(ressórrteh, mwéllyeh, primmerváirrer)*.
**Sprinkle.** Rociar *(rotheárr)*.
**Sprout.** Retoñar *(rettonyárr)*.
**Sprun.** Hilado *(illárdoh)*.
**Spunk.** Yesca *(yésker)*.
**Spur.** Espuela *(espwéller)*.
**Square.** Cuadrado, plaza *(kwudrárdoh, plúther)*.
**Squeak.** Crujir *(croo.hēēr)*.
**Squeaking.** Crujido *(croo.-hēēdoh)*.
**Squeamish.** Empalagoso *(empullergóssoh)*.
**Stable.** Caballeriza, establo *(cúbbullyerēēther, estúbloh)*.
**Stage.** Etapa *(ettúpper)*.
**Stagger.** Tambalear *(tumbu-lleárr)*.
**Stain.** Mancha *(múntcher)*.
**Stain with blood.** Ensangrentar *(ensúngrentárr)*.
**Stainless.** Intachable *(intu-tchúbbleh)*.
**Stairs.** Escalera *(esculláir-rer)*.
**Stammer.** Balbucear, tartamudear *(bullboothayárr, tarr-termoodayárr)*.

**Standard.** Norma *(nórrmer)*.
**Stamp.** Sello *(sélyoh)*.
**Star.** Estrella, astro *(estréll-yer, ússtroh)*.
**Starch.** (s.) Almidón *(úllmid-dón)*.
**Starch.** (v.) Almidonar *(úllmi-ddonárr)*.
**State.** Estado *(estúddoh)*.
**Station.** Estación *(estutheón)*.
**Stationer's.** Papelería *(pup-pellerrēēr)*.
**Statistics.** Estadística *(es-tuddísticker)*.
**Statue.** Estatua *(estúttoo.er)*.
**Statute.** Estatuto *(estuttōō-toh)*.
**Stay.** (v.) Quedar, -se *(ked-dárr, -seh)*.
**Stay.** (s.) Estancia, permanencia *(estúnthea, pairr-munnénthea)*.
**Stay.** Estancia *(estúnthea)*.
**Steal.** Robar *(robbárr)*.
**Steam.** Vapor *(vuppórr)*.
**Steel.** Acero *(utháirroh)*.
**Steelyard.** Romana *(rom-múnner)*.
**Steep.** Acantilado *(uckúnti-llárdoh)*.
**Stem.** Tallo *(túllyoh)*.
**Step.** Escalón, peldaño, paso *(escullón, peldúnyoh, pú-ssoh)*.
**Step-daughter.** Hijastra *(ih-hústrer)*.
**Step-father.** Padrastro *(pu-drústreh)*.
**Step-son.** Hijastro *(ihhús-troh)*.
**Staps, take.** Gestionar *(héss-tionnárr)*.
**Stereotypography.** Estereotipia *(estérreoh.típpea)*.
**Sterile.** Estéril *(estáirrill)*.
**Sterility.** Esterilidad *(esterílli-dud)*.

**Stern.** Popa *(pópper)*.
**Stewardess.** Azafata *(úther-farter)*.
**Stick.** Palo *(púlloh)*.
**Still.** Alambique *(úllum.-bēē-keh)*.
**Still.** (adj.) Quieto, tranquilo *(kee.éttoh, trunkēēlo)*.
**Still.** (adv.) Todavía, aún *(toddervēēr, ow.ōōn)*.
**Stimulate.** Estimular *(estím-moolár)*.
**Stingy.** Tacaño *(tuckúnyoh)*.
**Stipulate.** Estipular *(estippo-olárr)*.
**Stir (the soup). Stoke (the fire).** Atizar *(uttitharr)*.
**Stirrup.** Estribo *(estrēēboh)*.
**Stocking.** Media *(méddia)*.
**Stocks.** Cepo *(théppoh)*.
**Stomach.** Estómago *(estóm-mergoh)*.
**Stone.** (s.) Piedra *(pyéddrah)*.
**Stone.** (v.) Apedrear *(uppé-dreh.árr)*.
**Stone throw.** Pedrada *(pe-drúdder)*.
**Stool.** Taburete *(tubboorrét-teh)*.
**Stool, small bench.** Banquete *(bunkétter)*.
**Stop.** (s.) Parada *(purrárder)*.
**Stop.** (v.) Parar, detener, tapar *(purrár, dettennáirr, tuppárr)*.
**Stopper.** Taco *(túckoh)*.
**Store.** Provisión *(provis-seón)*.
**Stores.** Almacén *(úllmuthén)*.
**Storm.** Tempestad, tormenta *(tempestúd)*, torménter).
**Stove.** Estufa *(estōōfer)*.
**Straggler.** Rezagado *(rether-gúddoh)*.
**Straight.** Recto *(réctoh)*.
**Stranger.** Forastero *(forrus-táiroh)*.

**Strangle.** Estrangular *(es-trungoolárr)*.
**Strap.** Correa *(corráyer)*.
**Stratagem.** Ardid *(arrdēēd)*.
**Strategy.** Estrategia *(estrut-téh hear)*.
**Straw.** Paja *(púhher)*.
**Stream.** Arroyo *(urróyoh)*.
**Street.** Calle *(cúllyeh)*.
**Strength.** Fuerza *(fwáirrther)*.
**Strengthen.** Reforzar *(refforr-thárr)*.
**Stretch.** Estirar, tender *(es-tirrárr, tendáirr)*.
**Strike.** Huelga *(wélger)*.
**String.** Bramante, cuerda, cordel *(brummúnteh, kwáirr-der, corrdéll)*.
**Strip.** Gira *(hēērer)*.
**Stripe.** Raya *(ráhyer)*.
**Striped.** Rayado *(rahyúddoh)*.
**Strong.** Fuerte *(fwárrteh)*.
**Strophe.** Estrofa *(estróffer)*.
**Struggle.** (v.) Luchar *(loot-chárr)*.
**Struggle.** (s.) Lucha *(lōōtcher)*.
**Student.** Estudiante *(estoo-deúnteh)*.
**Study.** Estudiar *(estoodeárr)*.
**Stumble.** (v.) Tropezar *(trop-pethárr)*.
**Stumble.** (s.) Tropezón *(trop-pethón)*.
**Stun.** Atolondrar *(utóllon-drárr)*.
**Stupefy.** Embrutecer *(em-brootetháirr)*.
**Stupid.** Estúpido, tonto, torpe *(estōōpiddoh, tóntoh, tórrpeh)*.
**Stupidity.** Estupidez, sandez *(estooppidéth, sundéth)*.
**Stupity.** Atontar *(utton.tárr)*.
**Stupor.** Estupor *(estoopórr)*.
**Style.** Estilo *(estēēloh)*.
**Subaltern.** Subalterno *(soo-bultáirrnoh)*.

272

**Subdue.** Subyugar *(soob-yoogárr)*.
**Subject.** Súbdito, sujeto, asunto, tema *(sŏŏbdittoh, soohéttoh, ussŏŏntoh, támer)*.
**Subjunctive.** Subjuntivo *(soobhoontēēvoh)*.
**Sublime.** Sublime *(sooblēēmeh)*.
**Submission.** Sumisión *(soommisseón)*.
**Submit.** Someter *(sommettáirr)*.
**Subordinate.** Subordinado *(sooborrdinnúddoh)*.
**Subscribe.** Subscribirse *(soobscribbēērseh)*.
**Subscriber.** Subscriptor *(soobscriptórr)*.
**Subscription.** Subscripción *(soobscriptheón)*.
**Subsist.** Subsistir *(soobsistēērr)*.
**Subsistence.** Subsistencia *(soobsisténthea)*.
**Substance.** Substancia *(soobstúnthea)*.
**Substantive.** Substantivo *(soobstuntēēvoh)*.
**Substitute.** (v.) Substituir *(soobstittoo.ēērr)*.
**Substitute.** (s.) Substituto, suplente *(soobstittŏŏtoh, sooplénteh)*.
**Substraction.** Resta *(réster)*.
**Subterranean.** Subterráneo *(soobterrúnneo)*.
**Subtract.** Restar *(restárr)*.
**Suburb.** Suburbio *(soobŏŏrrbeoh)*.
**Subvention.** Subvención *(soobventheón)*.
**Succeed.** Tener éxito *(tennáirr éxittoh)*.
**Success.** Éxito *(éxittoh)*.
**Successively.** Sucesivamente *(soothessivvverménteh)*.

**Successor.** Sucesor *(soothessorr)*.
**Succumb.** Sucumbir *(soockoombēēr)*.
**Suck.** Chupar *(tchoopár)*.
**Suckle.** Mamar *(mummárr)*.
**Sudden.** Repentino *(reppentēēnoh)*.
**Suddenly.** Súbitamente *(soobittumménteh)*.
**Sudorific.** Sudorífico *(soodorríficksoh)*.
**Suffer.** Padecer, sufrir *(puddetháirr, soofrēērr)*.
**Suffering.** Padecimiento, sufrimiento *(puddethimmyéntoh, soōōfrimyéntoh)*.
**Sufficient.** Suficiente *(sooffithyénteh)*.
**Suffocate.** Asfixiar, sofocar *(ussfixeárr, soffoccárr)*.
**Suffocation.** Sofocación *(soffocutheón)*.
**Sugar.** Azúcar *(uthŏŏckarr)*.
**Suicide.** Suicidio, suicida *(soo.ithíddeoh, soo.ithēēder)*.
**Suit.** Traje *(trúhheh)*.
**Sulphor.** Azufre *(uthŏŏfreh)*.
**Sulphurous.** Sulfuroso *(soolfoorrósoh)*.
**Sum.** Suma *(sŏŏmmer)*.
**Summary.** Resumen *(ressŏŏmen)*.
**Summer.** Verano, estío *(verrúnnoh, estēē.oh)*.
**Summer residence.** Veraneo *(verrunnéh.oh)*.
**Summer resident.** Veraneante *(verrunneúnteh)*.
**Sumptuous.** Suntuoso *(soontoo.óssoh)*.
**Sun.** Sol *(sol)*.
**Sunday.** Domingo *(dommíngoh)*.
**Supercargo.** Sobrecargo *(sobbrehcárrgoh)*.

**Superficial.** Superficial *(sōō pirrfítheúl)*.
**Superfluous.** Superfluo *(so-opáirrfloo.oh)*.
**Superhuman.** Sobrehumano *(sobbre.oomúnnoh)*.
**Superior.** Superior *(soopairriórr)*.
**Superiority.** Superioridad *(soopairriorridúd)*.
**Suprenatural.** Sobrenatural *(sobbrehnuttoorrúll)*.
**Supper.** Cena *(thénner)*.
**Supplant.** Suplantar *(soo-pluntárr)*.
**Supply.** Abastecer *(ubbús-teh.thairr)*.
**Support.** (s.) Apoyo *(uppó-yoh)*.
**Support.** (v.) Soportar *(sop-porrtárr)*.
**Suppose.** Suponer *(soopon-náirr)*.
**Supreme.** Supremo *(soo-prémmoh)*.
**Sure.** Seguro *(seggōōroh)*.
**Surely.** Seguramente *(seg-gōōrer.ménteh)*.
**Surface.** Superficie *(soo-pairrfíthiéh)*.
**Surname.** Apellido *(uppel-lyēēdoh)*.
**Surpass.** Sobrepujar, superar *(sóbbrehpoohárr, soo-perrár)*.
**Surprise.** (v.) Sorprender *(sorprendáirr)*.
**Surprise.** (s.) Sorpresa, sobresalto *(sorpresser, sob-brehsúltoh)*.
**Surprising.** Sorprendente *(sorprendénteh)*.
**Surrender.** Rendir *(rendēēr)*.
**Surrendered.** Rendido *(ren-dēēdoh)*.
**Surroundings.** Alrededores *(úllreddidórress)*.

**Surveyor.** Agrimensor *(úg-grimensórr)*.
**Suspect.** Recelar, sospechar *(rethellár, sospetchárr)*.
**Suspicion.** Sospecha *(sos-pétcher)*.
**Suspicious.** Sospechoso *(sospetchóssoh)*.
**Sustain.** Sostener *(soste-nnáirr)*.
**Swain.** Zagal *(thuggúl)*.
**Swallow.** (s.) Golondrina *(góllondrēēner)*.
**Swallow.** (v.) Tragar *(tru-ggárr)*.
**Sweat.** (v.) Sudar *(sooddárr)*.
**Sweat.** (s.) Sudor *(sooddórr)*.
**Sweet.** Dulce *(dōōltheh)*.
**Sweeten.** Endulzar *(endool-thárr)*.
**Sweet-tooth.** Goloso *(gollós-soh)*.
**Swell.** Hincharse *(intchárr-seh)*.
**Swelling.** Hinchazón *(intchu-thón)*.
**Swift.** Veloz *(vellóth)*.
**Swim.** Nadar *(nuddárr)*.
**Swindle.** Estafa *(estúffer)*.
**Swing.** Mecer *(metháirr)*.
**Sword-wound.** Sablazo *(su-bblúthoh)*.
**Syllable.** Sílaba *(síllerber)*.
**Symbol.** Símbolo *(símbo-lloh)*.
**Symbolical.** Símbólico *(sim-bólliccoh)*.
**Sympathetic.** Comprensivo *(comprensēēvoh)*.
**Sympathy.** Simpatía *(sim-puthéar)*.
**Symhony.** Sinfonía *(sinfó-nnéar)*.
**Symptom.** Síntoma *(síntom-mer)*.
**Syndicate.** Agremiar *(ug-gremmeárr)*.

**Synonimous.** Sinónimo *(sinnónnimmoh)*.
**Synonym.** Sinónimo *(sinnónnimmoh)*.
**Syntax.** Sintaxis *(sintúckcis)*.

**Synthesis.** Síntesis *(síntessis)*.
**Syrup.** Jarabe *(hurrárbeh)*.
**System.** Sistema *(sistémmer)*.

# T

**Table.** Mesa *(messer)*.
**Table-cloth.** Mantel *(muntél)*.
**Table cover.** Tapete *(tuppétteh)*.
**Table service.** Vajilla *(vuhhíllyer)*.
**Tack.** (s.) Tachuela *(tutchwéller)*.
**Tack.** (v.) Virar *(virrár)*.
**Tact.** Tacto *(túcktoh)*.
**Tail.** Cola, rabo *(cōōler, rúbboh)*.
**Tailor.** Sastre *(sústreh)*.
**Take.** Tomar *(tommárr)*.
**Tale.** Cuento *(kwéntoh)*.
**Talent.** Talento *(tulléntoh)*.
**Talker.** Charlatán *(charluttún)*.
**Tall.** Alto *(úlltoh)*.
**Tallow.** Sebo *(sébboh)*.
**Tame.** Amansar, domar *(ummunsárr, dommárr)*.
**Tamer.** Domador *(dommerdór)*.
**Tap.** Espita, grifo *(espēēter, gríffoh)*.
**Tapeworm.** Solitaria *(sollittárrea)*.
**Tar.** Brea *(bráyer)*.
**Tariff.** Tarifa, arancel *(turríffer, urrunthéll)*.
**Task.** Tarea *(turráyer)*.
**Tassel.** Boria *(bórrear)*.
**Taste.** (v.) Gustar, probar, saborear *(goostárr, probbárr, subborreárr)*.
**Taste.** (s.) Gusto, sabor *(goostoh, subbórr)*.

**Tavern.** Taberna *(tubbáirner)*.
**Tea.** Té *(teh)*.
**Tea (meal).** Merienda *(merryénder)*.
**Teach.** Enseñar *(ensennyárr)*.
**Teacher.** Profesor *(proffessórr)*.
**Teaching.** Enseñanza *(ensennyúnther)*.
**Tear.** (v.) Desgarrar, rasgar *(desgurrárr, rusgárr)*.
**Tear.** (s.) Lágrima *(lúgrimmer)*.
**Tear, to pieces.** Despedazar *(despédduthárr)*.
**Telegram.** Telegrama *(telleggrúmmer)*.
**Telegraph.** Telégrafo *(telléggruffoh)*.
**Telephone.** (s.) Teléfono *(telléffonnoh)*.
**Telephone.** (v.) Telefonear *(telleffonneárr)*.
**Tell.** Decir *(dethēērr)*.
**Temerity.** Temeridad *(temmerridúd)*.
**Temper.** Templar *(templárr)*.
**Termerament.** Temperamento *(temperrermentoh)*.
**Tempered.** Templado *(templúddoh)*.
**Temple.** Templo *(témploh)*.
**Tempt.** Tentar *(tentárr)*.
**Temptation.** Tentación *(tentutheón)*.
**Ten.** Diez *(dyéth)*.
**Tenacious.** Tenaz *(tennúth)*.

**Tenacity.** Tenacidad *(tennassidúd).*

**Tenant.** Inquilino *(inkillēēnoh).*

**Tendency.** Tendencia *(tendéntheer).*

**Tender.** Tierno *(tyaírrnoh).*

**Tenderness.** Ternura *(tairrnōōrer).*

**Tendon.** Tendón *(tendón).*

**Tenmillionth.** Diezmillonésimo *(dēēthmillyonnéssimoh).*

**Tenor.** Tenor *(tennórr).*

**Tenth.** Décimo *(déthimmoh).*

**Tenthousandth.** Diezmilésimo *(dyéthmilléssimoh).*

**Tepid.** Tibio *(tíbbeoh).*

**Term.** Término, plazo, *(tairrminnoh, plúthoh).*

**Terminating.** Terminante *(tairrminnúnteh).*

**Termination.** Terminación *(tairrminnutheón).*

**Terrace.** Terraza *(terruther).*

**Terrain.** Terreno *(terrénnoh).*

**Terrestrial.** Terrenal *(terrennúl).*

**Terrible.** Terrible *(terrēēbleh).*

**Terrify.** Aterrar *(utterrárr).*

**Territory.** Territorio *(territtórreoh).*

**Terror.** Terror *(terrórr).*

**Text.** Texto *(téxtoh).*

**Textile.** Tejido *(tehhēēdoh).*

**Textual.** Textual *(textoo-úll).*

**Thank.** Agradecer *(ugruddetháirr).*

**Thanks.** Gracias *(grútheus).*

**That.** Aquel *(uckéll).*

**The.** El, la, lo *(el, lah, loh).*

**Theatre.** Teatro *(tayúttroh).*

**Theft.** Robo, hurto *(róbboh, ōrrtoh).*

**Then.** (adv.) Entonces, luego *(entónthess, loo.éggoh).*

**Then.** (conj.) Pues *(pwess).*

**Theory.** Teoría *(tayorrēēr).*

**There.** Allá *(ullyáh).*

**There is, are.** Hay *(i).*

**Thermometer.** Termómetro *(tairmómmetroh).*

**Thick.** Espeso *(espéssoh).*

**Thief.** Ladrón *(luddrón).*

**Thigh.** Muslo *(mōōsloh).*

**Thin.** (adj.) Delgado *(delgárdoh).*

**Thin.** (v.) Adelgazar *(addélguthárr).*

**Thing.** Cosa *(cosser).*

**Think.** Pensar *(pensárr).*

**Thinness.** Delgadez *(délguddéth).*

**Third.** Tercero *(tairrtháirroh).*

**Thirst.** Sed *(sedd).*

**Thirsty.** Sediento *(sedyéntoh).*

**Thirteen.** Trees *(trétheh).*

**This.** Este, esta, esto *(ésteh, éster, éstoh).*

**Thought.** Pensamiento *(pensummyéntoh).*

**Thousand.** Mil, millar *(meel, milyárr).*

**Thousandth.** Milésima *(milléssimmer).*

**Thorax.** Tórax *(tórrucks).*

**Threat.** Amenaza *(ummenúther).*

**Threaten.** Amenazar *(umménner.thúrr).*

**Three.** Tres *(tress).*

**Three hundred.** Trescientos *(tressthyéntoss).*

**Thee months.** Trimestre *(trimméstreh).*

**Thresh.** Trillar *(trilyárr).*

**Threshold.** Umbral *(oombrúll).*

**Thrill.** Apasionar *(uppússeonárr).*

**Throat.** Garganta *(garrgúnter).*

**Throne.** Trono *(trónnoh).*

**Throw.** Arrojar, tirar, lanzar *(urrohhárr, tirrárr, lúnthár).*

**Throw down.** Abatir *(ubbuttёёrr)*.

**Thunder.** (v.) Tronar *(tronnárr)*.

**Thunder.** (s.) Trueno *(trwénnoh)*.

**Thunderbolt.** Centella *(thentéllyer)*.

**Thundering.** Atronador *(uttronnadórr)*.

**Thursday.** Jueves *(hwévvess)*.

**Tie.** Amarrar, atar *(úmmerrárr, uttárr)*.

**Tie (games).** Empatar *(emputtárr)*.

**Tiger.** Tigre *(tёёgreh)*.

**Tight.** Estrecho *(estrétchoh)*.

**Tighten.** Estrechar *(estretchárr)*.

**Tightly.** Estrechamente *(estrétcherménteh)*.

**Tile.** Azulejo, teja *(uthoolléhhoh, téhher)*.

**Tiled-floor.** Embaldosado *(embúlldossárdoh)*.

**Time.** Tiempo *(tyémpoh)*.

**Time table.** Horario *(orrárreoh)*.

**Timidity.** Timidez *(timmiddeth)*.

**Tin.** Estaño, hojalata *(estúnnyo, óhherlútter)*.

**Tint.** Matiz *(mutteeth)*.

**Tip.** Propina *(proppёёner)*.

**Tire.** (v.) Cansar *(cunsárr)*.

**Tiredness.** Cansancio *(cunsúntheoh)*.

**Tireless.** Incansable *(incunsubbleh)*.

**Tireless.** Infatigable *(infuttigúbbleh)*.

**Tiring.** Fatigoso *(futtiggóssoh)*.

**Title page.** Portada *(porrtárder)*.

**Titular.** Titular *(tittoolárr)*.

**Toast.** (s.) Tostada *(tostúdder)*.

**Toast.** (v.) Toster *(tostárr)*.

**Tobacco.** Tabaco *(tubbúckoh)*.

**Tobacco shop.** Estanco *(estúncoh)*.

**Today.** Hoy *(oy)*.

**Toilet.** Tocado *(tockúddoh)*.

**Tolerable.** Tolerable *(tollerrúbleh)*.

**Tolerate.** Tolerar *(totlerrárr)*.

**Tomb.** Tumba, sepulcro *(tӧӧmber, sepӧӧlcroh)*.

**Tomorrow.** Mañana *(munyúnner)*.

**Ton.** Tonelada *(tonnellúdder)*.

**Tongs.** Tenaza *(tennúther)*.

**Tongue.** Lengua *(léngwer)*.

**Tonic.** Reconstituyente *(reckonstittooyénteh)*.

**Too much.** Demasiado *(demmússiárdoh)*.

**Tool.** Herramienta *(érrer.myénter)*.

**Tooth.** Diente *(dyénteh)*.

**Toothpick.** Palillo *(pullílyoh)*.

**Top.** Cima *(thёёmer)*.

**Topographer.** Topógrafo *(toppóggruffoh)*.

**Topography.** Topografía *(toppoggruffёёr)*.

**Torment.** (v.) Atormentar *(uttórrmenttárr)*.

**Torment.** (s.) Tormento *(torrméntoh)*.

**Torpedo.** Torpedo *(torrpéddoh)*.

**Torpedo-boat.** Torpedero *(torrpeddáirroh)*.

**Tortoise.** Tortuga *(torrtӧӧger)*.

**Torture.** Tortura *(torrtӧӧrer)*.

**Total.** Total *(tottúll)*.

**Touch.** Tocar *(toccárr)*.

**Tourism.** Turismo *(touríssmoh)*.

**Tourist.** Turista *(tooríster)*.

**Tow.** (s.) Estopa *(estópper)*.

**Tow.** (v.) Remolcar *(remmolcárr)*.

**Towards.** Hacia *(úthear)*.

**Towel.** Toalla *(toúllyer)*.

**Tower.** Torre *(tórreh)*.

**Town.** Ciudad *(thééoodúd)*.

**Town crier.** Pregonero *(preggonnáirroh)*.

**Toy.** Juguete *(hoogétteh)*.

**Trace.** (s.) Huella, pista, rastro *(wéllyer, píster, rústroh)*.

**Trace.** (v.) Trazar *(truthárr)*.

**Trace (draw).** Calcar *(cullcár)*.

**Tract.** Opúsculo *(oppõõscooloh)*.

**Tractable.** Tratable *(truttúbleh)*.

**Tradition.** Tradición *(trudditheón)*.

**Tragedy.** Tragedia *(truhhéddear)*.

**Train.** (s.) Adiestrar *(úddyestrárr)*.

**Train.** (s.) Tren *(tren)*.

**Traject.** Trayecto *(truy.éctoh)*.

**Tram.** Tranvía *(trunvéêr)*.

**Trample.** Atropellar *(uttroppelyárr)*.

**Tranquillity.** Tranquilidad *(trunkillidúd)*.

**Transatlantic.** Transatlántico *(trunsutlúnticoh)*.

**Transcendency.** Transcendencia *(trunsthendéntheer)*.

**Transfer.** (v.) Trasladar, transferir, traspasar *(trusluddárr, trunsferrêêrr, truspussár)*.

**Transfer.** (s.) Transferencia *(trunsferrénthéa)*.

**Transform.** Transformar *(trunsformárr)*.

**Transformation.** Transformación *(trunsformutheón)*.

**Transit.** Tránsito *(trúnsittoh)*.

**Translate.** Traducir *(truddoothêêrr)*.

**Translation.** Traducción *(truddooktheón)*.

**Translator.** Traductor *(traddooktórr)*.

**Transparency.** Transparencia *(trunspurrénthea)*.

**Transplant.** Trasplantar *(truspluntárr)*.

**Transport.** Transportar *(trunsporrtárr)*.

**Trap.** Trampa *(trúmper)*.

**Trapeze.** Trapecio *(truppétheoh)*.

**Travel.** Viajar *(veerhárr)*.

**Traveller.** Viajero *(vee.uhháirroh)*.

**Tray.** Bandeja *(bundéh.her)*.

**Tread.** Pisar *(pissárr)*.

**Treason.** Traición *(try.ilheón)*.

**Treasure.** (s.) Tesoro *(tessórroh)*.

**Treasure.** (v.) Atesorar *(uttessorrárr)*.

**Treasurer.** Tesorero *(tessorráirroh)*.

**Treat.** Tratar *(truttárr)*.

**Treatment.** Tratamiento *(truttermyéntoh)*.

**Tree.** Árbol *(árrboll)*.

**Tremble.** Temblar *(temblárr)*.

**Trembling.** Temblar *(temblórr)*.

**Tress.** Trenza *(trénther)*.

**Triangle.** Triángulo *(tree.úngooloh)*.

**Tribe.** Tribu *(tríbboo)*.

**Tribunal.** Juzgado *(hoothgárdoh)*.

**Tribunal.** Tribunal *(tribboonnúl)*.

**Tribute.** Tributar *(tribbootárr)*.

**Trinity.** Trinidad *(trinnidúd)*.

**Trinket.** Dije *(díhheh)*.

**Triple.** Triple *(trípleh)*.

**Triumph.** Triunfo *(tree.õõnfoh)*.

**Trivial.** Trivial *(trivveúl)*.

**Troop.** Tropa *(tróper)*.

**Trot.** (v.) Trotar *(trottárr)*.

**Trot.** (s.) Trote *(trótteh)*.

**Trousers.** Pantalones *(puntullónness)*.

**Truant.** Tunante *(toonnúnteh)*.

**True.** Verdadero *(vairrduddáirroh)*.

**Trumpet.** Trompeta *(trompétter)*.

**Trunk.** Tronco, cofre *(trónkoh, cóffreh)*.

**Trust.** (v.) Confiar, fiar *(confeárr, feárr)*.

**Trust.** (s.) Confianza *(confeúnther)*.

**Trusting.** Fiado, confiado *(feárdoh, confeárdoh)*.

**Truth.** Verdad *(vairrdúd)*.

**Try.** Probar, intentar *(probbárr, intentárr)*.

**Tub.** Cubo *(cõõboh)*.

**Tube.** Tubo *(tõõboh)*.

**Tuberculosis.** Tuberculosis *(toobairrcoolóssiss)*.

**Tuesday.** Martes *(márrtess)*.

**Tumour.** Tumor *(toomórr)*.

**Tune.** (v.) Afinar *(úffinnárr)*.

**Tune.** (s.) Melodía *(mellodéa)*.

**Tunic.** Túnica *(tõõnicker)*.

**Tunnel.** Túnel *(tõõnell)*.

**Turbulent.** Revoltoso *(revoltóssoh)*.

**Tureen.** Sopera *(soppáirrer)*.

**Turkey.** Pavo *(púvvoh)*.

**Turn.** Vuelta, turno *(tõõrrnoh)*.

**Turn leaves.** Hojear *(ohheárr)*.

**Turn (on lathe).** Tornear *(torrneárr)*.

**Turner.** Tornero *(torrnáirroh)*.

**Tusk.** Colmillo *(colmíllyoh)*.

**Tutor.** Tutor *(toottórr)*.

**Twelfth.** Duodécimo *(doo.oh.-déthimoh)*.

**Twelve.** Doce *(dótheh)*.

**Twenty.** Veinte *(véh.inteh)*.

**Twenty-eight.** Veintiocho *(ventiótchoh)*.

**Twenty-five.** Veinticinco *(ventithínkoh)*.

**Twenty-four.** Veinticuatro *(ventikwútroh)*.

**Twenty-nine.** Veintinueve *(ventinwévveh)*.

**Twenty-one.** Veintiuno *(ventiõõnoh)*.

**Twenty-seven.** Veintisiete *(ventisẽẽtteh)*.

**Twenty-three.** Veintitrés *(ventitréss)*.

**Twenty-two.** Veintidós *(ventidóss)*.

**Twin.** Gemelo *(hemmélloh)*.

**Twist.** Torcer, enroscar, retorcer *(torrtháir, enroscárr, rettortháirr)*.

**Two.** Dos *(doss)*.

**Twylight.** Crepúsculo *(creppõõscooloh)*.

**Typhus.** Tifus *(tẽẽfooss)*.

**Typography.** Tipografía *(tippoggruffẽẽr)*.

**Tyranny.** Tiranía *(tirunẽẽr)*.

**Tyrant.** Tirano *(tirrúnnoh)*.

# U

**Ugliness.** Fealdad *(fáy.ull.dúd)*.

**Ugly.** Feo *(fáy.oh)*.

**Ulcer.** Llaga, úlcera *(lyúgger, õõlthairrer)*.

**Umbrella.** Paraguas *(purrúgwus)*.

**Unaccomodating.** Intransigente *(intrunsihhénteh)*.

**Unbind.** Desatar *(déssut-tárr)*.

**Uncertain.** Incierto *(intháirr-toh)*.

**Uncle.** Tío *(ēê.oh)*.

**Unconditional.** Incondciional *(incondithionúll)*.

**Uncork, uncorer.** Destapar *(destuppárr)*.

**Under.** Debajo *(debbúh.hoh)*.

**Underline.** Subrayar *(soo-brahyárr)*.

**Undermine.** Socavar *(soc-kervárr)*.

**Underskirt.** Refajo *(reffúh.-hoh)*.

**Understand.** Comprender, entendre *(comprendáirr, en-tendáirr)*.

**Undertake.** Emprender *(em-prendáirr)*.

**Undertaking.** Empresa *(em-présser)*.

**Undervalue.** Menospreciar *(ménnospretheárr)*.

**Undo.** Deshacer *(déssu-tháirr)*.

**Undress.** Desnudar *(des-noodárr)*.

**Uneasiness.** Malestar *(mu-llestárr)*.

**Unedited.** Inédito *(inéddit-toh)*.

**Unequal.** Desigual *(dessi-gwáll)*.

**Unevenness.** Desnivel *(dés-nivvel)*.

**Unexpected.** Inesperado *(inesperrárdoh)*.

**Unfaithful.** Infiel *(infēê.él)*.

**Unfavorable.** Desfavorable *(desfúvvorrúbleh)*.

**Unfold.** Desplegar *(desple-ggárr)*.

**Unfortunate.** Infortunado *(in-forrtoonárdoh)*.

**Unhappy.** Infeliz *(infellith)*.

**Unheard of.** Inaudito *(in.ow-dēêtoh)*.

**Uniform.** Uniforme *(ooníffórr-meh)*.

**Uninhabited.** Deshabitado *(dessubbittárdoh)*.

**Union.** Unión *(oonéon)*.

**Unique.** Único *(ōōnikoh)*.

**Unite.** Unir *(oonnēêrr)*.

**Unity.** Unidad *(oonidúd)*.

**Universal.** Universal *(ooniv-vairrsúll)*.

**Universe.** Universo *(ooniv-váirrsoh)*.

**University.** Universidad *(oo-nivvairrsiddúd)*.

**Unjust.** Injusto *(inhōōstoh)*.

**Unlike.** Desigual *(dessigwáll)*.

**Unlikely.** Inverosímil *(inve-rossímmill)*.

**Unlimited.** Ilimitado *(illimmi-ttárdoh)*.

**Unmerited.** Inmerecido *(in-merrithēêdoh)*.

**Unpardonable.** Imperdonable *(inpáirrdonnúbleh)*.

**Unprovided.** Desprovisto *(désprovvístoh)*.`

**Unpunished.** Impunemente *(impoonerménteh)*.

**Unqualifiable.** Incalificable *(inculliffickúbbleh)*.

**Unrealizable.** Irrealizable *(irrayullithúbleh)*.

**Unstick.** Despegar *(déspe-ggárr)*.

**Unsure.** Inseguro *(inseggōō roh)*.

**Until.** Hasta *(úster)*.

**Unwrap.** Desenvolver *(dés-senvolváir)*.

**Up.** Hacia arriba *(úthea urrēê ber)*.

**Upholsterer.** Tapicero *(tup-pitháirroh)*.

**Upon.** Sobre, en *(sobbreh, en)*.

**Upset.** Trastornar *(trustorr-nárr).*

**Upsetting.** Vuelco *(vwélcoh).*

**Urge.** Urgir *(oorhéérr).*

**Urgence.** Urgencia *(oorhén-thear).*

**Urgent.** Urgente *(oorrhén-teh).*

**Urine.** Orina *(orééner).*

**Urn.** Urna *(ōōrner).*

**Us.** Nos, nosotros *(noss, no-ssóttross).*

**Use.** Usar, utilizar *(oossárr, ootillithárr).*

**Used.** Usado *(oossúddoh).*

**Useful.** Util *(ōōtill).*

**Useless.** Inútil *(inōōtill).*

**Useless, render.** Inutilizar *(inootillithárr).*

**Usher.** Ujier *(oohéérr).*

**Usual.** Usual *(oossoo.úll).*

**Usurer.** Usurero *(oossooorái-roh).*

**Usurpation.** Usurpación *(oo-soorrputheón).*

**Usury.** Usura *(oossōōrer).*

**Utensil.** Utensilio *(ootensí-lleoh).*

# V

**Vacant.** Vacante *(vuckúnteh).*

**Vacate.** Desocupar *(desoc-coopárr).*

**Vaccinate.** Vacunar *(vucco-onárr).*

**Vaccine.** Vacuna *(vuccōō ner).*

**Vacillate.** Vacilar *(vuthillárr).*

**Vagabond.** Vagabundo *(vug-gerbōōndoh).*

**Vagrancy.** Vagancia *(vu-ggúnthear).*

**Vagrant.** Vago *(vúggoh).*

**Vain.** Vano *(vúnnoh).*

**Vainly.** Vanamente *(vunner.-ménteh).*

**Valley.** Valle *(vúlyeh).*

**Value.** (v.) Tasar *(tussárr).*

**Value.** (s.) Valor *(vullórr).*

**Valve.** Válvula *(vólvooler).*

**Vanity.** Vanidad *(vunniddúd).*

**Vanquish.** Vencer *(ventháirr).*

**Variable.** Variable *(vurriú-bleh).*

**Variation.** Variación *(vurri.ut-heón).*

**Variety.** Variedad *(vúrri.ed-dúd).*

**Vary.** Variar *(vurriárr).*

**Vast.** Vasto *(vústoh).*

**Vault.** Bóveda *(bóvvedder).*

**Veal.** Ternera *(tairrnáirrer).*

**Vegetable.** Vegetal, legumbre *(vehhettúl, leggōō mbreh).*

**Vegetables.** Hortalizas *(orr-tullēēthus).*

**Vegetation.** Vegetación *(ve-hhettutheón).*

**Vehement.** Vehemente *(veh-hemménteh).*

**Vehicle.** Vehículo *(veh.iccoo-loh).*

**Vein.** Vena *(vénner).*

**Vein (mineral).** Filón *(fillón).*

**Velvet.** Terciopelo *(tairrthe-oppélloh).*

**Vengeance.** Venganza *(ven-gúnther).*

**Ventilate.** Ventilar *(ventillárr).*

**Verb.** Verbo *(váirrboh).*

**Verse.** Verso *(váirrsoh).*

**Vertibrate.** Vertebrado *(vairr-tibbrúddoh).*

**Vertibre.** Vértebra *(váirrteb-brer).*

**Vertical.** Vertical *(vairrtíckúl).*
**Vertiginous.** Vertiginoso *(vairrtihhinnóssoh).*
**Very.** Muy *(mõõ.ee).*
**Vessel.** Nave, vasija *(núvveh, vussééher).*
**Veterinary.** Veterinario, albéitar *(vetterrinárrioh, ullbaytárr).*
**Vex.** Hostigar, enfadar, fastidiar *(ostiggárr, enfudárr, fusstiddeárr).*
**Vibrate.** Vibrar *(vibbrárr).*
**Vibrating.** Vibrante *(vibbrúnteh).*
**Vice.** Vicio *(vítheoh).*
**Vicious.** Vicioso *(vittheóssoh).*
**Victim.** Víctima *(víctimmer).*
**Vigorous.** Vigoroso *(viggorrósoh).*
**Vigour.** Vigor *(viggórr).*
**Village.** Aldea *(ulldóyer).*
**Vine.** Cepa, parra *(thépper, púrrer).*
**Vine shoot.** Sarmiento *(sarmyéntoh).*
**Vineleaf.** Pámpano *(púmpunnoh).*
**Violate.** Violentar *(veolentárr).*
**Violence.** Violencia *(veolléntheer).*
**Violent.** Violento *(veoléntoh).*

**Violin.** Violín *(veolínn).*
**Virgin.** Virgen *(vírrhen).*
**Virtue.** Virtud *(veerrtúd).*
**Virtuous.** Virtuoso *(veerrtoo.óssoh).*
**Visa.** Visado *(vissúddoh).*
**Visible.** Visible *(visséébleh).*
**Vision.** Visión *(visseón).*
**Visit.** (s.) Visita *(vissééter).*
**Visit.** (v.) Visitar *(vissittárr).*
**Vitriol.** Vitriolo *(vittreólloh).*
**Vituperate.** Vituperar *(vittooperrár).*
**Vocabulary.** Vocabulario *(voccubboolúrreoh).*
**Vocation.** Vocación *(voccutheón).*
**Voice.** Voz *(voth).*
**Volcano.** Volcán *(volcún).*
**Volume.** Tomo, volumen *(tómmoh, vollõõmen).*
**Voluntarily.** Voluntariamente *(volluntárrearménteh).*
**Vote.** (v.) Votar *(vottárr).*
**Vote.** (s.) Voto *(vóttoh).*
**Voting.** Votación *(vottutheón).*
**Vowel.** Vocal *(voccúll).*
**Voyage.** Viaje (por mar) *(vee.úhheh porr márr).*
**Vulgar.** Vulgar *(voolgárr).*
**Vulgarly.** Vulgarmente *(voolgárrménteh).*
**Vulture.** Buitre *(bwéétreh).*

# W

**Wafer.** Oblea *(oblayer).*
**Wag.** Burlón *(boorlón).*
**Wage.** Jornal *(horrnúl).*
**Wagon.** Vagón *(vuggón).*
**Waist.** Cinto, cintura, talle *(thíntoh, thintõõrer, túllyeh).*
**Waistcoat.** Chaleco *(chulléckoh).*

**Wait.** Aguardar *(úggwarrdárr).*
**Waiter.** Camarero *(cúmmerráirroh).*
**Wake.** Despertar *(despairtárr).*
**Walk.** (v.) Andar, caminar, pasear *(undárr, cumminnárr, pusseárr).*

**Walk.** (s.) Paseo *(pussáy.-oh)*.

**Wall.** Pared, muralla *(purréd, moorúllyer)*.

**Wanderings.** Peregrinación *(perrigrinnutheón)*.

**Want.** Querer *(kerráirr)*.

**War.** Guerra *(ghérrer)*.

**Wardrobe.** Ropero *(roppáirroh)*.

**Warehouse.** (s.) Almacén *(úllmuthén)*.

**Warehouse.** (v.) Almacenar *(ullmuthenárr)*.

**Wares.** Género *(hénnerroh)*.

**Warm.** (adj.) Caliente *(cullyénteh)*.

**Warm.** (v.) Calentar *(cullyentárr)*.

**Warmed.** Acalorado *(uckúllerrárdoh)*.

**Warn.** Avisar, advertir *(uvvisárr, uddvairtēērr)*.

**Warranty.** Garantía *(gurruntéarr)*.

**Wart.** Verruga *(verrōōger)*.

**Wash.** Lavar *(luvvárr)*.

**Waste.** (s.) Despilfarro *(despillfúrroh)*.

**Waste.** (v.) Malgastar *(mulgustárr)*.

**Watch.** (s.) Pulsera, reloj *(pullsáirer, rellóh)*.

**Watch.** (v.) Vigilar, contemplar, velar *(vihhillárr, contemplárr, vellárr)*.

**Watchmaker.** Relojero *(relloh.háirroh)*.

**Watchmaker's.** Relojería *(relloh.herréar)*.

**Watchman.** Vigilante *(viggillúnteh)*.

**Water.** Agua *(úgwer)*.

**Water-closet.** Retrete *(rettrétteh)*.

**Watercolour.** Acuarela *(uckwurreller)*.

**Waterfall.** Catarata *(cútterrútter)*.

**Watering pot.** Regadera *(regguddáirer)*.

**Wave.** (s.) Ola, onda *(āwler, ónder)*.

**Wave.** (v.) Ondear *(onday.árr)*.

**Wax.** Cera *(tháirrer)*.

**Way.** Vía *(vēēr)*.

**We.** Nosotros *(nossóttross)*.

**Weak.** Débil, flojo *(débbil, flóhhoh)*.

**Weakness.** Debilidad, flaqueza *(debbíllidúd, fluckéther)*.

**Wear out.** Desgastar *(desgustárr)*.

**Weather.** Tiempo *(tyémpoh)*.

**Weathercock.** Veleta *(vellétter)*.

**Weave.** Tejer *(tehháirr)*.

**Weaving.** Tejido *(tehhēēdoh)*.

**Wedge.** Cuña *(cōōnyer)*.

**Wednesday.** Miércoles *(myáirrcolless)*.

**Week.** Semana *(semmúnner)*.

**Weekly.** Semanal, semanario *(semmunnúll, semmunnárreoh)*.

**Weigh.** Pesar *(pessárr)*.

**Weight.** Peso *(péssoh)*.

**Well.** Pozo *(póthoh)*.

**West.** Oeste *(owésteh)*.

**Wet.** Mojado *(mohhúddoh)*.

**Whale.** Ballena *(bullyénner)*.

**What.** Que *(keh)*.

**Wheat.** Trigo *(trēēgoh)*.

**Wheel.** Rueda *(rwédder)*.

**When.** Cuando *(kwúndoh)*.

**Where.** Dónde *(dóndeh)*.

**Which.** Cual *(kwull)*.

**Whichever.** Cualquiera *(kwulkyáirer)*.

**While.** (s.) Rato *(rúttoh)*.

**While.** (conj.) Mientras *(myéntruss)*.

**Whip.** Látigo *(lúttigoh)*.

283

**Whirlwind.** Torbellino *(torbe-llyēēnoh).*
**Whistle.** (s.) Silbido, pito *(sil-bēēdoh, pēētoh).*
**Whistle.** (v.) Silbar *(silbárr).*
**Who.** Quién, que *(kee.én, keh).*
**Whole.** Conjunto, entero *(con-hoontoh, entáirroh).*
**Wick.** Meche *(métcher).*
**Wickedness.** Maldad *(mul-dúd).*
**Wicket.** Postigo *(postēēgoh).*
**Wide.** Ancho *(úntchoh).*
**Widen.** Ensanchar *(ensun-tchárr).*
**Widening.** Ensanche *(en-súntcheh).*
**Widow.** Viuda *(vyōōder).*
**Widower.** Viudo *(vyōōdoh).*
**Wild.** Silvestre, salvaje *(sil-véstreh, selvúhheh).*
**Wild beast.** Fiera *(fee.áyrer).*
**Will.** Testamento, voluntad *(testerméntoh, volloontúd).*
**Wind.** viento *(vyéntoh).*
**Window.** Ventana *(ventún-ner).*
**Wine.** Vino *(vēēnoh).*
**Winepress.** Lagar *(luggárr).*
**Wing.** Ala *(úller).*
**Winter.** Invierno *(invyáirr-noh).*
**Wire.** Alambre *(ullúmbreh).*
**Wish.** Deseo *(dessáy.oh).*
**With.** Con *(con).*
**Within.** Adentro *(uddéntroh).*
**Without.** Sin *(sin).*
**Witness.** Testigo *(testēēgoh).*

**Wolf.** Lobo *(lóbboh).*
**Woman.** Mujer *(mooháirr).*
**Wonder.** Extrañar, pregun-tarse *(extrunyárr, preggo-ontárrseh).*
**Wood.** Bosque, madera *(bós-keh, muddáirrer).*
**Wool.** Lana *(lúnner).*
**Word.** Palabra, vocablo *(pullúbrer, voccúbleh).*
**Work.** Obra, trabajo *(óbbrer, trubbúhhoh).*
**Workman.** Obrero *(obrái-roh).*
**Workshop.** Taller *(tullyáirr).*
**World.** Mundo *(mōōndoh).*
**Worn out.** Gastado *(gustár-doh).*
**Worry.** (v.) Inquietar *(inkéa-tarr).*
**Worry.** (s.) Inquietud *(in-kéatúd).*
**Worse.** Peor *(payórr).*
**Worsen.** Empeorar *(empé-h.orrár).*
**Worst.** Pésimo *(péssimoh).*
**Worth, to be.** Valer *(vúlláirr).*
**Wound.** Herido *(errēēdoh).*
**Wrap.** Envolver *(envolváirr).*
**Wrinkle.** (s.) Arruga *(urrōō ger).*
**Wrinkle.** (v.) Arrugar *(urroo-gárr).*
**Write.** Escribir *(escribéar).*
**Writing.** Escritura *(escrittōō-rrer).*
**Wrong.** Malo, equivocado *(márloh, ekkivoccárdoh).*

# Y

**Year.** Año *(únnyoh).*
**Yearly.** Anual *(únnoo.úll).*

**Yellow.** Amarillo *(úmmerríll-yoh).*

**Yes.** Sí *(see)*.
**Yet.** Aun *(ahōōn)*.
**Yolk.** Yema *(yémmer)*.
**You.** Usted *(oostéh)*.

**Young.** Joven *(hóvven)*.
**Young lady.** Señorita *(senyorr̄ḗḗter)*.
**Youth.** Juventud *(hooventōōd)*.

# Z

**Zeal.** Celos *(thélloss)*.
**Zed.** Zeta *(thétter)*.
**Zenith.** Cenit *(thénnit)*.
**Zero.** Cero *(tháirroh)*.

**Zinc.** Cinc *(think)*.
**Zodiac.** Zodíaco *(thoddéuc-koh)*.
**Zone.** Zona *(thónner)*.

# NOTAS

## NOTAS

# NOTAS

# NOTAS